PRAISE FOR THE FIRST EDITION

'The best overall account of the background to the genocide, and the failure to prevent it ... the investigation is
hers, and hers alone. She discovered so much that we did
not know.' (Lt Gen. Roméo Dallaire, Force Commander,
UN Assistance Mission for Rwanda (UNAMIR), 1994,
and author of *Shake Hands with the Devil: The Failure of
Humanity in Rwanda*)

'Melvern offers a vivid picture of the role of Western
nations in abetting, ignoring and allowing Rwanda's
genocide.' (*New York Times*)

'Quite extraordinary: precise, and yet overwhelming; a
fine balance in the face of depravity ... Linda Melvern has
written an extraordinary account of the Rwanda genocide,
and the shocking failure of the West to lift a finger ... What
Melvern demonstrates so powerfully is that where Western
geopolitical interests are absent, Western morality and
"civilized" concerns are nowhere to be found ... A brave
and compelling book.' (Richard Falk, Princeton University)

'This is a devastating account of lies, deceit, complacency
and tragic neglect ... Linda Melvern deserves our thanks
for investing so much in breaking the silence and revealing
the truth.' (Glenys Kinnock, MEP)

'Linda Melvern has written a compelling description of
the most dramatic aspects of the genocide.' (Astri Suhrke,
International Affairs)

'Lifts the lid on the international community's failure
to prevent the genocide. Outlines how the slaughter was
aided and abetted by international indifference, loans and
weapons deals.' (Geoff Cumming, *New Zealand News*)

ABOUT THE AUTHOR

Linda Melvern is an investigative journalist and writer. For four years she was a reporter with *The Sunday Times*, including as a member of their award-winning Insight Team. Since leaving the paper to write her first book, she has written widely for the British press and also lectures on international issues. She is an Honorary Professor in the Department of International Politics, University of Wales, Aberystwyth. Her books include:

Conspiracy to Murder (2006)

United Nations (World Organisations Series) (2001)

The Ultimate Crime: Who Betrayed the United Nations and Why (1995)

The End of the Street (1986)

Techno-Bandits (1984) (co-authored)

A PEOPLE BETRAYED

the role of the West in Rwanda's genocide

Linda Melvern

New updated edition

Zed Books

LONDON | NEW YORK

A People Betrayed: the role of the West in Rwanda's genocide was first published in 2000 by Zed Books Ltd, 7 Cynthia Street, London N1 9JF, UK and Room 400, 175 Fifth Avenue, New York, NY 10010, USA

This new updated edition was first published in 2009

www.zedbooks.co.uk

Set in Monotype Plantin and Gill Sans Heavy by Ewan Smith, London
Index: ed.emery@thefreeuniversity.net
Cover designed by Rogue Four Design
Printed and bound in Great Britain by CPI Antony Rowe, Chippenham and Eastbourne

Distributed in the USA exclusively by Palgrave Macmillan, a division of St Martin's Press, LLC, 175 Fifth Avenue, New York, NY 10010, USA

A catalogue record for this book is available from the British Library
Library of Congress Cataloging in Publication Data available

ISBN 978 1 84813 244 3 hb
ISBN 978 1 84813 245 0 pb

CONTENTS

ABBREVIATIONS

ADL	Association Rwandaise pour la défense des droits de la personne et des libertés publiques
APC	armoured personnel carrier
BACAR	Banque Continentale Africaine Rwanda
CDR	Coalition pour la Défense de la République
CHK	Centre Hospitalier de Kigali
CIA	Central Intelligence Agency
CND	Conseil National pour le Développement
DAMI	Détachement d'Assistance Militaire et d'Instruction
DGSE	Direction Général de la Sécurité Extérieure
DMZ	demilitarized zone
DPKO	Department of Peacekeeping Operations (UN)
DSP	Division Spéciale Présidentielle
ESM	Ecole Supérieure Militaire
ETO	Ecole Technique Officielle
EW	early warning
FAO	Food and Agriculture Organization (UN)
FIDH	International Federation of Human Rights
ICRC	International Committee of the Red Cross
ICTR	International Criminal Tribunal for Rwanda
IMF	International Monetary Fund
MDR	Mouvement Démocratique Républicain
MRND	Mouvement Révolutionnaire National pour le Développement
MRNDD	Mouvement Républicain National pour la Démocratie et le Développement
MSF	Médecins Sans Frontières
NGO	non-governmental organization
NMOG	Neutral Military Observer Group (OAU)
NRA	National Resistance Army
OAU	Organization of African Unity
ONUSAL	UN Observer Mission in El Salvador

ORINFOR	Office Rwandais d'Information
Parmehutu	Parti du Mouvement de l'Émancipation des Bahutu
PDC	Parti Démocrate Chrétien
PDD	Presidential Decision Directive (USA)
PL	Parti Libéral
PSD	Parti Social Démocrate
QRF	Quick Reaction Force (UN)
RANU	Rwandan Alliance for National Unity
RGF	Rwandan government forces
ROE	rules of engagement
RPF	Rwandan Patriotic Front
RRWF	Rwanda Refugees Welfare Association
RTBF	Radio Télévision de la Communauté Française de Belgique
RTLMC	Radio-Télévision Libre des Mille Collines
SAP	Structural Adjustment Programme
SRG	Service Général du Renseignement de l'Armée (Military Intelligence, Belgium)
SRSG	Special Representative of the Secretary-General
UNAMIR	United Nations Assistance Mission for Rwanda
UNAR	Union Nationale Rwandaise
UNCIVPOL	United Nations Civilian Police
UNDP	United Nations Development Programme
UNESCO	United Nations Educational, Scientific and Cultural Organization
UNHCR	United Nations High Commissioner for Refugees
UNICEF	United Nations Children's Fund
UNOMUR	United Nations Observer Mission Uganda–Rwanda
UNOSOM	United Nations Operation in Somalia
UNPROFOR	United Nations Protection Force
UNREO	United Nations Rwanda Emergency Office
UPR	Union du Peuple Rwandais
WFP	World Food Programme (UN)
WHO	World Health Organization (UN)

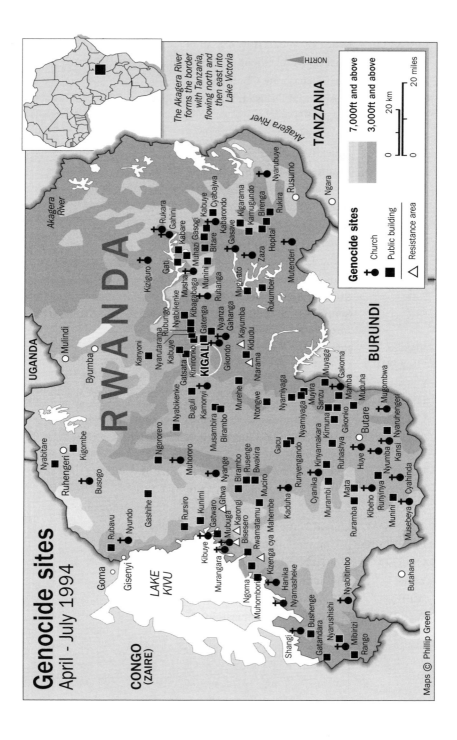

Genocide sites
April - July 1994

The Akagera River forms the border with Tanzania, flowing north and then east into Lake Victoria

NORTH

Genocide sites

✝ Church
● Public building
△ Resistance area

7,000ft and above
3,000ft and above

0   20 km
0   20 miles

CONGO (ZAIRE)

UGANDA

TANZANIA

BURUNDI

RWANDA

LAKE KIVU

Akagera River

Goma
Gisenyi
Nyabitare
Ruhengeri
Kigombe
Busogo
Nyundo
Rubavu
Mulindi
Byumba
Kigali
Gashihe
Ngororero
Muhororo
Kibuye
Murangara
Gatwaro
Mubuga
Bisesero
Rwamatamu
Mucuro
Kizenga cya Mahembe
Ngoma
Muhombori
Hanika
Nyamasheke
Shangi
Gatandara
Nyarushishi
Nyabitimbo
Butahana
Bushenge
Mibirizi
Rango
Nyarutarama
Kanyoni
Kabuye
Kimironko
Gatsata
Gikondo
Gatenga
Nyanza
Gahanga
Ntarama
Kidudu
Kayumba
Ngenda
Ntongwe
Murehe
Birambo
Musambira
Nyange
Gitwa
Karongi
Kaduha
Cyanika
Murambi
Mata
Ruramba
Kibeho
Musebeya
Munini
Runyinya
Cyahinda
Kansi
Nyamagabe
Runyengando
Gacu
Nyamiyaga
Kinyamakara
Ruhashya
Huye
Nyumba
Nyaruhengeri
Butare
Gikonko
Mugombwa
Muduha
Mamba
Gakoma
Muyaga
Sanzu
Kimuna
Muyira
Nyamata
Bwakira
Rusenge
Birambo
Kamonyi
Buguli
Nyabikenke
Kibagabaga
Muhazi Gasogi
Musha
Munini
Ruhanga
Mugesato
Kabuye
Gati
Gahini
Rukara
Kabare
Bitare
Zaza
Kabarondo
Gasave
Kamugundo
Nigarama
Birenga
Hopital
Rukumberi
Rukira
Mutenderi
Nyarubuye
Rusumo
Ngara
Kizguro
Gata
Rubungo
Kibumba

Maps © Phillip Green

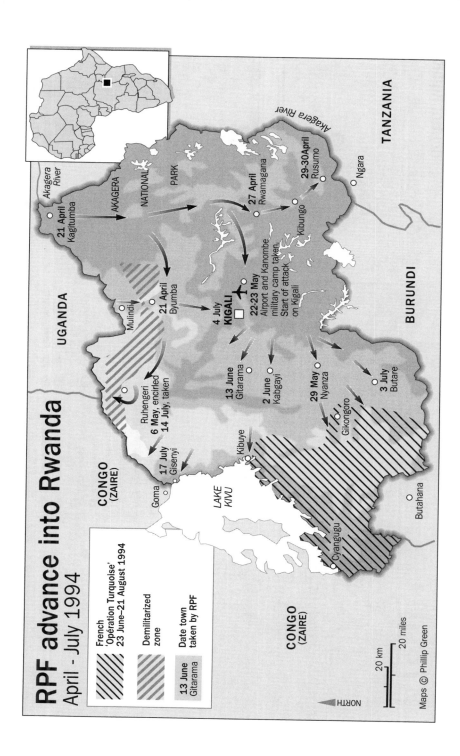

RPF advance into Rwanda
April - July 1994

TANZANIA

Akagera River

29-30April
Rusumo

27 April
Rwamagana

Ngara

AKAGERA

NATIONAL

PARK

Akagera
River

21 April
Kagitumba

Kibungo

22-23 May
Airport and Kanombe
military camp taken
Start of attack
on Kigali

UGANDA

Mulindi

21 April
Byumba

4 July
KIGALI

BURUNDI

Ruhengeri
6 May, encircled
14 July, taken

13 June
Gitarama

2 June
Kabgayi

29 May
Nyanza

3 July
Butare

17 July
Gisenyi

Gikongoro

CONGO
(ZAIRE)

Goma

Kibuye

LAKE
KIVU

Butahana

Cyangugu

CONGO
(ZAIRE)

French
'Opération Turquoise'
23 June–21 August 1994

Demilitarized
zone

13 June
Gitarama   Date town
            taken by RPF

NORTH

20 km

20 miles

Maps © Phillip Green

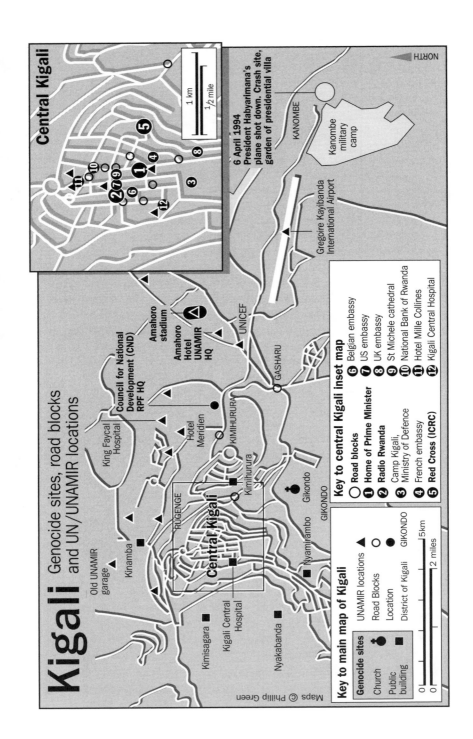

Kigali
Genocide sites, road blocks and UN/UNAMIR locations

Central Kigali

6 April 1994
President Habyarimana's plane shot down. Crash site, garden of presidential villa

NORTH

1 km
1/2 mile

Kanombe military camp

KANOMBE

Gregoire Kayibanda International Airport

Old UNAMIR garage

Kinamba

King Faycal Hospital

Council for National Development (CND)
RPF HQ

Amahoro stadium

Amahoro Hotel
UNAMIR HQ

Hotel Meridien

UNICEF

GASHARU

Kimisagara

Kigali Central Hospital

RUGENGE

Central Kigali

KIMIHURURA

Kimihurura

GIKONDO

Gikondo

Nyamirambo

Nyakabanda

Key to main map of Kigali

Genocide sites
- ✝ Church
- ■ Public building

- ▲ UNAMIR locations
- ◯ Road Blocks
- ● Location
- GIKONDO District of Kigali

0 — 5km
0 — 2 miles

Key to central Kigali inset map

- ◯ Road blocks
- ❶ Home of Prime Minister
- ❷ Radio Rwanda
- ❸ Camp Kigali, Ministry of Defence
- ❹ French embassy
- ❺ Red Cross (ICRC)
- ❻ Belgian embassy
- ❼ US embassy
- ❽ UK embassy
- ❾ St Michele cathedral
- ❿ National Bank of Rwanda
- ⓫ Hotel Mille Collines
- ⓬ Kigali Central Hospital

Maps © Phillip Green

1 | GENOCIDE, APRIL 1994

§ The people arrived in small groups, emerging slowly from the eucalyptus trees at the back of the school. Some of them were wounded. There was a girl, aged about six, with a machete wound in her head, and a boy with a gaping hole in his shoulder from a bullet. He did not cry. One man had a hand almost severed from a machete blow. Other people arrived at the front gate and some were running in terror, sometimes with militia in pursuit.

Soon there were families camped out in the classrooms, and when these became overcrowded people began to huddle together in groups on the playing field. They were on UN territory, which they believed no one would dare violate. Outside the school gates the militia brandished their machetes and hand grenades. They cruised around in jeeps, drinking beer, hurling vulgarities and chanting '*Pawa, pawa*', 'power', for Hutu Power.[1] The notorious Café de Gatenga, where militia congregated, was near by.

It was Friday, 8 April 1994. Here in Kicukiro, and all over the city, there were people fleeing in terror, to churches, to schools, to hospitals and to wherever they saw the blue United Nations flag, which was where peacekeepers were billeted. The best equipped and trained peacekeepers were from Belgium, providing the backbone of the mission known as the UN Assistance Mission for Rwanda (UNAMIR). There were 450 Belgians, and they were spread out in fourteen different locations all over the city. The largest group was located at this technical school, the Ecole Technique Officielle (ETO), run by Catholic Salesian Fathers. It comprised ninety Para-commandos from the second battalion of Flawinne, among the elite of the Belgian army. These soldiers were responsible for the central Kigali sector. Their code name was 'Beverly Hills' and their commander was Lieutenant Luc Lemaire. He had been in Rwanda for two weeks.

On the face of it, their assignment was unambiguous. It was classic peacekeeping, the provision of a neutral buffer between two enemies. A three-year civil war had ended and the UN was to oversee the peace agreement. For this to work effectively there had to be the consent of the parties; they would take part in joint patrols with the Rwandan army and gendarmes. Lemaire said nothing had gone right from the beginning: 'It was obvious to us that the gendarmes were playing around with UNAMIR ... in the end we stopped telling them the details of our patrols.'[2]

Lemaire welcomed the people, although he wondered how, with so little ammunition, he could protect them.[3] There were explosions near by and the sound of grenades and shooting. Then the shock news came, over the UNAMIR Motorola, that ten Belgian Para-commandos had been murdered by Rwandan soldiers. It had seemed impossible. The message urged them to continue their mission and to try to preserve life.[4] But Lemaire knew they could all be targets now and he tried to reassure the younger members of the contingent.

Lemaire told his commanding officers about the people at the school. He told them explosions could be heard all day and that a huge sweep of ethnic cleansing was taking place.[5] He estimated the number of people sheltering at the ETO to be several hundred. It was his duty to protect them, he was told.[6] Lemaire ordered defensive positions built around the perimeter fence. More people were arriving all the time. The people were traumatized, terrified, cold and hungry.

The food that priests had provided soon ran out. There was not enough water. There were insufficient medical supplies. Lemaire told headquarters that they had stopped treating the sick and wounded in order to keep the required reserves necessary for all UN personnel.[7] He telephoned the local offices of Médecins Sans Frontières (MSF) and the International Committee of the Red Cross (ICRC). He was told that it was impossible for anyone to get through the roadblocks to come to their aid.

A radio message came on Saturday, 9 April, in which Lemaire was ordered to prepare his men to leave; he was told that the entire Belgian contingent was pulling out of Rwanda. This was unbelievable. The people at ETO were all at risk from the militia. He radioed to ask what would happen to them.[8] No one had an answer. Lemaire asked a *bourgmestre* to assemble the crowd, and he stood on a chair to explain to the people that while the UN flag was flying over the school they were safe, but that this was not going to last.[9] He told them that the civil war had resumed and that the politicians in Brussels had decided to withdraw their soldiers from the UN mission. He advised them to disperse, to slip away under cover of darkness. The people were outraged and many of them pleaded for rescue, to be taken to UNAMIR headquarters a few miles away. Some people made plans to block the exits should the soldiers try to leave. There were several people who approached Lemaire later and asked whether, in the event of a pull-out, he would shoot them first, telling him that a bullet was preferable to being cut to pieces with a machete.

Lemaire spoke with a senior officer in the Rwandan army, Colonel Leonidas Rusatira, who came to the school.[10] Rusatira was the head of a Rwandan military academy, the Ecole Supérieure Militaire (ESM), and had been in government as the Director of the Cabinet in the Ministry of Foreign Affairs. Lemaire asked Rusatira whether, when the Belgians withdrew, he would make sure that Rwandan soldiers looked after the people. 'I thought this man might be enough of a human being to protect them,' said Lemaire. Rusatira said he had no soldiers at his command. Nevertheless, he brought sacks of rice to the school, although there was only enough for the children.

Lemaire considered escorting everyone to the headquarters of the UN mission, but he wondered whether there were enough peacekeepers to look after them even there. To move the people in small groups would require more than ninety soldiers. They risked attack en route.

§   On Sunday, 10 April, Lemaire was relieved to see French troops, but they had flown to Rwanda with orders only to get French nationals and Rwandan VIPs out of the country. The French soldiers, who were able to drive freely round the city, chose expatriates from the ETO crowds, selecting only three French and several Italian nationals. This angered Lemaire, and he told the French that they could at least take all the Europeans. Some 150 people were prepared for departure.

That day Lemaire was ordered to send soldiers to Gitarama, a town some forty miles away, to escort Belgian nationals to Kigali airport. He argued that this would diminish the security of the Rwandans he was protecting. The operation was cancelled, but for other reasons.

Lemaire's final order to withdraw from the ETO came on Monday, 11 April at 12.30. He faltered. He wanted the order confirmed. He said he contacted the most senior Belgian officers in order to be sure that his commanders knew what the consequences would be. The military log of the battalion records: 'Leave 2000 refugees at "Beverly Hills"?'[11] Colonel Luc Marchal, the commander of the Kigali sector of UNAMIR, confirmed the order.

'I did not want to leave,' Lemaire said some years later. 'But I did not think there was any other solution.'

All that was left was to plan the departure. If the people found out what was happening there might be a riot, so Lemaire decided the peacekeepers would try to leave quietly, as though going out on a mission. By chance a French jeep was passing, and as it drove on to the playing field, its soldiers were applauded by the crowds. They thanked the French for their protection. Then one by one the UN vehicles slowly began to leave the school grounds. Soon it was obvious what was happening, that the peacekeepers were sneaking away. 'We could not believe what they were doing ... just abandoning us when they knew the place was surrounded ... There were thousands of unarmed refugees ... it seemed unthinkable.'[12]

People tried to hang on to lorries but the Belgian soldiers brandished their weapons, and fired into the air. The French soldiers prevented people from getting too near to the UN peacekeepers. The French were promising that they would stay. But at 13.45 p.m., as the last Belgian soldier pulled out of the school, the French soldiers also began to leave. People were crying and screaming. The *bourgmestre*, a member of Rwanda's Parti Social Démocrate (PSD), the centre-left opposition party, tried to calm everyone, and told them that they must defend themselves. 'But we had no weapons, not even a stick,' a survivor later recalled.

'Not one minute after the UN left, the gendarmes and militia came,' said a survivor. They were firing their weapons at the people and throwing grenades into the crowd. People were being chased by militiamen wielding machetes, clubs and spears. Some people could not run because they were too young, sick or elderly.[13] Those recognized as Hutu were put to one side. The vice-president of the national committee of one of the militia groups, an agricultural engineer, Georges Rutaganda, was seen in a jogging suit, standing guard at a small entrance located on the side of the sports field. He was carrying a gun.[14]

In the crowd were pro-democracy opposition politicians and human rights activists, but the vast majority of people carried identification cards with the designation Tutsi. In the crowd was the minister of foreign affairs, Boniface Ngurinzira, who had helped to negotiate the peace agreement that had ended civil war and had provided for power-sharing. Two days earlier he had been rescued from his home by peacekeepers.

A large crowd estimated at more than two thousand people now made its way out of the gate with the intention of trying to reach UN headquarters a few kilometres away. But the column of people was stopped en route by members of the Para-commando battalion just near a factory, the Sonatube. They were all diverted, told that they were going to a place called Nyanza, where they would be safe.[15] A pick-up truck filled with members of the Para-commando unit passed them. The commander of the Para-commando unit, Major Aloys Ntabakuze, was there and the refugees walked past Colonel Théoneste Bagosora, a senior official in the Ministry of Defence, who was watching from his car. These army officers were coordinating and controlling the situation.[16]

'As we walked ... the soldiers and militia terrorized us with their grenades and guns ... they slapped and beat people up, stealing their money ... it was a long walk and the militia were everywhere,' a survivor recalled. 'The Interahamwe [militia] were armed with machetes, clubs, axes, spears and nail-studded metal sticks. Some women were forcibly taken away and raped.'[17] There was a torrential downpour and the people were wet and shivering in the cold.

At one of the crossroads, leaning on his vehicle, was Rutaganda, who was watching the proceedings. At one moment the soldiers ordered the people to sit down and cursed and insulted them for being Tutsi, telling them they were going to die. Then the convoy moved on again. 'As we walked along, the militia were hitting people with machetes. Some of the people who were wounded fell down and were trampled upon.'[18]

They came to a crossroads that led to Nyanza-Rebero, and when they reached a gravel pit near the Nyanza primary school they were told once more to sit down. It was late afternoon. A witness said that Rutaganda was instructing the militia how to proceed; there were hundreds of militia coming from different directions and they had machetes. Rutaganda directed them into position. One man carried a sack filled with grenades. The Tutsi who tried to escape by passing themselves off as Hutu were denounced and were killed on the spot.

'The Presidential Guard were watching us from a place that was higher than where we were,' a survivor recalled. After about half an hour a grenade was thrown into the crowd. Then the soldiers started firing. Some people tried to break through the militia but were struck down with machetes. A witness would later testify how he saw his child on his wife's back blown off by a grenade. 'We were so stunned that no one cried out ... it was only afterwards that you heard the voices moaning in agony ... then the Interahamwe came in and started with the machetes, hammers, knives and spears.' The survivors were mostly children who hid under the bodies. People in pain were told that they would be finished off quickly with a bullet if they paid money. Some girls were selected and their clothes removed and they were raped. The rapes continued well into the night. There were children crying over the bodies of their parents.

The next morning the militia came back to kill anyone found alive. The UN, said one of the survivors, had been their only hope of survival.[19]

Lemaire and his men ended that day at the airport. In the days to follow they provided military escorts for an emergency operation to get all expatriates out of Rwanda, with soldiers from France, Belgium and Italy – Para-commandos and parachute regiments, some of Europe's elite brigades – specially flown in for that very purpose. Once this operation was complete, it was the turn of the Belgian peacekeepers to leave, and Captain Luc Lemaire and the ninety soldiers from the ETO were among the first to fly home. When they arrived in Brussels, and were greeted by TV news crews on the tarmac, one of them took out his combat knife and shredded his UN blue beret. In the next three months massacres like the one at the ETO became commonplace as thousands upon thousands of people were killed in circumstances similar to these – in churches, schools, hospitals, health clinics, in sports stadiums and at roadblocks. The killing was vicious, relentless and incredibly brutal. It took place in broad daylight. Far from trying to conceal what was happening the perpetrators and organizers of the 1994 genocide of the Tutsi remained secure in the knowledge that there would be little international condemnation and that outside interference would be at a minimum.

The combination of revelations about the speed, scale and intensity of the genocide, the failure to intervene when it was threatened and the suppression of information about what was actually happening is a shocking indictment of governments and individuals who could have prevented it but chose not to do so even when the evidence was indisputable. It is a terrible story, made worse because the true nature of it continues to be deliberately distorted and confused.

2 | THE PAST IS PROLOGUE: RWANDA 1894–1973

§ The United Nations had been involved in the affairs of Rwanda since the creation of the organization in 1945, when the UN Charter – in many ways similar to the Covenant of the League of Nations – promised the colonized peoples of the world freedom, justice and protection. A special council was created, the Trusteeship Council, which was to oversee the transition to independence of the world's colonized peoples. Among the powers accorded the Trusteeship Council was the right to visit the territories placed under trusteeship. The first ever mission went to Africa in mid-July 1948. A group of four ambassadors visited Rwanda and Burundi, then officially known as Ruanda-Urundi, under Belgian administration, and Tanganyika, which was under British rule.[1]

Their report, published in October 1948, caused uproar. It condemned the British for having achieved great material success at the expense of the impoverished people of Africa. 'The Africans' economic and social world is still separated from that of the European by a wide gap.' It recommended that a tax should be levied to pay for health and education on the export of diamonds. The Belgian government was castigated for the common practice of whipping in its territories, especially during forced labour. In the General Assembly of the UN, Belgium was castigated for the subservient status and the suffering of Rwanda's 'Hutu masses', who were subjected to discrimination in all walks of life.

Both European governments dismissed the report as mischievous political propaganda. In London the Foreign Office did not accept the right of the UN to tell it how to discharge its responsibilities. The issue of colonialism was dominant in the UN; some states were increasingly vociferous about how slowly the great powers were applying Charter principles in the colonies. An increasingly effective anti-colonial bloc had been built around Egypt, India and Pakistan, a group beginning to enjoy support from the Soviets. As for the Americans, who rejected colonialism, they were torn by their close alliance with European countries. Washington was none the less worried about the radical nature of the department of trusteeship at the UN, and particularly about the influence of certain secretariat officials within it.[2]

A valuable and remakable description of Rwanda is provided in the 1948 report. The UN ambassadors had been surprised at the level of social and political control they found and believed that a system existed in the country which contained all the elements necessary for democratic development. Each sub-chief had a council composed of representatives, from all the social groups, appointed by selection with the consent of the family groups. In spite of there being no proper electoral system, there was a fairly democratic representation through which the desires of the lowliest person could be expressed. This enabled contacts between the leaders and the masses. The councils met frequently and dealt in the main with local matters.[3]

The UN ambassadors also noted a feudal system, which appeared to be based on cattle. Cattle were the pivot in an extremely complicated series of civil contracts and political relationships. 'The pre-eminence of man over the cow is still far from being established,' the ambassadors reported. 'All, even the most humble peasant, have but one desire; to own cows, no matter what the quality ... better two poor beasts than one good one.' The people of Rwanda counted their wealth in the number of their cattle. But most cows in Rwanda were of poor quality and of little use economically. Because of their high social value, cattle were not used as regular food and demanded a greater area of pasture land than the country could afford.

Rwanda was densely populated. The rainfall was irregular, with drought and soil erosion leading to the basic problem of how to feed all the people.

§ The European involvement in Rwanda had begun in 1894, exactly one hundred years before the 1994 genocide, when on 4 May the first European, a German count, Gustav Adolf von Götzen, was received at the Rwandan court by King Rwabugiri. The king claimed that his dynasty stretched back hundreds of years. He ruled a kingdom that included the whole territory of the present-day Rwanda together with other lands, now incorporated into Uganda and the Democratic Republic of Congo.[4]

The king, welcoming the German count, was unaware that ten years earlier, at the Berlin Conference of 1885, the European superpowers, knowing nothing at all about his country, had 'given' Rwanda to Germany. Von Götzen would become governor of German East Africa, and Rwanda was included in his territory. The Rwandan monarchy was allowed to continue. Germany kept only twenty-four military officers and six administrators in Rwanda.

Rwanda, a tiny mountain kingdom in the heart of Africa, was described by early travellers as a tropical Switzerland; one colonial official called it 'the pearl of Africa'.[5] It was said to be the most complex place in the Great Lakes and it certainly differed from all the others.[6]

The European visitors to Rwanda noted an intricate social order. It was basically feudal, with aristocrats and vassals. The administrative structure radiated from the centre, which was organized on four levels: province, district, hill and neighbourhood. The provinces were managed by high chiefs, although borders of the country were the responsibility of army chiefs.[7] The power radiated from the capital to the provinces. Each layer of the hierarchy was linked in a relationship of mutual dependence based on reciprocal arrangements regarding goods and services. This was known as *ubuhake*, and it referred to a contractual service in which a more powerful person could provide protection in exchange for work.

The history of Rwanda was told orally and controlled by the royal court, where various specialists lived, including dynastic poets, musicians, ritualists, exorcists of calamities, magicians, those who named the cattle, cooks and wine stewards.[8] There were elite families at court, the lineages said to have royal blood.

The story of Rwandan kings was told through a complex and symbolic language, Kinyarwanda, recounting the noble deeds of each Rwandan dynasty spanning forty-three reigns.

There was a wealth of oral literature, including some 300 historical tales and 175 dynastic poems.[9] These stories were used to glorify the court, and it is claimed today that these great myths convey a distorted and idealized version of events.[10] There were only a few notable families allowed to 'forge knowledge'. Only they possessed the wisdom to interpret the past. These court diviners were also said to be able to predict the future by interpreting past events.

There exists a relatively detailed record of central court history from the mid-eighteenth century, when the state's territorial holdings were expanded through the conquest of neighbouring regions.[11] In the last part of the eighteenth century, Rwanda was almost continually in a state of war, and at a time when military conquest was glorified. The strength of the kingdom of Rwanda was its permanent and professional royal armies. These royal warriors travelled the kingdom, bringing in their wake their vast cattle herds. Their ranks included experienced cattle rustlers, who drove the enemy herds to a safe place during battle.[12] The armies contained sections solely for servants and foragers, those who provided provisions for the soldiers.

As the state increased in size, so did the population and the size of the cattle herds. With special reserves created for the cattle belonging to the armies, the public pasture began to shrink. The farmers began to lose their land and became day labourers; others were forced to do extra work because they could not pay their tax burdens, usually a significant portion of the shrinking family crop. As new lineages found a place at court, so the taxes increased. 'The result', writes the historian Jan Vansina, 'was the general pauperization of the ... inhabitants of the country.'[13]

§ The king who welcomed Count Gustav Adolf von Götzen to his court, King Rwabugiri, was considered one of Rwanda's greatest monarchs, and said to have been not only a military genius but a political visionary. He created larger military forces and used increasingly sophisticated military techniques, including effective espionage.[14] More recent research tells of how he created murderous turmoil at court and how he institutionalized state violence. The king reduced the power of individual noble lineages by delegating authority to outsiders. A series of vendettas took place, and there was frequent denunciation for treason. There were executions every day, and attempts to exterminate all the male members of certain families. There was torture lasting several days, and it was exceptionally cruel.[15] Violence came to be seen as a key to ambition and success. The aristocracy was largely destroyed and society became increasingly violent.[16] The king's armies would plunder and pillage harvests and seize and rape girls and women. The exploitation of the masses continued with an increasing number of days set aside for services to the local chief known as *uburetwa*, although cattle herders were exempt.

It was in the royal armies, some historians believe, that the first systematic difference between Hutu and Tutsi evolved, for the cattle rustlers were called Tutsi and the servants were called Hutu.[17] A combatant was called Tutsi and a Hutu meant non-combatant. As most non-combatants were farmers, the elite eventually began to call all farmers Hutu.[18] For hundreds of years the court had used the word Hutu to refer to their servants – even those who were Tutsi. It was also used to describe everyone else who did not come from an illustrious lineage. The elite used the word Hutu to refer to 'rural boorishness or loutish behaviour'. The word Hutu also referred to all foreigners, for all outsiders were scorned. The Hutu came to be known as the vast majority, cultivating the soil and resembling most of the people living in the neighbouring countries of Uganda and Tanzania with typical

Bantu features. The Tutsi were usually taller, thinner and with angular features. In time the neighbourhoods were generally headed by Hutu, who obeyed orders from above, and most above this level were Tutsi; the monarchy was Tutsi and the king's army was mostly Tutsi, and Tutsi were favoured for political office.

There is a Rwandan dynastic myth which purports to explain the differences between Hutu, Tutsi and Twa. It tells how the king of all the earth had three sons, Gatwa, Gahutu and Gatutsi. To test them he entrusted to each a churn of milk. Gatwa quenched his thirst, Gahutu spilt the milk but Gatutsi kept his intact and so he was entrusted to command the others.[19] Today there is no consensus among historians or anthropologists on the origins of the divisions Hutu and Tutsi, so crucial to Rwanda's history. There is some evidence that the meanings attached to these categories changed significantly over time.[20] The identities altered, and the meanings evolved differently in different places.[21] There existed many criteria for the classification Hutu and Tutsi, including birth, wealth in cattle, culture, place of origin, physical attributes and social and marriage ties.[22]

Although the word Hutu would also come to mean 'subject' or 'servant' and the word Tutsi 'those rich in cattle', the differences were not solely based on wealth or class; there were Hutu and Tutsi in the same class. Tutsi pastoralists were as poor as their Hutu neighbours. But the word Tutsi did come to be associated with central government. These groups were not tribes, for the people shared the ancestral stories, and spoke the same language, Kinyarwanda. Long before Rwanda became a state, people were speaking variants of the language and were widely settled in the region.[23] There were no distinct areas of residence. The Twa, less than 1 per cent of the population, were pygmies and lived as hunter-gatherers.

One European interpretation, which was to be widely accepted, was that Rwanda was originally inhabited by the Twa, who were displaced by agriculturalists migrating northwards, and supposedly the ancestors of the Hutu. The Tutsi were said to have originated in the Horn of Africa, migrating south, and as foreigners they gradually achieved dominance over the other two groups. It was this theory which led to a view that the Tutsi were somehow a 'superior race',[24] and that Rwandans were fundamentally unequal. Some people were born to rule and to exploit while others were born to obey and serve.[25]

The idea that Hutu and Tutsi were distinct races appears to have originated with the English colonial agent and celebrated explorer John Hanning Speke, who 'discovered' and named Lake Victoria in 1859, in the year in which Darwin published *On the Origin of Species*. Speke visited the states of Karagwe and Buganda (part of what is now Uganda, on the border with Rwanda), and thought that there was a natural explanation for the divisions in the society that he observed. Speke would theorize that in this part of central Africa there was a superior race, quite different from the common order of natives.[26] So superior was the culture in central Africa that it must have come from somewhere else; it was impossible that 'savage negroes' could have attained such high levels of political and religious sophistication. The Tutsi ruling classes were thought to have come from farther north, perhaps Ethiopia, and were more closely related to the 'noble Europeans'. They were superior and too fine to be 'common negroes'. They had an intelligence and a refinement of feelings which were 'rare among primitive people'. Some missionaries thought that the Tutsi were descendants of ancient Egyptians: 'their ... delicate appearance, their love of money, their capacity to adapt to any situation seem to indicate a semitic-origin'.[27] Some still believe that present-day Rwandans encompass three different biological 'populations', and however one tries to explain the divide, the differences appear to be so deep that they may date back millennia.[28]

In Rwanda the words Hutu and Tutsi came to be used to define two groups linked through common experiences. The word Hutu would come to denote a peasant population, and the word Tutsi to mean overlords.

§ There were rebellions against the oppression of the masses during the reign of King Rwabugiri, when the Hutu and Tutsi classification would become more rigid.[29] There was an uprising in the north-west on the periphery of the kingdom in 1897 followed by an armed anti-Tutsi movement. This was significant, argues the historian Jan Vansina, for it showed that people were aware, even then, of Hutu and Tutsi divisions.[30] By the end of the nineteenth century, or so Vansina believes, Rwanda was already on the edge of an abyss.[31] There were rumours that a new king was going to come to liberate the downtrodden Hutu masses from their Tutsi oppressors. When the Europeans arrived, some considered this promise to have been fulfilled.

The Germans would rule Rwanda using the power structure in place; Count von Götzen believed that German policy must be to support the chiefs. The Germans favoured expansion and in 1912 helped the Tutsi monarchy to subjugate the areas to the north.

After the First World War and the defeat of Germany, the western provinces of German East Africa, Rwanda (Ruanda) and neighbouring Burundi (Urundi), were given to Belgium to administer as Ruanda-

Urundi under a League of Nations mandate. The greater part of the territory, Tanganyika, was given to the British. The League of Nations, which was intended to herald a new phase of human evolution, stipulated that the tutelage of the peoples in the colonies should be entrusted to advanced nations, which, by reason of their resources, experience or geographical position, could best undertake this responsibility. In the mandated territories there was to be 'fair and humane conditions of labour ... just treatment of the native inhabitant ... the prevention and control of disease'.

Ruanda-Urundi was placed under a category reserved for those countries for which self-determination was not considered feasible. Belgium was pledged by the League to ensure administration and promote development, free speech and freedom of religion. One remarkable report from the colonial archives, written in 1920, outlined the reality of Belgian policy towards Rwanda: 'We have a certain responsibility to the WaHutu ... we have to protect them against the injustices they often face ... but we will go no further. We find the Watutzi established since ancient time, intelligent and capable, we will respect that situation.'[32] The policy of the Catholic Church is shown by a priest who arrived in Rwanda in 1907 and who stayed until 1945, Monsignor Léon Classe. He wrote in 1930: 'The biggest mistake the government could make would be to do away with the Tutsi caste. This would lead the country to anarchy and communism, and to be viciously anti-European.'[33]

The policy of German indirect rule was gradually changed to Belgian direct rule with the power of the king eroded. In 1922 the king was obliged to have the assistance of a Belgian representative, and by 1923 he was forbidden to appoint regional chiefs. In August 1925 Belgian law decreed that the territory of Ruanda-Urundi should be subject to the laws of the Belgian Congo. The control of the territory Ruanda-Urundi rested with the minister of the colonies in Brussels, through a governor-general of the Belgian Congo and Ruanda-Urundi. The vice-governor-general of Ruanda-Urundi resided in Bujumbura and operated through a Belgian official known as a resident, based in Kigali.

In November 1931 the king, Mwami Musinga, who was against colonization, was deposed by the Belgian administration. There was little reaction from the League of Nations, even when the king was replaced with one of his more pliant sons, Mutara Rudahigwa. Rudahigwa became known as the king of the whites and he wore Western suits. He drove his own car. His conversion to Christianity in 1943 was part of a Belgian policy to encourage mass conversions. Christianity became a prerequisite for membership of the Tutsi elite.

By the outbreak of the Second World War Rwanda was divided into chiefdoms with Belgian administrators involved at every level of society. Money was introduced and so was education, although the latter was reserved for the sons of Tutsi chiefs.[34] A civil service was created using the members of the Tutsi oligarchy. Belgian rule was harsh and thousands of Hutu peasants fled to neighbouring Uganda to become migrant labourers. There was forced labour, particularly for road building, and routine beatings and corporal punishment were administered by hill chiefs. The introduction of coffee cultivation exacerbated the burdens on Hutu cultivators, expected to care for their own fields, while chiefs made increasing demands on their labour.[35] The Belgians exported both food and labour from Rwanda to serve the economic interests of neighbouring Congo; the food was destined for Katanga, the copper mining region. The recruitment of Rwandan workers for the mines in the Congo began in 1925. For the people of Rwanda colonization would bring new forms of exploitation and oppression and a loss of land and security.[36] It was oppression in many different forms which in turn brought about the cohesion of the Hutu group.

In 1933 the Belgian administration organized a census and teams of Belgian bureaucrats began to classify the whole population, either Hutu or Tutsi or Twa. Every Rwandan was counted and measured: the height, the length of their noses, the shape of their eyes. For many Rwandans it was not possible to determine ethnicity on the basis of physical appearance. Rwandans in the south were generally of mixed origin and most Rwandans of mixed origin were classified as Hutu.[37] Yet many people looked typically Tutsi – tall and thin. In the north mixed marriages were rare. Some people were given a Tutsi card because they had more money or possessed the required number of cows.

The divisions in society became more pronounced with the introduction of education. Although the monarchy had initially opposed missionary schools because of imposed conversions to Christianity, by 1946 King Mutara Rudahigwa was persuaded to dedicate Rwanda to Christ the King. There were three days of celebration. Catholic missions sprang up everywhere in Rwanda. When a school was opened – the Groupe Scolaire, in Astrida (now Butare) – to give administrative training, it was mainly for the Tutsi elite, producing agronomists, doctors and vets, and between 1945 and 1954 out of 447 students only sixteen were Hutu.[38] Most of the Hutu students who did acquire education found there were fewer jobs for them, and those who did eventually graduate from mission schools and seminaries took up posts in the lower administration, or became tradesmen and shopkeepers. Hutu women were not allowed an education at all. The Catholic Church encouraged the creation of a new Christian ruling class, to be composed entirely of Tutsi, and this in turn served to increase the resentment of the dispossessed Hutu.[39]

§ The UN, which replaced the League of Nations and established a Trusteeship Council in New York, sent five visiting missions to Rwanda between 1948 and 1962, and each report was more critical than the last, calling on the Belgian authorities to introduce a programme of democratization. Each time the Trusteeship Council paid Rwanda a visit, the Belgians responded with a gesture. In 1952 the Belgians introduced electoral procedures for advisory councils at four administrative levels. The Tutsi won the seats. The Tutsi administration remained entrenched and Tutsi won again in 1953, when elections were held at chiefdom level, but with the vote restricted. Rwanda remained a country under strict control over labour, land, education, wealth and power – all consolidated in the hands of very few.[40] A whole class of people now lacked secure access to land.[41] In 1954 the visiting mission urged the Belgian administration to give serious attention to the political education of the people. Belgium should recognize the growing forces of nationalism in Africa. In an election in September 1956, when men only were allowed the vote, it was only for sub-chief level. Only in the north of Rwanda, in Gisenyi and Ruhengeri, did the Tutsi incur electoral losses.

The northern region had been independent until the first decade of the century, when there was military defeat by German and Tutsi-led southern Rwandan troops. It had taken several military expeditions by the German Schutztruppen between 1910 and 1912 to subdue the Bakiga or mountain people in the north, and in spite of being incorporated into the Rwandan state, the Bakiga, known to have a distinct culture, were said to represent an independent Hutu tradition. There was a strong local solidarity and the people had their own history. There was bitterness towards both the Tutsi and southern Hutu about their subjugation. Their reputation was one of natural-born warriors.[42] In the north there had been substantial recruitment for the mines in neighbouring Congo. It was here that the ideology of Hutu Power, with its central idea of a 'pure Hutu nation', was forged.

The first serious political challenge to the Tutsi oligarchy came in 1957, when, in anticipation of another visit from the UN, a group of Hutu published a manifesto that demanded emancipation and rule by the majority. The manifesto was an effective appeal to Hutu solidarity, a rallying point for revolution, for it described the basic problem as being a political monopoly by one race, the Tutsi. The Hutu were condemned for ever as manual labourers. The cause was now one of ethnic discrimination, a view not shared by the king or his High Council. It was rural anger which encouraged an emerging national Hutu leadership, and the success of the campaign would depend on mass support, and an appeal to the growing consciousness of oppression among the poor. This group identity would be more important than hill and lineage. The leadership of this movement comprised mainly literate men who had been educated in church mission schools. There were key roles played at local level by educated Hutu schoolteachers and by the Catholic network of churches, with priests who could communicate with the people throughout the country. The Hutu had the support of many Belgian priests who worked in Rwanda, one of whom had helped to write the manifesto. Many priests came to identify with the Hutu masses. The priests understood the Hutu demand for liberty of expression, and an end to ethnic discrimination in the public service. The priests saw a powerless mass ruled by a callous aristocracy. There were Catholic journals willing to publicize the Hutu cause; a key ideological ingredient of this emerging Hutu revolution was the belief that Rwanda had been overrun by Tutsi invaders who had enslaved the Hutu.

In 1957, the report of the UN's visiting trusteeship mission was pessimistic; it found 'little hope for a rapprochement between the races' and called on Belgium to accelerate efforts to emancipate the Hutu. But when, in the late 1950s, Rwanda's first political parties were created, they were established along ethnic lines. The Parti du Mouvement de l'Emancipation des Bahutu (Parmehutu) was a Hutu party and called for an end to Tutsi colonization, before freedom from the Belgians. The opposition party, created on 3 September 1959, was mainly a Tutsi party, the Union Nationale Rwandaise (UNAR), which was pro-monarchist and which called for immediate independence from Belgium. Another party was the Rassemblement Démocratique Rwandais (Rader), founded by two moderate Tutsi, with the objective of economic and cultural development for both Tutsi and Hutu.

On 24 July 1959, Rwanda's forty-six-year-old Tutsi king, Mutara Rudahigwa, died in suspicious circumstances after having been given an antibiotic injection while in hospital. Belgian doctors maintained that he died from an allergic reaction, but there were rumours and suspicions and a certainty among the Tutsi elite that the Belgians had killed him with Hutu in on the plot. In the royal court an extremist group sought to destroy the Hutu leadership and there were brutal political assassinations. The political tensions increased, but the fuse was said to have been lit on 1 November 1959 when a group of young UNAR militants had attacked the Parmehutu leader, Dominique Mbonyumutwa, on his way home from mass at a Catholic mission in Gitarama. Violence spread from hill to hill and, according to the UN visiting mission report of 1960, some two hundred people died. Dozens of petitions were sent to the Trusteeship Council in New York from threatened Tutsi pleading for help. One of them read:

> the officials report that the fighting is between two groups of inhabitants which is not true … for a long time they have been living together, mixed up … killing and burning are being done during the daylight sometimes in the presence of so-called police … how can people with no proper communications have organised such a thing … please help innocent people from this destruction.[43]

Hutu began to attack the Tutsi authorities, burning Tutsi homes, and large numbers of Tutsi fled the country. The Hutu had huge numerical predominance, and a sense of injustice and of inferiority. A counter-attack was organized by the court with orders to the army to arrest Hutu leaders, and those captured were later tortured.[44] The Belgians portrayed the violence as a problem of race between Hutu and Tutsi, and on 11 November 1959 Belgium placed Rwanda under military rule. Its fortunes were entrusted to a Belgian colonel, an officer in the Force Publique in the neighbouring Congo. His name was Guy Logiest, and he came to Rwanda with a detachment of Force Publique soldiers and Belgian paratroopers. His major concern was to protect Hutu leaders. Military rule was imposed and Logiest was appointed as Special Military Resident.[45]

Logiest had a decisive effect. He later explained that to have supported the Tutsi at this stage would have meant a rapid move to independence – which he deemed 'harmful for the popular masses'. He said he opted instead for 'democratization', and the abolition of the Tutsi hegemony.[46] He immediately began to replace Tutsi chiefs with Hutu and announced to Belgian administrators that in future Hutu would be favoured within the administration. This would be called a 'social revolution'.

A UN Commission of Inquiry arrived in April 1960 and called for a conference in Brussels to reconcile the political parties. In June and July there were the first direct communal elections, and as predicted the Parmehutu won 71 per cent of the votes. The UNAR party claimed the vote was rigged and that the Parmehutu could not fail to win owing to the support of the Belgian administration. In June the new Tutsi king, Kigeli V, left Rwanda, never to return, and tens of thousands more Tutsi were forced to go in exile into neighbouring countries.[47]

There followed several UN-sponsored reconciliation conferences, and lobbying of the member states of the Trusteeship Council by the monarchists. In January 1961, while a UN reconciliation conference was taking place in Belgium, and a UN trusteeship commission was due in Kigali, Grégoire Kayibanda, a former schoolteacher, one of the original signatories of the 1957 Hutu manifesto and a founder of Parmehutu, organized a mass rally of communal councillors and *bourgmestres* at Gitarama and a vote was taken to abolish the monarchy. Rwanda was declared a republic. Kayibanda wanted no more UN tinkering in Rwanda affairs.[48]

At this direct challenge, the UN sent another mission and a referendum was organized to decide upon the principle of the monarchy, to run simultaneously with direct elections for a national assembly. The UN tried to supervise these elections, but there was intimidation and violence. Kayibanda, with Belgian help, had built up a network of cells; the most influential Hutu on each hill was made responsible for the people around him. In September 1961 Kayibanda's Parmehutu party won massively and the monarchy was abolished. The UNAR wanted fresh elections. There was a new wave of violence against Tutsi and another exodus of Rwandans to neighbouring states. The UNAR petitioned the UN to contest the fairness of the elections.

In December 1961, Kayibanda's government began the rapid expansion of a Belgian-trained Gendarmerie Nationale Rwandaise, a national guard, created a year earlier and now doubled in size to 3,000 soldiers. The Gendarmerie Nationale Rwandaise was responsible for the maintenance of internal security and units were stationed in each of the eleven prefectures and were commanded by Belgian military officers.

It was the escalating refugee crisis caused by Tutsi exiles, and the continuing violence in Rwanda, which prompted the UN General Assembly in February 1962 to establish a special commission of five member states to ensure that Rwanda acceded to independence as soon as possible and that the refugees would be able to return. There were by now an estimated 135,000 refugees in Kivu Province in the Congo, in Burundi, in Uganda and Tanganyika. Temporary camps had been set up and the refugees were dependent on government assistance. Their situation was precarious. There was an acute shortage of food. In Kivu, people in the camps were dying from hunger at a rate of fifty a day, and the number of refugees was growing; on average, 1,000 people were crossing into Uganda every week.

This UN commission was mandated to try to ensure human rights in Rwanda, the maintenance of law and order, and the peaceful withdrawal of Belgian military forces. On a visit to Rwanda in March 1962 it was discovered that the Tutsi ethnic minority had been brutally expelled from the social and political scene. The UNAR party leaders told the commissioners of the mass arrests of their members and acts of brutality against its officials, of torture and murder. The killing appeared to be systematic and seemed designed to eliminate the UNAR, and there were demands for an immediate judicial inquiry.[49] The commissioners reported to UN headquarters that there were roadblocks all over the country. At the entrance to each prefecture there was a roadblock. At each roadblock the identity of each traveller was checked. Travel permits were required to travel from one prefecture to another. These permits were not granted to members of the opposition. There was a curfew from 6 p.m. The government, under the pretext of combating the Tutsi terrorist bands known as 'Inyenzi', had taken extreme security measures. The commission reported that Rwanda was close to a police state, if not under a reign of terror. There was racism in Rwanda that bordered on 'Nazism against the Tutsi minorities'. This was created by the government, backed by the Belgian authorities. The hostility between the different ethnic groups had been artificially engendered in the last few years. The number of victims was estimated in the region of two thousand people.[50]

Kayibanda assured the UN commissioners that stability had been restored and that the recent violence was because the colonialists had created a problem where none existed. He maintained that his government wanted to see the return of the refugees. The commissioners did not believe him. Before they left the country they told Kayibanda of the 'vital importance which the international community attached to fundamental human rights'. In the eyes of the civilized world, that principle constituted the very basis and justification of a people's right to independence. The termination of trusteeship was set for July 1962, in three months' time. Unless there was national reconciliation, the commission concluded, the outlook was bleak.

§ It was to prevent any further UN interference in Rwanda's affairs that, on 1 July 1962, the monarchy was formally abolished and an independent republic was proclaimed by Grégoire Kayibanda, who was inaugurated as president. A constitution which came into force some three months later accorded the president both legislative and judicial power. He presided over a Council of Ministers and he could wield a veto over a new Assemblée Nationale. He could nominate and dismiss ministers, and decide all senior appointments in the military, the judiciary and in all state institutions. In the president's office in central Kigali were the presidential advisers, the *chefs de service*, each with a secretariat and each specializing in an aspect of government: finance, political affairs, foreign relations, judicial affairs, education, press relations. The president's own offices included a Directeur de Cabinet and a protocol office. A new constitution in 1978 further consolidated presidential power.

The deposed king, Kigeri Ndahindurwa, went to live in neighbouring Uganda, and from Kampala he called for the formation of a government of national unity and for help for the Rwandan refugees. A group of monarchists formed a secret organization which recruited about fifteen hundred men from refugee camps. They called themselves 'Inyenzi', or cockroach, a word that would be later picked up by their enemies.[51] On 14 November 1963 they invaded Rwanda from Burundi. They had brought with them three truckloads of arms bought by selling food supplied by voluntary agencies. They were intercepted by the Belgian-commanded National Guard. Another invasion took place on 21 December when at 4.30 a.m. about two hundred men, armed with bows, arrows and home-made rifles, crossed the Burundian border at Nemba. With local Tutsi joining the ranks, they numbered some six hundred men, and they attacked a military camp at Gako, stealing weapons and vehicles. Then they drove towards Kigali but were intercepted and at Kanzenze bridge on the Nyabarongo river they were decimated. The Rwandan Gendarmerie Nationale Rwandaise, commanded by Belgian officers, and armed with semi-automatic weapons and mortars, overwhelmed the invaders by sheer firepower.

There was panic in government. The rebels had been 25 kilometres from the capital and there were rumours that they had been helped by the internal opposition. A brutal reaction to the invasion was immediate and Kayibanda arrested opposition leaders. They were taken to Ruhengeri prison, where they were shot.[52] In the capital there were hundreds of arrests. These actions were said to mark the end of any further meaningful role for Tutsi in public life. Measures were taken for '*autodéfense civile*' in four southern prefectures. This entailed each prefect, supported by a government minister, calling meetings with *bourgmestres* in order to give necessary orders to peasants on how to combat the enemy. Three days later, and two days before Christmas, there began an organized slaughter of Tutsi. There were roadblocks everywhere, manned by civilians. The radio in Kigali repeatedly broadcast emergency warnings that a Tutsi plot was under way to enslave Hutu.

In the southern prefecture of Gikongoro, bordering Burundi, the prefect was persuaded that the Tutsi must be killed, otherwise they would kill every single Hutu. The killing began when, armed with spears and clubs, a group of Hutu started to kill every Tutsi in sight – men, women and children. Some five thousand people were murdered, and in the most atrocious and cruel circumstances. The killing was done by the local population, using whatever arms were available, mostly hoes and the panga, the long knife for cutting grass. There were the most hideous mutilations. Bodies and body parts were dumped in piles at the side of the road. At Shigira near the border with the Congo, some hundred Tutsi women and children committed mass suicide by drowning themselves in the river to escape attack by Hutu mobs.[53]

Some four weeks later, journalists from the Western press arrived and described the killing. So outraged was Western public opinion at what had happened that some would recall the Holocaust in Europe. How could it happen that people who had shared the history of the same state, and who could be distinguished neither by culture nor language, could behave in such a way? The British philosopher Lord Bertrand Russell said that it was the most horrible and systematic extermination of a 'people' since the Nazis' extermination of the Jews.[54]

The government version was that the Hutu population had run amok and that the local authorities had lost control. The official Rwandan government figure was 350 Tutsi invaders killed, and 400 civilian deaths. The exact number of people who died will never be known. The death toll was never established with any certainty: the World Council of Churches estimated between 10,000 and 14,000 people murdered and the UN estimate was 1,000–3,000 people.

There were few witnesses to testify. The French newspaper *Le Monde* carried a story in January 1964 that the Tutsi were being arrested, and in some places were being exterminated. Thousands had sought refuge in churches.[55] A fuller account was published in *Le Monde* a month later with a story from a Swiss professor who had been in the southern town of Butare. His name was Denis Vuillemin, he worked for UNESCO and he had written to the newspaper to publicly castigate the Belgian government. Under a headline, 'L'Extermination des Tutsi', Vuillemin said he was resigning his job because he refused any longer to represent Belgium, whose government, he said, was complicit in genocide. Vuillemin described how in Rwanda most Europeans working for aid agencies had been indifferent to the massacres. They thought that the persecution of the Tutsi was proof of the 'savagery of the negro'. Rwanda was under totalitarian rule, he explained, and no foreign news media maintained a regular correspondent there. Kayibanda's regime was increasingly bigoted and racist, he wrote. The government, instead of organizing development programmes, was doing nothing more than encouraging racial hatred. Vuillemin described how, in the December massacres, educated Tutsi had been arrested and thrown into prison and were beaten and left without food. In Cyangugu some eighty Tutsi were put on lorries and taken to a forest, thrown into a ravine and then shot. In Gikongoro it was a 'veritable genocide', the prefect, the *bourgmestres* and party officials from Parmehutu encouraging bands of killers to undertake a systematic extermination of Tutsi. The killing lasted for four days. Women and children were killed with clubs or were speared. Clothes were taken from corpses and the corpses thrown into the river. Vuillemin claimed that these events were no accident; the brutality was the product of carefully nurtured racial hatred.

'How can I teach under a UNESCO aid programme in a school where pupils are killed for the sole reason they were Tutsi? How can I teach pupils who will perhaps be assassinated in several months or several years?' Vuillemin asked.[56] The UN secretary-general, U Thant, asked a UN official from Haiti, Max H. Dorsinville, Officer-in-Charge of a UN peacekeeping mission in the Congo, to visit Rwanda. Dorsinville spent several days in Kigali, arriving on 30 December, and was assured by Kayibanda that all local authorities were being ordered to avoid 'reprisals'. Later on, the failure of Dorsinville to protest more strongly is said to have allowed the killing to continue until mid-January. Dorsinville made another visit in February. He reported to the UN secretary-general that the estimate of the dead varied between 3,000 and 45,000. Dorsinville would call the latter figure 'fantastic', and reported that, whatever the number of victims, the Rwandan government did not deny that there had been 'excesses'. The government had promised that an investigation would be held and assured Dorsinville that the culprits would be severely punished.[57]

The accusation of genocide against the Kayibanda government was unproven. The killings were widely accepted to have been the result of an extreme interpretation by local officials of the order to take 'all measures to defend the country' against external attack. There was further evidence that this was not genocide; there were 6,000 Tutsi refugees allowed to cross into Uganda and if this was genocide then these slow-moving and defenceless people would most probably have been killed. And within Rwanda the Tutsi who sought shelter at Catholic mission stations had suffered no reprisals.

In an interview with the Rwandan foreign minister, Lazare Mpakaniye, European journalists were told that the responsibility for the violence rested with the 'Inyenzi', who knew very well the reaction their invasion would provoke among the people. In March President Kayibanda addressed the issue: 'Who is guilty of genocide? Who organized genocide? Who came looking for genocide? Who wants genocide?' In a clear warning Kayibanda said that if there was an assault on Kigali everyone knew very well who would be the first victims – Tutsi.[58]

Some six months later a report in the *Atlantic Monthly* described how the 'Inyenzi' invasion in December had caused panic in government. The National Guard had been hard pushed to defend the borders. It had been decided that the defence of the country would have to rely on the civilian Hutu population. The worst slaughter had been in Gikongoro, where word spread that the Tutsi had taken Kigali and that the Mwami had been restored. Rwanda was by now in a state of constant military alert. The effect on the economy was disastrous and malnutrition was widespread. The presence of Tutsi refugees on the border made life impossible for those Tutsi inside the country, who were all regarded as suspect.[59] It was difficult to know how many Tutsi were left in Rwanda; those who remained were not allowed to leave, were branded as traitors and were subject to intimidation. By early 1964 there were a quarter of a million Rwandans living in camps outside Rwanda with a bare subsistence and inadequate medical services.

Later that year, in April, the Fabian Society in London published a pamphlet, *Massacre in Rwanda*, pointing out that whatever their past conduct and attitudes the Tutsi did not merit annihilation as a people.

§ Rwanda's first president, Grégoire Kayibanda, the founding father of Hutu nationalism, was authoritarian and secretive. He exercised strict control over appointments and nominations from the highest to the lowest level. He ruled through a small group of politicians who came from his home town of Gitarama. There was favouritism, corruption and censorship. The Hutu nationalists were part of a small elite educated at Catholic schools and links between Church and state became close. The second-largest employer, after the state, was the Church. Not less than 90 per cent of the population was Christian, and more than half of those were Catholic. Around the churches there grew schools, health clinics and printing presses for religious tracts. Contraception was banned, and so was prostitution. The Hutu were told to be proud to be Hutu, and the poor to bear their poverty with dignity.

The Church financed a bi-monthly newsletter, the *Kinyamateka*, with Kayibanda for some years its editor-in-chief.[60] He was close to Monsignor André Perraudin, a Swiss Catholic who arrived in Rwanda in 1950 and was appointed Archbishop of Kabgayi nine years later. He had taught and was later rector at the Grand Séminaire of Nyakibanda.

Perraudin was said to have influenced Kayibanda and supported the Hutu revolutionary movement. Not all members of the Church were as close to the regime and some priests preached in favour of reconciliation.[61]

The Parmehutu, Kayibanda's party, was the only party allowed to submit candidates for legislative elections, and, with rule by majority Hutu, Rwanda was widely considered to be a democracy. It was supposedly stable. The president lived modestly and his outward behaviour contrasted well with that of other African leaders. Rwanda continued to be supplied with technical and military aid by Belgium, and the fact that this was an apartheid system against Tutsi with a quota system for them was conveniently ignored. According to official calculations the Tutsi accounted for 9 per cent of the population, a figure that was contested, but Tutsi would be represented in Rwanda accordingly.[62] There were vigilante groups created to ensure that Tutsi were not acquiring more than their fixed quotas in schools and employment.

Kayibanda's reliance on regional power would eventually become his great weakness, and resentment would develop in the army about the large percentage of senior posts given to southerners. To deflect criticism, Kayibanda would respond with ferocious anti-Tutsi campaigns. He would also use events in neighbouring Burundi to further his ambitions. Because Rwanda and Burundi were administered as a joint colonial territory, and because there was violence between Hutu and Tutsi in both countries, the two were often linked. They are actually two distinct and self-contained states, although sometimes the events in one country triggered a reaction in the other. Burundi achieved independence in 1962, with a Tutsi minority dominating the majority Hutu. In April 1972 there was an abortive coup by Hutu and there followed massacres of Hutu of unprecedented magnitude. An estimated 200,000 Hutu were killed in a systematic slaughter which led to accusations of genocide, although one academic called it a 'selective genocide' to emphasize that the educated, the semi-educated, the schoolchildren, the employed – that is, the actual or potential Hutu leadership – were special targets.[63] In the US State Department it was estimated that in Burundi an attempt had been made to kill every Hutu male over the age of fourteen; every Hutu member of the cabinet had been killed, all the Hutu army officers, half the country's schoolteachers, and thousands of civil servants. In a special report produced by the Carnegie Endowment for International Peace, a congressional aide was quoted: 'By the end of May we knew it was genocide from officially classified information from the US State Department.'[64] Journalists began to write about events in Burundi and news stories prompted congressional interest. Senator Edward M. Kennedy told the Senate that the Hutu were being killed at the rate of 3,000 a day. 'Should not governments condemn the killings?' he asked.

The Belgian government called it 'veritable genocide'.[65] The French National Assembly urged action. The United States made diplomatic representations. It seems no other government raised the issue in the UN or in any other forum. In August, an official from the State Department explained: 'Genocide is a specific, legal term with a precise meaning. It boils down to trying to kill a whole people. The Burundi government didn't try to do that; they couldn't. You can't kill off 80 percent of your population. Perhaps they engaged in mass murder; they weren't guilty of genocide.'

At its meeting in 1973 at the UN Commission on Human Rights in Geneva, the Sub-commission on the Prevention of Discrimination and Protection of Minorities forwarded a complaint against Burundi for gross violations of human rights. But when the commission met in 1974 the only action was a working party established to communicate with the government of Burundi.[66] After a few days in the headlines, Burundi sank back into obscurity and the killing continued.

At least two hundred thousand people fled into Rwanda as a result of the massacres in Burundi, and for Rwanda's President Grégoire Kayibanda the events in Burundi were considered something to be exploited and manipulated for political advantage. He initiated a further crackdown against Tutsi and started a campaign to 'purify' the country.[67] The National Archives of Rwanda, those found in the Présidence collection, contain neatly typed lists of the names of Rwandans who in 1973 were ordered out of their jobs because they were Tutsi. These lists, dated February, were posted on public buildings: 'Those Tutsi who need not present for work tomorrow,' the decrees proclaimed.[68] Vigilante groups were established to reduce the number of Tutsi pupils in schools. There were Comités de Salut Publique created in each locality in order to check and verify every person's ethnicity and to ensure that in education and employment the 9 per cent quota was strictly enforced. In Butare, Hutu students formed tribunals to check the bloodlines of students to determine the 'pure Hutu'. Tutsi fled the campus and some of them were beaten by Hutu students with iron bars.

In charge of this nationwide anti-Tutsi campaign was the army chief, Major Juvenal Habyarimana.[69] Habyarimana, a northerner from Bushiru, was the first and the highest-ranking officer to have graduated in 1961 from Rwanda's newly established military academy.[70] He was trained by Belgian officers previously responsible for the Force Publique

Congolaise. The new army recruits received Para-commando and special forces training at Belgian military academies.[71] They were selected by Belgian officers from a Catholic secondary school in Kabgayi, and all but one of them were Hutu from the north.[72] They became known as the 'promotion Logiest', the class of Logiest. It was Colonel Guy Logiest who had wanted a modern army for Rwanda. A Belgian officer from Stanleyville, Major François-Louis Vanderstraeten, was appointed the first commander, and it was Colonel Vanderstraeten who, on 13 July 1963, handed command to Habyarimana, and promoted him to captain.[73] Vanderstraeten remained with the force as a '*conseiller technique*'.[74]

A total of 360 Belgian soldiers stayed in Rwanda after independence in 1962, and the army would become the strongest state institution. It was officially composed of 86 per cent Hutu and 14 per cent Tutsi, but in reality it was overwhelmingly Hutu. Habyarimana remained the commander-in-chief of the army and was later appointed minister of defence.

He seized power in a coup on 5 July 1973.

3 | THE RWANDAN PATRIOTIC FRONT

§ President Juvénal Habyarimana appeared to bring stability to Rwanda. He proclaimed the *coup d'état* in the name of a Committee for National Peace and Unity, and it was noticeable how the killing of civilians suddenly ceased. 'We can no longer tolerate ethnic discrimination,' Habyarimana declared in a radio address on 5 July 1973.[1] The committee, comprising fellow army officers – most of them from the first graduation year at the military academy – included one Tutsi. It would be called a bloodless coup, but a secret purge took place of some fifty-five members of the former government, including ministers, deputies, army officers and state functionaries, all of them imprisoned in the notorious Ruhengeri prison and starved to death.[2] Some of their family members were paid substantial sums for their silence about the disappearances.[3] The former president, Grégoire Kayibanda, and his wife were put under house arrest and were also starved to death.

Habyarimana retained his position as the head of the army, the National Guard and the minister of defence. There were new ministers appointed to government – all of them from the military. Habyarimana reinforced the regional rivalry and largely excluded from power those from the south, from the former president's power base. He came to rely on kinsmen from the north. Of the eleven officers who seized power with him, all but one came from the prefecture of Gisenyi, from the Bushiru, which included the communes of Karago, the president's own, and Giciye, where his wife, Agathe Kanziga, was born. She was from a well-established lineage.

At the centre of state power was the army, now called the Forces Armées Rwandaises (FAR). The officer corps was largely trained by Europeans, and it took four years to graduate from the Ecole Supérieure Militaire (ESM). This included training in commando tactics, guerrilla warfare and intelligence gathering. Some instructors had trained in France and Belgian officers served as lecturers.

The Gendarmerie Nationale, created in 1976, was somewhat different. It was created by French officers, part of a military assistance agreement which Habyarimana signed in 1975. France provided all the equipment

– vehicles and weaponry – and the training of recruits included courses in France. The gendarmerie was to be responsible for social control, mass mobilization and the restoration of public order. It was intended that there should be constant contact between national gendarmes and the population in order to 'inform and educate' the people. Intelligence gathering was a major role for the gendarmerie; the communal police on the hills of Rwanda were to regularly inform their local gendarme about citizen behaviour.

Both the army and the gendarmerie were given intelligence and surveillance capability for 'internal security'. The security services, however, the Service Central de Renseignements (SCR), were staffed by civilians and attached to the office of the president. An extensive filing system was created with files on individual citizens. This would eventually contain detailed information on some 44,000 people, who were overwhelmingly Tutsi.[4] This was called the Service de Recherches Criminelles et de Documentation (SRCD). Among non-communist countries Rwanda was probably the most controlled state in the world. Every Rwandan was mandated by law to carry an identity card showing his or her group, Hutu, Tutsi or Twa. Those who illegally changed this classification were subject to imprisonment, a fine or both.[5] No Rwandan was allowed to leave the prefecture without appropriate authorization. In February 1975 each prefect established a Council for Security. It was clear, even now, that the threat Rwanda faced was considered to be an internal one.

When in July 1975 military rule was formally abolished, a new political party came into being, the Mouvement Révolutionnaire National pour le Développement (MRND). Only MRND candidates were allowed to run for office. Every Rwandan, young or old, became a member. The party was everywhere, on every hill and in every family unit. Members of the party were appointed to run local administrations and senior party officials were Habyarimana cronies from the north of the country. The one-party system ensured that Habyarimana was triumphantly elected president in December 1983 and again in December 1988. He was the sole candidate. A devious man and a double-dealer, he was instrumental in teaching the people to adore him as the father of the nation. Internationally, Rwanda was portrayed as a democratic country with rule by the majority.

In this strictly controlled society Tutsi continued to be marginalized. The quota system was retained, allowing only a certain percentage of Tutsi to attend schools and universities. There was one Tutsi in a nineteen-member cabinet, one ambassador in the foreign service, two deputies in a seventy-seat national assembly, and two members in the central committee of the ruling party.[6] In the army, Tutsi were disbarred from becoming officers and Hutu soldiers were forbidden from marrying Tutsi.[7]

§ Rwanda's violent divisions might have been easier to heal and its tragic history somewhat different had it not been for the involvement of outside interests. None had more dramatic effect than that of France, for without France the dictatorship of Juvénal Habyarimana would never have lasted as long as it did. Two years after Habyarimana took power, in 1975, a military cooperation and training agreement was signed with Paris and, over the next fifteen years, France slowly replaced Belgium as the most important ally, offering financial and military guarantees that Belgium could not provide. So staunch an ally was France that Habyarimana would come to believe that French support for his regime was unconditional, regardless of the military or political tactics he used in order to remain in power.

From the time of the UN Trusteeship the French had been clear that their support was for 'the democratic Hutu party' in Rwanda and in favour of the 'Hutu revolution'. In 1963 an expert from the French Ministry of Foreign Affairs further elaborated on the policy towards Rwanda.

> Situated on the border between Francophone Africa and Anglophone Africa, Rwanda in years to come could effectively contribute to the development of French influence in the region ... And could be a jumping off point for cultural penetration of neighbouring countries.[8]

The first military links had been forged in 1965, when French attachés from neighbouring Kinshasa in the Congo sought military connections in Kigali. Their main contact was a young and ambitious minister of the National Guard, an army officer by the name of Juvénal Habyarimana. So close did these links become that the French ambassador in Kigali was able to predict that a *coup d'état*, should it occur, would be likely to involve Habyarimana as he had managed to accumulate virtually all the power in the land. Once the 1973 coup took place there was added impetus to the developing relationship with France. In the mid-seventies Belgium's former territories – Rwanda, Burundi and Zaire – were incorporated into the Franco-African family. Rwanda was regarded as a francophone bulwark against the neighbouring independent states of Tanzania, Uganda and Kenya. They were non-aligned and yet remained firmly in the anglophone sphere and were therefore considered hostile to French interests.

French relations with African countries were essentially founded on ties of friendship, believed the best way to maintain French influence in Africa.[9] This came through a policy of close relations between the presidential palace in Paris, the Elysée and African heads of state. President Habyarimana would become closely allied to President François Mitterrand, and considered him a personal friend.

The one problem that was never seriously addressed by either the regime or its French ally was the plight of the Rwandan refugees living outside the country, those people who had fled during the anti-Tutsi campaigns that had started in 1959. These exiled and stateless Rwandans had created the largest refugee problem on the African continent, and while the regime in Kigali denied these people the right of return, in neighbouring Uganda, where many were living, they were not accorded full rights of settlement. In western Uganda the Rwandans were the subject of prejudice, discrimination and sometimes persecution.

In October 1982, after years of disputes over land and jobs, the Rwandan refugee communities in Uganda were attacked by indigenous people, and there was looting and rape. People were beaten and some were killed. Some 35,000 head of cattle were stolen. More than 80,000 people fled towards the border with Rwanda and a few made it across before Rwandan guards closed the frontier. Some 10,000 people were then trapped, caught on a strip of land between the two countries barely two kilometres wide. People began to die and international agencies provided emergency aid. Rwanda agreed to resettle some 30,000 people in March 1983, but Ugandan persecution of Rwandan refugees continued, and in December thousands of Rwandans fled from Uganda to Tanzania. With an announcement in Kigali in July 1986 that the refugees would not be allowed to return because the country was not big enough, there seemed to be little hope of a political settlement.

The total number of Rwandans living as exiles has always been a matter of debate. One estimate put the total number at 2 million, which includes all those living in other African countries, and those in Belgium and North America. The government in Kigali estimated some 200,000. The United Nations High Commissioner for Refugees (UNHCR) estimated that by 1990 there were 900,000 Rwandan refugees in Uganda, Burundi, Zaire and Tanzania.[10]

When the first Rwandans had fled there had been hopes for a quick return, but as the years went by the camps took on an air of permanency. The incursions into Rwanda all failed. In Uganda, when President Milton Obote ordered the removal of non-skilled foreigners from public employment and a census was ordered, there were fears that the Rwandans might be expelled. The exiles were helped by the UNHCR.

Those refugees who fled as children acquired education and many gained scholarships to study in Europe and North America. Like other people who are stateless, these Rwandans set great store by education. These young and educated refugees kept in touch, forming clubs and associations. They lived in Quebec, in New York, Brussels, Nairobi and Dakar, and were doctors, lawyers and social workers. They produced regular newspapers and magazines. Most of them had no memory of Rwanda – and some had not even been born there – but for them it was considered to be a land of milk and honey.

The first organized grouping to be established in the refugee community in Uganda was the Rwanda Refugees Welfare Association (RRWF). In 1979 it evolved into the Rwandan Alliance for National Unity (RANU). This organization was more political and, as its name implied, it was created to oppose the divisive politics of Hutu nationalism. It operated in exile between 1981 and 1986 in Nairobi and then in 1987, when it changed its name to the Rwandan Patriotic Front (RPF), it transformed itself into an organization dedicated to the return home of the refugees. While the older generation feared that as in previous years an armed campaign would stand no chance, a new generation had grown up ready to fight, believing that it was the only solution to their refugee status. The RPF went on to establish groups in the diaspora and an intense fund-raising campaign was instigated; eventually there were RPF fund-raising cells in every country where Rwandan refugees were to be found. The leadership denied it was a Tutsi organization; its twenty-six-member executive committee was composed of eleven Tutsi and fifteen Hutu. It claimed support from all Rwandans opposed to the repressive and backward Habyarimana regime. The stated aim was to end the dictatorship for everyone. But while the RPF portrayed itself as a multiethnic movement seeking to depose a corrupt regime, there were many within Rwanda who remained suspicious; there was criticism of a lack of effort in forging links with opposition leaders within the country.[11]

From outside the country the RPF published an eight-point programme that included an end to Rwanda's ethnic divide and the system of compulsory identity cards. The RPF wanted a self-sustaining economy, an end to the misuse of public offices, the establishment of social services, democratization of the security forces, a progressive foreign policy and the elimination of a 'system which generates refugees'. Its leaders proudly proclaimed themselves to be Inkotanyi, the name that had described the king's royal warriors.

It was hardly surprising that a rebel army was created by the RPF, but it was the clandestine nature of the way this was achieved which was unusual. Waging a secret campaign, the RPF leadership encouraged the youth in the refugee camps, in order to obtain training and combat experience, to join the Ugandan army. One of these RPF leaders, Paul Kagame, would later explain how Rwandan recruits had been encouraged to take command positions. 'We saw each one as a future fighter in our force,' he said some years later.[12]

Kagame, a secretive, thoughtful, sober and intelligent soldier, had fled his home in Gitarama as a child in 1959. He had spent time in Cuba, sent there by the Ugandan government. In Cuba he sharpened his understanding of guerrilla warfare theory. 'When you wage armed struggle,' he said some years later, 'you have to combine that role with politics. The struggle is about what? How do you sustain it?'[13] Kagame already had direct experience of overthrowing a government. He had been one of Yoweri Museveni's original 1981 guerrilla group, and had been with his triumphant National Resistance Army (NRA) when it took Kampala by force in January 1986. This had been the first insurgent movement effectively to take power from an incumbent African government.[14] Uganda had been a country shattered by the brutal rule of Idi Amin and his successors. Museveni had re-established an effective central government.

When in 1981 the original decision had been taken by Museveni to oust Amin's successor, Milton Obote, he had only thirty-five men and twenty-seven weapons. This group was known as the Popular Resistance Army, and Museveni had attacked the barracks at Kabamba.[15] There were two Rwandans with him. One of them was Kagame and the other was Kagame's friend, a charismatic soldier called Fred Rwigyema. While Kagame eventually became a senior intelligence officer and the NRA's deputy head of military intelligence, Rwigyema was promoted to major-general, the NRA's deputy army commander-in-chief and Uganda's deputy minister of defence. Both men had learned that with a small group of insurgents it was possible to launch an armed struggle with few resources and overthrow a government.[16]

The Rwandans were natural allies of Museveni for during the Obote regime the Rwandan refugees had been persecuted. This was reason enough to help him. In 1982, when the refugee crisis occurred and Rwandans were trapped on the border between Uganda and Rwanda, many young Rwandans, rather than remain persecuted refugees, had joined the ranks of the NRA. A quarter of the soldiers in the 14,000-strong NRA were Rwandan, and up to two to three thousand were the sons of Rwandan exiles.[17] Many of Museveni's top commanders and officers were Rwandan. When he had fought Obote some sought to discredit Museveni by claiming falsely that he was a Rwandan Tutsi and an interloper who was interfering in Uganda's affairs. After his victory in 1986, Museveni consolidated his power, and began a military recruitment campaign in western and southern Uganda, from the Banyarwanda and Buganda areas. This increased still further the number of Rwandans in the ranks of the NRA as more refugees took up the opportunity of military training. Thousands signed up, hoping that what had successfully occurred in Uganda could now be repeated in Rwanda. Joining the ranks of the NRA was a first step along the road leading home.

These Rwanda recruits gained military experience. They took part in NRA campaigns to secure eastern and northern Uganda, which had been in almost constant insurrection. There was fighting at Acholi, Teso, Lango, Kasese and West Nile. The largest uprising against Museveni was led by a voodoo priestess, Alice Lakwena, whose supporters carried out suicide attacks. But the atrocities committed by the NRA during these campaigns provoked resentment in Uganda and the Rwandans were blamed for crimes against civilians. There were fears by people in Acholi and Lango that the intention was that the Rwandans were going to take their land.[18] While the Rwandan officer corps was doubtless an asset for Museveni, it was also a problem. There were increasing complaints among Ugandan officers that they were discriminated against in favour of Rwandans in the army. In response to these fears, in November 1989 the most famous Rwandan, Fred Rwigyema, was removed from office. This led to resentment in the ranks. But by now an RPF guerrilla force had been built within the Ugandan army and it included key brigade and battalion commanders. These RPF militants secretly comprised a well-trained, disciplined rebel force with much combat experience.

In August 1990, two members of Rwanda's political elite, Valens Kajeguhakwa, a Tutsi businessman, and Pasteur Bizimungu, a Hutu and a relative of Habyarimana, fled to Kampala. They described to the RPF a country on the verge of collapse, split north and south, and drained by corruption. The people of Rwanda were ready to welcome anyone who wanted to overthrow the regime.[19]

There are several indications that the regime in Kigali knew something of the RPF planning, with suspicions aroused by the Rwandan embassy in Kinshasa, in neighbouring Congo. The idea of using civil defence to protect the country was suggested in a confidential report written in 1989 when the Rwandan ambassador to Zaire warned the Ministry of Foreign Affairs that there was going to be an attack on Rwanda by outside forces. He had analysed the Rwandan population in Zaire, the Congo and Chad, the Central African Republic, Gabon and Cameroon. The country's enemies were said to be among those communities where there was a majority of Tutsi. Some of them were receiving military training in Uganda. He worried about the weakness of the Rwandan army and proposed that the youth of Rwanda learn armed combat for civil defence.[20] There is also a suggestion that French intelligence had picked up information, and it is noticeable that arms supplies from France increased dramatically in 1989.[21] In Nairobi the news agency Agence France-Presse picked up a rumour that Ugandan troops were massing on the Uganda–Rwanda border.[22]

What is certain is that the regime in Kigali had hoped that the refugee problem could be solved with the minimum repatriation. In February 1988 Rwanda and Uganda formed a joint ministerial commission as Kigali was beginning to claim that the RPF was 'encouraging' refugees to return home. The next year it was decided that the UNHCR should survey the refugee settlements to ascertain the numbers involved, beginning in October 1990. Talks were held to discuss the refugee problem with the Organization of African Unity (OAU) and the UNHCR.[23]

It was too little, and too late.

§   The invasion came on 1 October 1990, when several thousand Rwandan soldiers from the ranks of Uganda's army deserted their positions and invaded Rwanda, taking with them their weapons and supplies. These soldiers finally declared their true purpose, and, ripping the Ugandan military insignia from their uniforms, some two thousand of them, together with medical doctors, scouts and messengers, surged across a bridge into the Rwanda border town of Kagitumba. They moved steadily forward for several days and took the military town of Gabiro 60 kilometres inside the country. They had rallied to Fred Rwigyema, the popular 'Commandant Fred', who led the invasion of their country.[24]

It was a disaster. Rwigyema was killed on the second day, and so shocked were fellow officers that the news was not announced for two weeks. He had been a fearless fighter, a commander who had led from the front, and his death had caused immediate fears for the morale of the troops. On 7 October there was a counter-offensive by the Rwandan army and an RPF convoy found itself under attack from artillery fire from French Gazelle helicopters. It was the French military, come to save their ally from invasion. Hundreds of RPF soldiers deserted and fled back to Uganda. The RPF command, many of its officers and many of its fighters were killed. The RPF fell back at the end of October, seeking refuge in an area where they knew the Rwandan government forces would not follow, the inhospitable Virunga mountains in the north-west of Rwanda where some of the RPF fighters died from starvation and the cold.

Museveni denied supporting the invasion and claimed that the soldiers had stolen their Ugandan uniforms and equipment. International observers chose not to believe him. The soldiers in the RPF were thought to have had almost unlimited access to NRA hardware, including artillery, and a steady stream of ammunition, food and logistics, with the two armies sharing intelligence. Museveni was accused of playing a double game, of professing friendship with neighbouring Rwanda while allowing the preparation of an invading army.

According to senior RPF sources, Museveni had been told about the invasion plan but had rejected it, saying it would never work. Habyarimana was far too popular in the West and Museveni warned that if the RPF invaded, Habyarimana would receive a great deal of outside help. Museveni promised the RPF that if they would wait he would see to it personally that Habyarimana would let the refugees return. According to the RPF leadership, they only ever mentioned the invasion once to Museveni. They did not share Museveni's certainties, and believed that the racist regime in Kigali would never allow the refugees home. 'There would never be a political settlement, we were in no doubt of that,' said Patrick Mazimhaka, vice-president of the RPF. 'We knew that the repression in Rwanda could only get worse.'[25]

President Museveni's assessment was correct: the 1990 RPF invasion did attract international criticism. The amount of support given to the Habyarimana regime shocked the RPF leadership. President Sese Seko Mobutu from neighbouring Zaire sent his Division Spéciale Présidentielle (DSP), and Belgium sent 400 paratroopers to protect the 1,700 Belgian nationals living in Rwanda. France sent troops, ostensibly to protect its nationals, although the French were far more involved and French spotter planes did much to locate the retreating RPF soldiers. In Paris the RPF offensive was seen as a foreign invasion by a neighbouring state. It was considered to be part of a Ugandan plot, which, in turn, was part of an attack by 'les Anglo-Saxons', whose eyes were on French interests in Africa. In French conservative, intelligence and army circles the English-speaking RPF was anathema. To have abandoned Habyarimana would have been tantamount to handing Rwanda over to the rebels. In parts of the French military, Uganda was nicknamed 'Tutsi-land', and it was taken for granted that what Museveni wanted was a Tutsi empire. There were policy-makers in France who believed that in Rwanda they were supporting a democracy – with rule by a majority. This majority rule legitimized French military and diplomatic support for the regime.

When the RPF invaded in October 1990, Habyarimana immediately telephoned the Elysée Palace in Paris, where President François Mitterrand kept African affairs a family matter: his son, Jean-Christophe, headed his Africa office.[26] Present in the office that day was Gérard Prunier, a French political scientist, who was visiting on another matter. He heard Mitterrand's son say that the crisis would be over in a few months.[27]

French troops were dispatched to Rwanda three days after the invasion took place, with 300 French paratroopers, from the 2ème Regiment Etranger Parachutiste, stationed in the Central African Republic; they secured Kigali airport. Within a few days more than six hundred French troops were in the country to 'protect and evacuate French citizens'. These were special forces; there were two companies of parachutists and paramilitaries from the French secret service, Direction Générale de la Sécurité Extérieure (DGSE), and there were combat helicopters. These troops had specialized training in secret operations. Although the French troops were not officially allowed to use weapons, France nonetheless installed soldiers next to the government troops in the north. While military help was substantial, the requirement was discretion.[28] In reality the French had operational control of the counter-insurgency campaign, and provided much-needed expertise, including communications equipment. It was notable that from October 1990 the overall command of the French military operations bypassed the usual military hierarchy in the Ministry of Defence, with operational control given to senior officers in the Elysée Palace.[29] These would include Admiral Jacques Lanxade, who at the time of the 1990 RPF invasion had been strategic adviser to President François Mitterrand. Lanxade was appointed chief of staff in 1991, and continued to help to determine policy towards Rwanda. Both the defence and foreign affairs ministries objected to these unusual arrangements for they felt they were excluded from decision-making.

The December issue of the Hutu journal *Kangura* published a full-page photograph of President Mitterrand with the caption, in Kinyarwanda: 'Great friends, they stand by you during difficult times'.[30]

§ From October 1990 the Rwandan army expanded quickly from 5,000 to 28,000 men, requiring, inevitably, a sizeable purchase of military equipment. Rwandan soldiers, who had only ever been equipped with light arms, were now also to have heavier guns, grenade launchers, landmines and long-range artillery.[31] France was a major supplier but soon a second source of weaponry was found. In a dramatic reversal, the government of Egypt, which had always refused to sell arms to Rwanda, changed its policy.

We may never know the full facts of the Egyptian decision in October 1990. The sales would undoubtedly have helped to boost foreign earnings. Another factor may have been Rwanda's sudden change in fortunes, for some US$216 million of international funding had by then been earmarked for Rwanda, some of it from the European Union with sizeable bilateral contributions from France, Germany, Belgium and the USA. Rwanda's economy was now in the hands of the world's most powerful international institutions, the World Bank and the IMF. A recently signed agreement had made Rwanda the subject of a Structural Adjustment Programme (SAP) devised to try to prevent economic chaos. From now on Rwanda's perilous economy was to be shored up. There was to be fundamental reform – and with outside help, the creation of a sound financial system with low inflation.[32] This would involve changes in pricing and trade policies, reductions in the size of government, and the regulation of production in order to integrate countries into the international market economy. What was intended under an SAP was financial restraint.

Yet when it came to Rwanda there is evidence to suggest that part of the money provided was not used productively as intended.[33] A sizeable portion of quick-disbursing loans was diverted by the regime towards the acquisition of military hardware. And the military purchases of Kalashnikov assault rifles, field artillery – a powerful asset in the mountainous terrain – and mortars were made in addition to the bilateral military aid package provided by France.

The initial arms deal with Egypt was brokered by Dr Boutros Boutros-Ghali, then an Egyptian minister of state for foreign affairs who knew Rwanda well. Boutros-Ghali had recently overseen a state visit to Cairo by Rwanda's President Juvénal Habyarimana. Boutros-Ghali had not yet launched his campaign to become the sixth secretary-general of the United Nations. He was a professional diplomat, a lawyer and author of books and articles on international law and political science. The regime in Kigali was grateful for his personal intervention in the arms purchases. Egypt had cheap mass-produced weaponry for sale.[34] Buying weapons from Egypt, with its low production costs, showed a competitive advantage. It was Boutros-Ghali who had intervened with the Egyptian government on Rwanda's behalf, pointing out that military aid to Rwanda from Belgium had been cancelled.[35] The regime had been so desperate in the past to get Egyptian weapons that at one point it had asked for them as gifts. Egypt had always declined. The only gift had been the statue of a pharaoh, placed with fanfare in the centre of one of Kigali's strategic roundabouts.[36]

All this changed. And amid the strictest secrecy, on 28 October 1990 the first arms contract between Egypt and Rwanda was signed. It was worth US$5.889 million and it included 60,000 grenades weighed in kilos, some two million rounds of ammunition, 18,000 mortar bombs, both 82mm and 120mm, 4,200 assault rifles, rockets and rocket launchers. The Egyptian signature on the contract was that of Colonel Sami Said Mohamed, chief of the friendly-countries branch in the Egyptian Ministry of Defence, and the deal proceeded quickly. The first consignment of weapons, described as 'relief materials', was loaded at Cairo international airport and was flown to Kigali on the day the deal was concluded. The weapons were shipped to Rwanda in a Boeing 707 belonging to the Egyptian airline ZAS at a cost of US$65,000 for the round trip. Habyarimana gave authority for the money to be paid through the Commercial International Bank of Egypt. As a gesture of goodwill President Mubarak gave Rwanda a gift of two field ambulances, later shipped by sea. The Rwandan ambassador to Egypt, Célestin Kabanda, wrote to his foreign minister, Casimir Bizimungu: 'the personal intervention of Boutros-Ghali with his colleague in the defence ministry was a determining factor in the conclusion of the arms contract for he was following closely the events on our borders'. Bizimungu wrote directly to Boutros-Ghali on 31 December 1990 to thank him for his help in hastening the arms deal.[37]

The secrecy would be maintained and necessary because there were currently the most strenuous international efforts under way to prevent a civil war between the RPF and the Rwandan government forces. The Belgian prime minister, Wilfried Martens, had flown to Nairobi on 14 October to try to open negotiations between the Rwandan government and the RPF. There had been regional peace talks three days later between Habyarimana, President Yoweri Museveni of Uganda and President Ali Hassan Mwinyi of Tanzania. The talks were facilitated by Mwinyi, who feared the creation of a much larger refugee crisis. Two days before the arms deal between Egypt and Rwanda was signed, a ceasefire had been agreed between the Rwandan government and the RPF following diplomatic efforts by the Belgian government. But ceasefire or not, from now on Rwanda would become the third-largest importer of weapons in Africa, ranked behind Nigeria and Angola. An estimated US$100 million was spent on arms. For the next three years, among the military hardware that entered the country, there was a seemingly unstoppable flow of small arms and light weapons.

Some years later, when asked about these arms deals, Boutros-Ghali described his role as that of a 'catalyst'.[38] He was a minister of foreign affairs, he said, and it was his job to help armaments production through the sale of his country's weapons; he would have helped any government wanting arms from Egypt. Egyptian arms were cheap and the Egyptians prided themselves on the speed of delivery. As to the wisdom of arranging an arms deal while international peace efforts were under way, Boutros-Ghali said that he did not think 'a few thousand guns would have changed the situation'. His was a close relationship with the Rwandan regime. It had begun with his first official visit to Kigali in 1983, and most of the high-level Egyptian–Rwandan diplomatic dialogue was conducted through him.[39] When Boutros-Ghali first went to Rwanda on official business in the 1980s it had been Egyptian policy to create a friendly bloc of countries around the Nile basin. Then deputy foreign minister, Boutros-Ghali wrote to the Rwandan foreign minister offering closer cooperation, and the chance to attend a regional conference as a member of a group of central African states: Uganda, Sudan and Zaire in addition to Egypt. Rwanda is the source country of the Nile and Boutros-Ghali later described in his memoirs how he travelled southwards again and again, deep into the centre of the African continent, to the source of this great river, which had so impressed him as a child. He learned that not only the source of the Nile but that of humanity itself lay deep in Africa: 'Africa is the mother of us all, and Egypt is the oldest daughter of Africa. This is why I have loved Africa and tried so hard throughout my life to help her.'[40]

§ The internal reprisals by the Rwandan regime for the October 1990 invasion by the RPF were swift and terrible. Once again, just as in 1963, the killing was committed by peasants who had been persuaded by their local authorities to organize groups of '*auto-défense civile*'. On 11 October, in Kibilira, in the northern Gisenyi prefecture, local officials were instructed that the killing was part of the traditional communal work, *umuganda*. The targets were the Bagogwe, the poor and pastoral Tutsi who lived apart from Rwandan society in northern Ruhengeri. There were also killings in the sub-prefecture of Ngorolero in the prefecture of Gisenyi. A human rights group collected the following testimony.

> M ... saw his wife and six children killed. He hid because he thought
> it would be like 1959 and 1973 when everything was stolen and
> when only some of the men had been killed ... [this time] he saw his
> neighbour cut off the head of his wife with one machete blow, in front

of his children, while the wife of his neighbour killed a child on the back of a victim ... this woman killed this child, while she herself was carrying a child of the same age on her own back.[41]

Another witness said:

The old *bourgmestre* ... found a much more effective way of liquidating undesirables. He invited all the men from the area to a political meeting. Once arrived, the victims were given to the killers by the *bourgmestre*.

In Mutara, where some RPF rebels were in hiding, hundreds of Tutsi were killed during massacres organized by local officials who told peasants that the Tutsi were coming back to Rwanda to turn them back into slaves. There was evidence of the Rwandan army committing human rights abuses; dozens of people living on cattle ranches in north-eastern Rwanda were killed by Rwandan soldiers. In the lakeshore resort town of Gisenyi, the local authorities were joined by Rwandan soldiers who took Tutsi to the army camp to be killed. Within the ranks of the gendarmerie torture was described as endemic. In early October, prisoners in Byumba prison, all of them Tutsi, were reported to have disappeared. Amnesty International reported that human rights abuses in Rwanda were carried out both by government officials and the security forces. Amnesty received numerous accounts of prisoners being tortured and of mass arrests taking place. Most cases of torture occurred within detention centres in Kigali, these premises belonging to the gendarmerie.[42] There were cells in a single-storey building within a compound housing the presidential offices in Kigali where torture took place.[43]

In Kigali a curfew was imposed which served to imprison people in their homes, and an estimated five thousand people said to be 'RPF supporters' were arrested. Hundreds of people were detained in Kigali's Nyamirambo stadium, where they were told that should the RPF get anywhere near Kigali, everyone would be killed. There were people taken from the stadium to be tortured in the cells next to the office of the president in central Kigali. Some of them were never seen again.[44] To heighten fear of the RPF the Habyarimana regime staged a fake attack on the capital. The gunfire and explosions heard during the night of 4 October were intended to encourage citizens to make arrests of 'Tutsi suspects'.

There was one privileged insider at the time, a well-informed French gendarme, Colonel René Galinié, who was the defence attaché at the French embassy and who had been in Rwanda since 1988. In a series of telegrams to Paris, Galinié warned that the situation in Rwanda could turn into an ethnic war. He wrote that there were Tutsi in Rwanda who feared that genocide could take place if French and Belgian troops were not there to stop it.[45] In another telegram Galinié explained: 'Hutu peasants organised by the MRND are looking for Tutsi suspects in the hills, with massacres in the Kibilira region. ... The government forces are exploiting the loyalty of peasants who are taking part in military action ... [organized] as groups of auto-défense armed with spears and machetes.'[46]

In spite of the reporting by human rights groups of massacres in Rwanda, the French cut no aid, made no public complaint, issued no overt criticism. Only on 19 December 1990 did France take part in a diplomatic démarche when in a statement prepared jointly by the ambassadors of France, Belgium and Germany and the representative of the European Union in Rwanda, the following warning was issued: 'The rapid deterioration of the relations between the two ethnic groups, the Hutu and the Tutsi, runs the imminent risk of terrible consequences for Rwanda and the entire region.' In Brussels there was an outcry against the human rights abuses perpetrated by the Rwandan regime and, just days after the October invasion by the RPF, the Belgian government announced its intention to withdraw from Rwanda for good, citing a legal obligation to remain neutral in situations of war.

4 | AKAZU: THE OLIGARCHY RULING RWANDA

§ When the RPF invaded Rwanda in October 1990, Paul Kagame was in the United States, where he had just begun a military training course at the US Army Command and General Staff College at Fort Leavenworth, Kansas. He had immediately returned to take control of the defeated rebel force. It was Kagame, with his experience of guerrilla warfare, whose decision it was to move those still alive to the appalling conditions of the Virunga mountain range, leaving behind decoy units to stage attacks and to divert attention. It was in this inhospitable place that the RPF was reorganized. Despite the considerable hardships, there were new recruits arriving every day from the diaspora, and by 1991 the RPF had nearly doubled in size. Eventually the RPF would be credited as the most educated rebel army ever created. It reputedly had a high percentage of medical doctors in its ranks. From a ragtag band of fewer than two thousand men, Kagame created a 15,000-strong, disciplined light infantry army which, given all the circumstances, relied on resupply by foot.[1] For this reason his soldiers had high endurance levels. They were highly politicized. Each new recruit found political education to be a part of military training; there were 'political commissars' assigned to every unit in order 'to remind the soldiers why they were fighting'.[2]

Kagame believed it would be a protracted war. He also thought that if the RPF managed to increase pressure points in the north, then contradictions within Habyarimana's corrupt regime would cause it to self-destruct. There would be constant activity. 'Sometimes in a single day we would carry out ten different operations across Virunga and the northeast ... this made it very difficult for the government to have stability or the freedom to operate,' Kagame said some years later.[3]

After their disastrous invasion the RFP had sufficiently regrouped and rearmed that barely four months later it was able to mount a daring and dramatic raid on Ruhengeri, an important northern town and a Hutu stronghold. The first targets were grain warehouses and a government-owned farm with several hundred head of cattle, needed to feed their comrades. There was strong military resistance to their assault and only later on, after French paratroopers had been recommended for medals, would they realize that French soldiers had played a direct role in the defence of Ruhengeri.

The decision to attack a prison and free the 1,000 inmates was taken by Kagame. The attack prompted an immediate reaction from Kigali and an order from the president's office to the local commander, Captain Charles Uwihoreye, to kill all the prisoners. Uwihoreye refused the order and was thrown into prison in Kigali, and only released later when a human rights group took up his case.[4]

The successful attack on the prison was followed by looting of the bank and police stations. The RPF withdrew later that day carrying a sizeable quantity of stolen weapons in stolen jeeps, disappearing to their mountain hideaway. The Ruhengeri raid was a stunning humiliation for the regime. In retaliation and for the next three months the pastoralist Bagogwe people were again the targets of persecution. An estimated three hundred men, women and children were killed in the Gisenyi prefecture, in President Habyarimana's home region, the Bushiru. Roadblocks were erected in order to stop potential witnesses entering the area, and to prevent escape for the victims.[5] Once more there was evidence of the organized nature of the killing. In one commune buses were sent to collect the victims. There were instances of peasants being told that the killing was part of their community work, *umuganda,* and was necessary in order to get rid of 'enemies', and to eliminate the accomplices of the '*inkotanyi*'.[6] The goods and the land of the victims were distributed.

Over the next few months another key RPF victory was achieved with the seizure of the border town, Gatuna. By the end of 1991, the RPF controlled a swathe of land along the northern border, comprising an area constituting roughly 5 per cent of the country. The RPF now made its headquarters in an abandoned tea plantation at a place called Mulindi. There were ceasefires between the RPF and the Rwandan government in October and November 1990. In February 1991 there was another ceasefire. Each was renewed after violations. There were thus three years of sporadic fighting between the RPF and the Rwandan government army.

The president of the RPF was Colonel Alexis Kanyarengwe, a northern Hutu and former Rwandan minister of the interior who had fled Rwanda in 1980 after accusations that he was plotting against Habyarimana. His appointment signified a link between the RPF and the Habyarimana opposition in Rwanda. But during three years of civil war the RPF neither broadened its political base nor rallied large numbers of Hutu to its side. The civil war divided society; it created instability and near economic collapse.

§ The civil war had a devastating effect on Rwanda, displacing thousands of people, and having an impact on tea and coffee production. The war cut the road to the Kenyan port of Mombasa – Rwanda's main overland route to the outside world. It destroyed the fledgling tourist industry, which had become the third-largest earner of foreign exchange.

Although in Rwanda the levels of poverty remained high, during the 1970s and early 1980s economic and social progress had been made. The real gross domestic product (GDP) growth was of the order of 4.9 per cent per annum (1965–89), school enrolment increased and inflation was among the lowest in sub-Saharan Africa, less than 4 per cent per annum.[7] Coffee was cultivated by approximately 70 per cent of rural households, although it constituted only a fraction of the total monetary income of those who grew it. And 75 per cent of Rwanda's export earnings came from coffee. All coffee producers in Rwanda were smallholders and the government assured them a guaranteed price. This made the government a profit. A Belgian academic and expert on the region, Professor Filip Reyntjens of Anvers University, says that towards the end of the 1980s corruption in Rwanda was limited and he believed that human rights were more or less respected. Compared with other African countries, Rwanda was not so bad.[8] The Habyarimana years had begun with a campaign of development. Rwanda was endowed with one of the best road systems in Africa, post and telephone services, and there was an expansion of the electricity supply. It was a popular country for aid workers. Rwanda was beautiful and well organized. It was 62 per cent Roman Catholic and 17 per cent Protestant. The Churches controlled 80 per cent of health clinics and contraception was forbidden. Until the late 1980s Rwanda had been a small and poor but self-sufficient country with an average annual inflation rate not higher than 4 per cent. There were improving standards of public health and education, and Belgium, France and Switzerland poured in money. There were also fault lines. Rwanda had the highest, and growing, population density of any African country. In 1989 there was drought and famine in the south, and when the RPF invaded in October 1990 there was further loss of food production in the north, and the creation of 300,000 refugees, who lived in camps.

A lethal blow to Rwanda's economy had come in June 1989 when the International Coffee Agreement (ICA) had fallen apart, as a result of political pressure from Washington, acting on behalf of the large US coffee traders. World prices plummeted. In Rwanda, the Fonds d'Egalisation – the state coffee stabilization fund, which purchased coffee from Rwandan farmers at a fixed price – started to accumulate a sizeable debt.[9] Revenues decreased drastically and foreign earnings diminished by 50 per cent. Poverty increased. Very few countries had experienced such a rapid decline. Rwanda was a desperate case. The international financial institutions had concluded that with the imposition of a Structural Adjustment Programme (SAP), the levels of consumption would increase markedly and there would be recovery of investment, and an improved balance of trade leading to lower levels of debt. This depended on the speedy implementation of trade liberalization and currency devaluation and the lifting of all subsidies to agriculture, the privatization of state enterprises and the dismissal of civil servants. Rwanda signed the agreement in October and the first devaluation of the Rwandan franc was carried out in November 1990, barely six weeks after the RPF invasion. Intended to boost coffee exports, the devaluation was presented to the public as a means of rehabilitating the economy. But the fall in the currency contributed to inflation and a decrease in real earnings. There were large increases in the prices of fuel and consumer essentials. The state administration was in disarray; the biggest employer was the government, with 7,000 employed centrally and some 43,000 in local administration. The effects of the SAP were swift in coming. State enterprises were pushed into bankruptcy and health and education services collapsed. The incidence of severe child malnutrition increased dramatically, as did the number of recorded cases of malaria. The economic crisis reached its climax in 1992 when Rwandan farmers in desperation uprooted some 300,000 coffee trees, for the government had frozen the farm-gate price of coffee at its 1989 level. A significant profit was appropriated by local coffee traders and intermediaries, serving to put further pressure on the peasantry.

In June 1992, a second devaluation was arranged by the IMF, leading to further escalation in the prices of fuel and consumer essentials. Coffee production tumbled by another 25 per cent. The loan cooperatives that provided credit to small farmers disintegrated. The Food and Agriculture Organization (FAO) warned of the existence of widespread famine in the southern provinces. By early 1994 coffee production had collapsed. Rwandex, the mixed enterprise responsible for the processing and exporting of coffee, had become largely inoperative. Rwanda was descending into poverty and destitution and with fewer spoils for the governing elite. Military spending continued to increase, and by 1992 accounted for 71 per cent of the nation's budget.[10] It would appear no adequate warning system about military spending existed in either the IMF or the World Bank.

Another consequence of the October 1990 invasion had been the encouragement it gave to the emerging pro-democracy groups. They were supported in turn by the numerous human rights groups that had been created elsewhere in Africa. At the end of the cold war there had been hopes that, freed from the constraints of superpower rivalry, the brutal and corrupt regimes in Africa would change. There were widespread calls for democratization in Africa, echoed in Washington, DC. In June 1990, when President Habyarimana attended a Franco-African summit at La Baule, he had been informed by President François Mitterrand that a link was to be made by France between economic aid and political democratization. Mitterrand advised Habyarimana to introduce a multiparty system, and Habyarimana had quickly promised to liberalize. Rwanda was about to enjoy a higher profile during the forthcoming visit to the country of Pope John Paul II in September 1990. On 13 November Habyarimana announced that a multiparty system would be created. Later that month, the first independent party was established in exile: the Union du Peuple Rwandais (UPR). There was a wave of optimism and hope, but it was misplaced. Habyarimana continued to persecute journalists deemed to have written subversive articles, and the Mouvement Révolutionnaire National pour le Développement (MRND) and Habyarimana continued to benefit from state resources and access to the media. When a coalition government was created it included just one opposition minister.

§ President Juvénal Habyarimana lived in a large Swiss-style chalet set in a beautiful garden.[11] It was on the outskirts of the capital and close to an important military barracks. The house was minutes away from Kigali's international airport and was directly under the flight path. There were tennis courts, swimming pools and numerous summer houses for outside dining. The house had ebony woodwork, marble floors, brass fittings and white and gold reproduction Louis XV furniture. In a back bedroom, on the second floor, a secret stairway led from inside a wardrobe to a series of attic rooms. One of these rooms was the president's inner sanctum, a small, oppressive room with a tiny skylight. The dark green of the carpet matched the colour in the Rwandan flag. The attic also included a simple and unadorned private chapel where chosen visitors were taken to pray. But although the president and his wife were ostentatiously Catholic, and the word God figured in Habyarimana's speeches, in reality the couple consulted soothsayers and clairvoyants. Outside in the garden and some way from the house there was a small brick bungalow where their own special rituals took place.[12]

Habyarimana, a tall man, walked with a limp from an injury sustained during a parachute jump when he was the first Rwandan soldier, with much fanfare, to parachute on to Rwandan soil. He was educated by a French-speaking religious order, and he spoke fluent French. His links with President François Mitterrand were well known, and when in Brussels he would stay with the Belgian royal family. Habyarimana was closest to President Mobutu in neighbouring Zaire, and it was rumoured that Mobutu was particularly close to Habyarimana's wife, Agathe Kanziga.[13]

Although Habyarimana was considered the Mwami (king) of the Hutu, the real power in Rwanda was believed to reside with her. She was said to be so conniving and influential that the Rwandans nicknamed her in memory of a terrible character from Rwandan history, Kanjogera. Kanjogera was the former King Musinga's mother.[14] Kanjogera played a vital role as manager of the royal household, and was the focal point of all court intrigue. She held the power in the shadow of the throne.

Agathe was a member of a known northern lineage and she was proud of being able to trace her ancestral roots as a Hutu of the Bushiru.[15] Her husband had no such power base; there were even rumours that Habyarimana might not have been from Rwanda at all, but from Uganda. It was her family support which had apparently allowed Habyarimana to mount a *coup d'état* and oust the former president, Grégoire Kayibanda, a southerner. The northern grudge against southern Hutu was well known; the southerners were blamed for the subjugation of the northern lineages.[16] Had the RPF not invaded in 1990, some speculated that there might have been a different civil war, north against south. The northern Hutu were fearful of an end to their power and dreaded an eventual alliance between Tutsi, southerners and pro-democracy politicians.

During the Habyarimana presidency the north had been favoured for state sponsorship and rural investment, and this had particularly benefited the agricultural Bushiru, which was on the country's northern periphery.[17] When international investigators were later trying to unravel the social, economic and cultural development of the Bushiru, they found that the particular communes of Giciye, home of Madame Agathe, and Karago, that of her husband, had greatly benefited. This had been achieved through an association called the ADECOGIKA, a means by which international aid and development money was channelled to the region.[18] With Habyarimana as president access to power was granted only to those from northern prefectures.

Agathe was said to have surrounded herself with a tightly knit group of increasingly influential family members. This group would be given the name Akazu, meaning 'little house'. A personal network, it comprised her notorious brothers: Protais Zigiranyirazo,[19] alias Monsieur Z, former prefect of Ruhengeri, who had a fearsome reputation, and Séraphin Rwabukumba,[20] a prosperous businessman who ran La Centrale, an import company and quasi-monopoly, and who owned a large house in Belgium. This man was said to have diverted funds for arms deals and for a time he ran the National Bank of Rwanda. The Akazu was rumoured to operate a death squad, and one of the army officers involved was Colonel Pierre-Célestin Rwagafilita.[21] Akazu was credited with having contacts everywhere, including in local communes and prefectures; it had representatives in all of Rwanda's embassies, and its richer members kept bank accounts abroad.

When some years later, in 2007, Agathe Kanziga was seeking refugee status in France, the Commission for Refugees was told that she had been at the heart of the regime and was guilty of crimes perpetrated between 1973 and 1994, especially assassinations of political opponents after her husband's 1973 *coup d'état* and the planning of the Rwandan genocide.[22]

French intelligence is believed to have been particularly well versed on the power structures within Rwanda. In June 1991, an intelligence report revealed the existence of an 'inner circle of power' dominated by Agathe and her family members. This group was using ethnic hatred to increase its power. It was determined to resist democracy and, knowing that it would be suicidal to oppose reform directly, the group relied on propaganda to instil fear among the people. There were significant amounts of money being used to strengthen the army, and independent political parties were being sabotaged. The moderate members of the military, the cabinet, the young educated officers and the intellectuals were powerless. While this group maintained its grip on power the creation of democracy never stood a chance. And if anyone tried to impose democracy, the report warned, it would serve only to provoke resistance.[23]

In November 1991, the RPF issued a press release in Paris claiming that a military command unit was being used in Rwanda to eliminate political opponents.[24] There were other warnings. A French scholar, Jean-Pierre Chrétien, described how in Rwanda a racist ideology had not just recently erupted as a consequence of the RPF invasion but had been nurtured for decades. Chrétien wrote that if the importation of arms into Rwanda did not stop then the country would become a powder keg.[25]

A few months later, in the spring of 1992, the Belgian ambassador in Kigali, Johan Swinnen, received information from a Rwandan informant including a list of names of members of a secret group whose job it was to eliminate liberals and pro-democracy politicians. The members of this group included Protais Zigiranyirazo, the president's brother-in-law; Colonel Elie Sagatwa,[26] head of the president's own security network and his private secretary; François Karera,[27] deputy prefect in Kigali, who had been in charge of the logistics for a recent massacre of civilians in Bugesera in March 1992; Captain Pascal Simbikangwa;[28] Lieutenant Colonel Anatole Nsengiyumva,[29] head of G2 army intelligence; and Lieutenant Colonel Tharcisse Renzaho,[30] prefect of Kigali. Swinnen was provided a few months later with a document that had been sent to all sector commanders from the Rwandan Ministry of Defence. It described all Tutsi in Rwanda and all those living outside as the 'principal enemy'. Swinnen reported to Brussels: 'This secret group is planning the extermination of the Tutsi of Rwanda to resolve once and for all, in their own way, the ethnic problem and to crush the internal Hutu opposition.'[31]

There was information publicly available in France. A French journalist, Jean-François Dupaquier, writing for a weekly magazine, described a 'fanatical Hutu' group supporting a 'final solution'. This group had a propaganda weapon, a journal called *Kangura*, which published articles reminiscent of Nazi literature in the thirties. *Kangura* promoted the notion of a 'pure Hutu race'. He described the Interahamwe militia and how they killed with machetes. He wrote that in Rwanda human rights were abused with impunity.[32] Dupaquier tried to interest members of the French parliament in questioning their government as to why support was provided to such a terrible regime, but to no avail.[33]

In August 1992 a defector, Christophe Mfizi, went public to claim that Rwanda was ruled by an oligarchy from the north.[34] Mfizi had been a senior official of the MRND since 1976 and for fourteen years he had run the Office Rwandais d'Information (ORINFOR), which controlled Rwanda's press. Mfizi published an open letter in Paris revealing what he called Le Réseau Zéro (Network Zero), a group of people who had successfully infiltrated every part of Rwandan society: politics, the army, finance, agriculture, science and religion. These people treated the country like a private company from which a maximum profit could be squeezed. The president and the leaders of the MRND were enmeshed by this group and unable to escape. In order to retain power, the group was encouraging racism and regional division. Until it was destroyed, there was no chance of creating democracy in Rwanda.

Another public warning came two months later, on 9 October 1992, in a press conference in the Belgian senate in Brussels, when Professor Filip Reyntjens, along with Senator Willy Kuypers, described how in Rwanda a death squad called Réseau Zéro was killing people and creating havoc and instability with the intention of blocking the political opposition and sabotaging the process of democracy.[35] Reyntjens described how in June 1992 a street militia, the youth wing of the MRND known as the Interahamwe, had sealed the capital by erecting roadblocks. This operation had been controlled by senior figures in government. Reyntjens had travelled to Rwanda to investigate the killing of Tutsi in March in the Bugesera, a region where there was a higher percentage of Tutsi than anywhere else. An estimated three hundred people had been murdered. Reyntjens discovered that the death squad known as Réseau Zéro was similar to those operating in Latin America. Its membership comprised off-duty soldiers and militia. Reytnjens said his information had been corroborated and his informers were two members of the death squad and three others – including two high-ranking army officers. Some years later Reyntjens revealed that one of his sources had been Colonel Bonaventure Buregeya, the secretary-general in the office of the president, who had been one of the officers who had seized power with Habyarimana in 1973. Reyntjens implicated thirteen people, including those names mentioned in Ambassador Swinnen's earlier report. All of them were in command positions in the army, were working closely with the president or were related to him.[36] This group had local representation. In the Bugesera, for example, there was support from Fidèle Rwambuka, a *bourgmestre* in Kanzenze. Reyntjens discovered that seventy-five members of the Presidential Guard had been sent to the Bugesera dressed as civilians and that they had been armed with knives and pistols. There were Interahamwe militia who travelled to the Bugesera in Ministry of Works vehicles with petrol provided by Rwabukumba and Joseph Nzirorera, the secretary-general of the MRND and previously in 1989 the minister of public works.[37] He said there had been similar operations planned for the Gikongoro prefecture but this region had proved 'difficult for this sort of manipulation' and so the groups went to neighbouring Kibuye in August. There had been a dozen people killed, dozens of injured and several thousand people displaced.

Reyntjens described how Réseau Zéro comprised presidential family members from the Bushiru, business contacts and those who believed in a northern 'pure and strong Hutu' ideology.[38] Reyntjens had called for an independent and international inquiry into the human rights abuses in Rwanda.

Another of Reyntjens's informants had been Janvier Afrika, who claimed to be a former member of the death squad. He said he had worked for Rwanda's internal security services but he had become sickened by increasing violence. Afrika said that the killings of the Bagogwe in January–March 1991 had been organized at a meeting at which both the president and his wife were present.[39] He warned that a terrible and imminent danger awaited all Rwandans. The poison had been prepared, and was being administered to the country in small doses. Something had to be done.[40] Thrown into prison, he was interviewed there in January 1993 by Jean Carbonare, the president of a French human rights group, Survie. Afrika told Carbonare how some seventy members of a street militia known as the Interahamwe had killed Bagogwe people in Ruhengeri in early 1992.

The realities of Rwanda were never a secret. On 24 January 1993 Carbonare had broken down on a France 2 television news programme after a visit to Rwanda in which he condemned 'the magnitude and systematic massacres of civilians', which had nothing to do with 'ethnic conflicts' but rather involved 'an organized policy' in which 'the level of power implicated in this genocide, this crime against humanity was strikingly high – we emphasise these words'. He pleaded for help to protect victims. In the Paris-based *Libération*, on 9 February 1993, a journalist wrote:

> In the far hills of Rwanda … France is supporting a regime which for two years, with a militia and death squads, has been trying to organize the extermination of the minority Tutsi … the death squads, organized in a Réseau Zéro [Network Zero] by the President's clan, are operating a genocide against the Tutsi, as though it were a public service.

In March 1993 *Le Nouvel Observateur*, under the headline 'The killing fields of Réseau Zéro … ethnic purification in Rwanda', carried an article that queried France's 'inexplicable military help to a dictatorship'.[41]

A report produced by a Rwandan human rights group, ADL, for the years 1990–92 used the word 'genocide' to describe the massacre of the Bagogwe in the northern prefectures of Gisenyi and Ruhengeri.[42] In the newspaper *Le Monde*, journalist Stephen Smith published an article quoting the French ambassador in Kigali, Georges Martres, saying that stories of massacres were 'rumours'.[43]

§ A pro-democracy movement was continuing to grow and for the first time it looked as though there would be serious opposition to the one party, the Mouvement Révolutionnaire National pour le Développement (MRND). In March 1991 a group from Gitarama, the former President Kayibanda's region, established the Mouvement Démocratique Républicain (MDR). More parties were created: the Parti Libéral (PL), which had hopes of bridging the ethnic divide, and the Parti Démocrate Chrétien (PDC). This party had been difficult to establish given the support of the Catholic Church in Rwanda for the MRND. But soon there was a plethora of parties, including an emerging ecology movement.

In June 1991 a new constitution legalized the formation of political parties, and also provided for freedom of the press. A vibrant press came into being. Each time there was a concession towards democracy, however, there was violence, and violence soon became an integral part of political life. Youth gangs, attached to political parties, violently coerced support, and there was increasing lawlessness. The uneducated and unemployed youth were taken from the streets and formed into gangs, each of them including delinquents and petty criminals, with experts in thuggery. They would disrupt political meetings and would take control of their own neighbourhoods. The restrictions on freedom of movement and residence meant that the youth were forbidden from leaving the countryside to find work, and this was where 95 per cent of the population lived. Most of the country's youth lived in rural areas with little hope of a future, unable to inherit enough land to raise a family, and constantly in search of low-paid and temporary jobs. Rwanda's increasing population density and severe soil erosion led one former prefect to say that the problem of land scarcity was a 'time-bomb'.[44]

The Interahamwe was the best organized. It was attached to the MRND and would eventually become the largest and the best-known group. It was created in 1991, and in rowdy and intimidating groups it increasingly terrorized anyone who criticized the government. Its members were disciplined and it had leadership at the most basic neighbourhood level. Intended to be countrywide, the Interahamwe was to have committees in every one of Rwanda's 146 communes. There were plans for 200 militia members in each commune with one man for ten families. The Interahamwe had supporters in the Rwandan gendarmerie, in the Presidential Guard and within the Rwandan army. It was not just the new recruits who were given food, beer and clothing but also family members.[45] The best-trained members were given hand grenades. Some recruits were issued AK47 assault rifles, although these required requisition forms. The Interahamwe wore distinctive clothes and its members were equipped with cords and bayonets and provided with shoes to wear. Groups were organized to communicate with each other by blowing whistles, used effectively to call for reinforcements.[46]

Of all the youth gangs, the Interahamwe was the most militant, and it eventually became evident that members were receiving military training, including at a major army camp at Kanombe just on the outskirts of Kigali. There were rumoured to be several training camps, one of them in Mutara, another in the Bugesera and one in the forest of Nyungwe. One of the well-known camps was at Gabiro, near a hotel in the Akgagera game park, and another was in the north-western Gishwati forest, near the Hôtel Mont Muhe, which belonged to members of the Akazu. The youths sometimes lived in tents in the forest near Gabiro.[47] The recruits were taught to handle weapons and use explosives and eventually they were taught to kill, with the emphasis on killing at speed, cutting the Achilles tendon in order to prevent escape. The first time that the Interahamwe militia took part in the mass killing of Tutsi will probably never be known, although it is known that Tutsi were attacked and killed in November 1991 in the commune of Murambi, east of Kigali.[48]

The Belgian ambassador in Kigali, Johan Swinnen, reported to his Foreign Ministry that the Interahamwe, whose members had been recruited outside the Bugesera, had taken part in the killings there in February 1992. The local group of militia had been ordered to pillage and set fire to homes; in this way it was hoped to portray the killing as local ethnic disturbances. In fact the killing was well planned and Swinnen was told that a group of professional killers had also played a role. A commando group had been recruited at the national gendarmerie school, Ecole Nationale de la Gendarmerie, and, dressed in civilian clothes, the recruits had killed members of the local Parti Libéral (PL) and the Mouvement Démocratique Républicain (MDR).[49] These killings were widely reported. A group of five Rwandan human rights groups held a press conference on 10 March 1992 to reveal that the massacres were the work of local officials determined to ruin the 'new politics'. The deaths in the Bugesera had been directly linked to the effective use of propaganda.[50] There were news broadcasts on Radio Rwanda, at peak times, which claimed that an unknown group in Nairobi, associated with the Parti Libéral (PL), intended to kill twenty-two prominent Hutu. At the time the PL was actively recruiting in the region. This time peasants took part in the killing; they were told that this was a special collective work session. When local officials ordered the people to 'clear the bush', everyone knew this meant to clear the hill of Tutsi. The slaughtering of women and children was called 'pulling out the roots of the bad weeds'. More than three thousand people fled the area, their homes razed to the ground.

People were thrown in the rivers or were burned in their homes. Tutsi who tried to defend themselves were disarmed by government soldiers. There were reports that thousands of people had taken refuge in the Nyamata Catholic church, and that the church was surrounded. Many people died from hunger and exposure. There were extreme forms of harassment from local security forces.[51]

After the killings in the Bugesera, similar incidents occurred in the Kigali prefecture, in Kibuye, in Cyangugu and in Gisenyi. The government explained the killings in Bugesera as 'self-defence', and although 466 people were arrested, they were later released. The regime blamed the president of the PL, Justin Mugenzi.[52] The US and Canadian ambassadors[53] went to see President Habyarimana to express concern at the violence, although the French ambassador, Georges Martres, failed to join this démarche.[54]

Rwanda became more violent. Bombings were reported throughout the country, particularly in Ruhango, south-west of Kigali, and in the southern town of Butare. A series of terrorist attacks took place, and grenades were thrown into crowds. Five people were killed when a bomb exploded in a taxi in Kigali. All attacks were attributed by the government to the RPF or their supporters. In the countryside there were reports of Tutsi killed in Gisenyi and of MRND officials threatening those attempting to register opposition political parties.

In order to appease his Western backers, Habyarimana, on 6 April 1992, formed a new government. It looked as though for the first time the ruling MRND party would be sharing power. It was allotted nine ministries from a total of twenty.[55] There were women in government for the first time; one of them, Agathe Uwilingiyimana, became the minister of education.[56] Uwilingiyimana, a progressive politician, a Hutu from the south, was determined to end the ethnic divide in society. At the ministry she had tried to end the quota system for Tutsi in schools. Just a month after her appointment, on 8 May, she had been attacked in her home in Kigali by twenty armed men. Some three thousand women demonstrated in Kigali in support of her. The country was in chaos. Military spending continued to increase while the government was relying on food aid.[57] There was an epidemic of bacillary dysentery spreading through Byumba, and, in Rwanda, 500,000 cases of AIDS.

The international pressure for a settlement between the RPF and the

Rwandan government now included France, the USA, Belgium and the Organization of African Unity (OAU), under its secretary-general Salim Ahmed Salim. In May 1992, the USA became more actively involved and Assistant Secretary of State for African Affairs Herman Cohen travelled to Rwanda, where he was assured by Habyarimana of the progress towards democracy. But Cohen expressed his doubts in a report to Washington because of the massive military spending that was ruining the economy. By now the RPF had achieved a transition from rebel group to legitimate participant in the political process, a transition recognized when the RPF had talks with Cohen and with the OAU's secretary-general in Kampala in May 1992. That year there were preparatory talks between the RPF and the French government in Paris in June.

A communiqué of the US State Department issued in early 1993 maintained that the continuation of US aid depended on progress with reform and the pursuit of democracy, a policy much criticized later on. The attempt to instal a multiparty coalition government, under the trusteeship of Rwanda's external creditors, was considered by some to have been impossible.[58]

§ A ferocious anti-Tutsi campaign was launched on 22 November when in a landmark speech Leon Mugesera,[59] the vice-president of the MRND in Gisenyi, and a political science professor, addressed party militants in a rabble-rousing, racist speech which quite clearly incited the murder of Tutsi:

> … what about those accomplices here who are sending their children to the RPF … we have to take responsibility in our own hands … the fatal mistake we made in 1959 was to let them [the Tutsi] get out … they belong in Ethiopia and we are going to find them a shortcut to get there by throwing them into the Nyabarongo River. We have to act. Wipe them all out.[60]

The Interahamwe later chanted his words. Mugesera was one of the intellectual architects of the racist ideology which held that Tutsi were evil and clever, lazy and arrogant. At the time of the Mugesera speech the Rwandan minister of justice was a member of the opposition, a man called Stanislas Mbonampeka, of the Parti Libéral. A lawyer and human rights advocate, he charged Mugesera with incitement to racial hatred. A warrant was issued for Mugesera's arrest but he took refuge in a military camp and the police were too frightened to arrest him. Mbonampeka resigned. He was not replaced.

As Rwanda's economic situation worsened, and as negotiations took place in Arusha, the regime in Kigali received ever-increasing support from France. The French president, François Mitterrand, and his Africa Unit successfully kept the French public and parliament unaware of the policy of propping up the regime.

It was French technical and military training which allowed the Rwandan army to increase from 5,000 to 28,000, equipping it with modern weaponry. In the years of civil war France tripled financial aid to Rwanda.[61] French arms supplied to Rwanda in the years 1990–94 increased, including sales of light weaponry, grenades and ammunition.[62] Some weaponry was provided free of charge. An inquiry established some years later by the French senate found there had been thirty-one direct transfers of weapons to Rwanda in disregard of France's export procedures, and these supplies had been taken directly from French army stocks.[63] There was thought to have been a total of 146 contracts negotiated with France which did go through the approval procedure. This procedure included the prime minister, the minister of foreign affairs and the minister of defence in an oversight committee.[64]

It has been estimated that during the years 1991–92 at least US$6 million of arms from France was sent to Rwanda: mortars, light artillery, armoured cars and helicopters. By 1993 Rwanda was receiving US$4 million military aid from France. All this was under the terms of an amended 1975 military technical assistance accord which had entailed an initial modest annual transfer of arms.[65] The accord had been signed by President Valéry Giscard d'Estaing just two years after Habyarimana seized power. At the time 'Giscard the African', as he was sometimes known, wanted to expand France's African sphere to include Belgian and French-speaking colonial territories, including Zaire, where France became a principal arms supplier. The intervention in Rwanda was claimed to be under a treaty obligation to an ally which France was bound to honour. In 1992, the agreement was amended to an '*Accord de défense*'.

In June 1992 a 'Commandement des Opérations Spéciales' (COS) was created for Rwanda, comprising French special forces – including units from the Foreign Legion – and experts in covert action. The COS, directly under the command of President François Mitterrand, adopted a military doctrine first formulated in the fifties, which had been designed in response to the French defeat in Indochina. This doctrine had been adapted during the Algerian war and had become known as '*guerre révolutionnaire*' (revolutionary war), and it included methods of population control, special skills in psychological warfare, the use of propaganda, and the creation of an '*autodéfense*' militia. The COS was a political, military and secret force established by Admiral Jacques Lanxade, a former military adviser to Mitterrand until April 1991, when he had been appointed the head of the French armed forces.[66]

The documentary evidence about French military involvement that has survived, a part of it contained in a military archive in Kigali, includes an order at the most senior level to keep secret the extent of French help. A letter from Colonel Déogratias Nsabimana,[67] commander-in-chief of the army, dated 9 December 1992, pays tribute to French soldiers who were improving the government defences against the RPF in the north. 'The French work has been good but they must be more discreet,' Nsabimana wrote to the minister of defence. Although successive officials in the French government have denied that French paratroopers participated directly in the civil war against the RPF, there is evidence to the contrary. Aid workers saw French soldiers manning artillery positions during the fighting with the rebel RPF in January 1991. A French mercenary, Paul Barril, would later proudly claim that he knew a member of the French secret services who had single-handedly stopped an RPF advance in 1992.[68] French soldiers were seen controlling checkpoints in Kigali, demanding to see identity cards, arresting Tutsi and passing them over to the Rwandan army. The anti-Tutsi behaviour of French soldiers was noticeable.[69] The military training provided by France extended to the Presidential Guard, responsible for the president's security. The Détachement d'Assistance Militaire et d'Instruction (DAMI), the name used for French military cooperation, provided three officers to the Presidential Guard between November 1991 and February 1993, led by a French gendarme, Lieutenant Colonel Denis Roux.[70] This was eventually halted because of French concerns about the violent activities of the Presidential Guard.[71]

There was a credibility gap between the officially recognized cooperation with France and the reality. Colonel Bernard Cussac, the French military attaché (July 1991–April 1994), and the head of the French military assistance mission to Rwanda, once explained: 'French military troops are here in Rwanda to protect French citizens and other foreigners. They have never been given a mission against the RPF.'[72] The official aims of French military cooperation were to train the Rwandan army, to ensure the safety of French nationals, and to inform Paris about the local situation. And while claiming that there were only 600 French soldiers in Rwanda, with a creative manipulation of rotas it was possible to keep 1,000 soldiers there.[73] There is eyewitness testimony showing how French soldiers arriving at Kigali international airport bypassed border controls.[74]

When in October 1992 the supporters of an extremist Hutu party took to the streets to demonstrate against a peace agreement with the RPF, they were chanting, 'Thank you, Mitterrand. Thank you, people of France.' In Kigali the French president was laughingly called 'Mitterahamwe'.

5 | PEACE IN RWANDA? THE ARUSHA ACCORDS

§   It was thanks only to international pressure that negotiations began between the government of President Habyarimana and the RPF, pressure that came from France, Belgium, the USA and the Organization of African Unity (OAU). The negotiations opened in Arusha, Tanzania, in July 1992. They were the only hope for a peaceful resolution to the civil war.

It took thirteen months of talks to get the Rwandan government and the RPF to sign a peace agreement; without international pressure, given their differences and the problems, an agreement would never have emerged. So happy were they with the outcome that the diplomats involved called the eventual agreement, known as the Arusha Accords, one of the best deals ever negotiated in Africa. It was a truly international effort with the involvement of delegations from five African states: Burundi, Zaire, Senegal, Uganda and Tanzania. The negotiations were organized by the OAU with leadership provided by President Ali Hassan Mwinyi of Tanzania, whose government acted as facilitator. Four Western countries had observer status: France, Belgium, Germany and the USA. The talks were monitored by Britain, Canada, the Netherlands and the European Union from their local embassies. The OAU secretary-general, Salim Ahmed Salim, a Tanzanian and one-time front-runner for the job of UN secretary-general, had a high profile at these talks.[1]

The OAU had been involved from the start of the civil war, and its leadership had seen the RPF invasion of Rwanda not as aggression by a neighbouring state, but as an attempt by the children of exiled refugees to go home. One of the ceasefires that followed the outbreak of fighting in 1990 had provided for the presence in Rwanda of a fifty-member Neutral Military Observer Group (NMOG), provided by the OAU, to monitor the border between Uganda and Rwanda in order to prove that Uganda was not helping the invaders. A group of fifty officers was provided but it was plagued by serious logistical and financial shortages.[2]

The Arusha Accords provided for radical change. The triumphant signing ceremony came in August 1993 and the agreement was comprehensive and wide-ranging, providing for political, military and constitutional reform. Rwanda was to have a broad-based transitional government until a democratically elected government was installed. The presidency was to become largely ceremonial, with the president wielding less power than most constitutional monarchs. A neutral international force was to be deployed, to be followed by the withdrawal of French soldiers. The RPF and the Rwandan army would integrate; there would be disarmament and demobilization. The refugees would be allowed home. As a first step, a battalion of RPF soldiers would be stationed in Kigali.

The transitional government was to hold power for no more than twenty-two months until free elections, and it would contain representatives of the three political blocs: President Habyarimana's political party and its allies, the internal opposition parties, and the RPF. The accords named Faustin Twagiramungu of the Mouvement Démocratique Républicain (MDR), the largest internal opposition party, as prime minister during the transition.[3]

Some thought that the Arusha Accords were the best that would ever be achieved. Eric Gillet, a human rights lawyer who had contributed to a human rights report on Rwanda, said that he thought that all that could be done was done at Arusha. The trouble stemmed not from the accords themselves but from the fact that Habyarimana and his entourage did not want them to work, and did everything possible to prevent agreement. Gillet said: 'The human rights workers, whether Rwandan or international, were not fooled. We did not think that someone capable of organizing massacres would suddenly turn into a democrat. We saw what was happening. We kept telling the Belgian authorities.'[4]

There are critics of Arusha who claim that the accords served only to back the extremists into a corner, taking away all their power. The hardliners in the MRND party, the northern clique in the military and in the extremist new grouping, the Coalition pour la Défense de la République (CDR), were denied power in the transitional institutions. The MRND was reduced to five seats in the transitional government. If a newly independent judiciary were to be installed, then the culture of impunity would end. The corruption could be exposed, as would the regime's human rights abuses. There was no provision in the peace agreement for an amnesty for political, economic or human rights crimes. Any government figure, from the president down, could have been investigated and charged. All that was left to the extremists was their ideology of Hutu nationalism, and the means to attract sympathy to their cause.

The vice-president of the RPF, Patrick Mazimhaka, who participated in the negotiations in Arusha, says that no one in the RPF leadership believed for one minute that Habyarimana was sincere when he negotiated and signed the accords. It is Mazimhaka who tells a now famous story about Colonel Théoneste Bagosora, an army colonel from the Bushiru who had provided a direct link between Arusha and the extremists in Kigali. At one point during negotiations, Bagosora, a fervent anti-Tutsi, had packed his bags. Mazimhaka saw him standing in a hotel lift surrounded by suitcases and asked why he was leaving. Bagosora said he was going back to Rwanda to prepare '*apocalypse deux*', the second apocalypse.[5]

The RPF had put its faith in the international community, explained Mazimhaka, hoping that if neutral peacekeepers were provided then this would stop the worst from happening. Major General Paul Kagame had received assurances. 'The whole world will be watching,' Kagame says he was told by Western diplomats.[6] 'We thought Habyarimana would be isolated,' said Mazimhaka.

Whether or not to include extremists in negotiations and in government is an issue that bedevils peace agreements. A flashpoint during the Arusha negotiations was the exclusion from the process of the CDR.[7] The RPF would not countenance the CDR in government, arguing that it was an offshoot of the president's party, the MRND, a crypto-fascist gang that would not allow anyone with a Tutsi grandparent to join. The RPF argued that the CDR did not meet the requirement of an August 1992 protocol signed with the government that forbade the inclusion of parties that promoted ethnic intolerance. Habyarimana was in favour of the inclusion of the CDR and he was supported in this by French diplomats who argued that it was better to have the CDR in government where it could be controlled than out of government where it could not. The Tanzanians said the same. The obstinacy of the RPF leadership over this issue sent Western diplomats, both British and American, urgently seeking meetings with Kagame to persuade him to concede the inclusion of the CDR. The US ambassador to Rwanda, David Rawson, was forceful over the issue. According to the State Department desk officer for Rwanda, an inter-agency meeting to discuss Rwanda agreed as early as March 1992 that the CDR must be included.[8] Western governments saw the exclusion of the CDR as a departure from constructive negotiation, insisting that a more substantive role should be given to those who stood to lose power. The RPF delegates told everyone that the founder of the CDR, Jean-Bosco Barayagwiza, who worked as director of political affairs in the Rwandese Ministry of Foreign Affairs, was a fascist thug and that the CDR was the above-ground incarnation of the 'underground forces' murdering the opposition and the Tutsi, and running the country.[9] The RPF was blamed for intransigence. Overall the RPF achieved a high level of success in Arusha and proved superior in negotiation, for the government team was split between hardliners and members of a transitional government that Habyarimana had been forced to create.

Critics of the Arusha Accords describe the deal as a veritable coup for the RPF and Rwanda's internal pro-democracy opposition. The RPF prevailed over the CDR issue and the transitional institutions were to give equal representation to the RPF and the ruling MRND, at five members each. The balance of power would be shared between eleven members of the National Assembly, representing five of the smaller parties established since 1991. The prime minister and the minister of foreign affairs were to be drawn from the minor parties, with defence going to the MRND and the Ministry of the Interior to the RPF.

Just how sincere the Habyarimana regime was came to light afterwards, for while it engaged in negotiation in Arusha the regime entered into the largest of all the arms deals with a French company called DYL Investments for US$12 million, involving the purchase of 40,000 grenades, 29,000 bombs, 7 million rounds of ammunition, 1,000 truncheons, 1,000 pistols and 5,000 AK47s, the money to be paid in million-dollar instalments. Transport was in the hands of the OGA (Office Général de l'Air) and East African Cargo, a Belgian company.[10]

Soon after the deal was signed, the chief executive of Rwanda's bank, Jean Birara, took the risky and exceptional step of privately warning diplomats from Western embassies about the purchase. But to no avail. By late December 1993, so openly distributed were weapons in Rwanda that the Bishop of Nyundo, from north-western Rwanda, issued an unprecedented press release asking the government why arms were being handed out to certain civilians. The government's answer was that the locals had to defend themselves against rebel and guerrilla forces because there were not enough troops.

§ In the years immediately before the 1994 genocide there was a bewildering array of aid agencies involved in Rwanda and most of them were fully aware of the overt system of discrimination operated against the Tutsi. In 1993 there were thirty-eight non-governmental organizations (NGOs) in Rwanda. Nothing exists to show that any of the knowledge, even that which the Bretton Woods institutions possessed, about the reality in Rwanda was ever shared with the Western diplomats negotiating the peace deal in Arusha. The USA was actively involved in the peace process from 1991. For several months in 1991 a series of French and US meetings with the government and the RPF ran in parallel, while each kept the other informed. In early 1992, in the African Bureau of the State Department, the assistant secretary of state for Africa, Herman Cohen, convened an inter-agency forum which continued to meet for the next two years to coordinate American efforts.[11]

There were human rights groups gathering information. They reported extensively on the Bagogwe massacres in January 1991 and the February 1992 massacre at Bugesera, describing the involvement of military and local government officials. In some communes Tutsi had been repeatedly attacked, and the military had distributed arms to civilians who supported Habyarimana. In one case, Tutsi victims were buried in the backyard of a local government official. So bad did the situation in Rwanda become that, in January 1993, a group of international human rights experts from ten countries travelled to Rwanda and collected testimony from hundreds of people, interviewed witnesses and the families of victims, and reviewed numerous official documents. They published a report in March 1993 revealing that in the previous two years those who held power in Rwanda had organized the killing of a total of 2,000 of its people, all Tutsi, singly, or in small or large groups. There had been some ten thousand Tutsi and members of the political opposition arrested or detained without charge. Many people had been tortured or badly beaten; some were held incommunicado in military camps rather than in prison. The report made clear that those in power were guilty of serious, and systematic, human rights abuses. The authorities in Rwanda, at the highest level, including the president, were responsible for the violence and murder committed by civilians, soldiers and, increasingly, militia. The militias operated with impunity. Rwanda's judicial system was paralysed by political interference.[12]

The word genocide was not used in the report, being considered too highly charged by some of the group's authors, but a press release distributed with the report carried the headline: 'Genocide and war crimes in Rwanda'. This was written by William Schabas, a Canadian lawyer from the International Centre for the Rights of the Person and Democratic Development, based in Montreal, and a member of the investigating commission.[13] He had argued strongly for the word genocide to be used. Schabas was convinced that genocide in Rwanda was undisputable, citing the definition in the 1948 Convention on the Prevention and Punishment of the Crime of Genocide: 'acts committed with the intent to destroy a national, ethnical, racial or religious group'. Those acts were killing, causing mental harm, inflicting conditions of life calculated to bring about the group's destruction, imposing measures to prevent birth and transferring children from one group to another.[14] In Rwanda the intent to destroy Tutsi as a group was evident because of the hate propaganda.

In response to this damning human rights report, Habyarimana promised a ten-point set of reforms. At the time his chief propagandist, Ferdinand Nahimana,[15] who had helped to provoke the massacres at Bugesera, was on a tour of Europe and the USA, trying to convince the press and public that the international commission had been misinformed. There had been an internal Rwandan inquiry, Nahimana claimed, which found that local officials were responsible for the violence.

There was little international concern when the human rights report was published. The Belgian government recalled its ambassador from Kigali for consultations, and the Rwandese ambassador in Brussels was told that Belgium would reconsider its economic and military aid unless steps were taken to rectify the situation.

There was another report prepared when, from 8 to 18 April 1993, the Special Rapporteur for the Commission on Human Rights for Extrajudiciary, Summary or Arbitrary Executions, Bacre Waly Ndiaye, visited Rwanda. He had received allegations of grave and massive violations of the right to life in Rwanda. His report, published on 11 August, used the word genocide to describe the killings in Rwanda. The victims of violence in Rwanda, Ndiaye reported, were in the overwhelming majority of cases Tutsi, and so the Genocide Convention was applicable. The UN Commission on Human Rights was established in 1946 to filter and consider human rights complaints.[16] There are fifty-three member states represented on the commission, which is a subsidiary of the UN General Assembly. It meets annually, from February to mid-March. In 1992 and in 1993, the commission discussed Rwanda; both times, the confidentiality clause was used, a way to avoid embarrassment for the state concerned, and a way to allow the commission to approach the government in closed session.[17] These confidential discussions were conducted by a committee of five.[18] This was the first step in a process that could lead to the serious and public step of appointing a Special Rapporteur. Ndiaye accused the Rwandan government of using propaganda to create a situation in which 'all Tutsi inside the country were collectively labelled accomplices with the RPF'. He described an elite which, in order to cling to power, was fuelling ethnic hatred. Concerning massacres, he wrote: 'such outbreaks were planned and prepared, with targets being identified in speeches by representatives of the authorities, broadcasts on Rwanda radio, and leaflets … [and] the persons perpetrating the massacres were under organised leadership'. Local government officials were found to have played a leading role in most cases.[19] Ndiaye said later that for all the attention his report achieved he might just as well have thrown it into the sea. At the time of its publication the RPF and the Habyarimana regime had signed the Arusha Accords. From then on all efforts were concentrated on a rushed and desperate effort to implement them.

§ In early 1993, while the protocol that dealt with the distribution of seats in a transitional government was being negotiated in Arusha, there were violent demonstrations against the peace process organized by the MRND. The opposition parties launched counter-demonstrations. Three hundred Tutsi civilians were killed. At the negotiations in Arusha, Kagame was insisting that the whole issue was about fundamental change. What they were dealing with was a dictatorship that killed its own people.[20] He had spoken with survivors from the Bagogwe massacres, and then he suddenly pulled out of the negotiations in Arusha. On 8 February 1993, the RPF massively breached the ceasefire agreement,[21] ostensibly to stop the killing of civilians.

An RPF offensive was launched with 8,000 troops, the biggest military operation ever on Rwandan soil, driving back government troops and creating a wave of terrified people fleeing south, adding to the misery of those already displaced by civil war. By now 1 million people were homeless – one-seventh of Rwanda's population – living in huge camps where children were dying of starvation and dysentery.[22] The people in the camps were dependent on massive food aid for their survival. As a result of the exodus from fertile land, and fears that the next harvest could be down by 40 per cent, there were predictions of famine. Ndiaye's report had described the problems of the large number of displaced people as a 'time bomb with potentially tragic consequences'.

In Arusha there was speculation among the negotiators that the RPF attack had been launched because the next item on the agenda was the integration of the two armies. The offensive was launched to prove how strong the RPF was militarily, in order to get more of a share in the new Rwandan army.[23] If this was the intention then it succeeded. The invasion proved that the RPF, while less well equipped than the Rwandan army, was a superior fighting force. The RPF doubled the territory it controlled, reaching Rulindo, 50 kilometres from Kigali.

Once again French resources were used and the RPF fought helicopters and artillery fire, and there was radio-jamming by French operatives. The RPF could have taken Kigali, and Kagame said later that he wished he had carried on and taken the capital. The genocide would have been avoided. The RPF ended its offensive on 22 February when an accord was signed under which the RPF agreed only one condition – that a demilitarized zone be created in the territory now under RPF control.

The consternation in Paris at the military success of the RPF was expressed by Bruno Delaye, the head of the Africa Unit, who reported to President Mitterrand how great were the benefits now afforded to the RPF. Delaye bemoaned the fact that the RPF was benefiting from the 'benign complicity of the Anglo-Saxon world', and he wrote as much in a note to Mitterrand. The RPF had 'military support from Uganda ... Belgian sympathy for Tutsi ... [and] an excellent system of propaganda which makes the most of the unfortunate excesses [*exactions*] of the extremist Hutu'. Delaye believed that the situation for the French had become 'very delicate', and he wrote: '... we are at the limits of our strategy to indirectly support the Rwandan armed forces'. He continued: 'Our isolation on this internationally – the Belgians, the English and the Americans do not like Habyarimana – should steer us towards more offensive diplomacy.'[24]

The OAU publicly accused the French government of prolonging the conflict by supporting the Rwandan military, and for firing upon RPF positions in Ruhengeri. But France was undeterred and, on 20 February 1993, decided to send two more companies of troops.

The RPF attack in February had disastrous effects. The extremists' cause was strengthened by it and Tutsi were labelled RPF accomplices and Hutu members of the opposition regarded as traitors. The opposition split into two groups, pro- and anti-RPF. There was evidence emerging from human rights groups which showed human rights abuses by the RPF. According to the Ndiaye report for the International Federation of Human Rights, the RPF had executed at least eight local MRND officials. Because of the inaccessibility of the area where these events took place, Ndiaye said it was difficult for him to form an opinion, but the events needed to be investigated by an international team of experts. He reported that the RPF was willing to cooperate.[25]

The invasion damaged the fragile relationship which existed between the RPF and the opposition parties. There was speculation that the RPF did not really want a negotiated settlement. In a press release dated 25 February 1993, the CDR announced that the real RPF plan was to kill all the Hutu. The government should urgently 'provide the people with the means' to defend themselves.

In the Ministry of Defence in Kigali the idea was gaining ground that, in order to defend the country, a civilian self-defence network must be created. Habyarimana told his army sector commanders on 11 March that the population must begin to organize to defend itself. This idea was nothing new. It had been suggested earlier in 1991 in letters from Colonel Laurent Serubuga,[26] who was then in charge of military intelligence. Serubuga advised that only people approved by the local authorities should receive arms. Serubuga warned the president that army officers were sickened by the creation of political parties and the proliferation of the private press. The enemy was hiding behind freedom of expression as a means to gain power, and army officers wanted a law to stop such abuse of the press.[27]

A nucleus of Hutu extremists was now actively promoting the idea that in order to destroy the RPF something had to be done about the enemy within. Most of them came from the north-west of Rwanda. Their names are known.[28]

6 | PREPARING THE GENOCIDE

§ The prosecutors at the International Criminal Tribunal for Rwanda (ICTR) believed that Colonel Théoneste Bagosora and other northern army officers managed to legitimize their racist beliefs within the ranks of the army. The case they brought against the army officers was based on a claim that a large part of the planning for genocide had taken place in their offices, and the indictment against the military defendants on trial contains the allegation: 'From late 1990 until July 1994 [the defendants] conspired among themselves and with others to work out a plan with intent, to exterminate the civilian Tutsi population, and eliminate members of the opposition, so that they could remain in power.'[1]

The prosecution appears to have traced the roots of the conspiracy to 4 December 1991, when President Habyarimana, then commander-in-chief, held a meeting with more than a hundred officers from the military and gendarmerie. The army was dividing, splits were emerging in the ranks between moderates and hardliners on how best to respond to the RPF and whether or not a peaceful settlement could ever be reached. At this meeting there had been open and angry disagreement and President Habyarimana seemed to have been at a loss about what to do, and his power seemed to erode. One of the officers said later that it was as though a power vacuum suddenly opened up in front of them. A face-saving formula was devised with the creation of a military commission to agree policy on how best to defeat the enemy, 'in the military, media and political domains'.[2] Ten senior officers chosen for the commission included Major Aloys Ntabakuze, Lieutenant Colonel Anatole Nsengiyumva and Colonel Bagosora. A report was produced and an extract from it was circulated among Rwandan army officers. This was considered to be of some importance because it described 'the enemy' in a certain way: 'The Tutsis from inside or outside the country, who are extremists and nostalgic for power, who do not recognize and have never recognized the realities of the Social Revolution of 1959, and are seeking to regain power in Rwanda by any means, including taking up arms'. The secondary enemy was defined as: 'Anyone providing any kind of assistance to the main enemy'. The document specified that the enemy was recruited from within certain social groups, notably: 'The Tutsis inside the country, Hutus who are dissatisfied with the present regime, foreigners married to Tutsi women'. This part of the report was said to have been inspired by Bagosora. He was from the north, from the Bushiru, and his anti-Tutsi views were familiar to everyone.[3]

Bagosora did not try to hide his belief that the Tutsi did not belong in Rwanda because Rwanda was a Hutu country. He believed Tutsi were invaders, they were naturalized immigrants trying to impose their will. When Tutsi had first arrived in Rwanda they deceived the Hutu, who realized their true nature only after it was too late. Bagosora's version of history included a Hutu king called Mashira, killed by Tutsi along with his whole family. The Tutsi had cut off Mashira's genitals and hung them on a drum, the Kalinga, a symbol of royal power, a way of signifying the wiping out completely of the Hutu rival. In a document written after the genocide was over Bagosora described the two 'protagonists' in the Rwandan 'drama' as different people. In contrast to the Tutsi, the Hutu were modest, open, loyal, independent and impulsive; all Tutsi were dictatorial, proud, cruel, arrogant, clever and sneaky. 'The Tutsi are the masters of deceit, even going as far as comparing themselves with the Jews of Europe to gain the sympathy of this powerful lobby ... but the Tutsi have never had a country of their own ... with their arrogance and pride they are trying to impose their supremacy in the region.'[4] The RPF invasion in 1990 had been an attempted Tutsi takeover, he wrote. The danger was that the RPF would garner support from everyone who was excluded from power – all Tutsi, as defined by their ID cards, the political opposition and the regime's critics. These people, he warned, were an inherently disloyal 'fifth column'.

Bagosora was from Giciye – a neighbouring commune to Habyarimana's birthplace – and the heartland of the Bushiru. The son of a schoolteacher, and the eldest of six children, he went to a Catholic school, the Petit Séminaire St Pie X in the diocese of Nyundo, and from there, like many of his colleagues, he was recruited directly into the army. He went to Belgium to train, and in December 1981 had the singular honour to be the first Rwandan to attend the Etudes Militaires Supérieures de l'Ecole de Guerre Française, where he achieved a diploma in advanced military studies. On his return, he was given the command of the Kanombe military camp outside Kigali, and it was while he was the commander that the Tutsi civilians working in the camp were thrown out of their jobs. Many soldiers with Tutsi wives were dismissed from the army.[5]

Bagosora was ambitious, but his was no meteoric rise. He fell out of favour after marrying Isabelle Uzanyinzoga, from the south. But he built a power base as the president of the ADECOGIKA, an association that promoted investment in the Bushiru. Some officers said later that Bagosora had considered himself to be a possible successor to President Habyarimana and at his trial Bagosora himself admitted that in March 1991 he had tried to persuade Habyarimana to relinquish the presidency in his favour. He had been with Michel Bagaragaza, another northerner who was the head of the national tea export office.[6] Bagosora's younger brother, Pasteur Musabe, a director of the Banque Continentale Africaine Rwanda (BACAR), was also there.[7] Habyarimana had wanted Bagosora to be the chief of staff of the army but opposition politicians in the 1992 coalition government objected to the increasing influence of northerners. Afterwards, when the first international investigators came to look at Bagosora's role in what happened, they noted links with members of the French secret service (Direction Générale de la Sécurité Extérieure, DGSE), but this line of enquiry appears not to have been pursued.[8]

§ The prosecutors in Arusha believed that the strategy for genocide had been adopted and elaborated by political, civil and military authorities and that coordination had been a central element in the conspiracy.[9] In the judgment in the Media Trial, the ICTR South African president, Justice Navanethem Pillay, had said there was no single meeting, no dusty document discovered in a vault, that could be traced as the definitive first step in the genocide master plan.[10] There was not one single-minded and well-defined plot that had been clear cut from the beginning and which was followed through until the end. She noted, however, that as the story unfolded, through 1991 and 1992, 'there was a pattern the world community had missed'. The radical and military officials were working together, testing various killing techniques. Their experiments taught them that they could massacre large numbers of people quickly and efficiently and, based on early reactions, they could get away with it. All this was taking place as the country made its first faltering steps towards democracy and critics of the regime began to express themselves publicly. But the extremists had taken advantage.[11]

In later testimony for the prosecution, Professor Filip Reyntjens said he believed the 1992 massacres in the Bugesera had been a 'dress rehearsal'. He saw continuity between killings in 1991 in Murambi, the massacres in the Bugesera, those in Kibuye in August 1992, and other killings in early 1993 in the north-west. Reyntjens described: 'A number of mechanisms and perpetrators of crimes ... the use of

Presidential Guards ... preparing the fields through provocation'. It was the same when the genocide began, he said, but this time on a 'massive scale'.[12]

Some years later, in a report prepared for the US Holocaust Memorial Museum, it was determined: 'The heinous crimes committed in Nazi-occupied Europe, Cambodia, and Rwanda, for example, were all perpetrated with significant planning, organization, and access to state resources, including weapons, budgets, detention facilities, and broadcast media.'[13]

In Rwanda, in the years beforehand, the possibility of genocide was hardly a secret. The idea seems to have surfaced as situations changed and as different solutions to the RPF invasion were examined. One prosecution witness claims to have heard talk about the possible extermination of Tutsi as early as October 1990, just after the invasion, at a meeting in the northern prefecture of Gisenyi. He testified anonymously under the code-name ZF. He said the meeting was chaired by Bagosora and afterwards those present had gathered in small groups in the nearby canteen. 'They were calmly speaking about the extermination of Tutsi,' he told the court, '... you had to undo the enemy action and stop the extermination of Hutu by Tutsi.'[14] Senior political figures had attended, including Jean-Bosco Barayagwiza, a lawyer and the director of political affairs in the Ministry of Foreign Affairs. There was Joseph Nzirorera, the former minister of public works and now the secretary-general of the MRND. There was Protais Zigiranyirazo, the brother of the president's wife Agathe, a businessman and former prefect of Ruhengeri. There was Major Aloys Ntabakuze,[15] the commander of the Para-commando unit, and Lieutenant Colonel Anatole Nsengiyumva, who was the head of military intelligence (G2). One prosecution witness later described how Tutsi had been killed immediately after the invasion. Ntabakuze, who was sent north to the war zone, was said to have ordered the killing of a group of terrified people fleeing the fighting. 'Ntabakuze herded the people into two groups using their identity cards. Then he assembled the Tutsi in one place and killed them by throwing grenades at them.'[16] A report by Amnesty International the following year expressed concern about executions by the Rwandan security services; no one had been brought to justice, and this was a sign that the security forces were able to kill with impunity.[17]

When the defector Janvier Afrika[18] was interviewed in late 1994 he said that the idea of a 'final solution' to the 'Tutsi problem' had been suggested just after the 1990 invasion. The idea came from certain members of a death squad called 'Réseau Zéro' which had been created a year earlier.

The 'Réseau Zéro' was a vigilante group of some thirty people who were willing to help to eliminate opponents and dissidents. It was only after the invasion that 'mass killing' was organized.[19] Afrika claimed that from February 1991 to January 1992, new recruits received a four-month course in paramilitary training in the capital, Kigali. Regular planning meetings took place in a house owned by Captain Pascal Simbikangwa and Colonel Elie Sagatwa. They called the house the 'synagogue', the name thought to have been chosen by Mathieu Ngirumpatse, a former ambassador to Germany, where the MRND had strong links in the Rwandan community.[20] A certain number of Rwandan army officers had received military training in Germany. There were rumours afterwards that Hitler's *Mein Kampf* had been translated into Kinyarwanda by a Catholic priest.[21] Ngirumpatse was minister of justice in a government formed in 1991 and was appointed president of the MRND two years later. According to Afrika it was at the 'synagogue' that the dignitaries from the regime discussed clandestine operations and their murder victims. Sometimes President Habyarimana would attend.

The witness known as ZF said he believed 'Réseau Zéro' was the name of a radio network for people who did not want their conversations overheard: '… rather, they did not want other members of government, or officers, or members of the army to be aware of their activities and communications'. ZF claimed that in Rwanda there were small groups of well-trained killers, and the people called 'dragons' were in charge of these squads and were responsible for choosing their victims.

Another defector, Christophe Mfizi, in a statement he prepared for the international tribunal, urged prosecutors not to confuse the network with the Akazu, the name given to family members from the Bushiru, who were related to the president's wife Agathe. Mfizi said that Réseau Zéro was not a family mafia but a joint criminal conspiracy. It was central to everything that happened. The network, created by Protais Zigiranyirazo, had managed 'to sap the moral fibre of the country'. It had pushed the country's youth into the most extreme forms of violence. By 1992 Réseau Zéro had already devised a plan for massive killing with targeting of RPF 'accomplices' (*ibyitso*). Mfizi fled Rwanda in August that year, believing that all that was missing for a catastrophe was a lit fuse.[22] Just prior to Mfizi's defection a senior official in the MRND told him that should the RPF get anywhere near Kigali, then all Tutsi would be killed. Mfizi knew this already. In certain prefectures the Réseau Zéro had influence at cell level – the lowest administrative division.

In Kigali the drawing up of lists was said to have been an ongoing process and was first organized immediately after the RPF invasion of

October 1990.[23] The army, the gendarmerie and local authorities were given orders to prepare their own lists or update the existing ones. One prosecution witness said that Bagosora had instructed the general staff of the army and the gendarmerie to establish lists of people identified as 'accomplices'. The idea of genocide was sometimes openly expressed. 'They are very few,' Colonel Pierre-Célestin Rwagafilita told a French army officer in October 1990. 'We will liquidate them.'[24]

§ With the onset of a coalition government, in April 1992 President Juvénal Habyarimana was forced to remove several of the northern colonels from the army command. Colonel Théoneste Bagosora was one of them, but he was found alternative employment by the MRND, as the Directeur de Cabinet in the Ministry of Defence, effectively as its administrative head. And if Rwanda's political opposition believed that the retirement of certain officers would neutralize the hardliners, they were mistaken. A part of Rwanda's military intelligence archive shows how in the most influential department – that of military army intelligence – the chief of intelligence (G2), Lieutenant Colonel Anatole Nsengiyumva, continually warned of the dangers of a form of democracy involving the RPF and argued the Tutsi should never be allowed to share power. His voluminous reports, all copied to President Habyarimana, describe a public so terrified of the RPF that there was the possibility of a mass exodus should the Tutsi be allowed into government.[25]

'Before the people leave the country,' warned Nsengiyumva in a chilling prediction, 'they will massacre all the Tutsi.' Nsengiyumva described dissatisfaction within the ranks. 'Certain officers are asking whether or not civilians in the government are really capable of taking decisions in the national interest.' He reported that they would never accept a merger with the RPF. Some of the soldiers on the front line were thinking of desertion because the country was being sold out. Nsengiyumva's advice was that it must be made clear to France and the USA that Rwanda was a special case and that the intention of the RPF was to seize the power they had lost in 1959. They were going to re-establish the monarchy.[26]

A secret society was created in the army by a group of officers including Bagosora and Nsengiyumva. It was called Amasasu (the Alliance of Soldiers Provoked by the Age-old Deceitful Acts of Unarists, i.e. monarchists). Amasasu is the Kinyarwanda word for bullets. In January 1993, as the Arusha peace negotiations progressed, an open letter was sent to Habyarimana by Amasasu. It accurately predicted that the RPF was preparing a major attack.

A diary was found in Bagosora's house afterwards and a copy was given to Human Rights Watch. For the month of February 1993 in Bagosora's handwriting there are detailed notes for a 'popular' army to be created of local men. They were to be given military training either by the communal police or the military itself. Each cell and each sector must elect men to be responsible for defence; sixty trained men in each commune. There must be coordination between the military authorities and the local administration, communal councillors and local police. Starting on 1 February, there are a series of notes in which there is listed an order for 2,000 Kalashnikovs to 'bring to 5,000 the number for the communes'. Three to five weapons were to be distributed to each cell, and 'hand-grenades' is written next to a list of six communes. Bagosora was obtaining vehicles and finding storage for weapons. He refers to 'organizing information', and notes that a propaganda campaign, aimed at human rights organizations and the diplomatic corps, is assigned to a former Rwandan diplomat. He proposed that radio programmes should include the songs of Bikindi, a singer of anti-Tutsi songs.[27] Some of this bore a startling similarity to plans devised in 1963 when local groups were created for '*auto-défense civile*'. Bagosora was familiar with these operations, during which large numbers of Tutsi were killed, for he had included in his curriculum vitae the fact that in December 1963 he took part in 'campaigns' in the Bugesera against 'Inyenzi' (cockroaches), the name used for Tutsi.[28]

The idea for a system of '*auto-défense civile*', or a local civil defence force, seems to have surfaced with a plan to use civilians to protect the north of the country from the RPF, near the war zone. In September 1991 the idea was to extend this plan nationwide by way of mass mobilization so that in each cell there would be armed peasants – all of them MRND officials. In the summer of 1991 these plans were outlined by President Habyarimana's personal defence and security adviser, Colonel Augustin Ndindiliymana, who told a meeting of Rwandan military officers that a lack of money precluded compulsory military service. He said that when finance permitted a civilian militia would be created.

There is information about how '*auto-défense civile*' developed in a confession given later to the international tribunal by Jean Kambanda, the prime minister in the government that presided over the genocide. Kambanda said that after the RPF's 1990 invasion each communal officer had been obliged to write a report about local defence plans. Copies were sent to the *bourgmestre* and to army command.[29] Kambanda explained that eventually '*auto-défense civile*' became an integral part of the killing, and as the genocide progressed he had formalized the existing countrywide plan, and had signed decrees to that effect on 25 May 1994 with cabinet approval. Kambanda said the Interahamwe was eventually incorporated into the civil defence network: the militia was useful to encourage less well-trained and motivated civilians to kill people.[30] Through the use of civilian self-defence groups against non-combatants the system was transformed from a potentially legitimate form of civil defence into a means to commit genocide.

In January 1993, weapons had been distributed to communal police in certain communes in Rwanda. In the Ngoma, for instance, in the prefecture of Butare, eight new Kalashnikovs were added to a supply of twenty-six rifles as part of the civil defence network. By the end of that year there were hidden stockpiles of brand-new machetes, hoes, axes and picks in most communes, and each commune contained members of the Hutu 'Pawa' (Power) militia. The communes were divided into *quartiers*, each containing a representative of the MRND, responsible for ten houses. In the hills of Rwanda, there was constant surveillance of neighbour by neighbour, of peasant by local authority, with the active participation of the communal police and gendarmes. The militia was expanding. There were new recruits from the ever-increasing ranks of the unemployed, and thousands of young men regarded as delinquent. Some of the weapons purchased in the spending spree on light arms were passed by the armed forces directly to the militia. Some militia leaders were issued with AK47s, after filling out requisition forms; the distribution of grenades did not require paperwork.

The UN peacekeepers later found weapons stockpiled in secret locations in Kigali, put there by senior figures in the Ministry of Defence, and intended for use by the Interahamwe in Kigali. In Gitarama, a town with 150,000 inhabitants, there were 50,000 pistols and rifles, machetes and other arms. The UN peacekeepers would eventually determine that 85 tons of munitions had been distributed throughout the country.[31]

There were documents discovered afterwards in the offices of the Banque Nationale du Rwanda (BNR) in Kigali, a paper trail of the purchases for genocide – the invoices, bank statements, arms contracts, faxes and telexes to show how finance was made available to pay for its planning and execution. These documents were made available in August 1996 to two researchers: they were Pierre Galand, a former director of Oxfam-Belgium, and Professor Michel Chossudovsky, a Canadian economist and an expert in international development and finance. They had been commissioned by the post-genocide president of Rwanda, Pasteur Bizimungu, whose government faced a demand for the repayment of the debts incurred by the previous regime. Their inquiry investigated the indebtedness of Rwanda and covered the period 1990–94. Their work was funded by the United Nations Development Programme (UNDP).[32]

Under Rwandan banking regulations nothing could be bought or sold abroad without payment through the BNR, and there were millions of documents in this bank. Galand realized it was 'an extraordinary mine of material', and the two researchers spent whole days reading file after file of records. Galand remembers finding invoices to show how large amounts of beer had been purchased and stockpiled for the militia. They found bank accounts which showed how boots and clothes were bought for the militia using the military budget.[33] They discovered how food aid intended for famine areas had been sold to make funds available for the creation of the militia. They asked that some files be kept in the bank vault, including documents invaluable for future prosecutions, because they provided the proof of genocide planning. Midway through their work they had to leave Rwanda to fulfil professional commitments in Brussels, and when they returned to the bank, some weeks later, the vault had been emptied of many of the documents, which were now missing. Galand suspected that there were people working in the bank whose intention was to prevent full discovery, and he deduced that Rwandans, who had fled abroad and who were implicated in the genocide, were trying to protect themselves and paying bank staff to get rid of certain records. They managed to remove from the bank 'a series of records that were indispensable to the restitution of the paper trail of the financing of the genocide', he said. Both Galand and Chossudovsky urgently appealed to senior officials in the UNDP to help the new Rwandan government to protect their precious archives. 'Our requests to the international community were never really given an adequate response,' he said. They found some carbon copies of the missing documents in the basement archives of other ministries. The Rwandans had created an over-administered bureaucracy, said Galand. 'No minister ever wrote to another without taking multiple copies and providing one for the Prime Minister and the President.'

The conclusion reached by Chossudovsky and Galand was that without international finance there would have been no money available to expand the army, enter into substantial arms deals, buy the machetes and other agricultural tools, or the beer, petrol, clothes and food given to the armed forces, the militia and their families. Their eventual report provided details of exact amounts and payment records that showed how starting in 1992 large stocks of machetes and tools were imported. The following year half a million machetes and other agricultural tools were purchased and distributed throughout the country, including hundreds and thousands of hoes, axes, hammers and razor blades. According to bank records, US$4.6 million was spent on agricultural equipment in 1993 by Rwandan companies not usually concerned with agricultural tools.[34] Invoices show that most commercial concerns in 1993 imported machetes. One significant figure in the importation of machetes was Félicien Kabuga, whose wealth came from coffee exports and the import of household goods and clothes, a part of a system that allowed the elite to import goods free from the required import licences. Kabuga is considered today to be the principal financier of the genocide.[35] The documents in the bank showed a total of US$725,669 spent on 581,000 machetes; one machete for every third adult Hutu male. The machetes came from China, supplied between 1992 and 1994 by a company called Oriental Machinery. The invoices were filed under the heading 'eligible imports'. All imports were made easier because the World Bank/IMF had insisted on the liberalization of the import licence system.[36] Documents showed that this equipment was purchased with money from quick-disbursing loans from Western donors who entered into agreements with the regime that the funds should not be used for military or paramilitary purposes. Most crucially, Chossudovsky and Galand unearthed reports from auditors with clear warnings to the World Bank that there were funds being diverted to military spending.

While President Habyarimana had assured everyone that the purchases were legitimate in order to defend the country, the military equipment purchased in the two years prior to the genocide included a substantial amount of low-intensity weapons. The small arms – automatic weapons, machine guns, grenades and landmines – were less expensive to buy, to maintain and to conceal. These weapons contributed to the huge numbers of victims in the genocide, and to the speed of the killing. Although the total arms purchases between 1990 and 1994 were in the region of US$83 million, it is estimated that military expenditure was higher, for many of the purchases were hidden in the government budget. Within three years, impoverished Rwanda became the third-largest importer of weapons on the African continent.

The first arms deal with Egypt in October 1990 for US$5.889 million was followed by another in December in the order of US$3.511 million. By April 1991, the Rwandan government had spent US$10.861 million on Egyptian weapons. In June 1992, a further US$1.3 million was given to Egypt for weapons. In November 1992, 250 Kalashnikov assault rifles and 25,000 rounds of ammunition were purchased; in February 1993, 3,000 automatic rifles, AKM guns, each worth US$250, were purchased; later, another deal was signed to include 100,000 rounds of ammunition, and thousands of landmines and grenades.

In December 1991, with a contract in the pipeline worth US$1 million for 82mm bombs, fuses and charges, Egypt felt it necessary to remind the Rwandans of the importance of keeping the deals secret. Colonel Sami Said told the regime in Kigali that if the arms deals were to be made public, Egypt's relations with its allies would be compromised. In order to camouflage the deals, it was proposed that commercial trading should start and Egypt would buy Rwandan tea and coffee. The links between Egypt and Rwanda were strengthened and a military attaché was appointed to Rwanda's embassy in Cairo, which, by 1992, had become increasingly important.[37]

The largest arms deal between Egypt and Rwanda came in March 1992 and was for US$6 million of light weapons and small arms. The deal included 450 Kalashnikov rifles, 2,000 rocket-propelled grenades, 16,000 mortar shells and more than three million rounds of small-arms ammunition.[38] This time Rwanda asked whether it would be possible to pay in instalments. Egypt expressed reservations, insisting there be a guarantee of payment, and the French state-owned bank, Crédit Lyonnais, agreed to act as guarantor.[39] An arrangement was made for the money to be paid in $1 million cash instalments in London, deposited by the Rwandese government into a Crédit Lyonnais bank in Regent Street, into the account of the office of the Egyptian defence attaché in London. The payments were spread over four years. A further million dollars was to be paid for in Rwandan tea, which was to arrive in Cairo at the end of 1993.

Six weeks before the genocide, in February 1994, another contract was concluded between the Ministry of Defence in Cairo and the Rwandese government for $1 million of mortars and ammunition. Rwanda asked for urgent delivery. For the regime in Kigali, the Rwandan embassy in Cairo was pivotal. During the genocide, some US$1.4 million was transferred there, the money coming from the Banque Nationale du Rwanda, passing through the Rwandan embassy in Nairobi, then on to Cairo, where it was paid into the Commercial International Bank of Egypt. Whether or not this money was to pay for weapons has not been ascertained.[40]

South African dealers sold arms worth US$56.263 to Rwanda between 29 October 1990 and 29 May 1991. In 1991, substantial international financial aid had been promised under the Structural Adjustment Programme (SAP), amounting to more than US$170 million, including US$46 million from the European Community, $41 million from the

IMF, $25 million from the USA and $17 million from Belgium.[41] The weapons imports from South Africa included 20,000 R-4 rifles and 10,000 hand grenades, machine guns and 1.5 million rounds of ammunition for R-4 rifles. The money for these arms was paid into banks in Brussels, the Belgolaise and the Banque Nationale de Paris, and an account in the Volkskas Bank in Pretoria. The Chinese also provided weapons, but under a credit scheme of US$1 million for mortars, machine guns, multiple rocket launchers and grenades.

For three years, the Habyarimana regime used every accounting trick in the book to get enough money to pay for weapons. In bank records flagrant manipulations of funds were found; sometimes the same invoices were used two or three times to get at money from different donors. The Rwandan government's auditor, in a secret report to the Rwandan government, later complained: 'On several occasions double payments have been made into Rwandese commercial banks for the same import.' The regime even sold petrol on the open market to get money for the armed forces.

The experts who studied the paper trail, Chossudovsky and Galand, conclude that to arm and equip the *génocidaires* of Rwanda cost US$112 million. It is a mystery why the five missions sent by the World Bank to follow and supervise the Structural Adjustment Programme between June 1991 and October 1993 apparently failed to notice all this activity. Only in December 1993 did the World Bank suspend payment of a tranche of money because 'certain objectives had not been met', but even then it had already deposited, in a special account in the Banque Bruxelles Lambert, funds that would continue to be used by the regime until 31 May 1994 while the genocide was carried out.

Whatever the procedures in place, the unprecedented purchases of machetes and other tools, using money provided under quick-disbursing loans, seem to have passed through the system unnoticed. The arms purchases are a different matter. Several times World Bank officials raised the issue of the militarization of Rwanda with the regime. Indeed, the president of the World Bank, Lewis Preston, wrote to Habyarimana to raise the matter of military spending at a time when there was famine in the south and warnings from the International Committee of the Red Cross and the Food and Agriculture Organization that health and welfare provision in Rwanda was collapsing. This letter was dated April 1992, one month after the Rwandan government had concluded the $6 million deal with Egypt that had benefited from a guarantee from Crédit Lyonnais. In his reply, Habyarimana wrote that the increase in military expenditure was due to the civil war with the RPF and the need to defend the country from aggression from Uganda. He explained how just one fatal blow from the RPF would ruin all the efforts and sacrifice made by the Rwandan people to adhere to the World Bank programme. Habyarimana assured Preston that his aim was progressively to reduce military expenditure. In his reply, Preston reminded Habyarimana that the World Bank had agreed a safety net for the first stage of the SAP in order to protect those who were the most disadvantaged in the short term and to help ease poverty. 'I take note of your intention to reduce military expenditure and I encourage you to do it urgently,' he wrote.

The IMF seems to have been aware of military spending and a confidential briefing paper from 1992 betrays a sense of hopelessness about the continuing 'ethnic conflict'. It did not look as though the objectives of the IMF mission could be achieved. Even if hostilities ceased, it would take a long time to demobilize military personnel. The IMF mission decided to examine how to improve control over the government's spending.

At the end of 1992 the World Bank stopped negotiating with the regime.[42] At a hastily convened government meeting in Kigali, it was decided to cancel the latest arms deal and look for helpful gestures. The government decreed a reduction in the food rations given to soldiers and to their families, and a lowering of the salaries of civil servants. But the money saved was channelled to the military and the militia; there were lorries, purchased as agricultural imports, diverted to the army. In Kigali, the militia used hospital vehicles, filling them with petrol at the Ministry of Health's expense.

Although the SAP was based on the assumption that military spending would be kept under control, the budget of the minister of defence increased steadily. In Paris in June 1993, during a World Bank conference, a further US$120.3 million for Rwanda was agreed. As the global financial institutions operate in secrecy we may never know what was said about Rwanda at this conference. It would appear that a plea was made in favour of the regime by a World Bank official whose identity is not known, but who reminded the other delegates that at least the government of Rwanda was in control of the country.[43]

7 | THE HATE RADIO: RADIO-TÉLÉVISION LIBRE DES MILLE COLLINES

§ A torrent of propaganda now began in the media, a vile campaign against the minority Tutsi which was relentless in its incitement to ethnic hatred and violence. Among the first targets of this campaign was democracy itself, and any possibility that the Arusha Accords might actually work.

A new radio station called Radio-Télévision Libre des Mille Collines (RTLM) began to broadcast in July 1993, a month before the peace agreement was signed. This coincided with a number of cheap portable radios becoming suddenly available in the markets, and some radios were given free to local authorities.[1] The new station was immediately popular. It was rowdy and the disc jockeys used street language. There was pop music and phone-ins. Sometimes the announcers were drunk, particularly one of them, Noël Hitimana, whose jokes were offensive, vulgar and crude.[2] It seemed as though RTLM was designed to appeal to the unemployed, the delinquents and the gangs of thugs in the street militia. It broadcast mainly in Kinyarwanda and it revolutionized Rwandan broadcasting. Among a largely illiterate population, the radio station soon had a large audience who found it immensely entertaining. Using the FM frequency, the radio station had a style that was in direct contrast to that of the only other radio station in the country, the government-owned Radio Rwanda, which favoured a more formal approach. The new radio station carried commentaries and lengthy interviews.

The planning for RTLM began in November 1992. It was the inspiration of Ferdinand Nahimana, a history professor who was known for his work on the history of the 'Hutu nation' and whose main argument was that Tutsi were not indigenous to Rwanda.[3] He was a former director of Rwanda's information office, Office Rwandais d'Information (ORINFOR), where he had been responsible for Radio Rwanda. It was Nahimana who prepared the propaganda that was broadcast over Radio Rwanda and which had incited the murder of Tutsi during the massacres in Bugesera in 1992. Following the creation of a coalition government in April 1992 he was ousted from his post in an effort to ensure that Radio Rwanda had a more non-partisan stance. Nahimana, with a radio technician from Radio Rwanda called Joseph Serugendo, travelled to Brussels to buy equipment for a new radio station.[4] It was Nahimana who inspired the style of RTLM, and who planned the news bulletins.

Eight journalists worked for RTLM, and most of them had previously worked for pro-MRND newspapers or for the government. Not all programmes were in Kinyarwanda: there was a French-language programme presented by a former teacher, Georges Ruggiu, a Belgian citizen who had no journalistic experience at all.[5] The programmes were relayed to all parts of the country via a network of transmitters on two frequencies, the transmitters owned and operated by the government's Radio Rwanda. The documents incorporating RTLM contained a clause that it should 'create harmonious development in Rwandese society', to contribute to the education of the people and to 'transmit true, objective information'. The founders of RTLM were apparently 'encouraged by progress towards democracy'.[6]

The radio station was incorporated on 8 April 1993 as a jointly funded company with fifty original shareholders.[7] Forty of these shareholders were from the northern prefectures. The largest shareholder was President Juvénal Habyarimana.[8] On the list were businessmen, bank managers, journalists, army officers and government officials. Two people were authorized to sign RTLM bank cheques – Nahimana and Jean-Bosco Barayagwiza, a lawyer and the director of political affairs in the Ministry of Foreign Affairs. These two controlled and managed the radio, while Nahimana determined the content of the broadcasts. The International Criminal Tribunal for Rwanda (ICTR) concluded that RTLM had mobilized the population, and had whipped up the people into a frenzy of hatred and violence. The radio had been an integral part of a campaign to demonize the Tutsi.[9] It had circumvented key clauses in the Arusha Accords in which incitement to violence and hatred was barred from the political process. The pro-Hutu message of RTLM was anti-Arusha and anti-Tutsi. It would eventually broadcast the names of certain government opponents, individuals who 'deserved to die'. In October 1993, the Rwandan minister of information, Faustin Rucogoza, expressed his concern to both Nahimana and Barayagwiza about the race hate that was pouring over the airways. It made no difference. Rucogoza was preparing a case against the radio station for the Council of Ministers when the genocide began.

'I listened to RTLM,' said a survivor, 'because if you were mentioned over the airways, you were sure to be carted off a short time later by the Interahamwe. You knew you had to change your address at once.'[10] On 26 November 1993, an announcer called for the assassination of Prime Minister Agathe Uwilingiyimana, the pro-democracy opposition politician previously the minister of education.

The president of the board of directors of RTLM was Félicien Kabuga, the man who in 1993 had facilitated the importation of vast numbers of machetes, and who provided money for the Interahamwe. Kabuga was financial adviser to Habyarimana; his daughter was married to one of Habyarimana's sons. Kabuga financed *Kangura*, the bi-monthly tabloid newspaper that operated under the newly established freedom of the press. *Kangura* carried crude and venomous cartoons against the political opposition and against Tutsi. It used rough and common language. Just like the radio, *Kangura* peddled hate propaganda, and conveyed the message that Tutsi should be eliminated.[11] Its editor-in-chief was Hassan Ngeze.[12]

For those who found themselves denounced in its pages, the consequences could be fatal: 'Let us learn about the Inkotanyi [Tutsi] plans and let us exterminate every last one of them' (*Kangura*, 9, February 1991). In December 1993 *Kangura* predicted that President Habyarimana would be assassinated, not by a Tutsi but by a Hutu. 'There is no one more worried than Habyarimana himself,' *Kangura* told its readers.[13]

In December 1990 *Kangura* had published the Hutu Ten Commandments, which were instructions to mistreat and discriminate against Tutsi and which conveyed contempt and hatred for them.[14] The first three commandments referred to Tutsi women; the first commandment forbade marriage between Hutu and Tutsi because every Tutsi woman was a traitor and Hutu girls made more suitable mothers. There was propaganda against Tutsi women in the build-up to genocide and the hatred mobilized is thought to have encouraged the most inhumane acts of sexual violence that took place during the genocide. Tutsi women were portrayed as seductive agents of the RPF, a message that was conveyed repeatedly in *Kangura* and on RTLM. There were warnings to Hutu to be distrustful of Tutsi women, but also of Hutu men who had relations with them. Two commandments specifically referred to the role of Hutu women. There was hateful propaganda against Hutu women who advocated peace and power sharing and who opposed extremism. No other Hutu woman was more vilified than the transitional prime minister, Agathe Uwilingiyimana, who was portrayed as an 'accomplice to the Tutsi enemy'. By March 1994, Uwilingiyimana was being characterized in animalistic terms, for example as a rat eating money. By emphasizing Tutsi women's sexuality, *Kangura* played a role in encouraging a policy of rape.[15] The Tutsi population was portrayed as inherently evil and their extermination was necessary as a 'preventive measure'.[16] *Kangura* named Tutsi 'who owned a disproportionate amount of wealth'.

The radio and *Kangura* repeated the same messages, and the tactics used indicated a common strategy. Documents found later in the Rwandan government archives show the possible influence of a French psychologist, Roger Mucchielli, whose book on publicity and propaganda was published in Paris in 1970.[17] Mucchielli's work was said to have been influenced by the methods of the Nazi propagandist Joseph Goebbels.[18] A document in President Habyarimana's own archive shows how in August 1991 the committee members of the MRND were sent a twelve-page memorandum explaining Mucchielli's advice on how to attain and keep power. This involved turning the 'great mass of the ill-informed' into a 'political army'. Mucchielli advised that those who wished for power should never overestimate the intelligence of the masses. The public needed to be persuaded of common interest – and a common enemy. The opponent should be portrayed promoting war and slavery, and should be shown as responsible for sadistic cruelty. Another Mucchielli strategy included blaming one's own actions on the adversary.[19] Political opponents had to be isolated and attacked with lies, exaggeration and ridicule.

When the Arusha Accords were signed, *Kangura* warned that the agreement was a Tutsi plot. One *Kangura* issue, number 29, showed a machete on the cover with the headline: 'What weapons shall we use to conquer the Inyenzi once and for all?'[20] Copies of *Kangura* were read aloud at public meetings and at the rallies of the Interahamwe, who, wearing their black-and-yellow pyjama-suits and blowing whistles, unfurled giant banners bearing the face of Juvénal Habyarimana.

The Belgian ambassador, Johan Swinnen, warned Brussels several times that RTLM was destabilizing the country. He said later that not enough was done to try to neutralize the broadcasts.[21] In January 1994, three months before the genocide began, Swinnen told his Foreign Ministry that the broadcasts in Kinyarwanda needed to be translated but there were too few embassy staff to do the work and analyse the transmissions. A Belgian military intelligence officer in Kigali, Lieutenant Mark Nees, said that if RTLM had been prevented from broadcasting, then the genocide could have been limited, if not avoided.[22]

Most diplomats in Kigali did not take RTLM seriously. Neither the French nor the US ambassador was in favour of trying to prevent the radio from broadcasting. David Rawson, the US ambassador, argued that its 'euphemisms' were subject to various interpretations and that the USA believed in freedom of speech.[23] The US Agency for International Development (USAID) had launched a five-year $US5 million project in Rwanda that covered the promotion of responsible journalism.[24]

Swinnen raised the issue when he met Habyarimana on 3 March, only a few weeks before the genocide began. If the Arusha Accords were to succeed, Swinnen told the president, something would have to be done about the hate radio.

8 | NEW WORLD ORDER AND HIGH HOPES FOR A UN SUCCESS

§ A request to the United Nations Security Council for peacekeepers for Rwanda initially came from France. France lobbied hard for a UN presence and particularly after the massive RPF attack in February 1993 during which the rebel army had come within 23 kilometres of Kigali. At a cabinet meeting in Paris, President François Mitterrand had argued forcefully that the UN must get involved. 'We must pass it to the UN. It is incredible. One country attacks another and no one moves ... we should not have this responsibility ... we must urgently provoke a reaction from the UN,' the president had said.[1]

France blamed Uganda for supporting the RPF attack, an accusation denied by the Ugandan government. Uganda asked for a neutral monitoring mission to be established on the border with Rwanda and French diplomats agreed, wanting to prove claims that Ugandan logistics, supplies and weapons were being provided to the RPF. France was not alone in believing that Uganda's president, Yoweri Museveni, was knowingly supporting the rebels. The Canadian government, unconvinced by the Ugandan denials, had already urged Museveni to play a more positive role in peace efforts. The Canadians, significant aid donors to Rwanda, had also encouraged Britain to try to dissuade its Ugandan ally from permitting incursions into Rwanda from Ugandan territory. Canada feared the region would destabilize. The British Foreign Office denied any knowledge of Ugandan support to the RPF. The Canadian government of Prime Minister Brian Mulroney was unconvinced by the denial.[2]

The Rwandan government, shocked at the military success of the RPF, made a formal request to the UN Security Council on 28 February for a neutral monitoring force on the Ugandan border. The RPF responded on 4 March by calling for an expanded Organization of African Unity (OAU) mission to monitor a newly concluded ceasefire and to authorize an international force to maintain it. There had been OAU observers deployed to Rwanda the previous year.[3] The Security Council first became involved on 12 March 1993. In Resolution 812 the secretary-general was asked to examine the possibility of placing UN observers along the border. The resolution also provided for humanitarian assistance to the people of Rwanda. With the RPF attack there were now an estimated 800,000 people displaced by war. A UN mission was sent from New York headed by the secretary-general's military adviser, a Canadian, Major General Maurice Baril. The eventual recommendation provided for 100 military observers to be positioned on the Ugandan side of the 150-mile border with Rwanda. These observers were to patrol, observe and make sure a buffer zone was not breached, although they were active during daylight hours only.

After the signing of the Arusha Accords, French diplomats lobbied Security Council members to agree to a UN peacekeeping mission for Rwanda. They stressed that both sides in the conflict were committed to peace. There was speculation that France had put pressure on the regime of President Juvénal Habyarimana to sign the accords, and had promised him that French troops would never be withdrawn, not without the Rwandan government's agreement.[4]

The Arusha Accords called for a neutral intervention force during a twenty-two-month transition to democracy which was to ensure country-wide security. The French favoured a UN rather than an OAU mission and argued that the OAU lacked the means and the experience. A UN mission would involve the Security Council, of which France was a permanent member. There was significant reluctance about UN involvement from the USA and the UK. Both states had rejected the idea when France first suggested it in 1992. They argued for a lead role for the OAU – and so did the RPF.[5] The UN was overstretched with twelve peacekeeping missions already established.[6] There had been a dramatic increase in calls for UN help in a post-cold-war world. The Council was overwhelmed by problems; the missions in Cambodia, Somalia and the former Yugoslavia were proving particularly problematic. The scope of these missions had expanded from ceasefire monitoring and truce observations to electoral support, human rights monitoring, military demobilization, demining, humanitarian support and civilian police monitoring.[7] The UN's annual peacekeeping budget had increased from US$600 million to US$3 billion. The US was liable for 30 per cent of the total peacekeeping bill and Congress was reluctant to appropriate any large sums for the UN.

The arguments in favour of helping Rwanda were passionate. Nigeria, a non-permanent member, described the country as small and pathetic, one of the poorest in the world. Nigeria's ambassador, Ibrahim Gambari, pointed out that the USA was encouraging Rwanda to democratize, and there was a moral obligation to see it right through to the end.[8] UN resources were monopolized in former Yugoslavia, more there than anywhere else. For Rwanda, the Arusha Accords were the last, best hope.

The UN secretary-general, Dr Boutros Boutros-Ghali, lobbied hard for help for Rwanda. He argued that the mission in Rwanda was to be traditional peacekeeping. In a report to the Council, he outlined the concept of an operation and a deployment schedule, although this was much changed from a larger mission outlined by a UN reconnaissance team that had visited the area in August 1993.[9] In another report to the Council, submitted on 24 September, Boutros-Ghali indicated that implementation of the Arusha Accords depended on two conditions: that the two sides complied with their commitments, and that UN members provided the human and financial resources requested.

But Boutros-Ghali's relationship with the USA was at a low ebb. Under the UN Charter the secretary-general was intended to be independent of all states and impartial in his dealings with them, but from the beginning Boutros-Ghali's relationship with Washington was strained.

§ No secretary-general had ever taken the helm at a more propitious time than Boutros-Ghali. Every other secretary-general had been obliged to live with Security Council paralysis and ill will, but as his term began, in January 1992, a post-cold-war world led to a unified Council. Boutros-Ghali said that if he had been offered the job five years earlier, he would have turned it down: 'The UN then was a dead horse, but after the end of the Cold War, the UN has a special position,' he said.[10] In a historic gesture the Council had held its first meeting at summit level, a meeting billed as an unprecedented recommitment to the purposes and principles of the UN Charter. At the time the UK held the presidency of the Council and the summit meeting was claimed as a British initiative. The French delegation claimed it had been President François Mitterrand's idea.

The only concrete suggestion to emerge from the summit was a request to the new secretary-general to formulate ideas to guide peacekeeping, peace-enforcing and preventive diplomacy. Boutros-Ghali wanted an expansion of peacekeeping. He wanted the UN to play an enhanced role in the creation of democracy around the world. He believed that the UN had to become involved in national reconciliation processes, the restructuring and the rehabilitation of governments. He displayed great ambition for this newly relevant world organization. He said he wanted to shift the UN's emphasis from world development to human rights. He had been one of the leading advocates in 1978 of an African Charter of

Human Rights, a proposal that was adopted with the specific inclusion of the rights of peoples as well as of individuals. Some UN colleagues were sceptical about Boutros-Ghali's vision of global leadership. His style was forthright, outspoken and confrontational. He could have pursued a role complementary to that of the Security Council; instead, he began to compete with it, and this led to a dramatic falling out with the USA, the organization's most powerful member state.[11]

The US had abstained on the vote for Boutros-Ghali as secretary-general. The US president, George Bush, had favoured Prince Sadruddin Aga Khan.[12] Boutros-Ghali's candidature had also faced the complication of the rivalry between two permanent members of the Security Council, France and Britain, over which region of the African continent – francophone or anglophone – should provide the candidate. Four of the seven African candidates for the job were from English-speaking Africa, but Boutros-Ghali had the backing of the Arab League, which had twenty-one seats in the General Assembly. By August 1991, he had the promise of support from at least eighty-six assembly votes, quite clearly a majority, and this was a factor that the Council would take into account when it made its selection. President Mubarak gently reminded the Bush administration that Egypt had been a leading ally during the Gulf War. For Egypt, the candidature of Boutros-Ghali was a matter of national pride.

Most important to his candidature was the support of France. Boutros-Ghali was a personal friend of President François Mitterrand.[13] On the day of his selection by the Council – 21 November 1991 – Boutros-Ghali was in Bonn, and after telephoning the Egyptian president, Hosni Mubarak, he had telephoned President Mitterrand to thank him for helping his two-year campaign for office. 'He seemed to feel a personal victory in my election,' Boutros-Ghali wrote about this special moment.[14]

Boutros-Ghali portrayed himself as the African candidate, and he began his campaign for the job in 1991 with a tour of Africa. It was familiar territory. As the president of Egypt's Society of African Studies, he had known African leaders for fifteen years and had created a special fund for cooperation in Africa under his direction, with a budget of millions of Egyptian pounds, which enabled him to send hundreds of Egyptian experts to African countries.[15] There was an undercurrent of resentment among some diplomats from sub-Saharan African countries because Boutros-Ghali was the only light-skinned Arab African on the list of African candidates, and he lacked the wholehearted support of the Organization of African Unity (OAU), which had failed to make a choice from among seven other African candidates. Boutros-Ghali, described as a radical anti-colonialist, was a French-educated intellectual and scholar. He studied at the Sorbonne in Paris, receiving a doctorate in international law in 1949. Boutros-Ghali would be portrayed as a neutral; a man of the Third World, an African Arab, a Coptic Christian married to an Egyptian Jew, a man who spoke French. At sixty-eight his age was against him, but doubts were dismissed after President Bush's White House doctor gave him a clean bill of health.[16]

For France, there was no better outcome. French foreign policy was seeking a greater role and influence in the newly revitalized post-cold-war Security Council. Of the five permanent members, only France actively supported the candidacy of Boutros-Ghali. It had been Boutros-Ghali who had facilitated Egyptian entry into Francophonie, the worldwide association of nations that share the French language, an organization allowing France to pursue its interests and influence through culture and language. For the French, the appointment of a francophone as UN secretary-general was something of a coup.

§ For more than forty years UN peacekeeping, appropriately used, had been a useful device. It depended not on war-fighting soldiers but on troops trained in observation and the monitoring of ceasefires. The peacekeeper's weapon was not the rifle slung over his shoulder but his credibility; the UN soldier represented a world community of states and the Security Council's will for peace. The peacekeeper was not meant to solve conflict but to monitor compliance with already agreed ceasefires; these UN operations were solely dependent on the cooperation of the relevant parties for their effectiveness.[17]

A second phase of UN peacekeeping began with the end of the cold war when UN troops were expected to shoulder new burdens concerned with nation-building. The frequency of UN operations grew steadily; between 1989 and 1994 there were eighteen new missions, more than had been dispatched in the UN's first forty-five years. The Council became overwhelmed with high-cost, large-scale and open-ended missions. In Cambodia, Bosnia and Somalia peacekeepers found they needed to rely on the use of limited, but gradually intensifying, armed force, and there were tragic mistakes, when the Council sent peacekeepers into situations with orders they could not follow, and which the Council refused to change.

The UN's nemesis came in Somalia, a country in a state of anarchy since President Mohamed Siad Barre had been overthrown in 1991. Heavily armed gangs were preventing the delivery of food aid, and aid workers were being kidnapped and sometimes killed. An estimated 1.5 million people were starving to death and some 4.5 million more were threatened with malnutrition. This was classified the world's single worst humanitarian crisis, with warlords preventing the delivery of aid. George Bush, in the last weeks of his presidency, decided to send troops. 'Only the United States has the global reach to place a large security force on the ground in such a distant place quickly and efficiently and, thus, save thousands of innocents from death,' he had said.[18] When, on 9 December 1992, American troops stormed Somali beaches in the glare of television lights, there had seemed no limit to international humanitarianism. Bush sent 28,000 American soldiers to Somalia and a further 17,000 came from twenty other countries. There was already a small and under-equipped UN peacekeeping mission in Somalia that was stuck in barracks at Mogadishu airport. The Bush operation was called Restore Hope, and it was planned to stabilize the situation quickly and allow the aid to reach the starving. The operation was planned as a US mission, but given UN approval, and it was officially known as the Unified Task Force (UNITAF).

A month later, President Bill Clinton came to office. He said he was committed to UN peacekeeping. He promised to upgrade the size and professionalism of the UN headquarters staff. He was willing for US troops to come under UN command. Three months later, in March 1993, the command of the US operation in Somalia was transferred to the UN. The USA pulled out most of its troops but it left behind its 1,200-strong Quick Reaction Force, which would include an army battalion and a helicopter squadron. There would be 1,200 US troops for logistics. The new UN operation, although much smaller than UNI-TAF, was given more ambitious tasks. The US ambassador to the UN, Madeleine Albright, enthusiastically told the Council how the new UN Operation in Somalia (UNOSOM II) was about to embark on an unprecedented enterprise aimed at 'nothing less than the restoration of an entire country'. It was to restore law and order and compel the Somali militia to disarm.

But in spite of the rhetoric, in reality the UN mission was desperately understaffed and ill equipped and individual contingents continued to take orders from their national capitals.[19] It was a disaster, with UN troops trying to disarm militias in operations during which peacekeepers lost their lives. Then, in June 1993, twenty-three UN peacekeepers from Pakistan were murdered in one day, trying to inspect weapons that were under UN supervision. They were hacked to pieces by rampaging mobs. Fifty more were injured. These peacekeepers had lacked the most basic protective equipment. The Council immediately mandated the UN troops in Somalia to arrest the warlord allegedly responsible for inciting the crowds and to neutralize the radio station that was spreading anti-UN propaganda. Throughout the summer months an untold number of Somalis were killed as elite US troops, under US command, in raid after raid, tried to find the warlord. These US operations were outside the command and control of the UN, but it was the UN which was blamed. The other troop contributors to the mission objected to the US military missions. Italy threatened to pull out its 800 soldiers unless the USA stopped the 'Rambo-like' raids. 'It became a rogue operation,' a UN lawyer said in New York.

Worse was to come. On 3 October 1993, in a hail of bullets and missile fire, elite US troops, who were attempting to arrest the warlord, found themselves in a street battle with Somali fighters, and it is estimated that up to one thousand Somalis were killed. A total of eighteen Rangers, elite US troops, lost their lives, and eighty-four more were wounded. In a terrifying night-time firefight these US troops had to be rescued by a UN peacekeeping force of soldiers from Malaysia and Turkey driving Pakistani tanks. The USA eventually announced a withdrawal of its troops and urged all Western nations to do the same. The warlords were jubilant. Boutros-Ghali had warned that the US withdrawal would condemn the Somali people to a resumption of civil war. It would humble the UN and would show how without the presence of US troops, other countries were unwilling to provide their own soldiers.

There remained the image, broadcast around the world, of the body of a US soldier dragged behind a vehicle by his feet, through the dusty streets of Mogadishu, to a jeering and jubilant crowd. The Clinton administration distanced itself quickly and maintained that the doomed mission had been 'under the authority' of the UN. In turn, Boutros-Ghali tried to distance the UN, and he blamed the USA. The disastrous US raid had taken place without the UN in New York or the local command in Somalia being informed. The Clinton administration came under a barrage of criticism, including in Congress, where the president was accused of handing US foreign policy to feckless UN bureaucrats and to Boutros-Ghali, who had 'Napoleon-like' ambitions.[20] Congress immediately prepared a Peace Powers Act to make it impossible for the president to commit any more troops to UN operations.[21] The battle in Mogadishu had strengthened the hand of those in the US Defense Department who wanted nothing to do with the UN.

The Security Council commissioned its own report on what had happened in Somalia. When it was finished the Council tried to suppress it.[22] It concluded that the Council had lost control of the mission.[23] Its patchwork command structure had been as unstable as it was dangerous and never again should the UN undertake enforcement action within internal conflicts of states. The UN did not have the expertise, structure or resources to control forces in combat. 'The international community will be very careful in future,' said a peacekeeping official. 'We've learned … that [troop-contributing] states don't want to take casualties … you can't do coercive disarmament.'[24] Peacekeeping worked only with a clear mandate and a will on the part of the people to achieve peace.

The US troops were killed in Somalia two days before the Council was to vote on whether or not to provide peacekeepers for Rwanda. So determined was the US retreat from UN peacekeeping that some UN officials thought that Rwanda would be lucky to get anything at all.

§ On 5 October 1993 the Security Council passed Resolution 872, mandating the creation of the UN Assistance Mission for Rwanda (UNAMIR). It was designed specifically to cost as little money as possible.

The USA had wanted only a symbolic presence of 100 soldiers for Rwanda and insisted that any operation should cost no more than US$10 million a month. At the time, the US government owed US$900 million in unpaid assessments for regular and peacekeeping expenses. Congress, approving the 1994 budget, had just killed off a proposed peacekeeping contingency fund that was intended to allow the USA to contribute emergency start-up funds for peacekeeping operations.[25] The true cost of the UN mission in Cambodia had just become apparent at a staggering US$1.5 billion. The UN Transitional Authority in Cambodia (UNTAC) had been planned at US$600 million for an eighteen-month mission. There had been 22,000 military and civilian personnel serving there – UN troops, police monitors, election officials and civilian administrators. Its tasks were unprecedented, for it had been responsible for every aspect of rebuilding a shattered nation by organizing elections, supervising government and demobilization. Its reputation was for extravagance and corruption and a board of inquiry into its financial mismanagement had been set up. The problems had been immense, with the force deploying late in a deteriorating security situation. The civilian police component was a disaster in terms of its inability to bring criminals to justice.

When the mission for Rwanda was devised, in order to further cut costs, the USA argued for a reduction in the role of the peacekeepers and, with the support of Russia and the UK, substantially watered down the peacekeeping provisions of the Arusha Accords. Under the terms of Arusha, the peacekeepers were to ensure security throughout the country, but the Council decided that the peacekeepers should only 'assist in ensuring the security of the city of Kigali'. The agreement had provided that peacekeepers were to confiscate arms – 'the tracking of arm caches and neutralization of armed gangs throughout the country'. The peace terms also provided a comprehensive mandate calling for the collection of illegal arms, neutralizing armed gangs, and the protection of civilians at risk. The USA would have none of it. The operation for Rwanda was reduced to peacekeeping only. Peacekeepers observe, and they mediate. They do not seize weapons. The Arusha Accords specified that the peacekeepers should assist in providing the security of the refugees returning home, yet the eventual mandate for the peacekeepers in Rwanda was 'to monitor the process of repatriation'. It would have been useless, UN secretariat officials said later, to have tried to persuade the Council to approve a mandate more in line with the accords.[26]

Both diplomats and officials seem to have convinced themselves that Rwanda would be a success. So high were their hopes that some believed the mission for Rwanda would salvage the UN's battered reputation. This optimism would eventually lead to false political assumptions and unsound military decisions. The ambassador for New Zealand, Colin Keating, with a non-permanent seat on the Council, later blamed officials in the UN Secretariat for this optimism. They had been very discreet with their information about Rwanda. The non-permanent members of the Security Council came to see Rwanda not as the smouldering volcano that it really was, but rather as a small civil war. The situation was much more complex and dangerous than was ever revealed to the Council. The non-permanent members, in ignorance, were completely won over by the Arusha process and even more convinced by the joint Rwandan government–RPF delegation that came to New York. They saw only the positive: the end of the civil war.[27] Their decisions were based on the assumption that both sides would abide by the Arusha Accords. The British ambassador to the UN, David Hannay, claimed later that Rwanda had been 'landed on the UN's doorstep without adequate preparation or consideration'. It had been pressure from the French and other African countries which had overcome their qualms.[28]

After the vote in the Council to approve a UN mission for Rwanda, President Habyarimana stood at the podium of the General Assembly and told the UN membership: 'My country's recovery depends on the generosity of the international community.' He was right.

9 | PEACEKEEPERS: THE UN ARRIVES

§ In peacekeeping, the transition from dictatorship to democracy is the most dangerous time. It is the time used by extremists to make the most of a vacuum. Any delay or any hint of a lack of commitment serves only to encourage the hardliners who do not want peace. Under the Arusha Accords, a transitional government was to hold power in Rwanda until democratic elections were held. During a two-year period the UN peacekeepers were to monitor compliance with this agreement. Any delay in the arrival of the peacekeepers or failure to inaugurate the Broad-based Transitional Government, and the peace agreement could be derailed. Timing was crucial. Under the accords a neutral force was to be established in Kigali by 10 September – just thirty-seven days after the accords were signed. This defied all logic. The Security Council in New York had not yet decided to provide UN resources for Rwanda. In any event, the average time for the UN to deploy a peacekeeping operation was about six months. There were problems finding troops for Rwanda. Kofi Annan, a UN under-secretary-general and head of the UN's Department of Peacekeeping Operations (DPKO), described as 'incessant' the problems of getting countries to provide soldiers to serve in Rwanda.[1]

France offered soldiers, but the RPF was, naturally, opposed. In the end only Belgium, the former colonial power, came forward with a half-battalion of 400 of all ranks, and then Bangladesh offered 940 personnel, including soldiers, logisticians, military police and medical staff. Ghana offered 800 soldiers. The force commander chosen for the UN Assistance Mission for Rwanda (UNAMIR) was a Canadian, Brigadier-General Roméo A. Dallaire.[2] Dallaire was the Chief Military Observer of the UN Observer Mission Uganda–Rwanda (UNOMUR), already established by the UN Security Council with eighty-one military observers monitoring the 150-kilometre border. Dallaire had led a UN reconnaissance mission to Rwanda in August 1993 to examine the functions and resources needed. At the outset Dallaire had gone to UN headquarters in New York, where he discovered how low a priority Rwanda really was: there was no paperwork available in the Secretariat about the political and military situation in the country, and no reports on the Arusha Accords, even though UN officials had attended the negotiations. Much more interest was shown in crises in Liberia, Somalia, former Yugoslavia, Cambodia, Mozambique and Georgia.

The initial reconnaissance to Rwanda, which was led by Dallaire, had lasted twelve days. Dallaire visited the areas controlled by the RPF in the north and the government military positions, and he carried out a detailed survey of the forces, their structure and equipment.[3] Everyone Dallaire met, including representatives of the diplomatic community in Kigali, told him that the Arusha Accords were the last and best hope. Everyone stressed the urgency of implementation.[4]

Dallaire was a patient and principled soldier who had trained in an army proud of its tradition of peacekeeping. He was dynamic and charismatic in command. He had risen through the ranks, command-ing a troop, a battery, a regiment and a brigade. He was raised in a working-class area in the east end of Montreal; his father, a sergeant in the premier French-Canadian regiment, the Royal 22nd, had fought in Europe in the Second World War. His parents had worked in a local military supply depot. Dallaire's experience of UN missions was as brigade commander when his battalions had served in Cambodia and Bosnia. Dallaire brought the utmost dedication to this mission for Rwanda. He was a hard worker. And he was obstinate.

There was criticism afterwards that Dallaire was inadequately pre-pared for the realities in Rwanda. Dallaire himself said that had he known about the human rights reports then he would have insisted on a larger force.[5] Others believed that nothing could have prepared him, or anyone, for the reality they faced. Some years later Dallaire speculated about whether or not it had been like a Greek tragedy on the grandest scale. 'You sort of wonder ... when you look back at the whole thing, whether or not we were set up ... whether or not the UN and myself fell into something that was beyond our ability to manage.'[6]

The timing could not have been worse. On the day that Dallaire had arrived in Kigali to assume command of UNAMIR there was a cataclysmic event in neighbouring Burundi that would have the most terrible repercussions. In Burundi there had been startling progress towards democracy, a process that made the Habyarimana government appear indefensible. In the first successful elections since Burundi's independence in July 1962 a Hutu president had been elected, an astonishing achievement in a country that had traditionally been ruled by Tutsi. The whole process was destroyed on 21 October 1993, when the president, Melchior Ndadaye, whose election four months earlier had symbolized unity between Hutu and Tutsi, was assassinated by officers from Burundi's Tutsi-dominated army. His constitutional successor was also killed, along with most of the leadership of the democratic movement. Ndadaye had been a moderate. He had chosen a Tutsi prime minister and he had left the Tutsi army untouched. One of the reasons put forward for the coup was that negotiations were under way between Ndadaye's government and the French over a French military presence in Burundi. The army officers had not been consulted and they were suspicious of Ndadaye's new links with France, particularly in the light of the active support France was giving the Hutu government in Rwanda.[7]

Two days after the assassination in Burundi, a rally was held in the Nyamirambo football stadium in Kigali, where politicians from the former one-party Mouvement Révolutionnaire National pour le Développement (MRND) and the extremist Coalition pour la Défense de la République (CDR) had paraded with certain politicians from opposition parties. A speech was given by Froduald Karamira, once a moderate of the Mouvement Démocratique Républicain (MDR). This political party was a serious political threat to the MRND.[8] The MDR was the most powerful opposition party, and it had secured the control of the prefectures of Gitarama, Gikongoro, Kibuye and parts of Butare. An estimated 70 per cent of the total Tutsi population lived in these regions.[9] The MDR support did not extend to the north. The MDR was heir to the southern MDR-Parmehutu, which had ousted the Tutsi monarchy in 1959 and had first developed the exclusionist ideology underpinning massacres of Tutsi that had started in 1959.

In the Nyamirambo stadium that day Karamira had warned that 'the enemy was among the people'. In a rousing speech he said: 'We are not simply heating heads by saying we have plans to work ... We cannot sit down and think that what happened in Burundi will not happen here.' Karamira shouted: 'All Hutu are one power.'[10]

'Pawa, Pawa' was chanted over and over again. It was at this rally that the exclusionist ideology found a catchy name. From now on these words would be used as a rallying call. Karamira derided the president at the rally. The president was blamed for having conceded too much to the RPF. The Arusha Accords would never work, he said. He blamed the RPF commander, Paul Kagame, for the assassination of Ndadaye.

The next day Tutsi were targeted for violence in the streets of Kigali and there were rapes of Tutsi women.[11] There was speculation afterwards that what happened in Burundi spelled the end for Rwanda.[12] Where previously the democratic process in Burundi had encouraged pro-democracy activists, a propaganda coup was now handed to the extremists. The announcers on RTLM blamed the assassination on progressive politics, and on reconciliation with the Tutsi. The broadcasters claimed that the assassination was part of a plot to eliminate the Hutu completely. The Tutsi intended to dominate the entire region.[13]

There were massacres in Burundi following the assassination and an estimated death toll put the figure at between 35,000 and 50,000 people killed.[14] The Security Council in New York decided not to intervene, a decision greeted with considerable relief in the UN Secretariat, particularly in the DPKO, where there was mission overload.[15] Nor was the Western press interested in Burundi. The story of the massacres of civilians was not given much coverage.[16] There was speculation as to how this lack of reaction had encouraged the extremists in Rwanda, who came to the view that, whatever they did, outside interference and media interest would be at a minimum.[17]

One further consequence of events in Burundi was a flood of refugees fleeing the violence with an estimated 300,000 people crossing the Burundi border. Their only future was to live in Rwanda in miserable camps where there was soon a dysentery epidemic. An estimated nine thousand people died. A doctor with MSF-France, Jean-Hervé Bradol, later described a general indifference to the plight of these people among Rwandan officials and diplomats. By January 1994, 40 per cent of children under five in a camp in the prefecture of Kigali, not far from the capital, were suffering severe malnutrition.[18] The camps, with their large numbers of disaffected youth, were fertile recruiting grounds for Hutu Power. Another refugee crisis had been created in the north, where there were 800,000 people displaced, mostly Hutu, south of the demilitarized zone. Starting in February 1994, Tutsi refugees were coming home from Uganda, mostly men and boys of military age, and they were accompanied by large cattle herds, moving directly to the RPF zone and taking the land of the Hutus who had already fled. The RPF claimed not to be able to stem this flow of returnees, and yet it was clear that these people were being helped on their journey by the RPF. The regional representative for the UN High Commissioner for Refugees (UNHCR) told Dallaire that the returnees should not be assisted, for that would encourage an even greater movement of people. Aid for these people was eventually provided by independent agencies. The Rwandan army claimed that many of the displaced were recruited to the RPF. Because of unmarked minefields north of the demilitarized zone, peacekeepers were unable to effectively monitor the movement of refugees and arms from the Uganda–Rwanda border. The mines allowed the RPF to funnel the refugees into its own zone. 'The war started', Dallaire would recall, 'before we had fully grasped the nature of these events.' Their worst and most crippling handicap was their late arrival.

'We were too little too late. It was a grave error,' he said.[19]

§ The extremists watched UNAMIR's slow build-up. It was soon clear that the force structure given to the force commander, in particular the equipment, and the readiness level of his force, bore no relationship at all to what was really needed. Lieutenant General Dallaire lacked the barest essentials. He was reduced to borrowing petty cash from a UN agency. He lacked everything from ammunition to sandbags, fuel and barbed wire. The mission did not have essential personnel; there was no public affairs officer, no legal adviser, no humanitarian or human rights experts.[20] When Dallaire had devised the mission, he had asked for a minimum requirement of 4,500 troops.[21] This figure had been pared down by officials in the Secretariat even before being submitted to the Security Council. In the end, a total of 2,548 personnel had been agreed.

Their mission was to monitor the security of the city of Kigali within a weapons-secure area, monitor observance of the ceasefire and help with the formation of a new integrated army. They were to train local people to remove landmines, monitor the repatriation of refugees, and assist UN agencies in coordinating humanitarian assistance for the million refugees and displaced people.

The military component of UNAMIR was to comprise three infantry battalions, one engineer company, a transportation section with four utility helicopters, one logistics company, one medical platoon, and 331 unarmed military observers, a force headquarters, a movement control unit and a field hospital. There were to be twenty-two armoured personnel carriers (APCs) and eight military helicopters to allow for a quick-reaction capability. That was the plan. In fact, no military helicopters arrived. And only eight APCs were provided, of which only five were serviceable. They did not arrive until early March 1994, without tools, spare parts, mechanics or manuals and with limited ammunition. Their main weapon had never been test-fired. They were Czech-made BTR-80s, on loan only, and worn out from use in the UN mission in Mozambique. Before long they were inoperable. Dallaire said that it was not lack of effort or dedication and zeal which prevented the mission from ever achieving an effective state of operations or gaining the initiative from the belligerents in order to advance the peace process.[22]

The UNAMIR flag was raised for the first time in Kinihira, a northern hill in Ruhengeri, on 1 November, when the UN mission officially integrated with the UN military observer group. There was little to celebrate. Most of Dallaire's time and energy went into trying to sort out a logistics nightmare. He would spend more than 70 per cent of his time, and his principal staff's time, dedicated to battling with the UN's administrative and logistics structure, upon which his mission depended. Dallaire considered it a major achievement that UNAMIR was conducting any operational activities on the ground even six months after the mandate was approved. Apart from the 450 Belgian soldiers, all the contingents came from developing countries with their own weak logistics base at home. The Ghanaian battalion arrived without a single vehicle. Other vehicles for UNAMIR were coming by sea and then being driven overland to Kigali. There was petty theft during shipment, rendering vehicles defective – mirrors, filters and maintenance tools were missing. In Kigali, the peacekeepers had to wait for radios, tents, flak jackets and other material coming from the UN missions in Cambodia or Somalia. Dallaire said: 'I spent most of my time fighting the heavy mechanical UN system with all its stupidity ... we would order torches, and after a long delay they arrived without batteries ... Seeing to the most immediate needs stopped us from seeing what was reserved for us in the future.'[23]

The UNAMIR headquarters, in a bleak and concrete motel on the edge of eastern Kigali, were officially opened by President Juvénal Habyarimana on 17 November 1993. Habyarimana had welcomed the 'soldiers of peace, soldiers of hope' to his country.[24] But even as this ceremony took place there was a series of killings in northern communes when thirty-seven people were killed in five separate places. All the victims had just been successfully elected as members of local authorities, or were members of their families. The news of these killings was reported immediately by RTLM. At the end of the month other massacres took place; one of them was in Mutara, north of the Gishwati forest, when about twenty-five people were killed, including nine children. The children were murdered separately and their bodies were found the following day by a UN patrol. A UNAMIR inquiry was established but it failed to discover who was responsible. These were the first murders to take place since the UN's arrival and, because all the victims were Hutu, the RPF was widely blamed for them. A report on these events was sent in a coded cable to New York. It described how hands had been cut off, eyes pulled out and skulls crushed. Pregnant women were cut open.

The manner in which they were conducted, in their execution, in their coordination, in their cover-up, and in their political motives lead us to firmly believe that the perpetrators of these evil deeds were well-organised, well-informed, well-motivated and prepared to conduct premeditated murder. We have no reason to believe that such an occurrence could not and will not be repeated again in any part of this country where arms are prolific and ethnic tensions are prevalent.[25]

Dallaire's military assistant, Major Brent Beardsley, travelled north to investigate. The only survivor was a six-year-old girl who had been gang-raped. She lay in a local hospital in a coma and suffering spasms from brain damage. She was under UN guard. She died the following day. When Beardsley went to the place where these murders happened he found landmines preventing further enquiry. Beardsley was suspicious about the possible role of government Para-commandos from a nearby camp. These soldiers wore red cords around their waists and there had been red marks around the children's necks. It would have been extremely difficult for the RPF to have travelled from their base some hundred kilometres away to the northern stronghold of Ruhengeri. A board of inquiry was established comprising representatives from UNAMIR, the government and from the RPF. It completed its investigation in March 1994. The UNAMIR member of the board told Beardsley that he suspected the government extremists and soldiers were responsible for the murders and that they were part of a terror campaign to blame the RPF and strengthen anti-RPF feeling. But there was no conclusive proof.[26]

The culprits were never found. Every day for the next four months the announcers on RTLM issued a stinging rebuke to Dallaire and his peacekeepers for not finding out who was responsible for the killings. Listeners were told that Dallaire favoured the RPF.

There was a growing confidence among those whom Dallaire described as 'negative elements'.[27] At the end of November the extremist party, the Coalition pour la Défense de la République (CDR), issued a press release to the effect that the 'majority population' must be ready to 'neutralize its enemies and their accomplices'. In December, Dallaire described what he called a 'third force', which he described as 'ruthless and well organised ... a controlled and equipped terrorist force ...' He believed it to be responsible for the atrocities in the north.[28]

In December, most of the second half-battalion of infantry, a light unit from Bangladesh with some trucks, was deployed in Kigali. They had little operational experience; they were poorly trained and not a co-hesive unit. They had no logistics, no engineering equipment. They had arrived in Rwanda without bottled water or food in spite of instructions from New York that all contingents should be self-supporting for three months. The Bangladeshis were supposed to have provided a composite force of a medical company, an engineer squadron, a half-battalion of infantry and a movement control platoon.[29] They were to have provided a quick-reaction capability. Dallaire began training some of them but he found they were below acceptable operational standards. There were also problems with the Para-commandos from Belgium. These soldiers had come from the UN mission in Somalia where peacekeepers from both Canada and Belgium, as was later shown, had committed torture and in some cases the murder of Somalis. One disgraced Canadian regiment had been disbanded after the torture and beating to death of a young boy.[30] Some of the Belgian soldiers who arrived in Rwanda seemed conditioned to a peace-enforcement environment and there were instances of brutal racism. They were sent home for misconduct and lack of discipline and their replacements were briefed that their mission depended on cooperation with and the support of local people. At one point Dallaire contemplated the unprecedented step of recom-mending to New York that the Belgian soldiers be expelled from the mission.[31] Dallaire was surprised that the Belgian government had sent Para-commandos. Although they were suitable for enforcement opera-tions under Chapter VII of the UN Charter, they were not suitable for Chapter VI peacekeeping. In Canada they would have been considered unsuitable without a mandatory three-month training course.

The phase-one objective of UNAMIR's mission was to escort an RPF battalion into Kigali, a move that was intended to counterbalance the Rwandan army and deter aggression against RPF political leaders. This was a major operation; it had taken a convoy of ninety buses, lorries, coaches and jeeps from the RPF headquarters in Mulindi, a journey of some sixty kilometres. There were Belgian peacekeepers providing the escort and by the evening of 27 December the battalion was safely installed on the outskirts of the city, in a building previously housing the parliament. The extremists hated the whole idea and the chief of staff of the army, Colonel Déogratias Nsabimana, said the battalion was a 'Trojan horse'.[32] There were accusations that the RPF had infiltrated weapons and far more soldiers than the 600 allowed under the Arusha Accords.

With the RPF battalion established in Kigali, and in accordance with the Arusha Accords, the French troops withdrew.[33] French TV news crews showed an exchange of presents between Rwandan and French soldiers. Some French soldiers stayed behind. French military personnel from the Détachement d'Assistance Militaire et d'Instruction (DAMI) were recognized in civilian clothes in Kigali. And the infamous French mercenary, Paul Barril, adept at self-promotion, was there telling everyone he was an adviser to President Habyarimana.[34]

In these first months there were three separate incidents of ceasefire violations along the northern border with Uganda, and more than a dozen Rwandan government soldiers were killed. Rwandan army commanders told Dallaire that Ugandan battalions were crossing into Rwanda, although UN observers never reported any such occurrences. The supply lines operated freely, however, one of many ways the Ugandan government quietly supported the RPF.[35]

In spite of a failure to hold to the timetable outlined in the Arusha Accords, on 10 December the government side met the RPF in Kinihira, a hilltop with a magnificent view. They issued a joint declaration that peace was possible, and there was renewed optimism, and promises that every effort would be made to adhere to the peace agreement. Events elsewhere were not so reassuring. A teacher who had lived for twenty-seven years in Rukara, a rural commune in Kibungo prefecture, noticed how in December 1993 the Hutu youth had started to withdraw and to drink beer by themselves, and some youth wings of the political parties were being taught to shoot. They were holding rallies, speaking against Tutsi and the Hutu opposition. Sometimes they roughed up Tutsi. A nun from a Spanish order at Rukara said she believed that the Hutu had been informed that they would have to kill the Tutsi, but that they did not know when.[36]

In a clear and public warning from David Waller, Oxfam's regional specialist, Rwanda was described as more violently divided than at any time since independence. The war had done incalculable damage to the economy and the environment. The country stood on the brink of an 'un-chartered abyss of anarchy and violence'. There were too many historical, ethnic, economic and political pressures that were likely to push it over the edge.[37]

The only hopeful sign was a peace march on 1 January with an estimated six thousand people taking to the streets in Kigali with smaller numbers in Butare, Gisenyi, Gikongoro, in Kirambo, Biniga and Ruhuha.[38]

§ On 8 January 1994, there was a violent demonstration by the Interahamwe in Kigali and Rwandan gendarmes stood by helplessly in the face of a machete-wielding mob. The gendarmes had no communications equipment, no appropriate vehicles, and not even enough petrol. Nor did they have the will to act. The Rwandan gendarmerie had doubled in size in three years to 6,000. It had proved impossible to train so many recruits. Half of them had received only fifteen days' basic instruction.[39] Only 400 gendarmes performed a peacetime police role. There were three vehicles for them. In his initial reconnaissance mission report Dallaire had called the Rwandan gendarmes a disaster with weak discipline and poor morale. It was a military unit mainly used to defend strategic locations.

A turning point for the commander of the Kigali sector of UN-AMIR, a Belgian colonel, Luc Marchal, was watching the weakness of the gendarmes while they faced rampaging mobs. He said some years later that at this moment he had realized how few options there were. He had contemplated going to the rescue of the gendarmes, but there had been anti-UN slogans throughout the riot. It had seemed that the intention of the rioters was to provoke the RPF soldiers to break out of the parliament building barracks. There was intelligence information afterwards that this had been the intention. There were grenades and guns distributed among the crowd and a rumour had spread that Belgian soldiers would be killed. There was information that the demonstration had been pre-planned at a meeting the previous day at MRND headquarters. It was attended by the president of the party, Mathieu Ngirumpatse, the minister of defence, Augustin Bizimana,[40] the army chief of staff, Colonel Déogratias Nsabimana, the chief of staff of the gendarmes, General Augustin Ndindiliyimana, and the president of the Interahamwe, Robert Kajuga.[41] There were plans to store weapons in the homes of army officers, and if these locations needed protection from UN peacekeepers, then the Interahamwe would fight them off, with stones if necessary.[42] The whole of UNAMIR was now derided, with particular hatred reserved for the Belgians, blamed for having provided an escort for the RPF battalion's entry into Kigali.

Three times the inauguration of the Broad-based Transitional Government was planned, and three times it was postponed. Dallaire believed it was because the presidential clique wanted to retain power. The hostility towards Belgian troops worsened, and in one incident the Interahamwe surrounded a minibus full of soldiers and chanted at them, calling them 'Tutsi'. Threats were made against the owners of bars and shops in Kigali frequented by Belgian soldiers. A grenade was thrown into Marchal's headquarters and one night hundreds of grenades exploded. Dallaire asked UN headquarters for an intelligence-gathering capability but this was denied because it was contrary to peacekeeping policy. 'We were blind and deaf in the field,' Dallaire said later. 'The five permanent members ... possess high-tech information capabilities ... yet the UN is expected to operate in an information void.'[43]

In early December Dallaire had received a copy of an anonymous letter purportedly written by senior army officers. It was copied to all diplomatic missions and it warned of a 'Machiavellian plan' by President Habyarimana and of 'diabolic manoeuvres' to prevent the implementation of the Arusha Accords. There were going to be massacres spreading throughout Rwanda in order to persuade public opinion that Rwanda's problems were ethnic. The RPF would be incited to break the ceasefire and the civil war would resume. Opposition politicians were going to be assassinated, including the prime minister designate under the Arusha Accords, Faustin Twagiramungu (MDR),[44] and Félicien Gatabazi, the head of the Parti Social Démocrate (PSD), which was the second-largest opposition party.[45] The plot was devised by President Habyarimana with the support of a handful of military officers from his home region. The letter had been written because of 'revulsion against these filthy tactics'.[46]

What intelligence collection there was in UNAMIR was conducted by Dallaire's own military information office, comprising a Belgian officer and two French-African military observers. There were eighty-one unarmed military observers, as part of UNAMIR, whose job was to liaise at a local level, and who were posted all over the country. They were uniquely placed to gain the confidence of the local administration. They were the best informed, and their commander from Fiji, Colonel Isoa Tikoca, had years of UN experience. There were officers from sixteen countries, and Colonel Tikoca was supported by operations officer Lieutenant Colonel Somalia Iliya from Nigeria. Military observers consisted of commissioned officers from the rank of captain to lieutenant colonel. Their information was transmitted in the form of daily situation reports to Dallaire and then onwards to New York.

It was rare for unofficial information to be given to UNAMIR by local diplomatic or governmental sources. So concerned was Dallaire about the lack of intelligence-gathering that the UNAMIR command decided to bypass headquarters. Marchal appealed directly to Belgian military intelligence, the Service Général du Renseignement de l'Armée (SGR). This resulted in the creation of a two-person cell to report to UNAMIR headquarters in Kigali as well as to the Belgian military headquarters in Evere, outside Brussels. Eventually the cell controlled a total of five informers thanks to a small sum of money to pay for information.[47] The network was run by Lieutenant Mark Nees. At the end of December the intelligence cell was told that there were stocks of weapons stored at the homes of the militia leaders. There was a plan involving MRND leaders to undermine the credibility of the Belgian troops.

Dallaire created his own small intelligence unit using his own money. It comprised Captain Frank Claeys from Belgium and a military observer from Senegal, Captain Amadou Deme. The first thing they discovered was that the northern killings had been the work of Para-commandos from the nearby Camp Bagogwe.[48]

But it was not until 10 January that a source came forward who claimed to be from the heart of a secret Hutu network. This informer was introduced to them by no less than Faustin Twagiramungu, the prime minister designate. The informer was called Jean-Pierre and he agreed to meet Marchal the same night. They met by candlelight and both laid their pistols on the table. Jean-Pierre said that he was a former member of the president's security guard, who had worked as a chauffeur, and was now a senior trainer in the Interahamwe. His salary came from the ruling party, the MRND.[49] He told Marchal that 1,700 Interahamwe had been trained in Rwandan army camps and these men were now scattered in groups of forty throughout the city. Since the arrival of UNAMIR he had trained 300 men in sessions lasting three weeks. The focus of the training was discipline, weapons, explosives, close combat and tactics. He said that each of the twenty to thirty cells that he controlled could kill 1,000 people every twenty minutes. His job was to arm all the cells in the capital. In every cell there were militia armed with weapons with basic military training. Up until now Jean-Pierre had supposed that the Interahamwe had been created in order to protect Kigali from the RPF, but since October he had been ordered to register all Tutsi in Kigali. He was certain that it was for their extermination. He had come forward because he could not support the killing of civilians. Marchal remembered: 'What he told me was so enormous, it was so extraordinary. I was uneasy. I had not come to Rwanda to be James Bond. This was the work of a specialist intelligence officer.'[50]

Jean-Pierre said that the demonstration, held on 8 January, had been organized to trap Belgian peacekeepers and to kill them. There had been Para-commandos and gendarmes in plain clothes in the crowd as agitators. At the next attempt to inaugurate the transitional government, opposition politicians would be killed as they entered the parliament building. If Belgian peacekeepers reacted with force, then they would be killed in order to provoke a total withdrawal of UN troops from Rwanda. The president, claimed Jean-Pierre, had lost control of the extremists, and the people involved in these plans, from the Rwandan army and the Interahamwe, were in radio contact with each other. There was a direct link between the army chief of staff, Colonel Déogratias Nsabimana, and the president of the MRND, Mathieu Ngirumpatse. There were hundreds of AK47s, in secret stockpiles of weapons, throughout the city. Jean-Pierre was willing to go public but in exchange he wanted UN protection somewhere abroad for himself and his family.

Marchal made no promises, and he went straight to see Dallaire. They reached the same conclusion. It was necessary to put Jean-Pierre's claims to the test. If the weapons stocks existed they should be seized in order to expose the duplicity of the Rwandan government and reveal the political process as a sham.[51] Dallaire immediately wrote a coded cable to New York to inform the secretary-general's military adviser, a fellow Canadian, Major General J. Maurice Baril, of Jean-Pierre's claims. Dallaire wrote that he wanted to take action over the weapons cache in the next twenty-four hours and he recommended that the informant be given safe passage from Rwanda. Dallaire expressed reservations on Jean-Pierre's sudden change of heart, and stated that he had not ruled out that this was a trap. In the meantime they would prepare a detailed plan for a weapons raid.

In New York the Dallaire cable caused the utmost consternation. A claim later that it received routine treatment is simply untrue.[52] It was not Jean-Pierre's story which caused alarm, but the idea of weapons seizures. The deaths of twenty-three Pakistani peacekeepers in Somalia had happened only six months earlier, the troops killed during a weapons inspection, and this had been the incident that had ultimately led to the deaths of the eighteen US Rangers in Mogadishu. There was a meeting to discuss this new development with the secretary-general's military adviser, General Maurice Baril, the assistant secretary-general and adviser to the secretary-general, Iqbal Riza, and with Hedi Annabi, the director of the Africa Division in the DPKO. It was agreed that on no account was Dallaire to seize weapons. It was clearly outside his mandate.[53]

Kofi Annan, under-secretary-general and head of DPKO, explained later on that it had been reasonable to conclude that the Security Council did not want aggressive force used in this peace mission. Annan knew the restrictions placed on the budget and mandate of UNAMIR. A Chapter VI mandate under the UN Charter provided only for the pacific settlement of disputes. Both Annan and Riza were firmly of the opinion that only a political solution could minimize the violence in Rwanda. And Dallaire had not ruled out that the informer might be part of a trap to lure the peacekeepers. 'Force Commander does have certain reservations on the suddenness of the change of heart of the informant to come clean with this information ... Possibility of a trap not fully excluded,' his cable had ended.

Annan and Riza were both criticized in a UN inquiry for not briefing the secretary-general and the Security Council about this telegram.[54] Some years later, interviewed for a US television programme, Riza said he regretted the failure to take more heed of the information in the 11 January cable: 'All of us deeply regret it, all of us are remorseful about it ... yes, we failed.'[55]

The reply to the cable, signed by Annan, was addressed to the secretary-general's Special Representative in Rwanda, Jacques-Roger Booh-Booh, who had arrived in November. In every UN mission, it is the job of the Special Representative to implement the political objectives decided by the Council. The position is intended to provide cohesive, consistent leadership.[56] The response to Booh-Booh from Annan read: 'No reconnaissance or other action, including response to request for protection, should be taken by UNAMIR until clear guidance is received from HQ.'[57] Booh-Booh cabled back to say that he had met personally with Faustin Twagiramungu, and that Twagiramungu had told Booh-Booh that he had 'total, repeat total confidence in the veracity and true ambitions of the informant'. Booh-Booh responded that Dallaire was prepared to 'pursue the operation in accordance with military doctrine with reconnaissance planning and preparation ... if any possibility of an undue risk scenario presented itself the operation would be called off'. This time the reply came from Iqbal Riza, the UN official concerned with the day-to-day running of the operation at UN headquarters. It was addressed to both Booh-Booh and Dallaire and it told them that arms seizures were beyond their mandate: 'The overriding consideration is the need to avoid entering into a course of action that might lead to the use of force and unanticipated repercussions,' Riza wrote.[58] Annan and Riza had decided that the best way to handle Jean-Pierre's information was to tell President Habyarimana about it as quickly as possible. And so Dallaire and Booh-Booh duly met with the president and made it clear to him that the Security Council would hold him personally responsible for any violence. Habyarimana was told that he should report within forty-eight hours concerning the steps taken to recover the arms that had been distributed.[59] This diplomatic approach, devised by Riza and Annan, was grounded in traditional peacekeeping. Their intention was to evaluate how far Habyarimana had progressed in disarming the population, and dismantling stocks of weapons. If this approach failed to bring about a result, then the Security Council would be informed. Riza was baffled as to why UNAMIR, with some fifteen hundred troops, should take responsibility for seizing weapons when in Rwanda there were 28,000 troops and 6,000 gendarmes. Booh-Booh cabled Annan that the president appeared alarmed by the tone of their démarche and surprised at the detail they possessed. They had also told the president about the harassment of UNAMIR personnel and the violence against one ethnic group during a demonstration on 8 January. Habyarimana said he had been unaware of the demonstration. Booh-Booh and Dallaire also met the president of the MRND, Mathieu Ngirumpatse, and its secretary-general, Joseph Nzirorera. Both men denied that the party militia was involved in violence. Booh-Booh reported to New York that the president of the MRND had seemed bewildered by how specific their information was. Booh-Booh cabled New York: 'The President of the MRND seemed unnerved and is reported to have subsequently ordered an accelerated distribution of weapons.' Booh-Booh wrote that he thought the initiative to confront the accused parties with the information was a good one and might force them to decide on alternative ways of jeopardizing the peace deal.

Booh-Booh and Dallaire, also on instructions from New York, met three ambassadors in Kigali, from the USA, France and Belgium, and with the papal nuncio, Monsignor Giuseppe Bertello, the dean of the diplomatic corps, to tell them what Jean-Pierre had said. The three ambassadors expressed serious concern about the information and promised to consult their capitals. At a further meeting with the ambassadors on 13 January, Dallaire presented a letter from Jean-Pierre containing yet more information. The next day the three ambassadors met with President Habyarimana to express their own concern.

It was left to Colonel Luc Marchal to test Jean-Pierre's credibility. He sent Captain Amadou Deme with the informer to find the stocks of weapons. Jean-Pierre went straight to the headquarters of the MRND, where in the basement were 137 Kalashnikov assault rifles and ammunition. Jean-Pierre took Deme to see smaller caches of arms hidden in bushes and undergrowth at strategic crossroads in Kigali. Marchal recalled that he was stunned at the refusal of New York to allow weapons seizures. The whole point of their mission was to secure a weapons-free area in Kigali. 'It was the worst thing for us,' Marchal said, 'just to stay, and to watch, without reaction.' Marchal asked himself how a transitional government could be created in a country where there was a profusion of weaponry.

Dallaire tried several times to persuade New York to approve plans for the seizures of weapons. Booh-Booh wrote to Annan to complain that each day of delay in authorizing arms recovery would result in ever-deteriorating security. UNAMIR would soon be unable to carry out its mandate. The only major weapons seizure by the peacekeepers had taken place at the airport when, on 21 January, in a DC-8 belonging to East African Cargo, a consignment of 40 tons of ammunition arrived to be immediately confiscated by peacekeepers.[60] It had come from Châteauroux, France.[61] UNAMIR searched aircraft coming into Kigali and tried to monitor land routes, although this was not in the mandate. Apart from this one airport seizure, only sixteen weapons and just over one hundred hand grenades were seized.

Marchal told both his national authorities in Brussels and the Belgian ambassador in Kigali of the importance he attached to the information from Jean-Pierre. On 15 January, the Belgian ambassador in Kigali, Johan Swinnen, exerted his own pressure and told the government in Brussels that unless UNAMIR took immediate action, the weapons would be distributed to the Interahamwe. Swinnen believed that Dallaire's mandate certainly did provide for weapons seizures. The UN secretary-general, Boutros Boutros-Ghali, did not agree. On 14 January he warned that arms seizures could cause serious political repercussions.[62] Habyarimana telephoned Boutros-Ghali and told him that he needed all the help he could get, from the ambassadors in Kigali and from the UN. Boutros-Ghali told him that the UN trusted his leadership but that unless there was progress towards peace then the UN would be obliged to withdraw. A UN withdrawal would be a disaster for Rwanda, Habyarimana told Boutros-Ghali.[63]

On 16 January an estimated five thousand MRND supporters held a rally at the Nyamirambo stadium in Kigali. It was calm, as Jean-Pierre had accurately predicted it would be, for its main purpose was to distribute grenades. The following day, Marchal warned his army command in Brussels that it was 'imperative' Dallaire be given permission to seize weapons; it was vital to support Dallaire in his request to the UN. On 23 January, during a demonstration in Kigali, forty-seven people were killed. Dallaire appealed to New York for a broader interpretation of his mandate. Three days later, on 26 January, gunmen shot at Belgian peacekeepers, the security detail at Booh-Booh's residence. The Belgian ambassador in Kigali told his foreign minister that either UNAMIR was given a more forceful mandate, or the troops should be completely withdrawn.

At the end of the month, the Human Rights Watch Arms Project, in a detailed report, revealed that the Habyarimana regime had entered into arms deals with Egypt and South Africa and was also getting arms supplies from France. The country was awash with weapons. The researchers had obtained a secret document showing that the government had formed paramilitary 'self-defence' groups in select communities where human rights violations took place. The report noted:

> It is impossible to exaggerate the danger of providing automatic rifles to civilians ... In light of the widespread and horrifying abuses committed by Hutu civilian crowds and party militia armed primarily with machetes and spears, it is frightening to ponder the potential for abuses by a large number of ill-trained civilians equipped with assault rifles.[64]

10 | PEACEKEEPERS IN TROUBLE: FEBRUARY–APRIL 1994

§ Major General Roméo Dallaire never gave up hoping the peace plan would succeed. 'Once ministers were round a cabinet table, I thought they would be able to reach compromises,' he said.[1] If the Broad-based Transitional Government was established and the moderates took charge of key ministries and there was demobilization and a national army created, the extremists would be subdued and perhaps even marginalized. Colonel Luc Marchal, the officer responsible for the Kigali Weapons Secure Area, agreed with this assessment. Marchal liaised with Dallaire on a daily basis. There was mutual respect. Dallaire valued Marchal's experience in Africa; Marchal had served for five years, as a Para-commando, for Belgium's technical military cooperation in Zaire. He considered there was no better solution for Rwanda than the Arusha Accords. Although much criticized, the agreement had ended the civil war. In the first weeks of 1994, however, with a series of postponements of the swearing-in of the new government, there was political stagnation. The security situation deteriorated. At the end of January Dallaire warned New York about possible dangers to his peacekeepers and he listed alternative courses of action, including a return to Mulindi of the RPF troops in Kigali. He suggested the preparation of plans for a full evacuation of UNAMIR.[2] At a meeting with Major General Paul Kagame in Mulindi, Dallaire was told of the desperation of Rwandan refugees who had been promised a return home and who were being told to be patient. Kagame told Dallaire: 'Very soon we are going to face the situation that someone is going to have to be a winner.'[3]

On 3 February Dallaire warned New York in the strongest terms: 'We can expect more frequent and more violent demonstrations, more grenade and armed attacks on ethnic and political groups, more assassinations and quite possibly outright attacks on UNAMIR installations.' Dallaire estimated that every day of delay in authorizing deterrent arms recovery operations would result in an ever-deteriorating security situation. If the arms continued to be distributed then UNAMIR would be unable to carry out its mandate. 'If we do not take decisive action we run the very real risk of becoming potential targets.' He believed that the reluctance to allow a more proactive response was fear of creating 'another Somalia'.[4] There were rumours circulating of assassination plots against politicians. Dallaire agreed to provide UN security for the prime minister, and the President of the Assembly. There followed requests for protection from other moderate politicians, human rights activists and expatriate employees in UN agencies.[5]

For weeks cables passed backwards and forwards between the UN Secretariat and Dallaire about how peacekeepers could best help the Rwandan authorities to seize illegal weapons stocks. Annan made it clear that no action was to be taken without guidance from headquarters. And whatever else, the peacekeepers should only 'assist illegal arms recovery' on a case-by-case basis, and only when requested to do so by the government or the RPF. They were to do nothing that might lead to force or any unanticipated repercussions. The peacekeepers were to provide advice and guidelines only. They did not have the mandate or the capacity to 'take over the maintenance of law and order'.[6] This was not their role. Dallaire believed that New York no longer trusted his judgement.[7]

Both Dallaire and Marchal believed that determined and selective deterrent operations were needed to target confirmed arms caches and the individuals known to have weapons in their possession.[8] Marchal came up with a plan to enlist the Rwandan gendarmes in arms recovery and proposed that if the gendarmes took the lead, then military observers could monitor and advise. He began to train gendarmes. But UN headquarters questioned even this and asked for further clarification. Annan sent a cable to remind Dallaire of his mandate – to contribute to the security of the city, 'within a weapons secure area by the parties'.

Dallaire sent detailed situation reports, special incident reports and military assessments. He produced military and political analysis with options and recommendations. He repeated some sentences week after week. The phrase 'The situation is deteriorating significantly and all our resources are used to the full' is used seven times between 24 February and 5 April.[9]

At the beginning of February it was relatively quiet. Much of the violence stopped and gendarmes were more in evidence on the streets. The minister of defence, Augustin Bizimana, expressed regret to Dallaire about how little help had been given the peacekeepers. Bizimana promised a propaganda campaign to promote the work of the UN.[10] The sudden change of heart did not last. At the end of the month there was a deterioration in security, and so serious was the violence that it seemed it would spiral out of control.

On Sunday, 20 February, there was a national rally at the Nyamirambo stadium in support of the peace agreement. Stones were thrown at UN peacekeepers providing an escort for the prime ninister, Agathe Uwilingiyimana, whose transitional authority was provided for under the Arusha Accords. She was a member of the Mouvement Démocratique Républicain (MDR). The peacekeepers fired shots in the air. That night assassins tried to kill the prime minister designate, Faustin Twagiramungu, and killed one of his bodyguards. The following day the Interahamwe sealed the capital with roadblocks at strategic junctions. They stormed the Foreign Ministry and for several hours held hostages. The militia rampaged through the Constitutional Court and stole documents.

On the night of Monday, 21 February, Félicien Gatabazi, a charismatic and popular politician, who was secretary-general of the Parti Social Démocrate (PSD), was at the Hotel Méridien to meet with pro-democracy government ministers. Gatabazi had been chosen as the minister of public works in the not yet created Broad-based Transitional Government. He had been credited with ensuring PSD unity in the southern city of Butare, at a time when the opposition was splitting between anti- and pro-RPF positions. At around 11.30 p.m. he drove his Mitsubishi out of the hotel car park for the short drive home. As he approached his house several rounds of shots were fired and a gendarme in the back of his car was instantly killed. Gatabazi and another gendarme, both of them in the front, were injured. They managed to leave the vehicle and ran towards the house. The minister collapsed on his doorstep. By the time officers from the UN's civilian police contingent, CIVPOL, had arrived, Gatabazi was dead.[11] His body was placed in a child's bedroom, and when two CIVPOL officers, part of a team of investigators from Belgium, arrived they saw a Rwandan army doctor in uniform already there. They were forbidden from examining the body, but they got a chance to look at Gatabazi's vehicle, which was 100 metres from the house. On the right-hand side there were a number of bullet holes. Several cases of cartridges were in the road. There were four cartridges in the car for R-4 rifles, which were used by both Rwandan gendarmes and the army. The next day they returned to take photographs of the crime scene. They met with Kigali's public prosecutor, François-Xavier Nsanzuwera, but in spite of his best efforts they were unable to obtain permission for an autopsy.[12]

The assassination effectively ended the installation of the Broad-based Transitional Government, scheduled for the following day. The next morning Kigali was a ghost town. The only people outdoors were groups armed with machetes at the principal road junctions, watched over by peacekeepers and gendarmes. Dallaire believed that Gatabazi had signed his own death warrant, for the day before his murder he had been at a diplomatic supper for a visiting dignitary, and in a heated discussion he had directly insulted individual members of the MRND, accusing them of manipulating the political process.[13] He had accused the Presidential Guard of training militia in the Kanombe barracks.

On the day following the assassination there were huge demonstrations by PSD supporters in Gatabazi's home town of Butare. That afternoon the national head of the CDR, Martin Bucyana, was captured by PSD militants and lynched. Afterwards there were huge rallies of PSD supporters celebrating the murder of Bucyana as revenge for Gatabazi. There were terrified members of the CDR hiding in gendarmerie bases, and these events effectively brought the previously peaceful southern town into the civil war.[14]

In Kigali, in a poverty-stricken and overpopulated area called Gikondo, where Bucyana had lived, jeering mobs trapped Tutsi families in their homes. The militia screamed and chanted about how they were going to kill all Tutsi in Gikondo. Forty people were killed that night. Eighteen children were orphaned. Some families were escorted by gendarmes and officers from CIVPOL to Gikondo church as they were too afraid to stay at home. After this, some 130 Tutsi left their homes in Gikondo and went to stay with a man who made foam mattresses.[15]

That day, the RPF political leadership was to have arrived in Kigali for the inauguration of the National Assembly. But there had been an ambush by Interahamwe and Presidential Guard, in civilian clothes, waiting for them. The RPF convoy, travelling from their northern base in Mulindi, had been given an escort of UN military observers and Belgian peacekeepers. Dallaire had ordered the convoy to stay overnight in Mulindi but his order was ignored. When the ambushed happened, the Belgian peacekeepers and the UN military observers had immediately run for cover and abandoned the RPF guards, who were saved by colleagues who broke out of their CND base and rode to their rescue. One RPF soldier died and two were wounded. Dallaire said that the shame this incident brought on UNAMIR forces was never expunged. 'This was a disgusting situation,' he said later. It lowered his assessment of the Belgian contingent even further. It was fortunate that the RPF leadership was not on board the convoy; Kagame had been suspicious and had forbidden them to travel. Kagame said that he realized how little help the UN peacekeepers would be in any emergency.[16] He secretly reinforced the battalion in Kigali with arms and ammunition that were smuggled from RPF headquarters in Mulindi during troop rotation. The

RPF's Radio Muhabura broadcast a warning that the war was going to restart and the RPF had an excellent chance of victory.[17] There were large concentrations of RPF troops being trained and evidence of defensive positions dug on the north-west border of the demilitarized zone. It seemed to Dallaire that Kagame was realigning his forces, pushing for a good secure start line from which he could launch an offensive.[18]

While the US State Department issued a travel advisory for Rwanda,[19] Dallaire cabled UN headquarters to tell them that time was running out: 'Information regarding weapons distribution, death squad target lists, planning and civil unrest and demonstrations abound ... any spark on the security side could have catastrophic consequences.'[20] At the height of the violence on 22 February, Dallaire had withdrawn foot patrols from the streets of Kigali. He did not want his soldiers 'going into those volatile and darkened streets with a forewarned threat of an attack on UNAMIR having been started and on the Belgians in particular'.[21] The terror campaign seemed to be targeted at RPF supporters, 'and possible – unconfirmed – members of their ethnic group'.

Every day there were murders and banditry. The gendarmerie and communal police were handicapped in terms of personnel, equipment and training. The attempts to persuade New York that more UN civilian police were needed were unsuccessful. 'Locals are begging protection for their families or guarantees from the UN ...' one coded cable pointed out.[22] There were sixty officers from six countries in the CIVPOL contingent from Austria, Bangladesh, Belgium, Mali, Senegal and Togo. Originally intended to operate nationwide, there were not nearly enough of them to cover the whole country. They were limited to working with the Gendarmerie Nationale and the local police in Kigali. The Rwandan gendarmes were exhausted.[23] 'Even on a "normal" day it is difficult to know the exact number of deaths in Kigali and/or the cause of death ... we are following this aspect with particular attention because of the potentially explosive impact that the resurgence of Hutu/Tutsi ethnic violence could have ...'[24] President Habyarimana, when asked about the violence and insecurity, blamed the RPF for all the crimes.[25]

The UN's CIVPOL investigators continued their enquiries into the murder of Félicien Gatabazi and eventually an arrest was made. The manager of a bar called Las Vegas, a leader of the local Interahamwe, was taken into custody. The arrest took place in the presence of CIVPOL officers and François-Xavier Nsanzuwera. Afterwards there was pressure on Nsanzuwera to release the suspect. The pressure came from Captain Pascal Simbikangwa and from a former Presidential Guard, Captain Gaspard, who operated from the president's office. Nsanzuwera requested and was given UN security. In his own investigation, Nsanzu-wera had discovered the location from where the shots had been fired at Gatabazi's vehicle and he had found witnesses to the shooting. It was alleged that the manager of the bar had accompanied the four assassins, and that three of them were Presidential Guard.[26]

The Belgian CIVPOL officers wrote a draft Special Report into the murder of Gatabazi in which they made clear that the highest authorities may have been involved.[27] While in most cases in Rwanda a detailed investigation was impossible – owing partly to an inability to understand the language, Kinyarwanda – this time they wanted to question leading politicians and senior army officers, including members of the Presidential Guard.[28] They were determined to continue their enquiries, but their report was never more than a draft and no final version was ever issued by the head of CIVPOL, an Austrian police commissioner, Colonel Manfred Bliem. There was interference in the investigation from senior military officers and from officials in the Ministry of Justice. At one point the minister of defence, Augustin Bizimana, had advised CIVPOL that they needed a 'new orientation' regarding the assassination.[29]

The violence at the end of February 1994 had coincided with a visit to Kigali of the Belgian foreign minister, Willy Claes. Claes was shocked at what he found; the regime did not even bother trying to disguise the stockpiling of weapons, and arms were openly distributed to civilians. A Belgian photographer, Jacques Collet, who was travelling with the foreign minister, went to the city morgue and took photographs of some 120 bodies of people he found there, all of them murdered by the Interahamwe with machetes. The pictures were so horrific they were given limited circulation.[30]

Claes talked with the secretary-general's Special Representative, Jacques-Roger Booh-Booh, and there were doubts expressed on all sides about whether or not the Arusha Accords could be implemented. Booh-Booh emphasized to Claes the limitations of the mandate.[31] Dallaire told Claes that a lack of resources was causing him serious concern and Marchal, who had already tried persuasion with military authorities in Brussels, stressed to Claes that the peacekeepers might well have to defend themselves. In this event they would need munitions not usually supplied to peacekeepers. The Belgian contingent was spread out in fourteen different locations in Kigali.

Afterwards, in testimony to a Belgian senate inquiry, Claes claimed that he wrote a warning to the UN secretary-general, Boutros Boutros-Ghali, on 11 February, to tell him that unless the peacekeepers took firmer action UNAMIR might soon find itself unable to continue at all.[32] Before Claes had returned home, a telex was sent from the Belgian Ministry of Foreign Affairs to the Belgian permanent representative at the UN in New York to tell him that UNAMIR was in serious trouble. The peacekeepers were not capable of keeping public order. 'It would be unacceptable if Belgian troops were to find themselves as passive witnesses to a genocide about which the UN would do nothing.' This crucial telex, dated 25 February, continued, 'If the conditions deteriorate further, the UN and the Belgians can hardly, in reality, withdraw. UNAMIR must play a more active role ... and reinforce the credibility of the international community.'[33]

Claes claims that he told Boutros-Ghali that Dallaire was achieving nothing practical because he continually had to await instructions from New York. Dallaire needed a stronger mandate. Claes warned the USA that Habyarimana could be playing a double game and that it was in everyone's interests to avert a resumption of the civil war. The USA was already well informed. The US embassy's deputy chief of mission, Joyce Leader, was trusted and respected by Rwandan human rights activists, and well briefed about the extremists.[34]

Belgium's UN ambassador, Paul Noterdaeme, immediately sought a meeting with Boutros-Ghali, who told him that in the Council the USA and the UK were opposed to any help for UNAMIR purely for reasons of finance. UNAMIR was intended as a low-budget mission. Noterdaeme met with British and US diplomats and he found them unenthusiastic about UNAMIR.[35] He was told that at a forthcoming Council meeting, the USA was going to argue that unless the peace agreement was back on track in the next few weeks, then UNAMIR should withdraw completely. There was already a warning to this effect. In a speech given by Booh-Booh in Kigali, he had said that unless there was progress there was every possibility that the UN would pull out.

Later on, Dallaire was critical of Booh-Booh, claiming that he lacked a strategy. Booh-Booh had been considered pro-Habyarimana from the outset and his assessments to headquarters were generally much more optimistic than those of Dallaire.[36] He had boasted that those on the 'government side' were friends of his, and he told Dallaire that only a direct appeal from the secretary-general had brought him out of retirement, and he would have been happier running his banana plantation at home.[37] Booh-Booh claimed that Dallaire refused to stick to his military brief and interfered in politics.[38] Dallaire accused Booh-Booh of sharing his thoughts only with his close political advisers – all of them francophone Africans.[39] There was concern at UN headquarters about

Booh-Booh because he was a personal friend of Boutros Boutros-Ghali. Some senior officials thought his appointment 'unfortunate'.[40]

In March, while on leave, Lieutenant General Dallaire spent a few days at the UN Secretariat in New York and found that any interest there may have been in his mission was overshadowed by crises in former Yugoslavia, Mozambique, Haiti and Somalia. He met with Kofi Annan, under-secretary-general and head of the Department of Peacekeeping Operations, Iqbal Riza, assistant secretary-general, and the military adviser, Major General Maurice Baril. These officials had received all his cables and reports. He thought them decent men. They had supported him as best they could. He told them he urgently needed forty-eight more military observers to stem the flow of men and weapons across all borders which fed a not-too-surreptitious military build-up.[41] Riza said there would be no reinforcements. The USA was arguing that given the delays in the peace process the Rwanda mission should close. The French and the Belgians, however, were arguing that the mission's mandate should be renewed for a customary six months. A compromise was needed. Riza told Dallaire that one proposal was for a sixty-day extension. There was more bad news. France had written to the Canadian government to request Dallaire's removal as force commander. Dallaire speculated that this may have been because of references in some of his cables to the presence of French officers among the Presidential Guard.[42]

In spite of the increasing violence, and the recent publication of a report by Human Rights Watch giving details of the regime's continuing arms purchases, the press was paying little attention.[43] Le Monde carried a small story about the Egyptian arms deals, and in London the Guardian, in a short story on 23 February, reported the failure to implement the peace deal and a warning of 'a new wave of tribal killings'.[44] Dallaire and Marchal had held press conferences in Kigali to try to explain the role of the UN, but the local press was hostile and the international press, at a time when exposing what was going on could have made a decisive difference, was not interested at all.

The problems of Rwanda were hardly a secret. In Kigali an emergency plan, devised by the International Committee of the Red Cross (ICRC), and MSF-France, together with other organizations, saw four huge tents installed in the courtyard of the Centre Hospitalier de Kigali (CHK), a pavilion-style 200-bed hospital. They began to stockpile medicine and water and held discussions to decide which agency, in the event of large numbers of casualties, would collect the wounded from the streets, and who would provide emergency medical care. The chief delegate of the ICRC was a Swiss national, Philippe Gaillard, and in January he met Richard Dowden, the African editor of the British newspaper the *Independent*. Gaillard told Dowden that genocide was being planned. The militia was being armed by the government and plans were being laid to promote mass killing of Tutsi throughout the country. Dowden wrote later that everyone else he met had 'talked up' the Arusha process and only Gaillard had warned him of the likelihood of genocide. Dowden said he did not see anything 'sinister' on the streets of Kigali. He stayed for two days and then left. 'To write a sensational story about impending genocide would have been dishonest and irresponsible,' he wrote later.[45]

The head of MSF-France in Rwanda, Eric Bertin, an expert logistician, described the emergency planning in a fax to the headquarters of MSF-France in Paris. He explained that local clinics had been assessed for their capacity to treat wounded people. The ICRC had a surgical team in reserve for Kigali. The security situation worried Bertin. He wrote to Paris: 'It is beginning to be fearful ... we must respect our rules of security.'[46] During the fierce violence at the end of February, all aid workers had stayed at home, and it had not been possible to go south to the refugee camps. Bertin was helping to provide sanitation, water and medical help to the refugee camps in the Bugesera for people who had fled from Burundi and who were living in misery and squalor. In these camps children and old people were dying from starvation. In despair, some of the refugees had returned to Burundi and were murdered after crossing the frontier.

Dallaire suggested the redeployment of 250 peacekeepers from the demilitarized zone in the north to Kigali. This would free Belgian troops from static guard duty so that they could provide a mobile force for foot patrols, checkpoints, escort duties and reserve tasks. Dallaire wrote to headquarters: 'A faction seems to believe that with 1,000 UN troops in the demilitarised zone, UNAMIR can and will block the RPF, thus possibly leaving them free to continue the present delay in the formation of the broad-based government.' This cable revealed: 'We have lost the initiative and are rapidly losing any capability to respond to emergency situations. UNAMIR is losing credibility ... with the population ...'[47]

§ There were worrying reports from the UN military observers in the north. The Rwandan government soldiers had not been paid for weeks and in some areas there was looting. There was a sense of insecurity, and fears about the planned demobilization. In accordance with the Arusha Accords the Rwandan government army and the RPF were to merge. This requirement was a crucial part of the peace agreement. It was intended to unite the country. The merger of the two armies – and the disbandment of the Presidential Guard – had been one of the most difficult issues and had almost collapsed the Arusha negotiations. The government had wanted the RPF to share army command positions commensurate with the percentage of Tutsi in Rwanda. In the end, owing to the negotiating skill of the RPF and the weakness of the government negotiators, the Arusha Accords provided for joint command, down to field commanders' level.[48] The was considered a victory for the RPF, and so favourable that some experts thought it would never work. The US under-secretary of state for African affairs until 1993, Herman Cohen, was shocked when he heard what had been agreed, and he blamed 'the international community's obsession with getting a peace agreement'. There had been a lack of analysis and a failure to consider whether or not the accords could ever be implemented. Cohen thought the idea of stationing RPF soldiers in Kigali was folly and was bound to cause hysterical reactions among Hutu. But Kagame had argued that without protection the RPF political leaders in Kigali would be at risk. Kagame pointed out they were dealing with a regime that routinely killed its own people.[49] Some diplomats who took part in the Arusha negotiations warned that so advantageous was the military deal to the RPF that the hardliners would never accept it.[50]

In order to comply with Arusha the peacekeepers were to assist with military disengagement and the demobilization of some forty thousand soldiers. These plans advanced and meetings were held between officers from the Rwandan army and the RPF. Both sides seemed willing to make it work. There were discussions about assembly points and training centres and where to store surrendered weapons. The only practical arrangement was a contract for shipments of food for the demobilized soldiers. The food was starting to arrive in Dar es Salaam.[51] But no advice about demobilization was offered by UN headquarters, in spite of the considerable expertise which existed after the UN had success-fully carried out operations in Central America and Cambodia, and no financial provision was forthcoming in order to pay pensions, for retraining and employment.

As the peace agreement foundered Dallaire reported low-level intel-ligence about RPF preparations to resume the war. The monitoring of the Uganda–Rwanda border was hampered by a lack of equipment, especially helicopters. The military observers stationed with the RPF were at all times accompanied by RPF personnel.[52] Dallaire moved more UN military observers into the RPF sector. Some years later Dallaire claimed to have received information that the RPF was receiving shipments of weapons and ammunition from Uganda's National Resistance Army.[53]

The information collected by Dallaire's small intelligence unit in Kigali was increasingly alarming. A report was sent to him to reveal a 'death squadron' planning to murder opposition politicians. The head of the squadron was Protais Zigiranyirazo and the second-in-command Colonel Elie Sagatwa. There was information also available to Colonel Luc Marchal. On 10 February, he was told by Rwandan army officers that the Arusha Accords would never work. Later that same day, at a meeting with Interahamwe leaders in Kigali, Marchal heard that large numbers of Tutsi were going to be killed. There was intelligence provided about clandestine meetings, one of which took place on 25 February, when Robert Kajuga, head of the Interahamwe, had met local militia leaders, at which a system of communication was devised allowing the Interahamwe to keep in touch through telephones, whistles and runners. At another meeting, on 27 February, in the offices of the MRND, the compilation of lists of Tutsi was discussed.[54] Diplomats from African countries heard boasts that soon there would soon be no Tutsi left in Rwanda. Announcers on RTLM warned that RPF soldiers, stationed in Kigali, were planning to kill all the Hutu. The newspaper *Kangura* claimed that the UN peacekeepers were in Rwanda to help the RPF take power by force, and that the RPF was planning to kill the president. It was reported that 'something big' was about to happen.

A confidential warning was given to the governor of the Bank of Rwanda, Jean Birara, who was a relative of the army chief, Déogratias Nsabimana, and who had advised Birara to leave the country. Nsabimana said that three times there had been an attempt to provoke the 'final solution' and the next time he would be unable to stop it. There had been a plan to kill the president on 23 March, but it was cancelled.[55]

A prosecution witness, XXQ, claimed later that it seemed to him that the conspirators could not agree a start date; he had attended a meeting of junior officers and had been told that the civil war would resume on 23 February, and that the 'Tutsi and Hutu on the same side' would be eliminated.[56]

Some Tutsi who lived in Kigali planned an emergency evacuation. Others left the country. Some people began to sleep in churches for fear of being killed. One of the military observers, a Polish intelligence officer, Major Stefan Stec, said that everyone knew what was threatened. 'Genocide hung in the air,' he recalled.[57] Some Rwandan army officers were boasting that if Arusha went ahead they were prepared 'to liquidate the Tutsi'.[58]

The one issue now widely perceived as preventing the implementation of the peace agreement was the continuing refusal of the RPF to allow the extremist CDR to take part in the transitional institutions.[59] In an attempt to break the deadlock, Kigali's diplomatic community issued a joint communiqué which urged that the CDR be given a place in the forthcoming Broad-based Transitional Government. The communiqué included a guarantee that a commission of national unity and reconciliation would be created to ensure that every political party respected the principles of political ethics, the violation of which would lead to exclusion. If the CDR were to be accepted, there would be no further excuse for delay.[60] The initiative was led by the dean of the Diplomatic Corps, Monsignor Giuseppe Bertello, the papal nuncio. It was signed by the secretary-general's Special Representative, Jacques-Roger Booh-Booh, who had recently allowed the CDR to take part in discussions about the Broad-based Transitional Government. He had approved a list of deputies for the National Assembly, a list that included members of the CDR. The RPF issued a four-page letter in response. It was addressed to the UN secretary-general. It described the CDR as a fascist formation which should be outlawed. The letter raised the issue of human rights in Rwanda and quoted the International Federation of Human Rights Report of 1993 that had used the word 'genocide' to describe the killing of Tutsi. The letter included an official complaint against Booh-Booh for having insisted on the inclusion of the CDR, and so having breached a provision in the Arusha Accords which had excluded this extremist party.[61]

§ It was the Easter weekend. The Special Representative, Jacques-Roger Booh-Booh, was with Juvénal Habyarimana at the president's Lake Kivu house in Gisenyi. Booh-Booh claimed later that he had warned Habyarimana that his life was in danger. The president said he had already heard these rumours.[62]

On Sunday, 3 April, a news item was broadcast on RTLM warning that a 'little something' was about to happen in Kigali city, but that this would be camouflage for the final attack, or '*simusiga*'. Some years later an international courtroom heard the following RTLM recording: 'On 3rd, and 4th and 5th there will be a little something here in Kigali. And also on the 6th, 7th and 8th you will hear the sound of bullets and grenades.' It was the voice of Noel Hitimana.

On Monday, Prime Minister Agathe Uwilingiyimana held a reception for local administrators and army officers, including the head of the gendarmerie, Major General Augustin Ndindiliyimana, a southerner from her own commune, Nyaruhengeri. The following day, Tuesday, there was a news broadcast on RTLM stating that she had used the meeting to try to end the power of the northerners in the army. She was preparing a *coup d'état* and she was going to get rid of the president.

For several weeks Uwilingiyimana, a Hutu, had been increasingly critical of President Habyarimana. She had blamed the president for the continual delays in the peace process and for having engineered the divisions now destroying the opposition parties. She had questioned why weapons were being issued to civilians.[63] She also gave a frank interview to a Belgian journalist, François Ryckmans, a specialist on Central Africa who worked for Radio Télévision de la Communauté Française de Belgique (RTBF). She told Ryckmans how worried she was about a threatened UN withdrawal; she could not believe the Security Council would even think of abandoning Rwanda. Uwilingiyimana told Ryckmans that almost every day people were killed, whether poor peasants or political leaders. Famine was raging and people were dying of diseases, dysentery and malaria. 'You see ... we do not have institutions capable of negotiating with our donors in order to solve these problems.'

She continued:

When you have a dictatorial regime ... for twenty years how do you expect the officials of this dictatorship to give up power without any pressure? The international community really helped us to persuade the president that the war could end through negotiations ... in all his speeches he said he would fight the war to the end ... but the international community helped us change this. Why doesn't the international community go the last step? We have put pressure on ... but we think you must go slowly otherwise you will endanger lives. If we are abandoned the Rwandan people will be left to their fate ... What will happen? ... This is not the moment for pulling out. One last time we must make an effort ... to take the last step.

It was a last desperate appeal for her country. She was thirty-eight years old, a former chemistry teacher, and the first women to belong to the Mouvement Démocratique Républicain (MDR). The party was created in 1991 as the successor to Grégoire Kayibanda's MRD-Parmehutu party. She was the prime minister of a government that in accordance with the peace agreement was planned to last thirty-seven days. She said that President Habyarimana had thought she would be easy to manipulate but added: 'Someone has to speak for poor people, as they are the ones who are suffering.'[64] She believed that the people of Rwanda wanted peace. But their political leaders were showing a lack of goodwill, even irresponsibility, with ethnic differences being manipulated to sow confusion and division.

'Who will benefit from these divisions?' she asked. 'The president ... he has all the territorial power ... with all the *bourgmestres*, all the prefects, the *sous-préfets* and the MRND, and in three months, under the Arusha Accords, all this [power] was to have been wiped away.'

The Rwandan people were not ready to give themselves over to extremism: 'Extremists will always be wrong, whatever their ethnic origins,' she said. She spoke of how impossible it was to convene her cabinet. The hardline MRND ministers would not respond to her calls and refused to attend the meetings she scheduled.[65] She was ridiculed on RTLM, and accused of collaboration with the RPF. One broadcast called for her assassination.[66] She was guarded by UN peacekeepers. Uwilingiyimana knew her life was in danger but she remained principled and determined.

By April 1994 there were increasing concerns about security, and Dallaire wanted better defences at the airport. Each week UNAMIR was carrying out ninety foot patrols, 220 mobile patrols and twenty patrols by air, and providing twenty-five security escorts. At this stage Dallaire had 2,539 soldiers from twenty-four countries.

On Wednesday, 6 April, early in the morning, a Belgian peacekeeper saw Rwandans and a few Europeans living near Kanombe leaving for the airport, whole families carrying heavy bags. Someone else saw the Rwandan army setting up machine-gun posts at the military camp at Kanombe. In the afternoon there was reportedly heavy-weapons fire around the airport and roadblocks were erected in the Kimihurura area.[67] At around 3 p.m., guns were distributed from the back of a van in Nyarugenge commune, central Kigali.[68] Someone saw the Presidential Guard building roadblocks. Near the Hôtel Méridien, military families were being evacuated.[69] At about 4.30 p.m., according to Belgian peace-keepers, shopkeepers and traders in Kigali were told by the Presidential Guard to close their doors.[70]

Colonel Luc Marchal attended the weekly meeting of the chief of staff of the gendarmerie.[71] Most important now was a plan to seize weapons which had finally been approved by UN headquarters, using the Rwandan gendarmerie with assistance from UNAMIR. A first attempt to seize weapons had been a failure and none was found. The gendarmes were inept and news of the raid was leaked; the gendarmes would have to be better trained and more use would have to be made of CIVPOL officers. At this meeting, Colonel Augustin Ndindiliyimana had sug-gested that another search take place. A coordination meeting was held at which the final plans were made for an operation with peacekeepers, CIVPOL officers and gendarmes to be provided with UN vehicles. They were to seal and search a specific area within Kigali and seize all weapons found there.[72] It was decided, on Ndindiliyimana's insistence, that the vast majority of gendarmes in the city would be confined to barracks on Wednesday night, 6 April, in order to make ready for the weapons seizure the following day, the operation to begin with a 4 a.m. assembly on Thursday at Camp Kacyiru.[73]

In Belgian military intelligence (SGR) headquarters in Evere, Brussels, an official whose job it was to analyse intelligence had begun to issue warnings that if the Arusha Accords collapsed there were going to be thousands of victims. In testimony later on he said that no one, not even with all the information now available, would ever have imagined the scale of what was to come.[74]

11 | THE UN SECURITY COUNCIL: 5 APRIL 1994

§ On Tuesday, 5 April, the Security Council met to discuss what to do about its mission in Rwanda, established under Resolution 872 on 5 October 1993. Peacekeeping operations are given six-month operating periods, and after this expires the Security Council has to decide the conditions for extending or even ending the mandate.

There are fifteen members of the Security Council. Five of them – Britain, the USA, France, China and the Russian Federation – are permanent, and they wield a veto on all substantive decisions. Ten come from countries that are elected by the General Assembly to sit on the Council for two years. In April 1994 they were the Czech Republic, Djibouti, New Zealand, Nigeria, Oman, Pakistan, Spain, Argentina, Brazil – and Rwanda, recently voted a seat. This meant that the Rwandan government was well informed, with access as privileged insiders, as their UN ambassador, Jean-Damascène Bizimana, sat in the Council.[1]

The Council had received a report from the secretary-general, Boutros Boutros-Ghali, in which he gave an account of the delays in Rwanda's transition. The report described how most violent incidents in Rwanda could be attributed to armed banditry. His report was optimistic in tone and claimed that through their respect for the ceasefire the parties had demonstrated that they remained committed to the peace process. The peacekeepers continued to play a stabilizing role. He was encouraged that, in spite of tensions, the parties had maintained the process of dialogue. There was a brief mention of ethnic crimes, but the report did not include critical new intelligence from the informer Jean-Pierre. The Council members were not told about the 11 January cable, and were ignorant about the registration of Tutsi which the informer alleged was part of a plan for their extermination. When the UN's own official history of UNAMIR came to be written it included a claim that the Council was shown the cable.[2] There is, however, no record of a briefing on Rwanda to the Council at the time the cable was received.[3] The ambassadors deny they were shown the cable. Boutros-Ghali maintained that he had been away from New York in January and not in close touch with the Rwandan situation, and that he did not learn about the informer's claims until three years later.[4]

Boutros-Ghali's report to the Council also omitted details of a ten-page military assessment prepared by Dallaire which highlighted his serious deficiencies in capability and equipment; only later did Dallaire realize that the details of his assessment given to the Council had been watered down somewhere in the process of drafting the report. Later on, an insider claimed that Boutros-Ghali had no real interest in the views of his force commander.[5] With a coercive response ruled out, one strategy, already suggested by the USA, was to threaten that unless the peace agreement was implemented, the peacekeepers should withdraw. This could lead to a renewed civil war.

The presidency of the Security Council changes monthly, by alphabetical rotation. In April 1994 it was the turn of New Zealand, whose ambassador, Colin Keating, described a crowded Council agenda with desperate crises in Bosnia and Somalia. A list of agenda items extended from Iraq to North Korea and Haiti. There was little time for Rwanda.[6] During the Easter weekend, on Saturday, 2 April, Keating was telephoned at home to be told that Bosnian Serb troops were continuing to attack Gorazde, one of six designated UN safe havens. The UN commanders had requested NATO close air support. This issue alone would have dominated Council discussions. Only forty-eight hours earlier the mandate for the United Nations Protection Force in former Yugoslavia (UNPROFOR) had been extended for six months and the Council was increasing the numbers of peacekeepers there by an additional 3,500 troops.

Rwanda seemed quiet in comparison. But Keating was unhappy about the US idea to impose a time limit on UNAMIR. There was no evidence that this tactic worked; on the contrary, there were situations where it would be in the protagonists' interests to secure UN withdrawal. Such tactics risked playing into the hands of one of the parties and destabilizing the situation. If cuts were to be made to UN peacekeeping they should not be made in one of the African missions.

Keating said later that the Council had not been adequately briefed about Rwanda, and he complained about the quality of the reports submitted to the Council. 'We were kept in the dark,' he said. 'The situation was much more dangerous than was ever presented to the Council.'[7] Unlike the permanent five members of the Council with their extensive intelligence-gathering capabilities, the non-permanent members of the Council were largely reliant on UN reports. The ethnic complexity of the situation in Rwanda had been significantly underestimated. Nothing was forthcoming about human rights abuses in Rwanda. No mention was made of the 1993 UN Commission on Human Rights report which had revealed that the 1948 Convention on the Prevention and Punishment of the Crime of Genocide was applicable to Rwanda, and which blamed the Rwandan government for systematic human rights abuses.[8] The author of this report, Special Rapporteur on Extrajudicial, Summary or Arbitrary Executions Bacre Waly Ndiaye, said later that if he had been consulted by the Council he would have said that their mission for Rwanda was too weak to make any difference. President Habyarimana had no intention of sharing power. Ndiaye's recommendation would have been to take immediate and effective measures to protect civilians against massacres which, he said, had been described by the authorities in Kigali as 'spontaneous acts of anger' and 'self-protection'. The non-permanent Council members should have been exposed to the realities. 'With better information', said Keating later, 'the council might have proceeded quite differently.'

It is customary for the management of peacekeeping operations to be handled by officials in the Secretariat, in the same way governments delegate responsibility to their public service. The officials in the Secretariat were certainly of the view that it was their prerogative to manage UN missions. Keating found that any request for information by a member state was resented by these officials; they seemed to be of the opinion that states should not be allowed to micro-manage.[9] There was no mechanism at UN headquarters to quickly provide information to members of the Council.

When Boutros Boutros-Ghali became UN secretary-general, he had tired of the informal consultations held by the Council. Still determined to control the flow of information to the Council from the Secretariat, he had appointed a former Indian diplomat, Chinmaya Gharekhan, as his personal representative to speak on his behalf at Council meetings.[10] This appointment was a significant break with established procedure, for in the past the secretaries-general had regularly attended the Council informal consultations, where all the important decisions are made. Gharekhan wrote later that he believed that the great powers on the Council must have had a much better idea than the secretary-general about Rwanda.[11] It was the member states on the Council which had prime responsibility for peace and security.

Some ambassadors in the Council were slighted by Boutros-Ghali's failure to attend the informal meetings. He in turn became frustrated in his hopes for a cooperative and fruitful relationship with the Council.[12] In his memoirs Boutros-Ghali admits he did make some ill-judged remarks, for example when he characterized the conflict in Bosnia as a 'rich man's war' and contrasted reaction to this conflict with an alleged indifference to the collapse of Somalia. There was tension over Boutros-Ghali's determination to manage UN operations without any transparency or accountability to the Council. Somalia had shown how easy it was to lose control of a UN operation, and this had effectively eroded the Council's legitimacy and credibility.[13] The Council's own Commission of Inquiry into the Somali mission was kept under wraps. It had included adverse comments about the quality of UN staff reports and a failure of leadership and little coordination at UN headquarters.[14]

Keating believed that a lack of oversight was a classic recipe for disaster. The political accountability was with national governments on the Council and these governments had a right to know the details of peacekeeping. The governments had a particular duty to decide the issues when human life was at stake. 'We only dimly perceived the steady deterioration in the Rwandan ... situation,' Keating wrote afterwards. 'The deeper and more dangerous problem of a monumental threat to human life was ignored.'[15]

§ By 5 April 1994, when a decision had to be made about the mission in Rwanda, the USA was arguing that the mission should be closed completely. Somalia had robbed the USA of any enthusiasm for peace-keeping. President Bill Clinton, having come to office in January 1993 proclaiming a renewed commitment to the UN, was now committed to completely reversing his previous policy. In his first few months in office Clinton had been in favour of ambitious new UN operations. But now there was a determination to demonstrate a tough policy to an increasingly anti-UN Congress.[16] In the US Department of Defense there was a determination to avoid any more 'tribal wars' in Africa. The USA should be wary of being drawn into humanitarian efforts on the continent. The US ambassador to the UN, Madeleine Albright, previously full of enthusiasm for the UN, was now describing the Secretariat as 'programmed amateurism, and a near-total absence of contingency planning'.[17] In her memoir, however, she would admit that the USA had not provided the means to achieve the goals they had set.[18]

There was also a certain irritation within the Council towards Rwanda. The Council had not been involved in the peace process and it was felt that the Arusha Accords had boxed in the Council with a predetermined role for UN peacekeepers. France, always enthusiastic about the mission, now argued that the mandate of UNAMIR should be extended. France stressed the hopeful sign of a continuing ceasefire.

The Nigerian ambassador, Ibrahim Gambari, was also in favour of retaining the mission. Rwanda should be given a reasonable time to achieve democracy and certainly receive the resources and attention given by the UN elsewhere, particularly in the former Yugoslavia, where there were more UN peacekeepers stationed than in any other region in the world – an authorized deployment of 38,000 personnel, whose mandate included enforcement powers to protect safe areas.[19]

The UK's position was not to reinforce UNAMIR and to argue that the Arusha Accords should be complied with. Foreign Office policy towards Africa was mostly focused on anglophone and Commonwealth countries while Rwanda – considered to be in the francophone sphere – was outside Britain's area of influence.[20] Uganda, in the anglophone sphere, gave shelter to Rwandan refugees. Rwanda was important because it had the potential to spark diplomatic problems with France, and the British government was keen to limit any damage resulting from quarrels with the French about Ugandan support for the RPF.[21]

The British ambassador to the UN was David Hannay, who was regarded by younger diplomats in the Foreign and Commonwealth Office as the 'King of the Security Council'.[22] Hannay had a stellar reputation as one of the leading diplomats of his generation. In his memoir some years later he agreed that most Council members had not been at all well informed about Rwanda. The British had been particularly handicapped by a lack of information. 'We had no embassy there ... the British government had no idea of what was going on in Rwanda,' he said. 'The force was in place,' he wrote of UNAMIR, 'but with little to do.' For Hannay, Rwanda was an 'orphan of the international community'.[23] The UK was heavily involved in Bosnia, where British troops were serving with the UN and where there was a British commander, Sir Michael Rose. Hannay said he could not recall any Foreign Office reports on Rwanda at all.

Only later would it emerge that first-hand accounts were available to the British, in cables written to the Foreign and Commonwealth Office by the British high commissioner in Uganda, Edward Clay. Clay had visited Rwanda in March 1994. He had described Kigali as 'infested with armed and uniformed men'. He wrote: 'Over the period of our visit, individual killings, allegedly mostly of Tutsi, numbered between thirty and fifty dead.' The country was in the grip of a profound political crisis and administration almost impossible. The government was begging for funds to pay salaries. Clay described the 'wretched conditions' of the refugee camps where hundreds of thousands of people were living. He thought it would be useful to find out from Belgium how to get UK nationals out of Rwanda should the need arise.[24] The US government was also planning total withdrawal of all US nationals. The US Defense Attaché Office in Yaoundé, Cameroon, had already sent Lieutenant Colonel Chuck Vuckovic to Kigali to ensure that all 257 US nationals would be rescued if necessary.

At 7.10 p.m. on Tuesday, 5 April, the ambassadors filed from the room at the back of the Security Council chamber where their secret deliberations are held. In a formal and open meeting they unanimously agreed Security Council Resolution 909, which gave an unusually short four-month extension to the UNAMIR mandate, which was subject to review in six weeks' time. Unless the transitional institutions provided for under the Arusha Accords were established by then, UNAMIR would pull out completely.[25] The resolution also stipulated that economies be sought in the cost of the force. Moments before the vote was taken, Rwanda's UN ambassador, Jean-Damascène Bizimana, told the Council that, like the secretary-general, he was optimistic about peace. He praised the observance of a ceasefire by the parties, who were 'demonstrating their unwavering commitment to the peace process'.

There were diplomatic efforts elsewhere. A regional one-day summit meeting was held, attended by President Habyarimana and other regional heads of government, invited to Dar es Salaam by the president of Tanzania, Ali Hassan Mwinyi, the facilitator during the Arusha negotiations who was now concerned that the Arusha Accords were collapsing.[26] The summit was originally planned for 29 March, and its focus was to have been the ongoing crisis in neighbouring Burundi.

The meeting, held on Wednesday, 6 April, the day following the Council meeting, took place in a suite at the Kilimanjaro Hotel with President Mwinyi in the chair. Also present were President Yoweri Museveni from Uganda, and the vice-president of Kenya, George Saitoti. President Arap Moi had turned down the invitation at the last moment, but President Cyprien Ntaryamira of Burundi and Salim Ahmed Salim, the OAU secretary-general, were there.[27] The UN Special Representative, Jacques-Roger Booh-Booh, had been invited but chose not to go. The meeting reportedly turned into a humiliating experience for Habyarimana, for he was told that the delay in implementing the peace agreement was threatening the entire region. A renewed civil war would mean international isolation and empty bank accounts. Habyarimana was apparently shaken and agreed that power-sharing with the RPF was inevitable. He would no longer insist on the CDR taking part in government.

The president was to return home to Kigali late that afternoon. He had organized a meeting with the leaders of the political opposition, to take place on his return. He had given instructions that arrangements go ahead for the swearing-in ceremony on Friday of the Broad-based Transitional Government.

12 | FOUR DAYS IN KIGALI: 6–9 APRIL 1994

§ President Juvénal Habyarimana rarely travelled anywhere at night; it was a rule imposed by security. He was kept waiting in Dar es Salaam, however, as the regional summit had been delayed, and afterwards he had insisted on flying home, although he did cancel the meeting with politicians arranged for his arrival. His jet, a Mystère Falcon 50, was a gift from President François Mitterrand. It was four years old and spotless. Its maintenance was paid for by France, as were the three crew members, who were former French military officers, a pilot, a chief mechanic and a navigator. Apparently, President Cyprien Ntaryamira of Burundi asked Habyarimana for a lift home. Ntaryamira was tired and his own propeller-driven plane was slower and less comfortable. Ntaryamira's wife was in Kigali. His Air Burundi Fokker 28 could fly on later. Some people speculated that Habyarimana, not unaware that his life was in danger, wanted Ntaryamira on his plane for extra protection.

The aircraft was full. On board were Habyarimana's closest advisers: Juvénal Renzaho, a former ambassador to Rome and now the president's political counsellor; his private doctor, Dr Emmanuel Akingeneye; his private secretary, Colonel Elie Sagatwa, in charge of Habyarimana's personal security; the army chief of staff, Major General Déogratias Nsabimana; and Major Thaddée Bagaragaza, the commander of the Presidential Guard. Also on the plane were two Burundi government ministers, Bernard Ciza and Cyiaque Simbizi. Left behind in Dar es Salaam was Rwanda's foreign minister, Anastase Gasana, because, said Habyarimana, he did not want an opposition minister on his aeroplane.[1]

In Kigali, in the control tower of the Grégoire Kayibanda International Airport, a Rwandan air traffic controller had just begun the night shift. A colleague told him that the presidential jet, call sign 9XR-NN, was due. He noticed Presidential Guard in and near the tower. He said he had spoken with the Mystère Falcon pilot about his estimated time of arrival and, as a matter of procedure, he had alerted the emergency services. He telephoned the airport director, Cyprien Sindano. The pilot radioed that once he had landed he would be taking off again for Burundi. The traffic controller said he notified Bujumbura airport.

The Mystère Falcon was nearing the airport. 'At exactly 8.26 I could see the red lights of the plane as it approached,' the air traffic controller recalled. He continued: 'As it passed over Masaka Hill I saw three missiles, the first went over the aircraft and the third under but the second hit the aircraft and it burst into flames.' He radioed the pilot. There was no response. He immediately telephoned the airport duty manager and alerted the fire brigade. He thought the Mystère Falcon had crashed on to the runway. He said that almost immediately a Presidential Guard put a gun to his head, telling him he was going to kill him. The Presidential Guard was dissuaded by the Director of Civil Aviation, Stany Simbizi,[2] who had arrived in the tower, and said that the air traffic controller would be needed for interrogation.[3] There was a commotion. A Belgian C-130 plane was due to land and was beginning its approach. The Presidential Guard ordered the air traffic controller to talk to the pilot and to tell him that if he attempted a landing the plane would be shot at. The C-130 circled several times and then disappeared into the night sky. The Presidential Guard then left, taking the control tower log book and the controller's personal documents.[4]

There were three Belgian officers and one NCO stationed at the airport. They testified that within minutes of the crash there was the sound of heavy-weapons fire.[5] At the northern gate, Belgian peacekeepers, on their way to meet the Belgian C-130 transport plane, carrying supplies from Nairobi, were prevented from entering the airport by Presidential Guard, who took the keys to their vehicles. They became hostages. A Belgian captain whose group patrolled the interior of the airport spoke with an air traffic controller and relayed the news by radio to his commanding officer that the presidential jet had crashed. He was told the pilot had issued a distress signal.[6]

The perimeter of the airport was sealed by an impenetrable cordon of troops from the nearby Kanombe barracks. In Kimihurura, a residential area, there were roadblocks manned by Presidential Guard, established earlier.[7] The news that the president was due home had been broadcast on RTLM but the radio was now playing classical music. In Kigali, a rural capital spread over many hills, a maze of tree-lined roads connects at strategic roundabouts – and some roadblocks were now in place.

'I ran as fast as I could,' said a survivor. 'Even before the president died, the consciousness of the Hutus in our area had already been awakened ... they had been given a very clear idea. Hutus on our hill were always being called to secret meetings with the *bourgmestre*, councillors and other officials.'[8]

There was sporadic gunfire and explosions. In Kicukiro a critic of the government saw a checkpoint erected near his home: 'The checkpoint had been reinforced by people armed to the teeth ... cars were passing by full of people with machetes. Some even had guns ... my telephone was cut shortly after midnight ... It was clear massacres were about to begin.'

The Ghanaian deputy commander of UNAMIR, Brigadier Henry Kwami Anyidoho, made his way to headquarters at the Amahoro stadium, a short distance from the Hôtel Méridien. He took a circuitous route because of roadblocks. There was firing all over the city, and particularly coming from the Kimihurura district, where many politicians had their homes.

'Things happened very rapidly, as if they had been rehearsed,' he wrote later.[9] At Kigali's five-star hotel, the Hôtel des Mille Collines, owned by Sabena Belgian World Airways, the night staff discovered that roadblocks prevented them from going home. They stayed put.[10]

Lieutenant General Dallaire was at home when a military observer told him there had been an explosion at the airport. Soon afterwards he was told the president's plane had crashed. He called Colonel Luc Marchal to send a patrol to the crash site. A group of Belgian soldiers set out but were stopped at a roadblock. It was 9.35 p.m. They were disarmed and taken to the airport by Presidential Guard. The roadblock had consisted of a special unit created by French officers and called the Commando de Reconnaissance et d'Action Profondeur (CRAP). Shortly after the crash a section of CRAP, whose barracks were at nearby Camp Kanombe, was sent to the wreckage of the plane, which had split into pieces and fallen in the back garden of the presidential villa. These special troops were instructed to collect the bodies from the crash site.

The news that the president and all on board had perished in the jet was given to Dallaire by telephone by the prime minister, Agathe Uwilingiyimana. She told Dallaire she was now the titular head of the country, and she wanted her cabinet to meet. She was having trouble getting hold of her ministers; the moderate politicians were fleeing their homes and she could not reach the hardliners. She worried about how ministers would get through roadblocks.[11] She wanted an escort to take her to the news studios of Radio Rwanda to make an appeal for calm. Dallaire issued a red alert, for the third time since January, ordering the peacekeepers to barracks, doubling security and making the wearing of flak jackets compulsory. At around 10 p.m., he received a telephone call requesting his presence at a meeting of officers at Rwandan army headquarters. On his way he noticed that the Presidential Guard had been deployed.

The meeting began at 10.30 p.m. There were ten senior staff officers quietly taking stock. Some time after the meeting began they were told that the army chief, Major General Déogratias Nsabimana, had died in the jet. Other senior officers were out of the country. The minister of defence, Augustin Bizimana, together with the head of G2 (Military Intelligence), Colonel Aloys Ntiwiragabo, were in Cameroon. The head of G3 (Operations), Colonel Gratien Kabiligi, was in Egypt. The commander of the Presidential Guard, Major Thaddée Bagaragaza, and the head of presidential security, Colonel Elie Sagatwa, had been on the plane.

Colonel Théoneste Bagosora arrived shortly after the meeting began. He said he was late because he had gone to the Ministry of Defence, and that he was afraid of a trap, thinking there may have been a *coup d'état*.[12] Several officers remember that Bagosora wanted to chair the meeting. As the director of the office of the minister of defence, he was second only to the minister, and the minister was out of the country. Bagosora suggested the military take over the running of the country. But the officers did not agree. They were desperate to avoid the appearance of a coup. 'Not at the end of the twentieth century … not like this,' one of them said. One of the colonels suggested it would be more appropriate for Major General Augustin Ndindiliyimana, chief of the gendarmerie, to chair the meeting. But he did not want to. 'We could not believe it,' an officer recalled; he was critical of Ndindiliyimana's cowardice. Several times Bagosora left to take telephone calls in an adjacent room.[13] Writing about these events some years later, Bagosora described a 'fateful day', and remarked how extraordinary it was that so many people responsible for state security were either dead or out of the country.[14]

When Dallaire arrived at the meeting he was met by Bagosora. Several officers recalled how relieved they were to see him. 'We told him of our problem,' one of them said. Dallaire said that if the army took power, then the UN would leave. He suggested that Bagosora make contact with Prime Minister Uwilingiyimana. At that, Bagosora stood up and leaned towards Dallaire with his knuckles pressed hard on the table. He said she was inept and untrustworthy and that not even her own party trusted her. He did not want the Arusha Accords to be jeopardized, however, and he wanted to keep peace with the RPF. Bagosora said he would make every effort to ensure that the Presidential Guard returned to barracks. He readily agreed that UNAMIR should have access to the crash site. Dallaire did not believe him.[15]

Several officers suggested that Bagosora ask the MRND for a suitable candidate to replace the president, and it was agreed to appoint Colonel Marcel Gatsinzi as interim chief of staff; a known moderate, he was a member of the High Council of the army command, established under the Arusha Accords. They would all meet again in the morning. Before the meeting ended, Ndindiliyimana assured Dallaire that this was not a *coup d'état*. The military was keen to get the Arusha Accords back on track and ensure the creation of a transitional government. Dallaire suggested that peacekeepers patrol the streets accompanied by gendarmes, and that these patrols be allowed through army roadblocks. Dallaire was assured of cooperation, and was asked to keep watch on the RPF battalion housed in the Conseil National pour le Développement (CND), the parliament building.

Colonel Luc Marchal, who was trying to get to the meeting, crossed the city east to west and was delayed at a roadblock manned by the Reconnaissance battalion; an hour passed before he managed to negotiate his way through. When he arrived he thought Bagosora was quiet, guarded and genuinely shocked by the death of the president. Bagosora was known for openly expressing his views, and a few nights previously, at a diplomatic dinner, Marchal had heard Bagosora publicly advocate the extermination of Tutsi, arguing that so bloody and tragic had been the history of his country that this was the only solution.

At around midnight Dallaire accompanied Bagosora to the residence of the UN Special Representative, Jacques-Roger Booh-Booh. Booh-Booh asked Bagosora if a *coup d'état* had taken place and Bagosora assured him that it had not, adding that every effort would be made to adhere to the Arusha Accords. Bagosora once again objected to any contact with the prime minister. Booh-Booh said that he would arrange a meeting for nine o'clock the next morning with the US, French and Belgian ambassadors.

For the rest of the night Bagosora's movements are not known, but some time during the early hours he signed the first official announcement of the death of the president. It began: 'The Ministry of Defence has the profound sorrow in announcing to the people of Rwanda the death of their Chief of State.' The statement, read over Radio Rwanda at 6 a.m., ended with advice that the population stay at home and await further directives. On RTLM, the news was broadcast that Belgian soldiers and the RPF were responsible for the death of the president. The news was announced by Valérie Bemeriki, who claimed later that she was told this after telephoning the army command.[16]

At 1 a.m. on 7 April, Marchal drove through Kigali. He said it was quieter than some other evenings at this hour. Some of the roadblocks had been dismantled. Marchal did not think there had been a *coup d'état*: there was no great military presence on the streets, nor did it seem as though the reins of power had been seized in a carefully planned military operation.

§ At 2.38 a.m., Colonel Luc Marchal ordered Lieutenant Colonel Joe Dewez, commander of the 2nd Battalion of Belgian commandos, to send peacekeepers to the studios of Radio Rwanda, where the prime minister was to broadcast her appeal for calm. A detailed chronology of these events was compiled later by Colonel Dewez, who used the battalion log and other military records.

At 3.10 a.m., a group of Belgian peacekeepers was ready to depart, but the centre of the city, known as the presidential district, usually protected by numerous Rwandan army posts, was sealed by strategic roadblocks with light tanks. Another group of peacekeepers was ordered to escort the prime minister, Agathe Uwilingiyimana, from her house to the radio station. Ten Belgian Para-commandos – double the usual escort – travelling in four jeeps, set out. These peacekeepers had been in Rwanda for ten days.

The rumour was spreading that the Belgian peacekeepers had been responsible for shooting down the president's plane. At 3 a.m., a Belgian peacekeeper, stuck at a roadblock, and trying to negotiate his way through, was told that the Belgians were going to help Tutsi seize power. Marchal heard this rumour three hours later.[17] At the airport the rumour was circulating about an hour after the crash. By 6 a.m., through the UNAMIR radio network, a warning was given to all units about the rumours circulating that there had been Belgian involvement in the president's assassination.

One kilometre away from the prime minister's house, at the intersection with Avenue Paul VI and the Grands Lacs, a short distance from the St Michel Cathedral, the prime minister's UN escort was stopped at a roadblock. In accordance with peacekeeping policy, the escort radioed for gendarmes to come to help negotiate their passage. No gendarmes arrived. A Belgian peacekeeper, a captain, intervened and took the escort via a back road, farther up the hill. As they neared the prime minister's house there was the sound of intense gunfire.

Agathe Uwilingiyimana was with her husband, Ignace Barahira, a lecturer at the University of Butare, and their five children. She was being interviewed by Monique Mas of Radio France Internationale: 'There is shooting, people are being terrorized, people are inside their homes lying on the floor. We are suffering the consequences of the death of the Head of State, I believe. We, the civilians, are in no way responsible for the death of our Head of State.'[18]

Uwilingiyimana was receiving calls from friends telling her to go into hiding immediately. She refused. She said she had to take over the running of the country and ensure that there was calm. She telephoned the Belgian command at 3.40 a.m. to ask what had happened to her UN escort. She was told the peacekeepers were on their way and she was to stay at home. It had taken them three hours to make a journey that normally took fifteen minutes. Nearing the house, they were met by five Ghanaian peacekeepers assigned to nightly guard duty outside her gate. Their arrival was timed at 5.35 a.m. The officer in charge of the UN escort, Lieutenant Thierry Lotin, saw an armoured car belonging to the Presidential Guard. There was the sound of gunfire and grenades exploding near by.[19]

Uwilingiyimana was not ready to leave. She spoke to the minister of finance, Marc Rugenera, and said there must be a Council of Ministers meeting, but he said this would be difficult because of roadblocks. Uwilingiyimana wanted her escort reinforced. She tried unsuccessfully to get hold of the Rwandan army command.[20] A call from Booh-Booh told her that the army commanders would not talk to her. One of her gendarmerie escort remembered her saying that the situation was dangerous but that she felt protected by UNAMIR.[21] Lotin wanted her to hurry. He could see armed men crouched on rooftops. At 5.49 Lotin radioed that shots were being fired at the prime minister's house. He was told to take cover near their vehicles. Two jeeps were parked in the front garden, two more parked outside. In a radio message just before 6 a.m. Lotin was told to abide by the rules of engagement – to fire only if fired upon. If incidents arose the peacekeepers were to demonstrate non-aggressive and cooperative behaviour.

The Belgian peacekeepers nearing the offices of Radio Rwanda were stuck at a roadblock manned by gendarmes with armoured vehicles. They decided to park in a side road to sit it out, and the Rwandan gendarmes put planks full of nails in the road to prevent their departure. It was 6 a.m. On the other side of town, in the residential area of Kimihururua, at the home of the president of the Constitutional Court, Joseph Kavaruganda, there was a knock at the front door. It was Captain Cedeslas Kabera of the Presidential Guard.[22] The house was surrounded. Kavaruganda's son, in an earlier telephone call from Brussels, had pleaded with his father to make a run for it. Kavaruganda had told him it was too late.[23]

The 6 a.m. news bulletin on Radio Rwanda broadcast an official announcement that the president had been assassinated. At that moment a Para-commando company left barracks with orders to kill anyone who had an identity card proving them to be of the Tutsi ethnic group.[24] Immediately afterwards, in Kacyiru, the area was crawling with Interahamwe. 'They had already erected barriers ... and they were already killing people in the open,' said one resident. In Gikondo a young girl told her parents they must flee. There was no point, her mother said. 'They will kill us progressively.'[25] In Remera, at a Jesuit community, the Christus Centre, a mass in the chapel was interrupted by Presidential Guard. After scrutinizing identity cards, a group of seventeen Rwandans was taken by them into a room and killed with grenades and automatic weapons. In the north of the country, in Gisenyi, within hours of the plane crash, soldiers and militia had begun to kill civilians. Families were taken away on lorries, and told they would be safe, but instead they were taken to a public cemetery to be killed. One survivor said: 'They came into houses and took away people whose ID said Tutsi and anyone they decided looked Tutsi.'[26] In some sectors in the commune of Rubavu no one was left alive to bear witness. In the prefecture of Cyangugu, in a parish called Gisuma, a survivor said that gendarmes had turned up at around 5 a.m. and were killing with machetes and looting, and that the gendarmes were using explosives to break down doors.

§ At 6.10 a.m., at the home of the prime minister, Lieutenant Thierry Lotin noticed that a tank had been parked outside in the road. Lotin sent a message to the Belgian command at 6.44 to tell them that he was under fire.

Inside the house, Uwilingiyimana was trying to contact ministers in the government, but most of those she managed to reach feared for their lives. She learned that the minister of information, Faustin Rucogoza, had been taken away by the Presidential Guard. Her escort comprised fifteen UN peacekeepers – ten Belgian, five Ghanaian – together with ten Rwandan gendarmes. In such situations a directive provided for the Belgian officer to take command.

Lotin radioed at 6.50 to say that there were explosions and the sound of grenade launchers.[27] The prime minister's house was surrounded by perhaps twenty soldiers armed with guns and grenades. There were Presidential Guards on the roof of the house next door. There was a sudden explosion outside and at 8.20 a.m. Uwilingiyimana told Lotin that she wanted to run. Lotin radioed for advice and was told that if he followed her he would lose radio contact; their only communications equipment was in the jeeps. Lotin tried to persuade Uwilingiyimana to stay with them but she took flight with her husband and the children.[28] The youngest was three years old. Uwilingiyimana tried to climb a fence to reach her neighbour, the councillor of the US embassy, Joyce Leader. She had already called Leader for help. But the fence was too high and shots were being fired. Leader urged a peacekeeper who was trying to help to abandon the effort.[29] Instead the family clambered over the bamboo fence at the back of the house, the children still in their pyjamas. They were now in a compound run by the UN Development Programme (UNDP).

Momentarily confused, Lotin radioed UN headquarters. He was told to remain with their vehicles. But Lotin and his men, and the five Ghanaians, were surrounded by Presidential Guard. At about 8.30 a.m. a Rwandan major proposed that he would take them to safety if they disarmed. Lotin kept his head. He radioed again from the jeep. 'What shall I do?' he asked. His soldiers had the capacity to resist; each had an automatic rifle, half of them had revolvers and there were two semi-automatics in the jeeps. Lotin was told by Lieutenant Colonel Joe Dewez not to disarm but to negotiate.[30] The Rwandan soldiers were aggressive and told Lotin that if he did not comply it must mean he wanted to die. He was told by radio that it was now up to him.

Lotin was twenty-nine years old with a pregnant wife back home. He had two years' peacekeeping experience. Lotin radioed back at 8.45. Three of his men were disarmed and on the ground. Dewez told him it was better to do as he was asked. Lotin reflected, and then decided to disarm. He and his men were led to a minibus parked near by. A Rwandan major, Bernard Ntuyahaga, who worked for G4 (Logistics) in the Rwandan army, told them they would be escorted to a UN facility. With a Rwandan driver, Ntuyahaga accompanied them in the minibus. He claimed later that he was passing by chance.

The peacekeepers were taken a short distance to the Camp Kigali army barracks, where there was a UN military observer post at the entrance. Lotin and his men and the five Ghanaian peacekeepers left the minibus and, hands in the air, walked into the camp. An eyewitness noticed an adjutant who worked for G2 (Intelligence) tell the soldiers at the camp entrance that these were the Belgian peacekeepers responsible for the assassination of the president. The peacekeepers were immediately attacked with rifle butts and bayonets wielded by Rwandan soldiers. Only the quick thinking of a Togolese military observer managed to extricate the five Ghanaians. Some Rwandan army officers tried to stop the soldiers attacking the peacekeepers but failed.

The last message from Lotin came at 9.06 a.m., and he was communicating through a Motorola that belonged to a military observer stationed at the camp. Lotin told Dewez that he had no idea where he was but that he thought that he and his men were going to be lynched. Dewez asked Lotin whether he was not exaggerating slightly.[31] Dewez thought the peacekeepers were being 'roughed up' but he trusted the Rwandan army officers: he had trained with them and had friends among them. He believed the assurances of cooperation that had been given to Dallaire. Dewez thought the order to cooperate with the UN had not yet reached either the soldiers or the gendarmes. Dewez called Marchal's headquarters to let him know the men were prisoners and to ask for Marchal to contact senior officers in the Rwandan army to secure their release. 'Given the events in Kigali that morning,' one Belgian officer said, 'although the problems encountered by Lotin were serious, we did not think them exceptional, given what was happening elsewhere.'[32]

There were peacekeepers held hostage at the airport. The Belgian contingent of 450 was located in small groups in fourteen different places, all of them isolated. The airways were jammed with pleas for help from UN staff, aid workers and diplomats. There were reports that the Rwandan army, 7,000 strong, had begun to prepare its heavy armaments, a flagrant breach of the rules of the weapons secure area. There were 600 Presidential Guard, some of them on the streets. The only hopeful sign came later that morning from the airport, where, after the intervention of the Belgian ambassador, the peacekeepers at the perimeter fence were released. They had been surrounded by Rwandan soldiers and had sat it out, refusing to leave their vehicles.

§ At 7 a.m. Colonel Luc Marchal met with a senior officer in the gendarmerie, Lieutenant Colonel Innocent Bavugamenshi, who had come to tell him that a systematic search-and-kill operation was under way aimed at opposition politicians. Bavugamenshi had heard that among others the administrative head of the Ministry of Foreign Affairs, Déo Havugimana, had been killed. Bavugamenshi realized that Presidential Guards and gendarmes were evacuating MRND politicians and their families from their homes in Kimihurura. The Ministry of Defence had only recently transferred responsibility for the security of MRND leaders from the gendarmes to a unit of the army. Bavugamenshi was the head of the gendarmes responsible for the safety of the other political leaders and he immediately tried to organize gendarmes to protect the opposition politicians, but a lack of adequate equipment meant that he could not locate the commander of the gendarmes, General Augustin Ndindiliyimana.[33]

A contingent of Belgian peacekeepers in Kimihurura confirmed that Presidential Guards were carrying out systematic 'cleansing'. At 6.30 a.m. a firm response was ordered by Marchal, who wanted the peacekeepers reinforced and a platoon sent to the area. But the reinforcements were stopped at a roadblock by Rwandan soldiers. In Kimihurura, there were peacekeepers in the street where Félicien Ngango lived. Ngango, a lawyer and member of the Parti Social Démocrate (PSD), was to have been the president of the transitional National Assembly. He and his family were killed. At 11.38 a.m. a report from Kimihurura told of a search-and-kill operation against civilians. Only Rwandans were targeted, no expatriates or UN personnel. A witness recalled: 'Very early on Thursday morning we began to receive news of killings on the telephone. We learned that whole families had been wiped out.'

At mid-morning on 7 April, Marchal received a desperate call from the Canadian wife of an opposition politician, Landoald Ndasingwa, known as 'Lando', a prominent member of the Parti Libéral (PL), the first vice-president of the party and minister of labour and social affairs. Lando was at home with his two children and his mother. Five Ghanaian peacekeepers were protecting him.[34] Lando's wife wanted extra protection. Marchal doubted he could get any reinforcements because of the roadblocks. Then Lando himself came on the phone. Fifteen Presidential Guards were about to attack his home. Marchal heard a loud explosion and shots. 'It's too late,' Lando had said to him.[35] Later on, when Marchal was called to account for the death of Lando and his family, he had quietly explained to the interviewer: 'We were a minority on the ground.'[36]

Dallaire was told that the prime minister had taken flight at 9 a.m. He spoke over the phone to Iqbal Riza at UN headquarters, telling him that he might have to use force to protect her. Riza was adamant. He told Dallaire that he was not to fire unless fired upon.[37] Dallaire left UN headquarters to find her, but he was stopped at a roadblock outside the Hôtel des Mille Collines and ordered out of his jeep by Presidential Guards. He was obliged to walk, escorted by Rwandan soldiers. He was too late. Uwilingiyimana had been murdered. Her children were gone, rescued by a UNDP employee, M. Le Moal, and a Senegalese military observer, Captain Mbaye Diagne, who had taken them to the Hôtel des Mille Collines where Presidential Guards would later come looking for them.[38]

Earlier that morning Bagosora was said to have convened a meeting of the executive committee of the MRND to try to find a presidential successor, but the MRND was not ready to nominate anyone without approval from the party's national congress. At 9 a.m. Bagosora, in his Audi 1000, travelled the short distance to the residence of the US ambassador, David Rawson. No other diplomats turned up for the meeting. Bagosora was accompanied by Major General Augustin Ndindiliyimana, the chief of staff of the gendarmerie. Rawson asked Bagosora why there was gunfire and Bagosora replied that soldiers were unhappy about the death of the president and were firing in the air.

At 10 a.m. Bagosora arrived at the Ecole Supérieure Militaire (ESM), and was met by its commander, Colonel Leonidas Rusatira. Rusatira had been Bagosora's predecessor as the *chef de cabinet* in the Ministry of Defence and was the longest-serving officer, but recently he had been demoted and appointed director of the military academy. There were about a hundred people at the meeting, including Rwandan army officers who commanded sectors in Kigali, the commanders of the military camps, the officer from the Etat-Major, the headquarters staff, the gendarmerie, and the liaison officers with UNAMIR. There were officers from all over Rwanda, and it was remarkable how quickly the meeting was convened. It was chaired by Bagosora and Ndindiliyimana. As he had done the previous night, Bagosora suggested that the army take control of the country, but there was no agreement and it was decided instead to create a committee of public safety, a crisis committee, to re-establish stability and reunite members of the Broad-based Transitional Government in order to accelerate the Arusha Accords. During the meeting there was the sound of gunfire and grenades exploding at the army barracks, Camp Kigali, next door. A Rwandan army officer, Colonel Laurent Nubaha, the commander of Camp Kigali, interrupted the meeting, telling Bagosora that Belgian soldiers had been captured and taken to the camp.[39] Other witnesses said that the entire meeting knew that peacekeepers were being lynched not more than a hundred metres away.[40]

Dallaire had not yet arrived. It had taken him more than an hour to travel the short distance to the Ministry of Defence. Once he got there, a Rwandan officer had insisted on driving him to the ESM. Dallaire was accompanied by the senior Belgian duty officer, Major Peter Maggen. They passed Camp Kigali. Dallaire recounted later:

> I caught to my right side a brief glimpse of what I thought were a couple of soldiers in Belgian uniforms on the ground in the camp, approximately 60 metres. I did not know whether they were dead or

injured; however, I remember the shock of realizing that we now had taken casualties. I ordered the RGF [Rwandan Army] officer to stop the car. The officer refused, saying that the troops in Camp Kigali were out of control and it was not safe for even an RGF officer to go into the camp.[41]

Camp Kigali was a fortress; there were more than a thousand Rwandan soldiers there, plus several hundred soldiers in the Reconnaissance battalion. As Dallaire arrived at the meeting, a Togolese military observer approached him in a nervous and excited manner and told him that a number of Belgian peacekeepers were being held at Camp Kigali and that they were being beaten up. After the meeting was over, and still under Rwandan army escort, Dallaire returned to the Ministry of Defence to speak to Bagosora. Bagosora had made a brief visit to Camp Kigali and Dallaire had repeatedly and insistently asked to go there himself. Bagosora refused. He said that it was unsafe; the soldiers were rioting because, he claimed, the Belgian soldiers had fired on Rwandan soldiers. He promised Dallaire that he would ensure the camp was secure and would obtain the release of the peacekeepers. He also suggested that it might be advisable for the Belgian troops to be withdrawn from Rwanda because of rumours that they were to blame for the president's murder, hence the violent reaction in the army camp next door. It was difficult, Bagosora told Dallaire, because he was not in command of all the elements in the army. Dallaire wanted Bagosora to talk to the RPF at the CND to preserve the peace and prevent a resumption of hostilities. Dallaire remembers Bagosora briefing a senior officer about the release of the peacekeepers. That afternoon Bagosora spent time in his office in the Ministry of Defence writing letters, answering the telephone, signing documents. He was behaving as though this were a day like any other.

Dallaire thought the peacekeepers were being kept in the barracks, and that they would soon be released, like those at the airport. His duty was to the ministers who were to form the Broad-based Transitional Government. But the roadblocks prevented peacekeepers moving about the city. Dallaire wanted something done about the roadblocks, where people were at the mercy of the Presidential Guard.

Some time that afternoon Bagosora wrote a communiqué that was broadcast on Radio Rwanda at 5.20 p.m. It announced the creation of the crisis committee and assured the people of Rwanda that the situation would rapidly return to normal. Calm would be restored and they must reject hate and violence. The young must guard against vandalism. The communiqué emphasized the necessity of accelerating the creation of transitional institutions in line with the Arusha Accords.

The weaknesses in UNAMIR were now terrifyingly obvious. At 8.50 a.m. on 7 April, UNAMIR's Quick Reaction Force (QRF), with Bangladeshi soldiers and three armoured personnel carriers, was turned back from a roadblock, having been threatened with anti-tank weapons. Marchal and Dallaire had talked about the weakness of the QRF, wanting its soldiers to be replaced with troops from another country. Bangladesh was one of the UN's most important troop contributors, with 15,000 soldiers serving worldwide. Dallaire knew that in New York officials in the Department of Peacekeeping Operations (DPKO) had tried to obtain more soldiers for Rwanda but no one had offered anything. The Tanzanian contingent had never been deployed and Belgium had provided only half those requested. The sixty-strong Tunisian company, which was well led, well trained and disciplined, possessed no integral vehicles, communications equipment or logistics. The entire force lacked logistics, equipment, defensive stores and vehicles.

The Belgians, already weakened by being scattered in fourteen different locations, had only light arms. The UN guidelines for the mission, written in the UN Secretariat, had clearly stated: 'mortars and other heavy crew-served weapons are not required'. The Belgians had ammunition reserves 40 per cent below that required under standard military procedure. For weeks Marchal had been sending requests to Brussels for anti-tank weapons, heavy weapons and mortar bombs needed, in a worst-case scenario, to defend the airport. Belgium was the only troop contributor to UNAMIR to be able to provide this equipment rapidly. Marchal had never received a reply. Had these weapons been provided, the situation in which the peacekeepers now found themselves would have been entirely different. But they did not even have enough Motorola radios.

§ Dallaire found Lieutenant Thierry Lotin and his men that night, at the central hospital, the Centre Hospitalier de Kigali (CHK). In the gloom of a 25-watt bulb he just made out a pile of bodies, the ten peacekeepers in a heap, piled up like sacks of potatoes.[42] At first it seemed as though there were eleven of them.[43] Dallaire ordered photographs to be taken. He negotiated with the Rwanda gendarmerie for the bodies to be laid out with more dignity. A Rwandan colonel went to Camp Kigali and took money from the cash register behind the bar to pay somebody to wash the bodies.

Major General Augustin Ndindiliyimana, chief of the gendarmerie, loaned Dallaire his escort to return to UNAMIR headquarters. Ndin-diliyimana claimed afterwards he did not dare go home and spent the night at the Hôtel des Diplomates.

It took two days to get the bodies of the ten peacekeepers back to UN custody, where they remained, under guard, in a lorry in a hotel car park. Then a plane came to take them home. The autopsies showed that four of them died from weapons fire, three of them from blows to the head with a machete, one was stabbed with a bayonet, one died from a fractured spine due to a severe blow with a blunt object and one from injuries to his throat.[44]

It would take thirteen years for a trial to account for their murders. In 2007, in a courtroom in Brussels, a Rwandan army officer, Major Bernard Ntuyahaga, stood in the dock and pleaded not guilty, denying their deaths had been planned. Ntuyahaga had taken Lotin and his men in a white minibus to the army camp, and he said he spotted them, by chance, on the side of the road. His trial lasted eleven weeks and included testimony from the then prime minister of Belgium, Guy de Verhofstadt, who in 1996 had headed a senate inquiry into events in Rwanda. Verhofstadt told the court that he believed a plot had existed to kill Belgian peacekeepers.[45] For the prosecution, a Rwandan soldier, Lieutenant Grégoire Munana, said that Ntuyahaga had been ordered by superior officers to go to the prime minister's house to collect the peacekeepers and that he had known the fate awaiting them. There was evidence given in court that rumours had been spread beforehand that Belgian peacekeepers were preparing to assassinate the president. There were rumours that Belgian soldiers were to be killed. A Belgian lawyer who acted for President Habyarimana had been told by an MRND official in Brussels that Belgian peacekeepers would die.[46] Four months before, in December 1993, the prime minister, Agathe Uwilingiyimana, had told a Belgian journalist, Colette Braeckman, that she had heard ten Belgian peacekeepers were going to be killed in order to get the UN out of Rwanda. Braeckman said that on the night of the president's death, the wife of one of the French crew members had called the French embassy to be told that Belgians were responsible for the attack on the plane. The morning after the assassination, in the Rwandan embassy in Brussels, there was a claim that Belgian peacekeepers were implicated in the death of the president.

The defence in the Ntuyahaga trial argued that Habyarimana's jet had been brought down by the RPF and that the ten peacekeepers were suspected of being implicated in the assassination. This had been the accusation levelled against them at Camp Kigali moments before they were killed. One of the defence lawyers, Luc de Temmerman,[47] raised questions in court about the activities of the peacekeepers on the morning of Wednesday, 6 April, when Lotin and his men had gone to the Akagera National Park. Their mission, it was suggested, was to smuggle a missile for the RPF. Temmerman called this a 'mysterious mission' which had led to suspicion falling on them for complicity with the RPF in the assassination.[48] In court, a Belgian Para-commando who had accompanied Lotin to the Akagera that day denied this was the intention.[49] The court found Ntuyahaga guilty. He was sentenced to twenty years in prison. A life sentence, demanded by the prosecution, was rejected as the court determined he had been but one link in a long chain.[50]

A lasting and bitter controversy continues about why no attempt was made to rescue the peacekeepers. There was outrage in Belgium at their deaths. The most senior Belgian officers in UNAMIR, Lieutenant Colonel J. Dewez and Colonel Luc Marchal, came under a barrage of criticism. Dewez, who had thought Lotin was exaggerating the threat that morning, later explained to a Belgian senate inquiry:

> I had not come to Rwanda as a Para-commando to fight but as a blue helmet, a symbolic presence to help the Rwandans ... My perception of classic UN operations was that the UN does not fight ... I believed in the assurance, the night before, of the command of the Rwandan army that they would help us to assure security and order ... I was blinded by this logic, paralysed by it ... the fact that my men had been taken prisoner by the Rwandan army assured me that they were safe.

There were Belgian soldiers near by. Only a kilometre away there were thirty-six solders from Platoon B, 16th Company, with their fifteen-man command. These troops were separated from Camp Kigali by several roadblocks. Marchal explained that even had they known where Lotin was, the only way to liberate him would have been to negotiate with his captors. To have tried to fight the Rwandan army would have been suicidal. An attempted rescue would have drawn more peacekeepers into the army camp. The whole event may even have been a trap to drag them all in, and far more peacekeepers would have lost their lives.

'We had no armament, no equipment to face such a situation,' Marchal said. He had had every confidence in the Rwandan army. Some officers had, that morning, been cooperating with the peacekeepers and Marchal believed that a great many soldiers had not wanted to take part in the violence and were looking for a sign from the international community that would enable them to keep the peace and avoid a war.

In spite of the confusion and their lack of radio communications, there had been cooperation with the gendarmes. Only some gendarmes had refused to take part in joint patrols with UNAMIR. At some roadblocks there had been arguments among the gendarmes about whether or not militia should be allowed through without being disarmed.

Marchal said Dallaire's actions that day were quite rightly tailored to keeping the town calm. They were all vulnerable, including the unarmed military observers spread throughout the country with no protection at all.

Dallaire later explained just how vulnerable they were:

> Precipitous action in the context of the tense and uncertain security environment in Kigali that morning could have been the spark which would have ignited a wider conflict. This would have placed UNAMIR in an adversarial role … Had either Colonel Marchal or Lt. Colonel Dewez requested authority from me to conduct an assault on Camp Kigali to rescue the detained group under the conditions of that time my response would have been an outright refusal for such an armed intervention. The only solution reasonably available to us at that time was to continue to negotiate as a neutral force. The force had approximately two magazines, or forty-sixty rounds per person which could sustain a three minute fight at best.[51]

For the first two days Marchal thought that it would be possible to control the crisis, and that this was a similar situation to that in February when there had been a sudden deterioration in security. Two days earlier Major General Déogratias Nsabimana, who had been killed in the presidential jet, had talked to Marchal of his fears of an imminent attack by the RPF and a resumption of the civil war. Of their deficiencies, Marchal believed that the most serious was a lack of intelligence analysis: 'With decent intelligence analysis it would not have taken long to tell us that the priority was to protect the prime minister and the president of the Constitutional Court,' Marchal believed. The Rwandan army was now decapitated. There was confusion. 'We badly evaluated,' Marchal recalled later. 'We did not imagine the role of Bagosora in the shadows.'[52]

Afterwards, some of the Belgian officers who served with Marchal claimed that from the start of the crisis he was in direct contact with the Belgian foreign minister, Willy Claes, and that he had been given precise directives by Claes not to risk the lives of whites for those of blacks. Claes later denied any such suggestion: 'The mission was to save who we could … but the soldiers were there on the spot and it was up to them to judge what they could do,' said the former minister of foreign affairs.[53] A press attaché with UNAMIR, Vénuste Nshimiyimana, claimed later, however, that Marchal was in direct contact with Lieutenant General J. Charlier, his commanding officer in Brussels, and certainly for the whole of Thursday. It was Charlier who was in effective command of the Belgian half-battalion serving the UN.[54]

Only later was it ascertained that everyone, whether Hutu or Tutsi, who wanted power-sharing, or who had spoken out against Habyarimana and the northern clique, was on target lists: every journalist, every lawyer, every professor, every teacher, every civil servant, every priest, every doctor, every clerk, every student, every civil rights activist. All of them were hunted down in a house-to-house operation. The first targets were members of the never-to-be-constituted Broad-based Transitional Government.[55] The lists of the victims included the names of Tutsi shopkeepers and business people, the lists having been prepared in the military intelligence office, from where Colonel Anatole Nsengiyumva had written his reports to persuade the president of the threats of 'the Tutsi' to the country. And while the pro-democracy politicians were being killed, the Hutu Power politicians, the leaders of the MRND and others, were whisked away under the escort of the Presidential Guard.

The new chief of staff of the army, Marcel Gatsinzi, arrived in Kigali from Butare during the afternoon of 7 April and was shot at when his convoy approached the presidential district. Unharmed, he attended a scheduled meeting of the crisis committee at 7 p.m. Gatsinzi, Rusatira and Ndindiliyimana were in charge of the meeting.[56] Rusatira commanded the Ecole Supérieure Militaire in Kigali, but with only 100 soldiers at his command. Gatsinzi's battalion was in the south of the country, in Butare, and had been infiltrated by extremists.

That night, Bagosora claimed that he went to Kimihurura to get his family to the safety of the Kanombe military camp. He then visited the family of Habyarimana, paying his respects to the president's widow. Gatsinzi noticed that Bagosora had communications links with the elite units – the Reconnaissance and Para-commando battalions, with some eight hundred soldiers. All were in Kigali. On 7 April, before dawn, the Reconnaissance battalion had recalled to Kigali their armoured personnel carriers, which had been sent to Rambura, in the north, to evade UNAMIR control.

On Thursday morning, 7 April, there were massacres in Nyamata in the Bugesera. An accountant at the commune was seen to give beer to the Interahamwe in preparation for their 'work'. In the Kibungo prefecture early on Thursday morning, a forty-one-year-old cattle herdsman noticed wounded people fleeing from the direction of Murambi. They told him that Tutsi had been attacked all night long.[57]

In Ntarama, about an hour and a half from Kigali going south, the militia had started to burn Tutsi houses, forcing them to flee to the local church, where people thought they would be safe.[58] By nightfall on 7 April, the killing of Tutsi was taking place in the north-west in Gisenyi prefecture, in the south and north-east of Kigali prefecture, in Gikongoro prefecture and in the south-western town of Cyangugu. The next day the killing spread east and west.[59] 'I saw people running as their attackers ran after them with machetes ... I saw a lecturer from the university giving arms to the Interahamwe and telling them to do a good job,' said a survivor.

At roadblocks in Kigali the militia asked for identification cards at first, killing all those with the designation Tutsi, but this took too much time and became an irritation so the militia singled out those who were tall, with straight noses and long fingers. And then they killed those who looked educated and richer than others.

§ Major General Paul Kagame, commander of the RPF, was in his headquarters in Mulindi on 7 April. At around 1 p.m. he made a call to UN headquarters in Kigali. Kagame said he had just learned that the houses of some RPF supporters in Kigali had been surrounded by Rwandan government forces: 'I must inform you that we must act to protect our own,' his message said. This was an advance warning.[60] A second message from Kagame arrived fifteen minutes later: the peace-keepers must do all they could to protect the politicians who had been arrested. He was ready to send a battalion to assist government forces in preventing further civilian killings by 'renegade forces'. Kagame says that he suggested that he secure some areas, creating safe havens; there was no mandate in the world that could stop their combined forces ending the bloodshed.[61] Four messages were sent by Kagame and in the last one he proposed creating a common force with the Rwandan army in order to disarm the Presidential Guard.[62]

Dallaire did not trust these offers. Both sides were killing non-combatants. 'I needed troops from a third party,' he said. 'A strong UN force to stop the killings was absolutely essential.' To have cooperated with Kagame would have guaranteed losses among his thinly spread-out force. Dallaire relayed a message to Kagame that he was doing all he could to secure a ceasefire.

Tito Rutaremara, a senior member of the RPF political leadership, who was in the CND, was warning both Major General Augustin Ndindiliyimana and Colonel Théoneste Bagosora that the RPF would attack if the slaughter of civilians did not stop. Rutaremara said that the RPF soldiers were being goaded with victims brought in front of the CND. At 4.30 p.m. the RPF soldiers broke out and engaged the Presidential Guard. They went south-west towards the Rwandex factory. The government troops attacked the CND from the north and fighting lasted until nightfall. Witnesses testified to an attack that day by the RPF soldiers on the Compagnie Territoriale de Gendarmerie in Remera during which civilians, including children, were killed. That night Dallaire was asked by Gatsinzi to establish contact with the RPF command in order to obtain a ceasefire.[63] Other officers made requests to Bagosora to control the Presidential Guard. Bagosora ignored these requests.

On Friday morning, 8 April, Bagosora was to be found in the Ministry of Defence, where he was having a series of meetings with politicians. Armed escorts had been sent to collect various political figures and at I p.m. a group was assembled in the offices of the PSD party. A new president was chosen, Dr Theodore Sindikubwabo, a member of the MRND, who was elderly and in poor health. Over the next few hours an interim government was created whose legitimacy was said to come from the 1991 constitution. Later that day the French ambassador, Jean-Philippe Marlaud, called the Belgian ambassador, Johan Swinnen, to tell him about the new government. Swinnen immediately realized that all the ministers came from the extremist wing of the political parties, yet Marlaud was claiming that he thought the existence of this government would prevent a *coup d'état*.[64] Both Marlaud and the deputy defence attaché at the French embassy, Lieutenant Colonel Jean-Jacques Maurin, admitted later that they tried to persuade Bagosora to take control of the situation, and had insisted that the army must cooperate with UNAMIR.[65]

The new government was announced on RTLM by Valérie Bemeriki and Noël Hitimana. After Bemeriki had read out the names of the new ministers she began to giggle and told her listeners that, for some reason, the opposition members in the previous government could not be found. Perhaps, she said, they had 'resigned or simply wandered off'. She laughed again.[66]

The official swearing-in of Rwanda's new interim government took place on 9 April. The prime minister was Jean Kambanda.[67] An economist and banker, Kambanda later claimed to have been surprised by his appointment. In his inaugural speech he promised that his government would restore understanding between the people of Rwanda and provide security for them. The government would continue talks with the RPF and ensure compliance with the Arusha Accords.[68] Kambanda claimed later that the intention was for the military crisis committee to take power and appoint Bagosora as president, but the French ambassador and the Special Representative, Jacques-Roger Booh-Booh, had counselled them to adhere to the Arusha Accords. Kambanda claimed that the membership of the new government had been chosen by Bagosora and Mathieu Ngirumpatse.[69] Some witnesses testified later that the new government was created in the French embassy. On the morning after the assassination, dignitaries from the Habyarimana regime were seen gathering in the office of the French ambassador, Jean-Philippe Marlaud.[70] Among those present were Bagosora, Froduald Karamira, Justin Mugenzi, Jean-Bosco Barayagwiza, Hassan Ngeze, Jérôme Bicamumpaka and Ferdinand Nahimana. According to others, there were some two hundred Rwandans gathered at the embassy, and they included Félicien Kabuga, the financier, Protais Zigiranyirazo and Georges Ruggiu from RTLM and the banker Pasteur Musabe.[71] The interim government was presented to the crisis committee by Colonel Théoneste Bagosora, assisted by Colonel Laurent Serubuga and Pierre-Célestin Rwagafilita. It was described as a coalition government.

In New York UN officials welcomed the new government and thought that its creation would help to stabilize the country.[72] From now on, this government would portray the killing in Rwanda as the result of spontaneous Hutu grief caused by the assassination by the RPF of the president.

§ A first detailed assessment of the situation in Rwanda was sent to New York in a coded cable on 8 April. Dallaire described a campaign of terror that was well planned and organized, and led by the Presidential Guard. The violence was targeted at opposition leaders, the RPF contingent, the Tutsi ethnic group, the population in general, UNAMIR, and all UN offices, vehicles and personnel. His Belgian troops, the backbone of his operation, were isolated by roadblocks. They had no supplies of power or petrol. Ten peacekeepers were dead and he feared for the safety of the rest. The mission had food for less than two weeks, drinking water in some places for only one or two days and fuel for at most three days. He was critically short of ammunition and medical supplies. Although his primary task in Rwanda was the protection of politicians, given the murder of the prime minister and other ministers, this task was no longer possible. Kigali was in a state of war. Roadblocks prevented any movement. The security of his troops could not be assured. The moment he took further casualties he would run out of medical supplies and would be unable to evacuate. He could not assure the safety of the airport.

Dallaire raised the possibility that the peacekeepers might have to evacuate their civilian personnel, in which case he would need a different mandate and reinforcements. He would try to regroup smaller and more isolated units. He was trying to bring about a ceasefire between some two hundred RPF soldiers who had left the CND building and were fighting the Presidential Guard, but his telephone lines had been cut. He had a demoralized but brave Belgian battalion and an untrained, underequipped, below-strength unit from Bangladesh. Dallaire assured New York: 'There must be no doubt, that without the presence of UNAMIR the situation here would be much worse.' He wanted to know whether his mandate was still viable.[73]

The reply to his 8 April cable came from the Department of Peace-keeping Operations. He was to negotiate a ceasefire, not to risk further losses or take action that might result in reprisals. Dallaire later commented: 'An operation should begin with the objective and then consider how best to achieve it with minimal risk. Instead, our operation began with an evaluation of risk and if there was risk, the objective was forgotten. You can't begin by asking if there is a risk. If there is no risk, they could have sent Boy Scouts, not soldiers.'[74] It was a conclusion reached by Kagame, who asked why the UN had not sent Boy Scouts.[75]

In the first days, Dallaire thought this might be a power grab by the extremists, a military coup with the intention of eliminating all opposing politicians and ruining for ever the possibility of reconciliation with the RPF. For his part, Jacques-Roger Booh-Booh informed Kofi Annan that he was consulting with the new military crisis committee about security, and that the deaths of several ministers had created a power vacuum which could cause problems in the peace process.

The Interahamwe increased its control of the streets. On Thursday, 7 April, in Nyamirambo, in the south of the city, there were thousands of people sheltering at the St André School. Elsewhere in the city, in Gikondo, the whole area was sealed off as gendarmes and militia moved systematically from house to house killing people with machetes.[76] The eighteen children, orphaned in February, and who were being cared for in a local school, were all slaughtered.

The red-brick church, part of a large Catholic mission, was filling with people. The church was run by Polish Pallotti priests and nuns, and was set in terraced gardens surrounded by eucalyptus trees. The complex included a printing press, guest accommodation and a series of offices. On Saturday morning, 9 April, there were gendarmes searching the compound, saying they were looking for Tutsi. There were people hiding there beneath floors, in cupboards and in the rafters. There were an estimated five hundred people in the church and the priests organized a mass. As it got under way there was the sound of shooting and exploding grenades. There was a sudden noise as two Presidential Guards and two gendarmes burst into the church. They were followed by Interahamwe wearing their distinctive clothing, the *Kitenge*, multi-coloured trousers and tunics.

'The militia began slashing away with machetes,' a witness remembered. 'They were hacking at the arms, legs, genitals, breasts, faces and necks.' Some people were dragged outside and beaten to death. The killing lasted two hours. Then the killers walked slowly among the bodies, looting and finishing off the wounded.[77]

There were two military observers from Poland who lived in guest houses near the church, Major Jerzy Maczka and Major Chudy Ryszard.[78] Maczka had watched militia climb over the fence. When he tried to contact UNAMIR headquarters the radio channels were jammed. When he finally got through he was told that UNAMIR had no assets to deal with the protection of the local population and in any case slaughter was also taking place elsewhere.[79] Maczka had helped the wounded and with the priests carried them into the shade. He saw the nature of the injuries. Ears and mouths had been slashed, the genitals of men and women mutilated. Maczka took photographs. 'They did not limit their action to killing,' he said, 'there was bestiality.' There was a pile of identification cards with the ethnic designation of Tutsi burned in an attempt to eradicate all evidence that these people had existed. The next day the Interahamwe came back. They discovered injured survivors hiding in a small chapel. The militia poured petrol in through the windows of the chapel and threw in hand grenades.

A rescue was mounted for Maczka and Ryszard and they were found huddled together in the church. Their colleagues had taken UNAMIR's one serviceable Czech-made armoured personnel carrier (APC), using a three-man Bangladeshi crew who had objected to the whole idea. They had warned of the risks of going out into the city with an APC that could break down at any moment.[80] Two Polish military observers, Major Stefan Stec and Major Marec Pazik, based at headquarters, had insisted. They had served with Maczka and Ryszard in Cambodia. Also in the rescue mission that day was Major Brent Beardsley, Dallaire's staff officer.[81]

Once in Gikondo they had left the Bangladeshi crew with the APC and had walked into the church gardens. They saw the bodies of whole families who had been killed, including children, who had been hacked by machetes. There were terrible wounds to the genitalia. Some people were not dead. There was a three-month-old baby, the mother raped and the baby killed, with a terrible wound. There were children, some with their legs or feet cut off, and their throats cut. Most of the victims had bled to death. They heard how the Interahamwe had done the killing under the direction of the Presidential Guard. Stec returned to the APC. He wanted to get his camcorder. There must be proof. Stec said Gikondo should have alerted the world, for this was genocide. When he got back to UNAMIR headquarters, Stec says, he was told not to use the word.

Dallaire kept some convoys patrolling but after finding the bodies of Thierry Lotin and his men he pulled back and increased the size of the Belgian peacekeeping contingent at the airport. It was their only lifeline. His priority was the protection of the ill-equipped and poorly trained contingents, his civilian staff, and the people sheltering with them. It took Dallaire more than two weeks to find out where all his troops were and gain access to them. Because of the constant pressure from the Security Council to cut costs, most of his units had one or two days' water, a maximum of two days' rations, virtually no stocks of fuel and about twenty rounds of ammunition for each soldier.[82]

From the balconies in the concrete-block hotel that served as head-quarters, the peacekeepers watched. One of them was haunted by a killing only yards away: 'he just held him by his shirt and started dragging him … and just raised his machete and hacked him on the head … he did that twice and we were standing there watching him … after that he just rubbed his bloodstained machete on his buttocks, and then searched the victim's pockets … we all screamed at this'. Not long afterwards a tipper truck came by with prisoners who had been detailed to collect bodies from the streets.[83]

'Someone flagged it down and dragged the body from under the tree and threw it into the tipper truck which was almost full and people were moaning and crying, you could see that some were not dead.'[84]

13 | THE GENOCIDE EXPOSED

§ In New York, on Thursday morning, 7 April 1994 Kofi Annan, under-secretary-general and head of the UN Department of Peacekeeping Operations (DPKO), received a telephone call from Kigali. Three peacekeepers for certain, and probably more, had been murdered.[1] Later that day, Annan met with the Belgian ambassador to the UN, Paul Noterdaeme. The ambassador was under instruction to press for a stronger mandate for UNAMIR in order to protect the 1,520 Belgian nationals currently in Rwanda. The Belgian foreign minister, Willy Claes, wanted to know whether, under their current mandate, the UN peacekeepers could offer these people protection. Claes thought that what had happened in Rwanda was probably a *coup d'état*, and there would be widespread massacres.

Annan told Noterdaeme that he had already asked Dallaire to contact the Belgian ambassador in Kigali to see what he could do to help should an evacuation of Belgian civilians be necessary. Dallaire was doing his best to protect Rwandan politicians, and UNAMIR would try to 'prevent or reduce the massacres'. But it was up to Dallaire to see what was feasible. The force commander's first duty was the security of his soldiers, and he must do nothing to encourage reprisals. If UNAMIR were to be provided with a more robust mandate it would need to be re-equipped and reinforced. Nothing was more dangerous than to ask a peacekeeping mission to use force when its composition, armament, logistical support and rules of engagement denied it the capacity to do so. If UNAMIR were to use force, then authorization would be needed from the Security Council. Three permanent members, the USA, the UK and Russia, were already reluctant about the mission. A more forceful mandate would also require agreement from the countries with troops in Rwanda. Noterdaeme told Annan that if Belgians were going to be massacred, then Brussels had not ruled out flying a battalion into Kigali.[2]

Willy Claes spoke on the telephone to the secretary-general, Boutros Boutros-Ghali, who had arrived in Geneva from Minsk, Belarus, at the start of a three-week tour of Europe. Claes asked Boutros-Ghali for an immediate change in the mandate of UNAMIR to allow for enforcement action. Boutros-Ghali, according to Claes, said that he needed time to consult his experts. The next day, Friday, 8 April, Claes again contacted Boutros-Ghali, who again made it clear that the mandate could not be changed immediately; no one knew whether or not the members of the Security Council would agree to such a change.[3] Writing from Geneva, the secretary-general sent a letter to the president of the Security Council, Colin Keating, the permanent representative for New Zealand, in which he suggested the withdrawal from Rwanda of UNAMIR:

> It is quite possible that the evacuation of UNAMIR and other UN personnel might become unavoidable, in which event UNAMIR would be hindered in providing assistance under its present mandate and rules of engagement. The members of the Security Council might wish to give this matter their urgent attention. Should UNAMIR be required to effect such an evacuation, the Force Commander estimates that he would require two or three additional battalions for that purpose.[4]

Boutros-Ghali continued his scheduled European tour.[5] As the news from Rwanda worsened, his decision not to return to New York was seen in the Secretariat as inexplicable and irresponsible, and some believed it was a troubling abdication of leadership. Boutros-Ghali was an incessant traveller, and while he was abroad his officials found it harder to handle their responsibilities on a daily basis. This had been particularly true of the conflict in Bosnia. Boutros-Ghali later denied that his absence had made a difference and said that with secure coded telegrams he kept in constant touch with headquarters. There were as many as eight serious issues that demanded his attention, he said.[6]

While Belgian diplomats lobbied for a strengthened mandate for UNAMIR, Noterdaeme went to see British and American representatives. They told him that in the present circumstances the existing mandate for UNAMIR no longer made sense; indeed, both these countries were considering whether or not to pull out UNAMIR completely.[7]

The US decision to pull out all nationals was made some time on Thursday. This was communicated to Brussels with a request from Washington that the Belgian government exert pressure on the Security Council to allow their troops in UNAMIR to protect all foreign nationals in Rwanda, including 240 US citizens present in the country.[8]

A US military officer, Colonel Charles 'Chuck' Vuckovic, a defence attaché from the US embassy in Cameroon, was already in Kigali,[9] having arrived at the five-star Hôtel des Mille Collines some six hours before the presidential plane was shot down.[10] The plans for a total US withdrawal were already drawn up in accordance with standard procedure, worked out and refined with assistance from experts in the Department of State and the Department of Defense. The US community in Rwanda had been regularly briefed on the security situation and on the evacuation options. The order to leave came from the Department of State but it was Vukovic who took control of the operational administration of the plan, and he was praised later for his heroic job.[11] By Saturday, 9 April, the US citizens had left, travelling in a convoy of cars to Burundi, and protected by an armed escort of UN peacekeepers. But the UN civilians were the first to get out, some 150 people, in forty-two vehicles.

In Brussels, Claes was considering whether or not the Belgian troops in UNAMIR should be ordered to abandon their peacekeeping and start to rescue Belgians. He wrote to Noterdaeme in New York, 'for your personal information, if it gets worse, we have not excluded that the Belgian commander, in order to protect Belgians, should receive his orders directly from the government'.[12] Claes admitted afterwards that his one priority had been getting Belgian civilians out of Rwanda. After the deaths of the ten soldiers, he said, the preoccupation was to avoid any more Belgian deaths – at all costs. 'You could say that this is inadmissible,' Claes told a subsequent Belgian senate inquiry.[13]

The possibility of reinforcing UNAMIR to stop the mass human rights abuses taking place seems hardly to have been mentioned. Each time reinforcements were raised, it was only in the context of rescuing expatriates.[14] A Belgian senate inquiry would later show that in only one cabinet meeting was a plan discussed to stop the massacres, but it was dismissed as it would constitute interference in Rwanda's internal affairs. Noterdaeme's deputy, Alexis Brouhns, said that once or twice the idea of reinforcing the peacekeepers was suggested to UN officials in New York but they expressed reluctance. Noterdaeme said later that he had been approached by a French diplomat who warned him that on no account should the Belgians even think of reinforcing for whatever reason. It was too dangerous for Belgians in Rwanda because they were being blamed for the death of the president. The French diplomat said that he had recently spoken to Rwanda's ambassador to the UN, Jean Damascène Bizimana, and he thought that the Rwandans would probably adopt a more lenient attitude should the French decide to intervene for humanitarian reasons.[15]

Some years later it emerged that help for Rwanda had been discussed by three governments – those of France, Belgium and Italy. It was General Christian Quesnot, who was President Mitterrand's chief military adviser, who revealed this. Quesnot said the idea came to nothing. Giving evidence to a senate investigation in France, Quesnot claimed that he had suggested an intervention by France in order to 'stabilize' the Rwandan army, re-establish order and stop the RPF. The plan was apparently rejected by the prime minister, Edouard Balladur.[16]

The focus of attention now turned, following the US and UN lead, to an emergency withdrawal of all expatriates. There were troops provided immediately by the Belgian, French and Italian governments, their specific orders to rescue expatriates only. No Rwandans were to be rescued. The plan needed the help of Lieutenant General Dallaire. His instructions came from New York, in a cable from Riza on 9 April, telling him that only in rescuing expatriates was he to take any risks. 'You should make every effort not to compromise your impartiality or to act beyond your mandate,' Dallaire was told. 'But you may exercise your discretion to do [sic] should this be essential for the evacuation of foreign nationals.' Riza added: 'This should not, repeat not, extend to participation in possible combat except in self-defence.'[17] Dallaire discovered that some of the peacekeepers were no longer taking his orders, in particular the Bangladeshi contingents.[18] A later cable from headquarters, signed by Annan and Riza, told him that if events moved in a more negative direction then it might be necessary to conclude there was no other option but the total withdrawal of UNAMIR.

The evacuation of the expatriates from Rwanda began at dawn, on Saturday, 9 April, when a contingent of 190 French soldiers flew into Kigali International Airport and, with no warning to UNAMIR, occupied it and installed artillery and anti-aircraft weapons. Later that day, a further 400 French troops landed at the airport; some of them had stolen UN vehicles parked there. The first French plane landed in Kigali at 3.45 a.m. It was carrying tons of ammunition and, according to a Senegalese peacekeeper who had watched it unload, the boxes were put on to Rwandan army vehicles, and taken to Kanombe military camp. The French government has always strenuously denied this.

The French military, having secured the airport and the road from the airport to the French embassy, now began their operation to safely escort the French staff at the embassy, and certain Rwandan VIPs sheltering there, whom the French were to fly to France. These included Séraphin Rwabukumba, and others central to the ruling clique, including the Hutu Power ideologue Ferdinand Nahimana and his family.[19] In the first French aircraft were the president's widow, Agathe, and two of her daughters, one of her sons and two of her grandchildren. Later on, French troops escorted sixty children from the St Agathe orphanage from Masaka to the airport, accompanied by thirty-four 'helpers'; Tutsi at this orphanage were abandoned.

Some expatriates drove south to Burundi or took their cars to the airport. Those Rwandans who did manage to board the European convoys were taken off at roadblocks and killed; sometimes these murders were witnessed by French and Belgian soldiers. At the airport, a Russian woman had to abandon her Tutsi husband. She had to argue on the tarmac to get her children on the plane. A survivor recalled: 'We were told they could not take us. We pleaded with them, pointing out the danger. Some of the children were screaming. But they told us that they were forbidden from taking Rwandese out of the country ... we were in so much fear that we were shaking and could hardly talk.'

The head of the MSF-France operation in Rwanda, Eric Bertin, had 126 expatriate staff and hundreds of nationals working in five different centres. There had been an MSF presence in Rwanda since 1990. Bertin had received a telephone call from a colleague who had described how fifty wounded people, waiting in emergency tents in the Centre Hospitalier de Kigali (CHK), had been dragged from the courtyard and murdered.[20] The killers had thanked the MSF staff working there for providing a Tutsi collection point. Bertin said he realized then that Rwanda was now beyond the limits of humanitarian help, and on Sunday, 10 April, he made the decision to pull everyone out. His office in Paris told him that a surgical team was needed now, and they were discussing the provision of emergency medical care with the International Committee of the Red Cross (ICRC).[21]

Bertin left Rwanda that same afternoon. He described later the strange feeling of being driven to the airport in a Rwandan army truck driven by a Rwandan soldier, but with French soldiers providing the escort. The French military quite clearly had control over the Rwandan army and he wanted to know why the French officers did not simply stop the killing. The French were driving freely around Kigali. While the UN peacekeepers wore bullet-proof vests, the French soldiers did not. Bertin knew the killing was organized and that it was predetermined. He had watched militia arrive at his neighbour's house looking for Tutsi, for *Inyenzi*, the 'cockroaches'. Bertin heard about a UNICEF health officer, Bertrand des Moulins, who had just buried two people in his back garden. He lived near the Hôtel Méridien,[22] and late in the morning on Thursday, 7 April, a Presidential Guard had arrived looking for his cook and nightwatchman, both of them Tutsi. The Presidential Guard shot dead a Rwandan couple in their early twenties, relatives of the cook who had come to him for safety. Bertin said he knew that all Tutsi were targets. 'We did not use the word genocide but we knew that's what it was,' he said later.[23]

The departure of the French from Rwanda was a hurried exit. When the French embassy in Kigali closed on Tuesday, 12 April, there remained behind a huge mound of shredded paper, filling an entire room, floor to ceiling. All around the city now, every Western office was closing. Every UN agency, every aid agency, every development and cooperation mission, and every embassy, all apart from that of the Chinese, was shutting. To this day no one has been able to explain why this sudden exodus took place. No abandonment had occurred elsewhere, no similar evacuation from Burundi after the assassination of two presidents in the space of six months.[24] The scenes of farewell were dreadful, as friends and employees pleaded with Europeans for rescue. One woman who worked for the World Health Organization (WHO) saw twenty-eight people shot.[25]

In a matter of four days, almost all the expatriates had left.[26] A total of 3,900 people of twenty-two nationalities were safely out of the country.

§ The chief delegate of the ICRC in Rwanda, Philippe Gaillard, had been in the country for nine months. In that short time he had built a network of contacts and was trusted at the highest levels – in the army command, the RPF, and militia groups, including the Interahamwe. It was Gaillard who was to decide whether or not ICRC would stay on. It was his personal choice, or so the ICRC president, Cornelio Sommaruga, had told him. Sommaruga said that Gaillard was the expert and that it was his decision to take; only Gaillard possessed the necessary skill of negotiating a safe area for a hospital.

Gaillard said he had known immediately what was happening in Rwanda. The killing was not peculiar to Africa, as many now supposed. And it was no repetition of Somalia. This was an apocalypse, as seen in the works of Bruegel, in the cast of monsters descending into the hell of Dante. A medieval scholar for many years, Gaillard had joined the ICRC after a chance meeting and had been immediately accepted for an induction course at the Geneva headquarters. In March 1982, he was sent to Iraq, visiting the prisons to meet with Iranians captured during the Iran–Iraq war. He had spent ten years in Argentina, El Salvador and Colombia. Rwanda was to have been an easier mission.

When the presidential jet crashed Gaillard was in the CND with the RPF battalion discussing the provision of food aid for people displaced by the RPF in the north. That night Gaillard sheltered with two of his colleagues in the damp basement while the building was being shelled. No one could sleep. They listened to RTLM. One of the announcers, Noël Hitimana, claimed that the Belgians had assassinated Habyarimana. Tito Rutaremara, a senior RPF official, did not believe that Habyarimana was dead and thought that the news of the crash was no more than a pretext to shell the CND with the RPF inside it. Rutaremara spoke to the prime minister, Agathe Uwilingiyimana. She said she thought she would be killed.[27]

The next morning Gaillard and his colleagues watched in horror while people were murdered with machetes in front of the building. People ran screaming in terror, chased by soldiers and machete-wielding militia. A row erupted between an enraged RPF officer, desperate to intervene, and a UN officer who told them they must not. Gaillard described the killing as 'instantaneous'.[28] Gaillard's immediate concern was to regroup the ICRC delegates and their families. There were thirty-five expatriates and 130 local people employed by the ICRC, and some of them were pleading for rescue over the telephone. A colleague told Gaillard of the murder by the Presidential Guard of an opposition politician.

It was against all advice that Gaillard left the CND. At the first roadblock his car was stopped by Rwandan soldiers, some of whom were drunk. Gaillard was ordered out of the car. He approached a captain and immediately received a blow to the stomach from a Kalashnikov assault rifle. Gaillard was told to hand over his car keys. Gaillard, a small and skinny man, responded firmly. 'My name is Philippe Gaillard. What's yours?' The captain did not answer. Gaillard told him that he was on his way home and that he lived near the Ministry of Defence. His neighbour was Colonel Bagosora and he fully intended to report the state of these soldiers, and their lack of discipline. Gaillard was allowed to pass. 'Bluff ... game of poker,' he said some years later. He had been terrified.[29]

The city seemed silent. As he drove, Gaillard remembered thinking that everyone who had tried to run was probably dead.[30] Later that first day he managed to regroup all the delegates, the Rwandan staff and their families, into the ICRC delegation. There were soon 500 people in a space where fifty people used to work. Gaillard held a meeting. There was no need for him to explain what was happening. They all knew. There was a stampede to leave but the ICRC was going to stay on. He was sorry he could not speak to them individually, nor could he take questions, and they must appoint a spokesperson. He organized travel home for all non-essential staff.

Of the twenty-six delegates who remained with him, twelve were medical personnel. Gaillard told them that if it became too hard for them, their duty was to tell him. One delegate, a strong man both mentally and physically, confided later that, even with years of service, he was trembling. Gaillard thanked him for his honesty and made arrangements for him to leave. A Swiss male nurse who had worked for the Red Cross all over the world never worked again after Rwanda. He told Gaillard that his mind had been macheted. 'Everyone cracked up, at some time or another,' said Gaillard. 'Many of us not until it was over.'[31]

And so, on a Kigali hillside, they created an emergency field hospital, the ICRC together with personnel from MSF-France. It was an unforgettable sight. There were giant flags, twenty-square-foot sheets carrying the Red Cross symbol on all the roofs of the buildings and even hanging in the trees.[32] This had been a girls' convent school, next to the ICRC delegation, known as the Centre des Soeurs Salésiennes de Dom Bosco. There were a number of classroom buildings which were quickly transformed into a 200-bed hospital with two operating theatres, and two rooms for minor surgery. It was on the Avenue de Kiyovu, which, in the civil war to come, would become a changing front line between the RPF and the Rwandan government soldiers. The hospital was shelled several times.

There was a delivery of supplies to the hospital late on the afternoon of 13 April, when an ICRC convoy carrying a doctor, an anaesthetist and three nurses arrived. The convoy had travelled north from Bujumbura with 18 tons of medical supplies. A team of six people from MSF-France also travelled with it, and 5 tons of medical equipment. The next day, Jean-Hervé Bradol, who had travelled with the lorries, visited the CHK. There were an estimated one thousand bodies in the morgue.[33] Patients told Bradol how killers came at night to drag Tutsi from the hospital to kill them.[34]

Soon, the ICRC had a routine. Every morning a convoy of ambulances left the hospital to tour the streets to search for the wounded. These rescue teams included Rwandan volunteers, ICRC delegates and MSF medical staff. Bradol described searching through piles of bodies tossed into ditches, having to decide which of the wounded to lift into the ambulance. 'All the choices were difficult,' he said. Only the most seriously wounded were taken to the hospital, only those who would die unless they received treatment. Children were a priority. It was pointless to rescue Tutsi men. They were bound to be killed at roadblocks. The Red Cross vehicles would eventually display special permits, signed by the army commander, Major-General Augustin Bizimungu. Some militia could not read and so Bradol would point to his signature. He would explain that this was the seal of the Ministry of Defence. Bradol bought beer and cigarettes at roadblocks, and joked and laughed with the militia. One of them once asked Bradol whether he could work for MSF because he did not like what he was doing.[35]

Bradol was in no doubt about the organized nature of the killing. 'There was no anarchy, no chaos,' he recalled. Although described as a popular and sudden uprising, it was not. Bradol had seen a popular uprising in Somalia. There was no comparison. If this had been a popular uprising they would not have been able to circulate. 'In Kigali, there was order,' he said. One army officer confided that every day a lorry-full of arms and ammunition was distributed during a tour of the roadblocks.

Sometimes they had to argue to stop the killing of their wounded; one militia had wanted to throw grenades into the back of an ambulance. 'We tried to make contact with them,' Bradol said, 'to create relationships with them.' Each day the Red Cross visited the CHK, where two Rwandan surgeons continued to carry out operations, mostly on wounded Rwandan government soldiers, and if the wounded were too numerous they would send some to the ICRC hospital.

Bradol went to Gikondo. The parish was now completely surrounded by roadblocks.[36] As he entered the area, militia told him there was no point collecting the wounded because all Tutsi in Gikondo were going to be killed. When Bradol left Gikondo, the militia looked under his vehicle to see whether anyone was hiding there. The rescue teams would make every effort to get back to the ICRC hospital before 1 p.m. After that the militia were too drunk and high on drugs to make negotiation possible. 'When we got back to the hospital it was always a feeling of relief … it was the only place where you knew no one was going to be killed,' said Bradol. They watched from the hospital grounds as people were killed on the hill opposite. On one occasion a group of people trying to reach the hospital was killed just yards from the door. Bradol remembered one of their first casualties, a girl of six. She had a machete cut across her face. 'How could anyone look at a child of six, and lift a machete to her?' Bradol asked himself, and he worked out the angle at which the killer had wielded the blade.[37] The child was the same age as his daughter. After this, and day after day, Bradol saw dozens and dozens of mutilated children. The word genocide did not enter his head, he said. But he knew for certain that an extermination plan against the Tutsi was under way.

§ Two days after the killing in the church gardens in Gikondo, on

Monday, 11 April, a description of what happened there was published in a French daily newspaper, *Libération*. It was written by Jean-Philippe Ceppi, who had himself seen the mutilated bodies.[38] Only a dozen people had survived the killing and they were all dying. Ceppi described the roads around Gikondo, and how all over the city there was murder taking place. Everywhere there were sounds of screams and gunfire. The Presidential Guard, carrying lists of victims, toured the city in APCs. The Interahamwe battered down doors, chasing Tutsi from house to house, and room to room. Nowhere was safe for them. The French daily *Le Monde* also provided a description of Gikondo, on Tuesday, 12 April, with a piece written by journalist Jean Hélène. He described how the victims were mostly Tutsi and speculated that by the time the RPF reached Kigali, all Tutsi would be dead.[39]

Ceppi had met Philippe Gaillard in Gikondo. Gaillard was there with an ICRC medical team to look for survivors. Gaillard told Ceppi this was genocide, and Ceppi used the word in his article. He described how the RPF was advancing on Kigali, and according to some reports was only 15 kilometres from the capital. 'But by the time they arrive', Ceppi speculated, 'the genocide of the Tutsi will already have taken place.' After this, the word genocide seems to have disappeared, and for the next few weeks the Western press would describe nothing of the sort, preferring 'tribal anarchy' or alternatively 'an orgy of ethnic violence'. Rwanda was portrayed as a failed central African nation suffering from a centuries-old history of tribal warfare and a 'deep distrust of outside intervention'.[40] In these first weeks, this view bolstered the arguments that nothing could be done to stop the killing.[41]

An article was written about Rwanda by Roger Winter, the director of the US Committee for Refugees. Winter had known the country since 1983 and had returned home to the USA from a visit there. His article explained how the violence was political in nature, and the killing part of a conspiracy by an extremist clique determined to cling to power, using ethnicity to achieve its ends. Winter's article was rejected by the *Washington Post* and the *New York Times* and was eventually published in the Toronto *Globe and Mail* on 14 April.[42]

There were Great Lakes experts in the USA, with extensive knowledge, but they were ignored. Catharine Newbury, a political scientist, and her husband, David Newbury, a historian, had known Rwanda for thirty years, living and working there and learning Kinyarwanda. In 1994, both were teaching at the University of North Carolina, Chapel Hill. They did all they could in the weeks and months to come to change perceptions, and to galvanize public demand for something to be done to protect the civilians at risk. They made hundreds of phone calls in order to place stories to explain what was really happening. Not even their fellow experts on Africa believed what they were saying, and thought they were exaggerating the death toll. Catharine Newbury tried unsuccessfully to speak to Madeleine Albright, the US ambassador to the UN. These academic experts were never given a chance to explain.[43]

In a harsh rebuke after the genocide was over, an international inquiry concluded that, although the news coverage had been handicapped by danger on the ground, the Western press, in characterizing the genocide as tribal anarchy, was fundamentally irresponsible. The media's failure to report that genocide was taking place, and thereby generating public pressure for something to be done to stop it, contributed to international indifference and inaction, and possibly to the crime itself.[44]

§ Three times Lieutenant General Dallaire was told to plan a total withdrawal of UNAMIR. The first occasion was when the UN Special Representative, Jacques-Roger Booh-Booh, ordered him to begin a withdrawal. Dallaire replied that Booh-Booh could issue all the orders he liked, but UNAMIR was staying. 'I will not withdraw,' Dallaire said. There were an estimated fifteen thousand people now under UN care. What would happen to them? On Sunday, 10 April, Dallaire received a telephone call from the secretary-general's special political adviser, Chinmaya Gharekhan. Gharekhan said Dallaire must plan a withdrawal. Dallaire again said it was out of the question; if UNAMIR pulled out the situation would only get worse. Dallaire needed a new mandate, and a modest reinforcement of 5,000 soldiers to put an end to the massacres.[45]

A call from the secretary-general, Boutros Boutros-Ghali, who was in Bonn, came on Tuesday, 12 April. He came straight to the point. He spoke about a complete withdrawal, but Dallaire explained that this was not even to be contemplated. Boutros-Ghali failed to persuade him otherwise. Later, Boutros-Ghali pointed out that asking for a plan to be prepared did not necessarily mean that the plan would be carried out.[46]

In the UN Secretariat, among those officials dealing with Rwanda, there could have been no doubt about the dangers to those people trying to shelter with the UN or about the nature of the killings. In a coded cable dated 8 April, Dallaire had been quite specific. He had described a well-planned, organized, deliberate and orchestrated campaign of terror. There were indications of large-scale massacres, and Tutsi were the targets.[47] Dallaire was formulating concrete proposals for reinforcements needed to stop the killing. He believed that a show of force by the UN, with tanks and guns, would intimidate the gangs roaming the streets, making the most of what he called 'a balance of fear'. Even taking into account the dangers of a renewed civil war between the RPF and Rwandan government soldiers, a modest expansion of UNAMIR of between 2,500 to 5,000 troops could knock out the radio station inciting the militia to kill. Protected sites could be established for civilians. He did not believe that his Chapter VI mandate, dealing with the pacific resolution of disputes, prevented him from taking action. He had written his own rules of engagement in which it was quite clear that he could prevent crimes against humanity. Clause 17 specified:

> There may also be ethnically or politically motivated criminal acts committed during this mandate. I will morally and legally require UNAMIR to use all available means to halt them. Examples are execution, attacks of displaced persons or refugees, ethnic riots, attacks on demobilised soldiers etc. During such occasions, UNAMIR military personnel will follow the ROE outlined in this directive in support of CIVPOL, and local authorities or in their absence UNAMIR will take the necessary action to prevent any crime against humanity.

Only a lack of means prevented him from taking action.

Some people have questioned the validity of Dallaire's judgement about reinforcements, and claim that his estimate is problematic given the determination of the extremists. Three years after the genocide ended one study concluded that Dallaire had been right; the Carnegie Commission on Preventing Deadly Conflict, the Institute for the Study of Diplomacy at Georgetown University and the US army undertook a project together to assess it and assembled, at a conference, a panel of senior military leaders. A report was published based on their discussions and Colonel Scott Feil of the US army pointed to a consensus view that a force with air support, logistics and communications would have prevented the slaughter of half a million people. UN forces, backed by air power, could have protected Rwandan civilians with little or no risk to soldiers.[48] The window of opportunity had been between 7 and 21 April at a time when the political leaders of the violence were still susceptible to international influence. The expansion of genocide to the south could have been stopped; it was relatively contained at this point. An intervention would have altered the political calculations of the extremists as to whether they could get away with it. A larger force was needed after 21 April. By then the genocide had spread.

Colonel Luc Marchal is convinced that if the European forces that came to rescue the expatriates had not pulled out, then the killing could have been stopped. There were already 2,500 peacekeepers in Rwanda, and 2,000 of them could have taken part in a rescue mission. There were 500 Belgian Para-commandos, part of the evacuation forces, and 450 French and 80 Italians from parachute regiments. In Kenya there were 500 Belgian Para-commandos, also a part of the evacuation operation. In Burundi there were 250 Rangers, elite US troops, who had come to help ensure the safety of American nationals. There were 800 French troops on stand-by in the region. Together with moderate Rwandan soldiers, these would have constituted an ample force to restore calm. In this scenario, the RPF would have had no valid reason to mount an offensive. It was not explained where a coherent, unified military command structure would have come from.

For the peacekeepers of UNAMIR, the final departure of the troops that came to rescue the expatriates was an affront to their mission. It was unbelievable that they could leave, knowing the dangers. Dallaire said that it was inexcusable by any human criteria. '[That we] were left to fend for ourselves,' he said, 'with neither mandate nor supplies – defensive stores, ammunition, medical supplies or water – with only survival rations that were rotten and inedible – is a description of inexcusable apathy by the sovereign states that made up the UN, that is completely beyond comprehension and moral acceptability.'

14 | THE SECRET MEETINGS OF THE SECURITY COUNCIL

§ The meetings held by the Security Council to discuss what to do about Rwanda took place behind closed doors. These meetings used to be held in public, and it was possible to hear the options discussed, but nowadays the debates take place in a side room and it is here that the deals that make up UN policy are concluded. These closed meetings are known as 'informals', effectively allowing each government to hide its policy from public scrutiny. Throughout the genocide the Council met twice daily and sometimes long into the night, and the individual views of each government would have remained secret for ever were it not for an account of the meetings, a remarkable 155-page document – an invaluable primary source.[1] This account gives a unique view of the Council's secret world, and without it a reckoning of the failure over Rwanda would be incomplete. The document shows, for example, that for the first three weeks of the genocide the Council hardly discussed the organized killing of civilians. It was not a priority. The idea of reinforcing with a modest number of troops in order to save lives was not even an issue.

There were multiple crises and, in April 1994, the Security Council was preoccupied with a worsening situation in Bosnia, where a Serb bombardment of the so-called safe area of Gorazde was dominating both the Council agenda and the international news headlines. But having established a mission for Rwanda, the Council was now responsible for its future, and the future of UNAMIR would, from now on, dominate any time the Council allocated to Rwanda. Those states that had advocated a tough line on compliance with Arusha a few weeks earlier – the USA and the UK – were now inclined to carry out their threat to withdraw the force, although the immediate concern in the Council was whether or not it was possible to get a ceasefire in the renewed civil war. One of the ambassadors occupying a non-permanent seat, Karel Kovanda of the Czech Republic, recalled: 'No one was sure what, if anything, needed to be done. Into this absolutely bizarre situation came the big powers ... who said they could do nothing.'[2]

There were briefings from Secretariat officials and one of them, Iqbal Riza, assistant secretary-general, a member of Boutros-Ghali's inner cabinet, said that in the first week there was confusion. All assessments coming from the field, apart from one, concerned the resumption of the conflict. Only in a cable on 8 April had there been any detail about organized killing. This was the cable in which the force commander, Lieutenant General Dallaire, had described to New York a deliberate campaign of terror, initiated principally by the Presidential Guard, since the morning after the death of the president. In the same cable a report from the secretary-general's Special Representative, Jacques-Roger Booh-Booh, attributed the worsening of the security situation to the fighting between the Presidential Guard and the RPF. Riza said that in the first week they were under the impression that they were dealing with a breakdown in a ceasefire, except for one sentence, in one cable. Dallaire later queried this claim and said his daily situation reports and his more frequent telephone calls had made it abundantly clear that genocide was looming. Riza said: 'Possibly we did not give all the details ... And if we did not, I really can't tell you what happened then to prevent us from giving those details.'

On Monday morning, 11 April, the Council was informed that there were thousands of people seeking safety wherever they could, gathered in hospitals and in churches and wherever they saw the UN flag. The routine morning meeting held by senior officials from the Department of Peacekeeping Operations (DPKO) had been told that ten UN peacekeepers were dead, and the rest of the Belgian force could be marked for assassination. The RPF battalion in Kigali had broken out of barracks and was fighting the Presidential Guard. The RPF was on the move, invading through the demilitarized zone (DMZ) in the north, an offensive that had begun on Friday, 8 April. There were reports of carnage. Access to the airport was increasingly precarious. The evacuation of expatriates was under way. That weekend, they had watched the Republican leader in the Senate, Robert Dole, say about Rwanda on the CBS news programme *Face the Nation*: 'I don't think we have any national interest here ... I hope we don't get involved there. I don't think we will. The Americans are out, as far as I'm concerned in Rwanda. That ought to be the end of it.' In Washington the attitude of the administration of President Bill Clinton was camouflaged in news spin. At a daily press briefing, when asked whether or not the USA, now the only superpower, had a responsibility to lead an international effort to restore order in Rwanda, Michael McCurry, the State Department spokesman, answered that the situation would be under review at the

UN, the appropriate place for such discussions. Other officials, off the record, were letting it be known that the American strategy on Rwanda was to keep expectations as low as possible, a decision rooted in the appalling peacekeeping mission in Somalia.

The next day, Tuesday, 12 April, at a meeting between Boutros-Ghali and Willy Claes in Bonn, Claes announced that the Belgian military was pulling out of UNAMIR. Claes said that the situation was deteriorating drastically and was going to get rapidly worse. All the UN troops were at risk, he claimed. The whole of UNAMIR should pull out. Claes said later that Boutros-Ghali had agreed with this analysis.[3] Boutros-Ghali maintains that he argued with Claes against a Belgian withdrawal of troops,[4] and that he knew at once that the position of the remaining peacekeepers would now be untenable, unless of course the Belgian troops were replaced with equally well-trained troops from somewhere else. After this meeting the Belgian government launched a diplomatic campaign to try to persuade everyone else of the wisdom of a total UNAMIR withdrawal. Claes telephoned his counterparts in Washington, London and Paris to argue for it. He explained that the Belgian press was in an uproar because of the deaths of the Belgian soldiers; public opinion was demanding that the troops come home. Claes claimed the reaction was similar to that in the USA after the deaths of their soldiers in Somalia.[5] When asked later why the Belgian government had made such strenuous efforts to achieve a total withdrawal of UNAMIR, Claes replied: 'The fear of losing face ... did play a role.'

After the meeting in Bonn, Boutros-Ghali wrote a letter to the president of the Security Council, the New Zealand permanent representative, Colin Keating, to inform him officially of the Belgian decision. It was dated 13 April. The letter records: 'I have asked my Special Representative and the Force Commander to prepare plans for the withdrawal of UNAMIR, should this prove necessary.'[6]

On Tuesday, 12 April, Riza told the Council of 'chaotic, ethnic, random killings'. But most of his briefing concerned the interim government and its move from the fighting in Kigali to Gitarama. The non-permanent members of the Council requested the views of the force commander and the secretary-general. They would continue to do so in the days ahead. But the views of the force commander were never forthcoming to them and complaints surfaced that no options had been presented and that the secretary-general was absent from New York.

At this point, and with US diplomats expressing doubts about the viability of the force, it was the UK ambassador, David Hannay, who came up with options. The first possibility, Hannay said, was to reinforce the troops and give the peacekeepers a stronger mandate to intervene to halt the bloodshed. But this, Hannay warned, would be a repetition of Somalia. Peacekeeping was not appropriate for civil war, for situations where there was no peace to keep and where fighting factions were unwilling to cooperate. Inadequate efforts were worse than no efforts at all. Second, UNAMIR could pull out completely but the negative signal to public opinion would be damaging. Third, the troops could stay on, although he did query what they could effectively do, for there was no evidence that UNAMIR was in any position to protect civilians. The fourth and last idea was to pull most of them out, leaving behind 'some elements'. Although this might initially attract public criticism, it seemed to be the safest course. Hannay warned the Council that the decision could not be delayed.

The USA agreed. No country should be expected to send soldiers into this chaotic environment. It was doubtful whether the peacekeepers could even be resupplied. If the UN failed to protect its own soldiers, then the Security Council would have serious difficulties obtaining any more troops for other UN operations. The USA did not want to be seen to be responsible for the gradual depletion of an isolated force, but the peacekeepers could be flown out and kept in a neighbouring country and then go back in at some later date. It was highly improbable that an outside force could halt the terror in Rwanda.

The Nigerian ambassador, Ibrahim Gambari, pointed out that tens of thousands of civilians were dying all the time. The meeting adjourned. They would ask the views of the secretary-general, and those states contributing troops to UNAMIR. The Council thought of one action: it called for a ceasefire. The African group at the UN was one step ahead. It urged the Security Council to take action at once to protect the lives of civilians and reinforce UNAMIR.[7]

§ The RPF offensive had begun along an 80-kilometre demilitarized zone in three main axes, putting into place a plan long in preparation. Its aim was to defeat an army three times its size and with far superior weaponry. In a radio address on the RPF station, Radio Muhabura, it was announced there had been a 'bloodbath' in Rwanda inflicted by the Presidential Guard. Almost the entire government was wiped out. A new government had been formed comprising those who were opposed to the Arusha peace agreement. A military communiqué announced that the RPF was to fight the 'murderous clique' that had taken over in Rwanda; the RPF was willing to work with Rwandan government soldiers in order to bring the murderers to book.[8]

The lead element of the RPF moved east along the border with Tanzania, a central axis of soldiers went through Byumba, and the western thrust advanced through Ruhengeri, where there was preparatory bombardment to draw out a large concentration of Rwandan army forces. Some soldiers in the central thrust moved towards Kigali. In this way, Major General Paul Kagame held down the Rwandan army on central and western fronts. Throughout the advance, the RPF used mortar fire to maximum advantage and, after a period of sustained fire, often succeeded in intimidating the government forces and cutting off supply lines. The RPF advance on the east was amazing for its speed. The first battalion group from the brigade on the eastern front, some fifteen hundred soldiers, entered Kigali on 12 April, only four days after the start of the campaign and covering a distance of some seventy-five kilometres. The soldiers moved in small numbers, during the night, infiltrating their heavy weapons and combat supplies and carrying out dawn attacks.

The sound of heavy machine guns, multiple rockets and artillery fire could be heard in the city on 13 April, as attacks by the RPF came from the east and north-east. The main bombardment was focused on the barracks of the Presidential Guard, the most fortified part of the city. The Guard held on, and for the next eight weeks, on this front line, there would be no more than 100 metres separating the RPF from the Presidential Guard. Once arrived in Kigali, the RPF troops joined their troops already in the city, and the CND building would become their base. It was where RPF casualties were evacuated for medical attention. But the RPF held only a portion of the capital, and the battle for Kigali lasted three months.

In the weeks to come the Rwandan army would become expert in well-planned and -executed withdrawals at night, when whole areas fought over were often found to be empty in the morning. The Rwandan army lacked an established line of defence; if they had advanced on the RPF battalion in the CND building, they could have defeated that single battalion. Instead, the army held back and allowed the RPF to form a firm base, linking up with its battalions from the north. There were several front lines in the RPF offensive, and Kigali was divided into RPF and government-held zones. Where there were no soldiers, militia ruled the streets. Neighbourhood boundaries were defined by roadblocks, with their piles of bodies. Major General Paul Kagame said he knew the genocide was under way in the first week. As his troops advanced they had evidence of it. There were similarities in the stories survivors were telling, and people with machete wounds were searching out RPF bases.[9]

The Rwandan army's new commander and Gatsinzi's replacement was Major General Augustin Bizimungu. He had previously commanded the Ruhengeri garrison. The army had low morale. In comparison, the militia showed strong political indoctrination and an effective command structure. Sometimes the militia were to be seen intimidating government soldiers at roadblocks. While the RPF advanced, the image of them broadcast on RTLM became increasingly horrific, with people warned that Tutsi soldiers were devils who killed their victims 'by extracting various organs ... for example, by taking the heart, the liver, the stomach ... the cruelty of the *Inyenzi* [cockroach] is incurable, the cruelty of the *Inyenzi* can only be cured by their total extermination'.[10] This was the final attack, the announcers said, using the Kinyarwanda word '*simusiga*', a word used to describe genocide.[11] The war had to be waged with no mercy.[12] The announcers justified the call to kill all Tutsi by identifying them with the RPF. They warned that the RPF was going to exterminate all Hutu. People were encouraged to tell the radio station where people were hiding. In one of her broadcasts, Valérie Bemeriki read out the names and addresses of thirteen people, together with where they worked, and even their nicknames. She urged that they be found. The radio broadcast the vehicle number plates of those who were trying to escape, and they read on air the addresses of where people were hiding. They broadcast requests from civil servants or from militia leaders who needed a resupply of ammunition, or grenades.[13]

Dallaire had pleaded with New York for permission to neutralize the station: 'It was inciting people to kill, it was explaining how to kill, telling people who to kill, including whites, including me.' On 18 April, the RPF mounted a machine-gun attack on the studios and broadcasting was stopped, but only temporarily, and it resumed within hours.[14]

There was some control of the situation by state authorities, using RTLM. The country was run via the airwaves, and RTLM was from the beginning the only government institution that seemed to operate effectively. The radio station was an integral part of national and local government planning. There had, for instance, early on, been a broadcast telling drivers of heavy goods vehicles to present themselves at the offices of the prefecture in Kigali. The drivers were needed for the garbage trucks and the bulldozers, to collect and bury the bodies littering the streets. Gaillard provided petrol for these trucks. A sub-prefect later confided in him that 67,000 bodies had been collected in this way.[15]

RTLM once broadcast that Gaillard was a Belgian, putting his life at risk. A gang of Interahamwe stopped him at a roadblock and Gaillard had to argue, to show them a photograph of his family home in Switzerland,

St Pierre de Clages, in the Valais, where a tiny twelfth-century village is dwarfed by mountains. Gaillard told them there were no mountains in Belgium. And then he drove to the offices of RTLM and spoke to the announcers. They broadcast a racist retraction to the effect that Gaillard was too brave, too intelligent and too motivated to be a Belgian.

Gaillard kept in touch with everyone – including the announcers at RTLM, the leaders of the Interahamwe, the Rwandan army commanders and RPF officers. 'Dialogue was the cornerstone of our security,' he said, 'more important than protective vehicles or bullet-proof vests which are signs of fear and of aggressive force.' Once, because of overcrowding, Gaillard decided to move a hundred wounded people to another hospital in Kabgayi, in a Roman Catholic diocese, some forty kilometres away. As the convoy set out, RTLM began to broadcast that RPF rebels were hiding in the vehicles. The convoy was stopped by a mob of Interahamwe and Gaillard was obliged to wage a furious round of negotiations, including driving at great speed to find army commanders in order to obtain written permission to continue unhindered. The radio station eventually broadcast a denial that any RPF were in the convoy.

To stay informed and ahead of developments, Gaillard established an information-gathering unit in the delegation offices with twenty-four-hour monitoring of Radio Rwanda, of RTLM and the World Service of the BBC. With an ICRC technical expert and a scanner, he picked up the communications of the Rwandan army, the RPF and UNAMIR. All these messages were noted and collated. He monitored UNAMIR channels thanks to a Motorola that Dallaire had given him to keep in touch. Gaillard put a map of Rwanda on his office wall, and showed where the next battle in the civil war would be fought. Each night, at a briefing, he explained to the medical teams the progress in the war. Gaillard said the briefings were a way to hold them together. They had supper together every night, and he would read from the one book he had with him, Arthur Rimbaud's *Une Saison en Enfer* (A Season in Hell). Gaillard hoped that the poems would have a similar effect to prayer, to calm them. Rimbaud was with them as a friend, he said later. On the day when the interim government abandoned Kigali, the ICRC administrative coordinator, Jean-Pascal Chapatte, got hold of some Pauilhac 1986 for $5 a bottle, the wine looted from an empty embassy. That night Gaillard dreamed he was alone in a convent in the centre of New York, and New York was in flames.[16] Jean-Hervé Bradol, from MSF, said later that Gaillard's steely determination was noticeable; he had tremendous intellectual strength, unusual in the field of humanitarian aid. He had told them that the fine words of politicians were meaningless, and that a stronger moral authority existed in the poems of Federico García Lorca than in the Universal Declaration of Human Rights.[17]

He became a regular feature on the streets of Kigali. Always smartly dressed, wearing a white shirt, a jacket and tie, Gaillard would cajole the Interahamwe as though they were old friends, laughing and joking, as he continued to negotiate freedom of movement for the ambulances.[18] He was, according to Prime Minister Jean Kambanda, the only person who ever talked about the intensity of the massacres.[19]

Gaillard watched the miserable spectacle when the interim government fled to Gitarama, almost a week after the genocide began, on Tuesday, 12 April. A convoy of cars had set out from the Hôtel des Diplomates and there had been a hurried scramble, women and children crying, ministers carrying their own suitcases. Everyone desperately piled into cars, parked in a long line in the circular driveway. There was no solidarity; one minister was left behind and had to ask a colleague for a lift. The car belonging to another minister ran out of petrol and Gaillard offered him some, explaining to a curious onlooker that one day the service might be repaid. Thousands of people left Kigali for Gitarama the following day, a column of people stretching about five kilometres, moving slowly along the road and out of the city.[20] Some Rwandans travelled in Mercedes saloons with armed civilian escorts. One reporter with Associated Press described a bulldozer with dozens of people clinging to it and twenty people in the bucket at the front. The city was looted – including the Central Bank. Colonel Bagosora had telephoned Lieutenant General Marcel Gatsinzi, who was for the moment the chief of the army, and told him to prepare armed guards to escort the government's hard currency from the vaults to the interim government in Gitarama. Gatsinzi had refused,[21] but Bagosora moved the money anyway, by organizing a detachment of soldiers. There exists only a rough estimate of how much money there was, but it filled several trucks. The year's taxes had just been collected and the amount was later estimated at 24 billion Rwandese francs (US$170 million). The Rwandan currency stolen is estimated at twice that in circulation at the time. There was also foreign currency and gold in the vaults.[22]

Gatsinzi, together with other moderate officers, kept his distance from the interim government. They tried for peace, on 12 April, when ten senior officers published a communiqué to propose a meeting with the RPF in order to examine ways of creating the institutions required under the Arusha Accords. Nothing came of it. Gatsinzi was relieved of his command on 17 April and replaced by Colonel Augustin Bizimungu, now promoted to major general.[23]

The arrival in Gitarama of the interim government brought in its wake the Presidential Guard and more than a thousand Interahamwe. It might have been possible to have spared the prefecture from genocide because the prefect there, Fidèle Uwizeye, was opposed to the killing, and had organized the *bourgmestres* to defend the prefecture. Once the interim government arrived and arms were distributed, however, and with a concerted campaign of hate propaganda from RTLM, the opposition was soon destroyed.[24] And the genocide continued to spread.

Marcelline lived in the commune of Taba in Gitarama. The Interahamwe rounded up her family and killed all the men. The women were made to dig graves to bury the men, and then throw the children in the graves. 'I will never forget the sight of my son pleading with me not to bury him alive ... he kept trying to come out and was beaten back. And we had to keep covering the pit with earth until ... there was no movement left.'[25]

§ The debate in the Security Council is often shaped by recommendations from the secretary-general acting on advice from officials in the UN Secretariat who receive all the cables from UN commanders. When it came to Rwanda no such recommendations were forthcoming. Some of the non-permanent members speculated that either the Secretariat had no options at all, in which case it was not up to the task of managing the conflict, or it was overwhelmed with problems to the point of paralysis.[26]

Colin Keating, the president of the Security Council in April, continued to ask for more information from the force commander, particularly on the consequences for UNAMIR once the Belgian peacekeepers withdrew.

The letter to the president of the Security Council, written in Bonn by Secretary-General Boutros Boutros-Ghali, and dated 13 April, which confirmed the Belgian decision to pull out, was greeted with consternation. The letter stated that unless the Belgian contingent was replaced by another 'equally well-equipped', then it would be extremely difficult for UNAMIR to carry out its tasks; in these circumstances, Boutros-Ghali had asked the Special Representative and the force commander to prepare plans for the withdrawal of UNAMIR.[27]

Some of the non-permanent members were surprised. Was this all the secretary-general had to offer after a week?

The UK ambassador, David Hannay, found the letter far from adequate. The secretary-general seemed to think, quite bizarrely, that if the Belgians were to stay on, then all would be well. It was not right to give the impression that two battalions could protect the civilian population of Rwanda. The peacekeepers, with their limited capacity, could not protect civilians. If a small military presence was left behind, then it could encourage the parties to move back to the peace deal. The French delegation wanted to know why the secretary-general had assumed that Belgian withdrawal would lead to an automatic pull-out on the part of UNAMIR. There was every reason for the Belgians to leave Rwanda, for every Belgian national was a target, but if everyone left then the situation would deteriorate further. A US representative said it was unfortunate for the secretary-general to appear to blame Belgium for a total withdrawal; while it was not possible to pull the plug completely, the ambassadors should remember Somalia. The best course was to leave a skeletal group of peacekeepers and pull out everyone else.

Boutros-Ghali defended his letter. Some years later he explained that he was trying to put pressure on the Security Council to authorize a new force; he had requested the force commander to prepare plans for withdrawal, 'unless we received additional forces'. He wanted a strengthened mission and an enforcement operation and said that his views were not well received.[28] There was a briefing to the Council on 13 April by Iqbal Riza. He offered the ambassadors an update on the progress of the battle for Kigali, and told them that the RPF would not agree to a ceasefire. The situation was deteriorating, Riza said. Dallaire was conducting some rescue missions and he continued to try for a ceasefire. There were an estimated 14,000 Rwandan refugees sheltering with the UN and the protection of these people required more resources. But there remained a question mark over how prolonged this protection could be, and the Council must consider whether peacekeeping should involve such tasks. Gambari, for Nigeria, wanted to know whether Africa had fallen off the map of moral concern. They discussed a draft resolution from Nigeria suggesting that peacekeepers be allowed to 'enforce public order and the rule of law and create temporary state institutions'. The resolution pointed to the thousands of innocent civilians being killed but, although it was circulated among ambassadors, it was never tabled. It stood little chance. A US ambassador, Karl Inderfurth, told them of a strong feeling in Washington that peacekeeping was not appropriate for Rwanda. The USA would not be pushing in the Council for total withdrawal, but the Council should consider the future of the mission. China disagreed. China, the only country not to have closed its embassy in Kigali, pointed out that there was no immediate danger to the remaining UN peacekeepers. Only the untrained contingent from Bangladesh was in a panic. The others – the sixty Tunisians and the

800 Ghanaians – were doing useful work under the force commander. The Rwandan ambassador, Jean-Damascène Bizimana, representing the interim government, had sat impassively throughout all these exchanges. With a non-permanent seat on the Council, Rwanda had the right to participate in procedural decisions, and the right to block the required consensus on presidential statements.[29] Bizimana was debonair and a fluent French speaker and was in a superb position as part of a vitally important propaganda campaign waged by the interim government to persuade the world that the deaths in Rwanda were the result of civil war. He circulated a letter on 13 April, written by the interim government's minister of foreign affairs, Jérôme Bicamumpaka, claiming that the situation in Rwanda was improving and that the presence of UN peacekeepers was helping to stabilize the country. This letter explained that because of the death of the president, the military and the people of Rwanda had 'reacted spontaneously', and started to attack 'those under suspicion'. A new government had been created and was giving great hope to the people. A press release from the RPF was ignored. Dated 13 April, it was a first notification to the Council that genocide was under way. A ceasefire would only allow the criminals to continue committing atrocities, it said.

At an informal meeting of the Security Council on Thursday, 14 April, there was a spirited defence of the secretary-general by another of his senior officials, Alvaro de Soto, who was assistant secretary-general in the Department of Political Affairs. Although the secretary-general was touring Europe, said de Soto, he was in constant contact with UN headquarters, with the force commander and the Special Representative. It was not accurate that Boutros-Ghali was in favour of total withdrawal, but the problem was that the peacekeepers were prevented from carrying out their mandate. The secretary-general had formulated two options: UNAMIR could remain as it was without the Belgians or it could be reduced. Both options were predicated on a ceasefire. The delegate for Oman called for written proposals. Spain wanted to know why no mention had been made of a possible change in the UNAMIR mandate. France thought that any mission in Rwanda would have to serve some useful purpose. The UK thought that the Secretariat should be more precise about the minimum force level which could remain behind. The USA said that what the Security Council needed was a resolution to provide for the orderly evacuation of the mission.

The following day, Friday, 15 April, Willy Claes, the Belgian foreign minister, wrote to Boutros-Ghali, once again to officially notify him that the Belgian peacekeepers were pulling out but this time to recommend that the whole of UNAMIR be withdrawn. Based on an intimate knowledge of events, the scale of the massacres that peacekeepers were witnessing, together with a deteriorating military situation, there was no alternative and no chance of a ceasefire. While they delayed their decision, the Security Council was increasing the risks to the soldiers. Claes asked Boutros-Ghali to give an instruction to the force commander to release immediately the Belgian soldiers from UNAMIR.[30] Following this letter there was a diplomatic blizzard from Belgium in order to persuade everyone that the entire mission should immediately get out. Boutros-Ghali was inclined to believe that Belgium, the former colonial power, understood Rwanda much better than either the Special Representative or the force commander.[31]

Later that day a disagreement developed between Belgian diplomats and the officials in the DPKO. Kofi Annan did not favour a complete pull-out, and he argued that this would only make the humanitarian situation worse. Dallaire had faxed a long and urgent wish-list of supplies, including water, fuel, medicine and flak jackets. The UN's Field Operations Division had no cash and no method for crisis resupply. A Belgian diplomat saw Dallaire's wish-list and joked about his optimism.

Another cable arrived from Kigali the following day. It was from Major Marec Pazik, one of the Polish military observers who had discovered the Gikondo massacre. He was now employed as humanitarian plans officer, and he faxed to UN headquarters the details of those people who were sheltering nearby in the Amahoro football stadium. There were 5,000 people, and 2,402 of those were children under the age of fifteen. The majority were orphans whose parents had been massacred. There was no food. There were two local doctors without equipment or medicine. Twenty people urgently needed limb amputations, 150 people were seriously injured, there were 150 cases of malaria, 115 with serious diarrhoea, 205 people with bronchitis, 32 with dysentery, and 15 with chickenpox.[32] In the stadium, at a makeshift clinic under one of the spectator stands, they were handing out small sachets of apricot jam. 'It's all we have got,' said someone. 'We have to give them something.'[33]

On Friday, 15 April, the Nigerian ambassador, Ibrahim Gambari, held a private meeting with Colin Keating. He advised Keating to pay particular attention to the views of the force commander and told him that Belgium's reaction was slightly hysterical, owing in part to historic and domestic concerns. Keating also met with Belgium's UN ambassador, Paul Noterdaeme, who told him that when the Belgian peacekeepers left, there would be a bloodbath. UN officials told Keating that peacekeeping was suitable only for the most benign environment and that the Council was reaping what it had sown by putting in a force with inadequate equipment, inadequate training and lack of firepower. Without the Belgians, UNAMIR was going to be in very deep trouble. Other troop-contributing governments would soon withdraw their troops and UNAMIR would disintegrate. It would be the UN's most ignominious failure.

In the Council meeting that day, Gambari made a plea for reinforcements. He said that however weighty the advice from Belgium, they should realize that no other country had withdrawn its troops – not Ghana, not Bangladesh. The peacekeepers had a vital role to play to protect the population and promote a ceasefire. The USA objected. A total withdrawal was all that was acceptable. The UK thought a compromise could be reached by leaving a token force behind. The UN could hardly leave two battalions in Rwanda to be slaughtered. Gambari said that the troops on the ground were at least accomplishing something, but the USA was adamant. If a vote were to be taken, based on an 'independent assessment' of the situation in Rwanda, they would have no choice but to decide that there was no role for peacekeepers. The Council's primary obligation was to ensure that each UN mission was do-able. Their priority was the safety of UN personnel. Afterwards, the US ambassador, Madeleine Albright, who had actively promoted this policy, would deny any knowledge of what was happening in Rwanda. 'It would be weeks before most of us understood the nature and scale of the violence,' she would claim. There was confusion about who was to blame for the killing.[34] But she did believe that the USA was 'on the wrong side' and she had left the room to telephone Anthony Lake, the National Security Adviser. He had told her to calm down. Lake, who could have made Rwanda a priority within the administration, chose not to do so, and was largely silent on the issue.[35] The Council adjourned for the weekend.

The details of this informal meeting were immediately relayed to the interim government. The next day, Saturday, 16 April, a cabinet meeting decided to push ahead with 'pacification' in the south – the word 'pacification' was used to describe the genocide. In all, there would be seventeen cabinet meetings held by the interim government to discuss which directives to give local bureaucrats in order to 'pacify' their areas.

One of the first decisions of the government had been to summon Rwanda's prefects to ensure that, in the weeks to come, each would obey instructions.[36] A minister was designated for each of the eleven prefectures whose job was pacification. Prefects passed orders to *bourgmestres*, who alerted councillors, who held meetings to inform all residents of 'the work in hand' – clearing their areas of Tutsi. Sometimes the councillors went from house to house to sign up all the young males for 'the work'. Administrative officials in possession of birth and death records knew exactly how many Tutsi lived in each area; during the genocide, they kept track of the dead.

The prime minister, Jean Kambanda, broadcast an announcement on RTLM to tell the population to search out the enemy, by which he meant those who 'do not share our opinion'. Kambanda ordered the construction of roadblocks. He distributed arms and ammunition. He ordered, incited and helped other ministers, prefects, *bourgmestres* and other local officials to exterminate the Tutsi and pro-democracy Hutu.[37] The massacres in Rwanda were the result of a chain of command and a prepared strategy. The genocide was a conspiracy at national level, but without the complicity of the local and national civil and military authorities, the large-scale massacres would not have taken place.

§ On Thursday, 14 April, a Red Cross ambulance was stopped at a roadblock in Kigali. Six wounded people were dragged from the back by militia and shot. An RTLM broadcast had announced only minutes before that the Red Cross was transporting 'enemies of the Republic disguised as fake wounded'.[38] Earlier that day the same ambulance had passed the same roadblock with no problems, but it was raining then. When it rained, the roadblocks were not manned. But in the early afternoon the sun was shining and armed civilians and soldiers had returned; this time there was a man with a sub-machine gun, and there had been a recent distribution of grenades. The ambulance was in a convoy with two cars and was driven by a Rwandan who worked for the Red Cross. This stretch of road had one checkpoint every 100 metres.[39]

Gaillard was furious and he immediately suspended the collection of wounded from the streets. He gave an interview to a journalist in which he asked what was the point of saving people only to see them killed. He drove to the studios of RTLM. He shared a beer with some of the announcers, and asked them to counterbalance the broadcasts in order to guarantee respect for the Red Cross emblem. Gaillard later spoke to ICRC headquarters in Geneva and a press release was issued appealing for the Red Cross to be allowed to assist the wounded. There were articles in the Western press about the ambulance killings, which, for the interim government, was unwelcome attention. A subsequent broadcast announced that ambulances were allowed to circulate. Gaillard said later: 'The assassination of these wounded allowed us to save thousands more.'

On 15 April Gaillard went to Nyamirambo, south of Kigali, where a week earlier dozens of people had been killed in a church. Several days afterwards, hundreds of people sheltering in a mosque had also been murdered, the massacre preceded by an announcement on RTLM that Tutsi were hiding there. Nyamirambo had a large Tutsi population; in the months before the genocide started, Tutsi living in other communes had moved there for safety.

The news continued to leak about large-scale killing, and a report of a massacre in the parish of Musha, 40 kilometres miles east of Kigali, appeared in a Belgian newspaper, *Het Volk*. The details were later picked up by other Western media. Associated Press reported that this was the biggest massacre reported so far, an attack on 13 April in a church in which hundreds of people had been sheltering. The Presidential Guard had kicked in the door, opened fire with semi-automatic weapons, and thrown in grenades. 'Afterwards they attacked defenceless people with knives, bats and spears. There were 1,180 bodies in my church including 650 children,' the pastor, Danko Litrick, had said.[40]

But journalists were leaving now. On 14 April a group was taken by UN peacekeepers from the Hôtel des Mille Collines to the airport, and as they prepared to leave the hotel, there were dozens of Rwandans in the lobby, crowding around them and begging to be allowed to go with them. On the road to the airport they saw houses burned and shops looted, and in one place corpses piled in a heap. Five journalists remained behind.[41]

The peacekeepers were now faced with the withdrawal of the Belgian contingent. Colonel Luc Marchal was incredulous. 'Under no circumstances could we leave,' he said. 'This was the point of view I expressed to my superiors until the moment when the political decision was made to leave UNAMIR. Our political leaders should have known that in leaving … we would condemn thousands of men, women and children to certain death.'

On Sunday, 17 April, Dallaire wrote a long cable to UN headquarters. It began with his thoughts on the Belgian contingent: 'These men were our best trained, experienced, equipped and motivated … even though they suffered heavily with the loss of their comrades.' He outlined his problems. 'A radical change of key staff at such a critical moment is most distressing and may cause us some serious degradation of control in the force.' He was pessimistic about a ceasefire. A report sent by two military observers who had been in Gisenyi when the genocide began estimated that in one massacre 10,000 people had died. The news was relayed to New York.[42] The RPF was adamant that the priority and the precondition of any ceasefire must be the stopping of massacres behind government lines by groups armed with machetes. The killing was the work of some soldiers, gendarmes and groups of militia who were increasingly organizing themselves. In the Rwandan army, Dallaire told New York, the hardliners had pushed aside the moderates: 'The stopping of the massacres may become more and more difficult as the local groups/militia are becoming seemingly bolder ... The ethnic killings are continuing and in fact unconfirmed reports indicate it is even increasing in scale and scope in the areas just ahead of the RPF advance.' His knowledge about events elsewhere was limited. With the departure of most of the UN military observers the mission had lost its eyes and ears: 'New York may very well know more about what is going on than UNAMIR with intelligence information (satellite, EW, etc.) from its members of the situation outside Kigali.' He explained that behind RGF lines, massacres of Tutsi, pro-democracy Hutu and sympathizers with opposition parties were taking place. Bodies littered the streets and posed a significant health hazard.

> RTLM radio broadcasts inflammatory speeches and songs exhort-ing the population to destroy all Tutsis ... It appears now that the Presidential Guard initiated the ethnic attacks and then handed this task over to the militia like the Interahamwe ... and then withdrew to Butare and Gitarama. In Kigali, frequent roadblocks are established, ID cards checked and Tutsis executed on the spot ... these massacres have been witnessed from a distance by UN troops. The militia have displayed drunkenness, drug abuse and sadistic brutality. They do not respect the UN flag, the Red Cross or any other human symbol. They will not hesitate to stop any convoy and attack its Rwandese passengers or even the UN guards. Without our present rules of engagement we are confronted with the dilemma of enforcing the security of persons under our protection. We have attempted to smuggle out small numbers and have been successful to date but it is only a matter of time until a confrontation occurs.

Dallaire was receiving a torrent of requests from expatriates who had left Rwanda and who now wanted the peacekeepers to rescue the Rwandans they had abandoned. These people were often in places where there were thousands of people. 'Any attempt to rescue, let alone even identify, the individual will lead to a mob attack,' he explained. Most of the large concentrations of people were in militia-controlled areas and the risks of rescue had to be assessed: 'Does UNAMIR risk an armed confrontation, for which we are not equipped, protected or mandated, at considerable risk to the safety of our own troops, to attempt to save these people, or do we leave them for possible extermination?'

An armed confrontation would substantially increase the threat to the peacekeepers. Any withdrawal of UN troops would then have to be undertaken under hostile conditions: 'If this mission is to be changed into a peace enforcement scenario to stop the massacres and rescue threatened civilians, then a change in mandate will be required and the mission must be reinforced with men, weapons and equipment.' Rescue and protection were more and more dangerous. The commander of the Bangladeshi contingent was under his own government's orders not to endanger his soldiers.[43] In the first hours, the Bangladeshi soldiers had run for cover to the Amahoro stadium and had even refused entry to a group of Belgian peacekeepers who were being threatened by an angry crowd. The Bangladeshis would not even allow Bangladeshis sitting in an armoured personnel carrier to help the Belgians by dispersing the crowd. Later, an internal Bangladeshi report noted: 'When the crisis began discipline deteriorated ... some soldiers refused to obey orders, arguing that ... this was not in a peacekeeping mandate ... exaggerated reports were sent back to the Ministry of Defence and there was panic ... We saw men crying. Our level of training and motivation for peacekeeping was a shame for us.'[44] Dallaire wanted the Bangladeshi troops to be withdrawn. They were a handicap and used precious resources, water and food. There were junior Bangladeshi officers who told Dallaire that if Bangladeshi troops were stopped at roadblocks with locals in the convoy, they would hand them over, rather than use their weapons. There was a widespread mistrust of this contingent, and it meant that most of the rescue missions would have to cease; with the departure of the Belgian troops it would become more and more difficult to move around the city.

The long cable from Dallaire included the paragraph:

> ... the militia and self-defence groups controlling important arteries and areas of the city ... they are a very large, dangerous and totally irrational group of people ... The force simply cannot continue to sit on the fence in the face of all these morally legitimate demands for assistance/protection, nor can it simply launch into chapter VII type of operations without the proper authority, personnel and equipment ... maintaining the status quo on manpower under these severe and adverse conditions is wasteful, dangerously casualty-causing and

demoralising to the troops ... either UNAMIR gets changes ... in
order to get into the thick of things ... or it starts to thin out.

The next day in New York, Annan and Riza began to argue the
position that with no prospect of a ceasefire they must report to the
Council that a total withdrawal of UNAMIR needed to be envisaged.[45]
Everyone was preoccupied with the civil war, including officials in the
DPKO, in the secretary-general's suite of offices on the thirty-eighth
floor, and in Security Council meetings.

There was an assumption that only a massive and dramatic intervention would succeed in Rwanda, and that this was out of the question.
No attention was given to the contribution that the peacekeepers could
continue to make, even without reinforcements. Dallaire and the deputy
force commander, Brigadier General Henry Kwami Anyidoho, knew that
reinforcements were the only answer and that stopping the killings was
far more important than bargaining for a ceasefire.

15 | GENOCIDE SPREADS

§ Colonel Luc Marchal hung on at Kigali International Airport with the last of the Belgian peacekeepers for as long as he could. Three times he ignored final orders from General José Charlier, the commander of the Belgian army. Marchal wanted to give Dallaire enough time for the Ghanaian troops to move to Kigali from the DMZ, in spite of a shortage of vehicles, and dig in.

Marchal wrote a letter to the force commander, Lieutenant General Dallaire, to tell him that he was leaving under protest. The consequences of the Belgian withdrawal were clear to them all. Marchal wanted it on record that, in his estimation, the result would be a bloodbath. Thousands of people were going to be slaughtered. He was told to keep quiet but years later his anger was undiminished: 'To dare to take this decision, and then to dare to try to persuade everyone else to adopt the same attitude, is inexplicable, inexcusable.'[1] Only weeks before, Willy Claes, the Belgian foreign minister, had visited them and praised the UN peacekeepers, telling them how vital their work was in Rwanda. Claes said then he would back them to the hilt.

Marchal handed over his command on 19 April, at 9 a.m. At 11.30 a.m., with a final salute, he boarded a plane. Dallaire said: 'I stood there as the last Hercules left ... and I thought that almost exactly fifty years to the day my father and my father-in-law had been fighting in Belgium to free the country from fascism, and there I was, abandoned by Belgian soldiers. So profoundly did I despise them for it ... I found it inexcusable.'

The Ghanaian battalion was redeployed to the airport and Canada kept a C-130 plane flying from Nairobi.[2] Without this source of resupply the garrison would have collapsed completely. There were times when Dallaire ran out of everything, even food. At one point a Canadian Hercules was sent to Somalia, to Mogadishu, to fly in Canadian rations. It was able to land only when there was a lull in the fighting; on these occasions it would wait on the runway with engines running, for between five and ten minutes, as near as possible to the airport building, allowing those who were getting out to make a dash for it. Each time it landed, Dallaire was there. His determination and obstinacy helped to persuade the Canadian government that the mission must not be abandoned.[3] It appears the pilots never received the recognition they deserved.

When the genocide began, Dallaire had been short of water and fuel. There had been no reserve stocks before 6 April, even though the issue had come up again and again in his daily reports to UN headquarters. There was no blood bank for the forces, no way of screening or storing blood and no essential drugs. Throughout the genocide, emergency electrical and communications facilities were kept operational by four UN civilian employees who had volunteered to stay behind with troops.[4]

Dallaire wondered whether the idea in New York was to weaken his mission to the point where withdrawal was the most rational action.

As the Belgian troops prepared their departure the shelling intensified, and two mortar rounds hit the airport. On Tuesday, 19 April, thirty shells were fired by the government army directly at the Amahoro stadium, killing forty-five people and injuring hundreds more. The ICRC and MSF personnel managed to get out some of the more seriously wounded people and distribute some food to others. The RPF had taken control of this whole area on 8 April, telling Dallaire that because his headquarters was sheltering the prime minister designate, Faustin Twagiramungu, rescued by peacekeepers, the UN risked an attack from the Rwandan government Para-commando unit at the airport. The presence of the RPF prevented the harassment of the people sheltering in the stadium by Rwandan government soldiers, but it encouraged almost constant shelling.

To the outside world, the killing in Rwanda continued to be portrayed as tribal, preordained and impossible to prevent, and although on 13 April the RPF had called what was happening genocide, the word does not appear to have resurfaced publicly again until 19 April, two weeks after the genocide began, when the executive director of Human Rights Watch, Kenneth Roth, wrote to Ambassador Colin Keating to point out that the killing in Rwanda was neither random nor inevitable and the atrocities were spreading: 'We urge your attention to the fact that the Rwanda military authorities are engaged in a systematic campaign to eliminate the Tutsi ... the organised campaign has become so concerted that we believe it constitutes genocide as defined by Article II of the Convention on the Prevention and Punishment of the Crime of Genocide.' Roth called on all parties to the Genocide Convention, including the five permanent members of the Security Council, to take steps to suppress and punish genocide. Roth urged that the peacekeepers be allowed to remain in place as they were essential to safeguard the estimated 25,000 Rwandans under UN protection. But genocide was not something which governments were prepared to confront. David Rawson, the US ambassador to Rwanda, now back in Washington, was quoted: 'If you get into a stalemate, and trench warfare in which the country totally exhausts itself, and there is anarchy in the countryside, then we could have taken a step backward into Somalia.'[5] In at least one US department, the fact of genocide was recognized. James Woods, the Deputy Assistant Secretary for African Affairs at the Department of Defense, said: 'Never mind that the American press, which was poorly represented anyway, hadn't quite got it right yet, at all, in fact … there was plenty of evidence around if you'd wanted to use it.' There had been information for a couple of years, Woods said, to the effect that extremists in Rwanda were planning to do something like this. 'It was known that this was planned, premeditated, carefully planned, and was being executed according to a plan with the full connivance of the then Rwandan government. This was known.'[6] An official at the State Department recalls that it was increasingly clear that the massacres amounted to genocide after the interim government had fled Kigali. By Thursday, 21 April, it was certain. 'We knew that this was a systematic effort to exterminate Tutsi … we were certain this was genocide.'[7]

§ For two weeks Rwanda's second city, Butare, had remained untouched by genocide, and thousands of people fleeing the massacres elsewhere, from the prefectures of Kigali, Gikongoro and Gitarama, sought refuge and protection there. The city had a high percentage of Tutsi, and Jean-Baptiste Habyalimana was the only Tutsi prefect in the country. Habyalimana was educated in the USA, and he had gained a PhD in engineering. He had refused a good job offer to return to Butare, which was Rwanda's intellectual heartland, and was known for its liberal traditions and ethnic tolerance. In Butare, Tutsi and Hutu had lived together for centuries. It was where the National University was located. Under its colonial name, Astrida, it had been the administrative capital of Rwanda.

A week after the killing began, on Wednesday, 13 April, RTLM announced that there were Tutsi hiding themselves among people fleeing to the prefectures of Gitarama and Butare. In response, Habyalimana, determined to calm the people, ordered that meetings be held throughout the prefecture. Four days later he was named on RTLM by Valérie Bemeriki and accused of working for the RPF. On 18 April, the interim government dismissed him and he was captured at his home and then sent to the headquarters of the interim government in Gitarama, where he was executed.[8]

Jean Kambanda, the prime minister in the interim government, travelled around the country and went to the prefectures of Gitarama, Gisenyi, Cyangugu and Kibuye to incite, encourage and direct massacres. He gave an interview to RTLM during which he said: 'the population must search out the enemy and this enemy is Tutsi and Hutu who did not agree with our [government] policy'. He was in Butare on 19 April at the inauguration of a new prefect, Sylvain Nsabimana, together with the president of the interim government, Theodore Sindikubwabo. They addressed local dignitaries and gave rousing speeches. Kambanda described what was happening as a final war: 'It must be finished ... the state, the military, the people have decided to wage this war, and to win it.'[9] Their speeches were broadcast by RTLM. The following day the new prefect held a meeting at which a discussion took place about what should happen to the 'infiltrators'. There were smaller meetings throughout the prefecture. Some time that morning a first victim was Rosalie Gicanda, the eighty-year-old widow of Mutara Rudahigwa, the King of Rwanda, who had died in 1959.[10]

Interahamwe came from Kigali by bus, and were put up in hotels near Butare airport. The Presidential Guard arrived and, as in Kigali, their first targets were selected from lists. One witness remembered how, on 21 April, people were rounded up in Butare: 'I saw them driving groups of people ahead of them, behind came the soldiers with their guns ... they took them down to the valley and killed them with nail-studded clubs, with hoes and machetes, I heard no shots ... only the cries of horror and pain.' That day, soldiers rounded up students from the National University cafeteria, and those with Tutsi identity cards were taken to the arboretum and shot. There students, representing Hutu Power, searched the university to pull Tutsi from their hiding places. Some six hundred bodies were found later in a mass grave where Tutsi students were taken. In the Groupe Scolaire, the first high school to be established in Rwanda, there were an estimated six hundred orphans and several hundred people, all attacked by Interahamwe. The people had been separated into two groups on the basis of their identity cards. It is estimated that three thousand people died here. After these attacks there was feasting, singing and dancing. The government representative in the prefecture of Butare, who was responsible for its 'pacification', was Pauline Nyiramasuhuko, the minister for the family and the advancement of women who would later stand accused of taking part in perpetrating massacres. There was evidence collated by Human Rights Watch to suggest that in the prefecture of Butare the killing was happening more frequently than anywhere else in the country. At several places, thousands of people were killed at a time, in health clinics, in schools, on playing fields, in markets.[11]

In Gikongoro, the killing began almost as soon as the prefect was replaced. The British-based African Rights estimated that in the commune of Karama, a total of 43,000 people were killed. One witness described how the parish was rocked with the deafening explosions of grenades and shooting which lasted all day inside the church and in both the secondary and primary schools, where people had gone for safety. At first the men tried to fight back, but they had only stones.[12] It is estimated that 100,000 people were killed in large-scale massacres in the prefecture of Butare. The genocide spread.

§ The secretary-general's report on Rwanda arrived at the Security Council on 21 April. It is dated 20 April, and Under Secretary-General Chinmaya Gharekhan claimed it was finalized on 19 April. It presented no new options, nor did it give a clear picture of the situation in Rwanda. It reflected the views of the interim government. It focused on civil war, and described 'anarchy and spontaneous slaughter'. The killing had been started by 'unruly members' of the Presidential Guard. It described widespread killings with both 'political and ethnic dimensions', with deaths in tens of thousands. It did not mention the organized nature of the killing of Tutsi. It claimed that murders of moderate cabinet ministers and the killing of the ten Belgian soldiers had been carried out by unruly soldiers. It made no mention of the efforts of peacekeepers and military observers to rescue and protect civilians. Boutros-Ghali clearly believed that the most important task was a ceasefire in the civil war. There was no mention of organized and extensive massacres. This report framed the violence in terms of the breakdown of the peace process. A plan to protect civilians, which had been discussed by officials in the Secretariat, was not contained in the report.

In portraying what was happening in terms of civil war, the report undermined the moral case for military intervention; military intervention in a civil war was presented as totally impractical, and would lead to a repetition of events in Somalia. The first option, an enforcement operation 'to coerce the opposing armies to stop fighting', would need the strongest possible mandate – Chapter VII of the UN Charter – and would require 'an immediate and massive reinforcement of UNAMIR'. The report noted that the UN troops had performed courageously in dangerous circumstances, but could not be left at risk indefinitely with no possibility of their performing the tasks for which they had been dispatched.[13] The two other options were either a complete withdrawal or a token group of some 270 UN military personnel to promote a ceasefire and assist in the resumption of humanitarian relief.[14]

The UK ambassador, David Hannay, expressed disappointment with the report. He had expected a choice of options based upon the opinions of the force commander and the secretary-general's Special Representative in Rwanda. He dismissed the very idea of reinforcements. The Council only had to think back to Somalia. What exactly would they be asking these troops to do? It seemed quite clear that they could not possibly wage a war against the RPF or the Rwandese troops, nor take over the country and try to deal with two heavily armed groups. If a ceasefire were to be agreed the following week, needing UN military observers, then the UK would consider such a request very seriously. He was opting for leaving a token force. They must make up their minds quickly. Some years afterwards, Hannay explained that anyone seeking to understand 'the policy paralysis' that overtook the Council could not afford to ignore 'the heavy shadow of Somalia which hung over the Council'.[15]

Nigeria disagreed and argued that there should be UN reinforcements instead. Ibrahim Gambari told them that none of their options met with his own government's approval, and what they needed to do was to work out a force level adequate to protect 14,000 people who were sheltering under the UN flag. Was the UN to do nothing to help these civilians?

There was a short recess, and in a more relaxed atmosphere a group of the non-permanent Council members had a quiet briefing from the secretary-general's Canadian military adviser, Major General Maurice Baril, who was from the same French Canadian brigade as Dallaire. From the beginning of the crisis they had been in daily telephone contact. Baril told them quietly that Dallaire was trying to feed 25,000 desperate Hutu and Tutsi fugitives living in internment-camp conditions. The peacekeepers themselves were living in the filthiest conditions. There was not a military commander in the world who would leave a force exposed in such a way. Dallaire's soldiers were 'exhausted, confused and questioning the responsibility of their superiors'. They were constantly in fear. The Bangladeshi government had warned that unless there were reinforcements with heavy equipment, including APCs, to secure the safety of the troops, they would be relocated to a neighbouring country. There was already desertion, with Bangladeshi soldiers leaving by road and taking UN vehicles. The military situation was hopeless, with the RPF advancing south, and against determined resistance. Dallaire, with the means at his disposal, was unable to defend the airport from a determined attack. The Rwandese army was strengthening its position and blocking the runway at night. The airport was the only lifeline, as the roads were lined with ambushes on both sides, especially at night. Every hour of delay in taking a decision was an hour closer to losing the airport.

Afterwards, Colin Keating said that he believed that most of the Bangladeshi contingent would vote with their feet, leaving in utter chaos. Without the strength of the Belgian contingent, UNAMIR was unsuitable for anything other than a benign environment. But Keating argued against a total UN withdrawal. If everyone left, no one would get back in. A small contingent could later be built up again. A UN presence would symbolize continued concern and preserve the Council's reputation. Keating knew that Dallaire was willing to take action to save lives. A small number of troops, in particular from Ghana, were willing to stay on. Their existing mandate – Resolution 872, which stipulated that UNAMIR maintain security in Kigali – was sufficiently flexible to allow for whatever robust action Dallaire thought necessary. The USA remained unconvinced. Their officials did not refer to Somalia, but everyone knew the atmosphere of caution regarding UN peacekeeping that existed in Washington. A major policy review was under way.

At around 10.30 p.m. on 21 April, the fifteen ambassadors filed wearily from their informal discussion room into the Security Council chamber to formally vote on Resolution 912. It was the first decision since the genocide began, and under its terms the majority of the UN peacekeepers were to be withdrawn from Rwanda, leaving behind a small group with the force commander 'to mediate between the two armies and facilitate human relief ... to the extent feasible'. The resolution was tailored to fit a situation in which a civil war had resumed.

It would later be called one of the most ignominious resolutions in Security Council history. 'It was not a resolution that went forward with any enthusiasm on my part,' Keating said. 'But I am still convinced it was the only decision.' That night a UN press release explained that UNAMIR had been 'adjusted' and the Council had now authorized a force level of approximately 270 in order to secure a ceasefire, to assist in the resumption of humanitarian relief and to 'monitor and report developments'. It was Baril who telephoned Dallaire to tell him that he could give the order, and the withdrawal had begun within hours, at first light. Within two days most of the UN peacekeepers were gone.

In recriminations later on, Chinmaya Gharekhan was scathing about Council behaviour, and how no one had wanted to take responsibility, and had preferred the secretary-general make a recommendation.

Gharekhan claimed that the secretary-general had wanted to suggest reinforcements but was told by his advisers there was not the slightest chance of the Council agreeing. 'The UN ought perhaps to have taken a moral, principled stand,' Gharekhan wrote some years later. 'This would have upset major powers, but would have kept the UN's or at least the Secretary-General's credibility intact.'[16]

Afterwards, the Council had immediately turned its focus to former Yugoslavia. The following day, on 22 April, the so-called safe haven of Gorazde fell. Gorazde was filled with some 60,000 people, one-third of whom had fled to the town from surrounding villages. The war was commanding front-page news. In the West, there was a strong lobby insisting on enforcement measures to prevent the killing of civilians. On 27 April, the Council authorized an increase in the strength of its mission, UNPROFOR, with 6,550 additional troops. The Serbs had tested the Security Council and NATO resolve. It was human rights abuses in Bosnia which would be considered to be the UN's ultimate humiliation.

§ In a clearly illegal act, Dallaire and his deputy, Brigadier Henry Kwami Anyidoho, who was the commander of the Ghanaian contingent, defied the Security Council and kept more troops than the 270 they were allowed. Lieutenant General Dallaire had asked for a residual force of 1,200, but the Council had thought otherwise. Dallaire gave everyone the option to stay or leave, and those who stayed believed that UNAMIR still had a viable role. 'We believed in Dallaire,' one of them said later, 'and we believed in this mission.' The residual force of some 470 troops comprised mostly Ghanaians, plus forty Tunisians.[17] It was troops from Ghana who ensured that UNAMIR did not capitulate, for without them no one would have been able to stay. The determination of Anyidoho and the government of Ghana did not falter, and he wrote later: 'The President, Jerry John Rawlings, fully supported my decision for the Ghanaian contingent to stay despite the fact that others decided to withdraw.'[18]

In spite of the near-hopelessness of it all, and even after the main force had pulled out, there were constant telephone calls from UN offices in New York and Geneva, from people who wanted rescue for Rwandan friends and colleagues, their former employees who were missing. The peacekeepers were wary. After one successful mission, and after seeing a group of people safely on to a Canadian C-130 on 21 April, the Kenyan authorities had sent the people back to Kigali from Nairobi. There were forty-seven of them, returned for failing to have an adequate visa or passport. The peacekeepers' anger and despair were palpable. 'Each rescue mission poses a direct threat to the lives of UNAMIR soldiers,' cabled Dallaire to New York. 'Our efforts cannot be wasted in such a way.' His peacekeepers were constantly asked to do more to help expatriates, missionaries and Rwandans who were missing. 'My force was standing knee-deep in mutilated bodies, surrounded by the guttural moans of dying people, looking into the eyes of children bleeding to death with their wounds burning in the sun and being invaded by maggots and flies. I found myself walking through villages where the only sign of life was a goat, or a chicken, or song-bird, as all the people were dead, their bodies being eaten by voracious packs of wild dogs.'[19]

The stench in the city worsened. A Polish military observer, Major Stefan Stec, described the smell of bodies as so bad that it was like living on top of rotting meat. There were thousands of unburied bodies in the streets of Kigali and a large number of scavenging animals – rats, birds and dogs – were spreading disease. Rwanda's countryside was littered with dead. Some people were dismembered and there were reports of body parts stacked neatly, and instances where the militia had joked about cutting the Tutsi down to size by chopping off their hands and feet. Laetitia Ugiriwabo, aged ten, said:

> Some people dressed in uniforms and carrying guns came into the church. They asked everybody to come out with their arms in the air … They made us sit in the sun and then searched people for money. They separated the boys from the women. They … removed baby boys from their mothers' backs … Then they macheted the men, including the babies right in front of us … they brought a tractor to take the bodies away.

In Gikongoro prefecture, in a parish called Murambi, a large-scale massacre began at dawn on 21 April. Thousands of people had been urged by Catholic priests to shelter in a technical school on a hilltop at the end of a narrow road. The priests said that all Tutsi would be safe, but Rwandan soldiers surrounded the school. The water supply was cut. When the massacre began, the Interahamwe went from building to building, throwing grenades through windows. People outside were beaten or slashed to death. There were sixty-four classrooms full of people. The killing lasted several days and thousands perished.

A survivor recalled: 'She said, "Ah, you have given birth to another *Inyenzi*" … and she picked up a stick and killed my child.'

On 22 April, a second road convoy of the ICRC reached Kigali from Burundi. It carried doctors, nurses and medical supplies. In Gitarama prefecture, two ICRC delegates had begun to try to provide care for 100 people. Two more ICRC teams had entered Rwanda from Zaire, one going to the Gisenyi area, and the other to Cyangugu, where delegates were hoping to gain access to 5,000 people in a stadium surrounded by Rwandan gendarmes and militia. The people had initially sought refuge in the cathedral and were later herded into the stadium. There were reports that sixty people, pulled out from the crowd, had been executed. Missionaries said that some 10,850 people had been killed in Cyangugu town. In a press release on 20 April, the UNHCR reported that 16,870 people had been killed in nine villages around Cyangugu. A Hutu man in Cyangugu, who opposed the CDR, had been killed by having parts of his body cut off.[20]

On 23 April, Mark Doyle, a BBC journalist who had stayed on in Rwanda and won Dallaire's respect through his persistence, reported that up to 100,000 people had been killed in Rwanda in the past eighteen days. That day, a *New York Times* editorial began: 'What looks very much like genocide has been taking place in Rwanda.' It continued: 'The wider horror is that the world has few ways of responding effectively when violence within a nation leads to massacres and the breakdown of civil order.' The paper reported how the Security Council had 'thrown in the bloodied towel'. It might be unsettling, but the withdrawal of the UN peacekeepers fairly reflected the unwillingness of most UN members to recruit a force big enough to stop a 'genocidal conflict'. Most troubling of all was the uncertain fate of thousands of Rwandans who had sought the protection of UN peacekeepers. All of them could now be slaughtered.

'Yet what other choices really exist?' the editorial asked. Somalia had proved ample warning against plunging into an open-ended 'humanitarian mission'. The USA was arguing that keeping a UN presence, however reduced, was better than nothing. 'But it is scant comfort to Rwandans who in good faith sought UN protection ... the horrors of Kigali show the need for considering whether a mobile, quick-response UN force under UN aegis is needed to deal with such calamities. Absent such a force, the world has little choice but to stand aside and hope for the best.'[21]

Two days later, on Monday, 25 April, a British emergencies officer working for Oxfam, Maurice Herson, who was on the Burundi–Rwanda border, telephoned his headquarters in Oxford and said he had talked to people fleeing to Burundi and, jotting some figures on the back of an envelope, he believed that the reported death toll of 100,000 was hopelessly misleading. Herson estimated that perhaps half a million people had been murdered in the past three weeks. The killing was planned and systematic. He did not want to use the word genocide, but it was appropriate. The next day, Tuesday, 26 April, Herson called again. He was more agitated. The UN was going to do nothing, he said, that much was clear. Even if it did, it was too late. Everyone would soon be dead.

In Oxford a serious discussion took place. Could Herson be right? Was it genocide? And if it was genocide, what should they do with such information? The press officer, John Magrath, thought Oxfam must go public, for it would at least provide a moral and legal stick with which to beat the Security Council. How else could pressure be exerted? A week earlier the Oxfam director, David Bryer, had sent a fax transmission to David Hannay at the UN, to Douglas Hurd, the UK Secretary of State for Foreign and Commonwealth Affairs, and to Baroness Lynda Chalker, who was the UK minister for overseas development. Bryer had advised them that what was needed in Rwanda was troop consolidation, reinforcements and a Chapter VII mandate. More information was arriving at Oxfam and it was grim and detailed. Alfred Sakafu, Oxfam emergencies officer, speaking by phone from Tanzania, told Magrath that hundreds of bodies were clogging the Kagera river flowing from Rwanda. Magrath wrote a press release using the word genocide, but he did not issue it. He wanted the advice of an Oxfam employee in Kigali who he believed might still be alive.

A campaign by MSF was by now under way. Keating was given a briefing by the general director of MSF-Belgium, Jean-Pierre Luxen, who advised that what was needed was the establishment of humanitarian corridors and civilian protection zones within Rwanda. Luxen described in detail the witness testimony of Dr Rony Zachariah, an MSF medical coordinator, who had been working in a hospital in Butare. Zachariah had seen forty wounded male patients dragged from the hospital by Interahamwe and soldiers. They were killed behind the hospital because they were Tutsi. Their bodies were later removed by prisoners supervised by soldiers. On the night of 22 April, all Tutsi patients had been removed from the wards to make room for wounded Presidential Guards who had been flown to Butare by helicopter from the fighting around Kigali. Zachariah had tried to ensure the security of his patients by negotia-ting with a military captain who was responsible for the welfare of the Presidential Guard, but shortly afterwards around 170 wounded Tutsi, among them children, were taken out in groups and either beaten or hacked to death. Three nurses were taken away. One of them was a Hutu but she was seven months pregnant and married to a Tutsi. 'She apparently had to be killed because her baby would be Tutsi at birth,' Zachariah had reported. 'I tried to intervene between the soldiers, but they told me that these people were on their list.' He saw that the lists were typed and several pages long. He heard one of the soldiers say, 'This hospital stinks with Tutsi. We must clean up.'[22] Zachariah had returned to Brussels determined that the perpetrators would one day be judged for this crime, and he did, eventually, give testimony for the prosecution at the International Criminal Tribunal for Rwanda (ICTR).[23] Keating duly told the Security Council what Luxen had said. The ambassadors were stunned into silence.[24] Luxen had pleaded with Keating for help for Rwanda. Keating remembers that the word genocide was used.

On the following day, 28 April, Keating received a letter from the RPF representative in New York, Claude Dusaidi, who had previously been a teacher in Canada. Dusaidi had not given up hope that the West would send reinforcements. He thought that so far the Council had failed to grasp the principle involved. In his letter he explained that a carefully planned campaign was under way to exterminate the Tutsi ethnic group. It continued: 'When the institution of the UN was created after the Second World War, one of its fundamental objectives was to see to it that what happened to the Jews in Nazi Germany would never happen again.' Dusaidi wrote that in accordance with the Genocide Convention, the international community was legally obliged to act.

But in Washington, attempts were continuing to avoid the word altogether. On Thursday, 28 April, during a press conference, a State Department spokeswoman, Christine Shelley, was asked whether what was happening in Rwanda was genocide. Shelley said:

> The use of the term genocide has a very precise legal meaning, although it's not strictly a legal determination. There are other factors in there as well ... When in looking at a situation to make a determination about that, before we begin to use that term we have to know as much as possible about the facts of the situation ... This is a more complicated issue to address, and we're certainly looking into this extremely carefully right now. But I'm not able to look at all of those criteria at this moment.

One of the journalists present, Alan Elsner of Reuters, said that, looking back on it, it sounds utterly ridiculous: 'These were all kinds of artful ways of doing nothing,' he said.[25] The only gesture was a telephone call to Colonel Théoneste Bagosora, from US Under-Secretary of State for Africa, Prudence Bushnell. She demanded he put an end to the massacres and sign a ceasefire. Bagosora's response was to send an immediate cable to the army high command to tell them of the urgent need for diplomatic action to counteract RPF lies.[26]

That same day, at a press conference in Brussels, the president of MSF-Belgium, Réginald Moreels, described the killing as genocide. And Oxfam issued a press release. The headline read: 'Oxfam fears genocide is happening in Rwanda'. It was the first UK non-governmental organization to do so. But there was hardly a flicker of interest. Another story was now grabbing the headlines. There were thousands and thousands of people pouring out of Rwanda into Tanzania in the fastest exodus the world had ever seen. Whole communities were on the move, not fleeing genocide, but the advancing RPF troops. In each of these communities on the move were groups of Interahamwe. Unlike those fleeing to the south into Burundi, these people had no wounds. At first, the Tanzanian officials had disarmed them and huge piles of machetes were to be seen at border posts.

Magrath noted how at the time large numbers of journalists had been covering the South African elections. He dryly recorded in his diary: 'The South African elections were over and all the crews were diverted to Tanzania – the refugees became the story, not the genocide.' While genocide was happening, the number of reporters in Rwanda never rose above a maximum of fifteen. In South Africa, in early May, for the inauguration of Nelson Mandela as president, there had been 2,500 accredited press representatives.[27]

The RTLM broadcasts now told the people of Rwanda that 5 May was going to be designated 'clean-up day', the day when no more Tutsi should be left in Kigali. It was the day when they planned to bury the body of Juvénal Habyarimana. Aware that the attention of the world could shift in their direction at any time, Hutu Power now attempted to tighten its grip by reactivating a civilian 'self-defence programme', ostensibly to fight the RPF. Unlike the militia, which had been controlled by political parties, the defence groups in each commune were intended to be under the control of local administrators. Perhaps Hutu Power wanted more control over the killing, making sure there were sufficient weapons, and that roadblocks would continue to be manned. These local groups could hunt Tutsi in less accessible sites than churches and schools.[28]

Dallaire warned UN headquarters that a new round of massacres was likely, and that people under UN protection would now be targeted. There had been a broadcast on RTLM that Dallaire was an RPF accomplice who had helped the RPF to infiltrate Kigali. The RPF was claiming to have intercepted the communications of the Rwandan army, revealing a plot to kill Dallaire, a plot that had the support of a member of Jacques-Roger Booh-Booh's staff. Dallaire received a call from Ottawa to tell him that a friendly government had warned that his life was at risk.

His senior officers assumed that this friendly government was the USA. If US intelligence knew this, what else did they know?[29] Canadian army command ordered Dallaire not to leave headquarters without an escort.[30] It was reported that the French were putting pressure on the Canadian government to remove Dallaire from command.

Once more, the director of Oxfam, David Bryer, wrote a message to the UK ambassador to the UN, David Hannay, in which he invoked the killing fields of Cambodia. Bryer was also desperate to alert the press to what was happening, but their focus was elsewhere.[31] Later on, research by Human Rights Watch showed that most of the large-scale massacres were almost over.[32]

§ On Friday, 29 April, the Security Council finally addressed the question of genocide. Ambassador Colin Keating, whose presidency of the Security Council was to be over at the end of the month, proposed a Presidential Statement to recognize that genocide was happening, thereby invoking the 1948 Convention on the Prevention and Punishment of the Crime of Genocide. Keating believed that if the Security Council were to officially acknowledge it, then under the terms of the convention the members of the Council were legally bound to act. All but Djibouti, Nigeria and Oman had signed the convention. Keating found support from Argentina, Spain and the Czech Republic. The Czech ambassador, Karel Kovanda, had already confronted the Council with the word genocide a day earlier, telling them it was scandalous that so far 80 per cent of Council efforts had been spent discussing withdrawing the peacekeepers, and 20 per cent trying to obtain a ceasefire in the civil war. 'It was rather like wanting Hitler to reach a ceasefire with the Jews,' he told them. What was happening in Rwanda was genocide, conducted by the interim Hutu regime. The Council had simply avoided the question of mass killing. After the meeting, diplomats from the UK and the USA took Kovanda to one side and quietly told him that on no account was he to use such inflammatory language outside the Council. It was not helpful.

A draft of the Presidential Statement was submitted. It included the paragraph:

> The horrors of Rwanda's killing fields have few precedents in the recent history of the world. The Security Council reaffirms that the systematic killing of any ethnic group, with intent to destroy it in

whole or in part constitutes an act of genocide as defined by relevant provisions of international law ... the council further points out that an important body of international law exists that deals with perpetrators of genocide.

The draft reminded the interim government of its responsibility to immediately discipline those responsible for the brutality.

There were strenuous objections to the draft. The British ambassador, David Hannay, did not want the word genocide to be used. If the word were to be used in an official UN document, then the Council would become a 'laughing stock'. To name this genocide and not to act on it would be ridiculous. Nor did the USA want the word to be used. China also argued against. And so did the Rwandan ambassador, who continued to point out that the deaths were the result of civil war. He was supported by the French ambassador, Jean-Bernard Mérimée. France was opposed to condemning only one side – the interim government – without criticism of the RPF for human rights abuses. The ambassador from Djibouti was supportive and said later that he was against the statement because it was 'sensationalist'.

Keating next tried the somewhat desperate measure of threatening a draft resolution, tabled in his national capacity. This would require a vote, and a vote was always taken in public. This would expose the positions of each country to public scrutiny. A compromise was reached. Thanks to the drafting ability of the British, known for framing resolutions with mind-numbing ambiguity, a watered-down statement was eventually issued, and while the statement quoted directly from the Genocide Convention, it did not use the word genocide.

> The Security Council condemns all the breaches of international humanitarian law in Rwanda, particularly those perpetrated against the civilian population, and recalls that persons who instigate or participate in such acts are individually responsible. The Security Council recalls that the killing of members of an ethnic group with the intention of destroying such a group in whole or in part constitutes a crime punishable by international law.

The statement recognized that the massacres were systematic, although it did not identify the targets, but it did describe how 'attacks on defenceless civilians have occurred throughout the country, especially in areas under the control of supporters of the armed forces of the interim government of Rwanda'. To satisfy demands from the French, that massacres had also been conducted by the RPF, the statement continued: 'The Security Council demands that the interim government of Rwanda and the Rwandese Patriotic Front take effective measures to prevent any attacks on civilians in areas under their control.' The statement appealed to all states to refrain from providing arms or any military assistance to the two sides in Rwanda and reiterated the call for a ceasefire. It provided that the secretary-general 'investigate serious violations of human rights law'.[33]

The close adviser of the secretary-general, Chinmaya Gharekhan, was scathing of Council behaviour, believing that it had reached the 'depths of sterile, absurd, and totally meaningless discussion'. The members of the Council were suffering from a guilt complex. This meeting, said Gharekhan, had been 'the pits'. He wrote later: 'They wanted to demonstrate to others, and to themselves, that they were concerned.' The Presidential Statement, he said, was 'rubbish'.[34]

For hours the Council had discussed the use of the word genocide – from 11 a.m. until the final vote the following day at 1.15 a.m. on Saturday, 30 April. Keating said: 'We ended April exhausted but hopeful that the first few weeks of May would bring action to reinforce UNAMIR with a real force capable of doing what Dallaire had been urging.'

§ On the day of the lengthy debate, Boutros Boutros-Ghali, suddenly, recommended a reversal of the decision to withdraw the peacekeepers. In a letter to the Council he suggested that they reconsider Resolution 912, which had mandated a reduction in the force levels. Boutros-Ghali was apparently regretting that he had not thrown his full weight behind the first alternative – to reinforce, a suggestion from his report a week earlier. He told the Council that the force commander had reported a further deterioration in Kigali. There was a humanitarian catastrophe. He urged them to think about what action, including forceful action, was necessary to restore law and order and to put an end to the massacres: 'Such action would require a commitment of human and material resources on a scale which the member states have so far proved reluctant to contemplate. But I am convinced that the scale of human suffering in Rwanda and its implications for the stability of neighbouring countries leaves the Security Council with no alternative but to examine this possibility.'

The letter was greeted with silence. Gharekhan claimed afterwards that the Council would have liked to ignore the letter but the media were already talking about it.[35] Others were surprised by the secretary-general's continuing failure to suggest detailed options to the Council. Options for action had been discussed at length by officials, and with the force commander. Why Boutros-Ghali failed at this stage to guide the Council has never been explained. And now, in a largely unnoticed press release issued in New York, the RPF announced that the time for UN intervention was past. The genocide was almost complete. The RPF was now insisting on the removal of the Special Representative, Jacques-Roger Booh-Booh, insisting he be replaced by someone more competent. The RPF demanded that Boutros-Ghali should urge all countries to ostracize the perpetrators of massacres. Two extremists had been openly welcomed on a visit to Paris on 27 April, Jérôme Bicamumpaka, the foreign minister, and Jean-Bosco Barayagwiza, the leader of the CDR. They had met the prime minister, Edouard Balladur, the foreign minister, Alain Juppé, and Bruno Delaye, who was the head of the Africa Unit in the Elysée.[36] President Habyarimana's widow, Agathe, was now living in a luxury apartment in Paris, and she made an official visit to Cairo from 17 until 23 June, when she was accorded full diplomatic honours and given the Salon d'Honneur at Cairo's airport.[37] The contact between Lieutenant Cyprien Kayumba, chargé d'affaires at the Rwandan embassy in Paris, and Jean-Pierre Huchon, head of the military mission at the French Ministry of Cooperation, was frequent.[38] In May, Huchon received Lieutenant Colonel Ephrem Rwabalinda, chief adviser to the Rwandan chief of staff.

Prunier testifies that there were frantic efforts being made by officials in the Africa Unit to 'save their allies'. The French government was secretly delivering ammunition to the Rwandan army.[39] This was later denied. According to French officials, there were no legal and official deliveries of weapons to Rwanda after 8 April. The RPF later discovered that the governments of France and Egypt had hosted high-level talks with members of the interim government and appeared 'to be masterminding the current proposal for the deployment of a UN intervention force as a result of those talks'. The RPF wanted both Egypt and France to be censured.[40]

It was business as usual for the extremists, relying on two important allies – France and Egypt. Throughout the genocide, with money looted from government coffers, the extremists resupplied their stocks of weapons on the open arms market. There are letters and invoices, bank statements and money transfers, a paper trail to show that, once the genocide was under way, $US13 million of Rwandan government money passed through the Banque Nationale de Paris. Money was also transferred from the government system to Rwandan embassies in Washington, Moscow, Kinshasa, Bonn and Tokyo and to the Rwandan consulate in Pretoria.[41] Four days after the genocide began, the newly installed interim government made contact with Mil-Tec, a company with offices in London, to order $854,000-worth of arms and ammunition; later, the interim government paid a total of US$4 million to this company for arms shipped on 18 April, 25 April, 5 May and 20 May.[42] In the murky depths of arms trafficking, the paper trail always ends up offshore, and Mil-Tec was incorporated in Douglas, the Isle of Man, with a correspondence address in Hove, East Sussex. It bought and flew weapons to Hutu Power from countries all over the world. As an offshore company it was exempt from a UN arms embargo imposed by the Security Council on 17 May.[43] Under British law, UN arms embargoes are enforced by means of statutory instruments, and on 24 June 1994, when the arms embargo statute was drafted by government lawyers, they failed to include the Crown dependencies in the enabling legislation.[44] Thanks to this loophole thousands of rounds of ammunition, bombs and grenades were flown by Mil-Tec from eastern Europe and from Israel.[45]

As far as is known, not one single British-manufactured weapon was shipped, so no export licences would have been necessary. The arms did not arrive in, nor did they leave, the UK. In Britain, with the shipment of weapons from third countries, there was then no obligation to report arms sales. The Security Council set up an inquiry into the arming of the former Rwandan government forces.[46] This International Commission of Inquiry was chaired by Ambassador Mahmoud Kassem of Egypt, an appointment made by Boutros-Ghali, to collect information and investigate reports relating to the supply of arms to former Rwandan government forces.[47]

One arms sale uncovered by this commission concerned Colonel Théoneste Bagosora, who, during the genocide in May, had negotiated an arms deal in the Seychelles. The government of the Seychelles had been acting on the basis of an end-user certificate issued by the government of Zaire, authorizing the sale. A Nigerian-registered aircraft carrying arms from Malta to Goma on 25 May 1994 included Bagosora among its passengers.

Research undertaken by the arms division of Human Rights Watch established that on five occasions in May and June 1994 weapons were delivered to the Rwandan government army through neighbouring Goma, and that these arms came from the French government or French companies operating under government licence.[48] The French government strenuously denied this.

16 | THE WORLD SHUTS THE DOOR

§ Towards the end of April, a logistician with Médecins Sans Frontières (MSF) France, René Caravielhe, watched as a young boy slowly approached the International Committee of the Red Cross (ICRC) hospital in Kigali. The boy had bare feet and he was wearing a dirty Coca-Cola T-shirt and ragged trousers. He was not crying, but he looked sickened. The boy told Caravielhe that there had been a massacre not 500 metres from the hospital and two children were still alive. He told Caravielhe where the place was but he would not go himself.

When Caravielhe and a colleague reached the spot they found a gang surrounding the bodies of a family, and spitting on them. Caravielhe later wrote the following description:

> Jean de Dieu, eleven, was curled up, a ball of flesh and blood, the look in his eyes was a glance from nowhere ... without vision; Marie-Ange, aged nine, was propped up against a tree trunk ... her legs apart, and she was covered in excrement, sperm and blood ... in her mouth was a penis, cut with a machete, that of her father ... [nearby] ... in a ditch with stinking water were four bodies, cut up, piled up, their parents and older brothers. We took the two children in our arms and we were about to put them in the car when a jeep came past, full of men with weapons, and they started to laugh sadistically. The fact that we had children in our arms did not temper their aggression, and we had to go through the same sort of palaver as usual ... There was a torrential downpour which was fortunate, and we were allowed to put the children in the car and we left for the hospital ... [one day] another word will have to be coined more terrible than the word horror, in order to describe this sort of thing ... this sort of thing was a daily experience for volunteers still in Rwanda. To get back to the hospital we had to go through roadblocks where there were children, grenade in one hand and a machete in another.[1]

After several days, Jean de Dieu told them his age. He explained that boys and men had put their penises in his mouth and then they had beaten him. He had watched while these men killed his parents and hurt his sister. Marie-Ange came out of her coma some days later. She refused to eat or drink but she did find the will to live, probably because she was among other children. Caravielhe ended his dispatch with the words 'the laughter of children, although they are amputees, is the strongest medicine in the world'.

As April came to an end, the ICRC issued the most strongly worded statement in its history. In a clear message to the Security Council the statement demanded that everything be done to put an end at once to the 'terrifying mechanism' of the killing. Whole families were being exterminated in the most atrocious circumstances. The ICRC was providing a drop of humanity in an ocean of appalling suffering.[2]

On Saturday, 30 April, in an interview reported by Reuters, Lieutenant General Dallaire said that unless the international community took action, it would be unable to defend itself against accusations of doing nothing to stop genocide, but later, in a coded cable, officials at UN headquarters questioned his use of the word. That same day, Dallaire travelled 80 miles east of the city to Byumba for a two-hour meeting with Major General Paul Kagame. Dallaire carried with him a ceasefire proposal from the interim government providing for a return of both armies to the positions of 6 April, an end to massacres, and a return for all displaced people.

Kagame was scathing. This whole idea, he said, had been devised by the French at a recent and secret meeting in Kinshasa with the interim government. 'You are the representative of the UN here,' Kagame said. 'You know who's doing what and who says what.' Dallaire said that the time might have come for UNAMIR to be reinforced. Kagame told him it was too late; it would be an empty gesture. Only the RPF could put an end to the massacres. Nothing would be allowed to slow his advance. If UN peacekeepers came between the RPF and the government troops, then they would be treated as the enemy and engaged. Kagame said that his aim was to save as many people as possible from the killing machine that had been set up in the interim government zone. This whole thing was the UN's fault for failing to provide the right mandate at the right moment. The RPF had consistently brought to everyone's attention the alarming preparations for these massacres. Everyone had been warned.[3]

The RPF was gaining ground, infiltrating men and material into Kigali at night and slowly and systematically expanding their area of control. The RPF drove government forces back into their camps, seizing key terrain and dominating key crossroads. Dallaire described this military advance in a cable to New York: 'The blitzkrieg nature of their offensive as was seen in the first days of the war has slowed and has been methodical in its application with the focus of their main effort the strangling and capture of Kigali.'

§ On Sunday, 1 May, Rwandan soldiers, convalescing in a hospital in Butare, had slaughtered twenty-one children, the survivors of other massacres, and thirteen Rwandan Red Cross workers trying to protect them.[4] The children had been segregated by their killers into Hutu and Tutsi. The killings were reported by Peter Smerdon of Reuters, who also described how UN peacekeepers had tried unsuccessfully to escort some of the 300 people who were trapped at the Hôtel des Mille Collines in Kigali.[5]

The people sheltering in the hotel were mostly well-connected Tutsi and pro-democracy Hutu. There were doctors, journalists, a senator, business people and students. The hotel had harboured the five children of the prime minister after the assassination of their mother on 7 April. They had been hunted down; a dozen soldiers and militia had come to the hotel lobby looking for them. These soldiers had threatened that each and every door in the hotel would be blown apart until the children were handed over. Only a Senegalese peacekeeper, Captain Mbaye Diagne, persuaded them otherwise, and they had gone away. That night the children were evacuated in a French convoy and Switzerland accepted them as refugees.[6] Those taking refuge in the hotel were under constant threat. The manager, Paul Rusesabagina, said that he was once told by an army officer to get everyone out of the hotel in thirty minutes. Rusesabagina asked where the people would go, and he said afterwards that he was told that this was not his problem. Using the one working telephone line, Rusesabagina, who was in close touch with senior army officers, claimed that he managed to get the threat lifted.[7] In reality, it was a group of Tunisian peacekeepers who kept the military and militia at bay. A feature film, *Hotel Rwanda*, released in 2004, is said to have been based on events here, but it does not recognize the righteous stand and heroism of those UN officers who stood at the entrance.[8]

On Tuesday, 3 May, an attempt was made to get some of the people out of the hotel to the airport. A UN military observer, Major Stefan Stec, had stood in the lobby and read out the names of those allowed to go. 'I had a Schindler's list of the people we were allowed to save,' he said, 'only those with the right visas to enter Belgium.' A few blocks away, at the St Famille church, there were 5,000 starving people. Every night militia came to kill. 'We did nothing for them because no one there had any visas,' Stec recalled.[9] There were similar sites with large concentrations of people throughout the city, and an increasing number elsewhere, and by mid-May there were ninety-one such sites – with only enough UNAMIR soldiers to stand guard at four of them.[10] Lieutenant General Dallaire sent patrols several times a day to orphanages, schools and churches. He hoped that a military observer presence would deter the killers, and just as at the Mille Collines, it seemed to work. The need was so dire that he ordered military observers to spend the night with the most threatened refugees.[11]

The convoy that was to leave the Hôtel des Mille Collines was readied by Ghanaian peacekeepers, but the Interahamwe got wind of the plan. An instant broadcast over RTLM radio announced the names of the people – some of them well known – who were going on the convoy. A mile into the journey, at a checkpoint manned by Presidential Guards, the convoy was stopped. Everyone in the first car was ordered to get out and sit down on the road. The luggage was looted. Then François-Xavier Nsanzuwera, who was a Hutu, and Rwanda's deputy attorney-general, was rifle-butted to the floor.

'They beat everyone very badly … some young women suffered very serious injuries … they slapped children who cried,' remembered Nsanzuwera.[12] The Interahamwe arrived and one of them shot at Nsanzuwera but missed. One bullet hit a Presidential Guard. Nsanzuwera remembers how the peacekeepers with the convoy had sought protection in their vehicles. The prefect of Kigali, Tharcisse Renzaho, had intervened and ordered the convoy to return to the hotel.

There were by now an estimated twenty thousand people trapped in Kigali, starving and desperate. There were thousands of people taking refuge in two Catholic churches, St Paul and St Famille, and in the Hôtel Méridien and the King Faisal hospital, a recently built medical facility in the RPF zone, which had never opened. Each night the Interahamwe came to drag people away. In mid-April, at the St Famille church, the Interahamwe and Presidential Guard selected 120 men and boys, one by one, and called out their names from lists. They were taken outside and shot. Most victims were political activists, businessmen, students or young men who looked like Tutsi.[13] Again, in mid-June, sixty teenage boys were chosen – two boys who turned out to be Hutu were released and then two more chosen in their place – and herded to a pit outside the church compound to be killed. The crime was described to a UN military observer by a priest. When the observer relayed the news at UNAMIR headquarters, an RPF colonel who was there for talks, Frank Mugambage, wept. Four days afterwards, UN peacekeepers mounted an operation to rescue as many as they could from St Famille. There was a scramble for the buses and trucks and terrible scenes as people were clubbed by government soldiers who were insisting that names be read from a list. People pleaded for rescue. One small boy, no older than five, had run past the guards and leapt on to a flat-bed truck as it drove away. The onlookers cheered. A later rescue mission from the church by RPF rebel forces, operating well within enemy territory, and with carefully planned artillery support, took 600 people to safety.[14]

§ Just after capturing the town of Rusumo on the Tanzanian border on 4 May, Major General Paul Kagame met with Western journalists. They asked him why there was no ceasefire. Kagame said that the interim government was a 'clique of murderers' and a ceasefire was impossible without an immediate end to the massacres. He wanted the Presidential Guard disbanded and RTLM shut down.

Rwanda was nearing the top of the foreign news schedules now, owing to the massive exodus across the Tanzanian border. On Sunday, 1 May, a quarter of a million people crossed into Tanzania in twenty-four hours, creating the world's largest refugee camp. The images of this mass movement of people were spectacular and there was demand for news coverage.[15] The front page of the *New York Times* carried a report about how officials in the Clinton administration were examining ways of 'helping to organize and pay for military intervention in Rwanda by neighbouring African countries'. The idea was at a preliminary stage.[16]

Some journalists stood on the bridge over the Kagera river at the Rusumo Falls, and had watched as bodies passed by underneath. A BBC producer, Tom Giles, who had just flown from London to cover the refugee crisis, later wrote about seeing: '... bodies by the dozen, bloated and obscene ...' Towns and villages lay abandoned. 'For nearly three weeks in April,' Giles wrote, 'after its first days had passed, the story of one of the Twentieth Century's worst crimes had failed – in an age of global satellite broadcasting – to make the top of the TV news bulletins.' It would take another six weeks before the full graphic horror of the genocide would be broadcast on the BBC.[17] A British print journalist at Rusumo Falls noted: 'Hundreds and hundreds must have passed down the river in the past week and they are still coming,' and then in an effort to explain what was happening the journalist wrote: 'A terrible genocidal madness has taken over Rwanda. It is now completely out of control.'[18]

As their invasion continued, the RPF soldiers were discovering that their promised land had the foulest stench, and was mostly empty. There were Tutsi, children and women, with terrible machete wounds coming to their bases. Kagame, in an interview some years later, said that he had never seen the world more hopeless or helpless. He stopped looking at the massacre sites. He feared the effect on his actions.[19] 'All those claiming to be civilized had turned their backs ... I knew that we were alone,' he said. They would have to sort out the problem themselves. 'I developed contempt for those people in the world who claimed to stand for values of moral authority,' he added.

In the first week in May, the UN secretary-general, Boutros Boutros-Ghali, assumed a higher profile. Having publicly called for reinforcements at the end of April, he now appeared on US television, on ABC *Nightline*, interviewed from Geneva by Ted Koppel.[20] Koppel began: 'Tonight, Rwanda. Is the world just too tired to help?' He reminded viewers of the thousands of deaths of the recent past – in former Yugoslavia, in East Timor, in Angola, in Burundi, in Tajikistan and Nagorno-Karabakh. Rwanda had the misfortune to come at the tail-end of a particularly noxious stretch of history. A film clip showed President Bill Clinton, that same day, who had been asked about Rwanda. 'Lesson number one is, don't go into one of these things and say, as the US said when we started in Somalia, "Maybe we'll be done in a month because it's a humanitarian crisis" ... Because there are almost always political problems and sometimes military conflicts, which bring about these crises.'

Before the *Nightline* interview went live, Boutros-Ghali told Koppel that a modest reinforcement of 5,000 troops could have prevented the slaughter. This surprised Koppel, who remembered that, only a week earlier, the Security Council had decided to withdraw soldiers from UNAMIR. On air, Boutros-Ghali explained to Koppel some of the problems involved in obtaining troops for Rwanda. He had written letters to heads of state all over the world asking for troops. Koppel asked him why it was taking so long. Boutros-Ghali explained that there was a general fatigue, and that there had been the same reaction to requests for troops for all peacekeeping operations. Rwanda, however, required intervention. He added: 'because it is a question of genocide ... I am sure that we have the capacity to intervene'.

Ted Koppel: 'You appealed to the Security Council the other day?'

Boutros-Ghali: 'Yes, Friday ...'

Ted Koppel: 'For direct intervention ... You got absolutely nowhere with them.'

Boutros-Ghali: 'We have to repeat the appeal ...'

He said that if troop offers came from African countries, then this might encourage other nations to help. But leadership over Rwanda rested with the Security Council. It was up to the major countries, the permanent members.

The next day in Washington, the position of the Clinton administration became clearer during a press conference given by the National Security Adviser, Anthony Lake. Lake explained that America could not solve other people's problems. Nor could America build their states for them.

> When I wake up every morning and look at the headlines and the stories and the images on television of these conflicts, I want to work to end every conflict. I want to work to save every child out there. And I know the President does, and I know the American people do. But neither we nor the international community have the resources, nor the mandate to do so. So we have to make distinctions. We have to ask the hard questions about where and when we can intervene … these kinds of conflicts are particularly hard to come to grips with and to have an effect on from outside, because basically, of course, their origins are in political turmoil within these nations. And that political turmoil may not be susceptible to the efforts of the international community. So, neither we nor the international community have either the mandate, or the resources, or the possibility of resolving every conflict of this kind.[21]

The press conference marked the publication of the first comprehensive review of US policy towards multilateral peace operations. The review, months in preparation, and post-Somalia, was known as Presidential Decision Directive number 25 (PDD-25), and it set strict limits on future US involvement with the UN. From now on this would depend on certain criteria: whether or not US interests were at stake, whether or not there was a threat to world peace, a clear mission goal, acceptable costs, congressional, public and allied support, a working ceasefire, a clean command and control and a clear exit point. Rwanda failed every criterion bar one: the USA would consider contributing to a UN peacekeeping operation if there was 'urgent humanitarian disaster coupled with violence'.

The directive reflected the view from the Pentagon that there was only one mission for an army: to fight and win its nation's wars. The former chairman of the Joint Chiefs of Staff, General Colin Powell, when once asked about a UN standing army, had replied: 'As long as I am chairman of the Joint Chiefs of Staff, I will not agree to commit American men and women to an unknown war, in an unknown land, for an unknown cause, under an unknown commander, for an unknown duration.'[22] Rwanda was the first UN operation to come up against the presidential directive.[23]

At a press conference in Kampala, Uganda, President Yoweri Museveni accused the interim government of using genocide to eliminate the opposition. This government was a criminal band, not unlike the Nazis. If people understood what was going on in Rwanda, then the whole of the international community would hunt down the perpetrators.

§ Lieutenant General Dallaire sent a cable to headquarters on Friday, 6 May, to warn that the civil war was intensifying. The RPF had launched a major attack and the city centre had been bombed. A Canadian transport plane had been forced to take off within minutes of touching down. The interim government, via the prime minister, Jean Kambanda, was calling for mass mobilization. 'We have men, munitions, a united government, a united army and we have to win,' he announced. Everyone must be armed, Kambanda said, with the provision of weapons a government priority, even if this prevented the 'normal importation of goods'. Kambanda was speaking from the safety of Kibuye. A month earlier, in Kibuye prefecture, there had been a quarter of a million Tutsi. By the time Kambanda made this broadcast, it is estimated that more than 200,000 of them had been killed.

A month had passed since the genocide began. There were no options for action. The presidency of the Security Council in May had fallen to the Nigerian ambassador, Ibrahim Gambari, and he asked the UN secretary-general, Boutros Boutros-Ghali, for 'contingency planning' regarding the delivery of human assistance and support for the displaced people in Rwanda. A resolution was presented to the Council by Spain, New Zealand, Argentina and the Czech Republic – calling for reinforcements. But the UK and the USA argued that future action in Rwanda should be taken primarily through the efforts of African countries. In the opinion of the UK ambassador, David Hannay, the Organization of African Unity (OAU) had a 'key role to play'.

But Boutros-Ghali had already approached the OAU, and consulted with Hosni Mubarak, the president of Egypt, appointed the next OAU chairman. The OAU secretary-general, Salim Ahmed Salim, had received a letter from Boutros-Ghali requesting that African states contribute troops. In response, Salim Ahmed Salim had pointed out that given the magnitude of the Rwandan tragedy, there should be efforts under UN auspices, with all that implied in terms of political engagement and resource commitment. 'This has been the practice in other situations of dire need elsewhere in the world. It must not be set aside in the case of Africa,' he wrote.

A first and tentative official recognition of genocide came in the first week of May when the UN Human Rights Commissioner, José Ayala Lasso, in a press conference in Geneva, said that he was 'inclined to accept' the definition. Lasso was going to Rwanda to see for himself, and to gather information.[24] His was a new appointment.[25] The idea of appointing a commissioner, a human rights supremo, had come a year earlier, at a landmark human rights conference held in June 1993 – the World Conference on Human Rights, held in Vienna, Austria. There had been 7,000 participants and 800 organizations that had hoped to forge 'a new vision for global action on human rights', and the appointment was intended to give human rights a higher profile. The idea had found enthusiastic support within the administration of President Bill Clinton. Lasso, the first incumbent, was a former Ecuadorean foreign minister, appointed by Boutros-Ghali, and he had no human rights background.

Lasso stayed two days in Rwanda, 11–12 May, during which time he met Colonel Théoneste Bagosora and Major General Augustin Bizimungu, chief of staff. Bizimungu told Lasso that he would do all he could to ensure that 'hostages' in Rwanda were freed, but he did not control the militia. Lasso went to the Hôtel des Mille Collines and watched as Bizimungu assured everyone 'in the presence of the UN's most senior human rights official' that all the people there would soon be set free. Bizimungu explained that the killings were due to the spontaneous anger of the people at the assassination of their president. Lasso met Major General Paul Kagame. Kagame told him that the entire international community should be calling for an end to the killings. In an appeal on Radio Rwanda, Lasso said both sides should cease hostilities and allow 'the population to go to the destination of their choice'.

Lasso wrote a report when he got back to Europe appealing to both sides to avoid human rights abuses.[26] He described 'wanton killing' of more than 200,000 innocent civilians. He noted all the relevant international human rights instruments, to which Rwanda was a party, including the Convention on the Prevention and Punishment of the Crime of Genocide.[27] He was no more specific than this.

A more direct approach came from the president of the ICRC, Cornelio Sommaruga, who wrote an article for the *International Herald Tribune*, in which he condemned the press and governments for failing to give Rwanda the attention it warranted. All states had a responsibility to act.[28] The ICRC was building a larger presence, in five locations – in

Kigali, Byumba, Gisenyi, Kabgayi and Kibungo – and the delegates were witness to the most appalling suffering of thousands of sick and wounded people who were continually at risk of brutal murder at the hands of soldiers and militia. Sommaruga had spoken with Philippe Gaillard. Gaillard had travelled to Kabgayi, where 30,000 people were trapped, the families who fled massacres elsewhere in the prefecture of Gitarama, and near the headquarters of the interim government. The ICRC had opened a sous-delegation in Kabgayi on 12 May. When they arrived the militia slaughtered seven people in front of them.[29]

Kabgayi, an imposing convent on a hilltop with a large church and several buildings, was known as the Vatican of Rwanda. But now people were crammed so tightly into the primary and secondary school and the health centre that they could not move. There was no clean water and hardly any food. About a dozen people a day died from starvation and the corpses were bloated and unburied. A foul stench was everywhere.

'Every day soldiers came to the camp to take away Tutsi to kill ... at night soldiers went through the classrooms looking for victims ... it was terror time ... in addition to killing people they came to take girls and women to be raped and afterwards they were brought back,' a survivor recalled. Near by there was a hospital where wounded government soldiers were treated, and some of them would come to the camps to kill Tutsi for sport. The militia once took people away in stolen Red Cross vehicles.

Kabgayi was later described as a concentration camp. 'There were unburied corpses ... everyone coughed, as dust and dirt seeped into their lungs,' a foreign correspondent, James Schofield, wrote. The ICRC delegates were forbidden from going inside the camp and lived in a house outside the camp perimeter.[30]

Sam Kiley of *The Times* had also been to Kabgayi and published a description on 14 May. He had interviewed Father Vjeko Curic, who had a reputation as the only white man south of Kigali. A Franciscan priest from Bosnia, he was trying to find food for Kabgayi. He had negotiated his way through thirty roadblocks during his journey from the border with Burundi. He had seen hillsides literally covered with bodies, and he thought that half a million people had been killed.[31] Kiley met a representative of the interim government, Pauline Nyiramasuhuko, the minister of the family and women's affairs. She told Kiley that the Rwandans were a peaceful people but that the militia had been armed in order to weed out 'Tutsi extremist infiltrators' sent by the RPF. The Tutsi plan, she said, was to exterminate all the Hutu. Kiley spoke with Major General Augustin Bizimana, the minister of defence. Bizimana told Kiley that that people had been afraid they would be wiped out by the Tutsi and RPF infiltrators. Bizimana admitted that innocent people had been killed, and these had included Tutsi who supported the interim government, and Tutsi who had never even heard of the RPF. The armed forces were beginning to gain control of the militia. 'It's very difficult to end these hatreds,' he said.

Gaillard tried to persuade ministers in the interim government to see Kabgayi for themselves: 'They [the interim government] were disorganized, they were powerless and incapable of putting a stop to the murdering madness of systematic massacre they had helped to organize ... some of them.' Gaillard described the poor of Rwanda as the damned of the earth, for they had accepted, like manna from heaven, the racist insanities pouring over the airways.

The MSF-France doctor Jean-Hervé Bradol was by now back in Paris, where his organization was conducting a concerted press campaign to explain that genocide was happening and to make the case for urgent military intervention, not to stop civil war, but to put an end to the killing. On 16 May, Bradol appeared on French television news to say that the deaths in Rwanda were not the result of a civil war but of a deliberate and planned extermination. The MSF had never seen killing such as this. The French government bore a special responsibility for having armed and trained the perpetrators. The newscaster, Patrick Poivre d'Arvor, seemingly surprised, ended his interview describing what was happening in Rwanda as a 'veritable genocide'.[32] On 18 May, MSF-France took a page in the newspaper *Le Monde* to print an open letter to President Mitterrand to point out that doctors could not stop genocide. France must take action immediately to protect the population of Rwanda.

§ A detailed plan to protect the sites where people were sheltering was sent to UN headquarters on 12 May by Lieutenant General Dallaire. He had been told that at a recent informal meeting of the Security Council, the UK ambassador had insisted that before any resolution to address Rwanda's humanitarian emergency, there had to be a formal document and a budget. Dallaire's cable included a map showing ninety-one sites, and the name of each one, where a total estimated number of 756,000 people were trapped and in danger. They urgently needed protection. Dallaire suggested that rather than waiting, and losing time, the paperwork could be done afterwards. A locally overwhelming presence of UN forces was needed.[33]

The Security Council, having requested a further report from

Secretary-General Boutros Boutros-Ghali, waited a week for it to arrive. When it did, the day following Dallaire's cable, 13 May, it contained details of an original plan, already prepared by Dallaire, to airlift a standing brigade, some 5,500 well-armed and trained soldiers, into Kigali, to protect civilians at risk, and provide security for humanitarian operations. This was a minimum viable force.[34] Boutros-Ghali told the Council that for such an operation to work, the troops had to be highly mobile. The operation would be called UNAMIR II, and would require sixteen helicopters and teams of military and civilian police. The key to success was speed of deployment, and it was intended that the troops be airlifted as soon as the Council authorized the resolution. The longer the delay, the greater the risk of not achieving its purpose. Protected sites could be patrolled and monitored by peacekeepers. The airport could become a neutral zone under the control of the UN. The operation could begin with the immediate dispatch to Kigali of 800 soldiers from the Ghanaian battalion who had been evacuated to Nairobi when UNAMIR was reduced, and who were currently languishing in an aircraft hangar, but these troops had to be provided with the protection of APCs. If countries could provide already formed infantry brigades, this would mean that deployment could be rapid.[35]

There were immediate complaints from US diplomats. Madeleine Albright, the US ambassador, was now championing the new Presidential Directive on peacekeeping, and in accordance with this directive her staff argued that the plan for Rwanda was inadequate and lacking in field assessments. She agreed with the UK that there must be more detailed preparations, a clearer concept of operations, a breakdown in the costs, and an idea of the duration of any mandate. The USA suggested, albeit discreetly, that the plan, rather than a serious strategy for a realistic and do-able mission, was a public relations exercise by Boutros-Ghali. Boutros-Ghali was openly critical of the Security Council for 'shocking behaviour' and for meekly following the US lead in denying the reality of the genocide. He was particularly scathing about Albright. She was always waiting for instructions from Washington. 'As the Rwandan genocide continued, she was apparently just following orders,' he wrote later.[36] He said subsequently that the blame for the inaction over Rwanda rested with the USA. They were prevailing upon governments to with-hold relatively trivial sums to stop genocide.[37]

Throughout May there were determined attempts by the UN's Department of Peacekeeping Operations (DPKO) to obtain both troops and military equipment for Rwanda. If armoured personnel carriers could be found, then the Ghanaian battalion could return to Kigali.

There were urgent requests for APCs sent to a total of forty-four member states known to have a spare military capacity. Then, on 28 May, a call came from an official in the Pentagon. The USA had forty-eight APCs in storage in Germany. If the UN wanted them, they could be leased for $US4 million. The USA already owed the UN more than 1 billion dollars in back dues. This was the only offer and so negotiations started in order to move the APCs at once. The Pentagon then insisted that only when the lease was signed could the transport of the equipment begin, and then it would take two weeks to get the APCs to Uganda, which had the nearest large airport. The Pentagon organized its own transport from the storage location in Germany to Uganda – at an extra charge to the UN of US$6 million. When the equipment arrived at Entebbe there were no heavy machine guns or radios, rendering them useless in terms of a self-defence capability. The UN came under a barrage of criticism for incompetence and waste in its procurement of equipment, yet it was later discovered that a commercial contractor would have delivered the APCs to Entebbe for much less than the USA charged. Three months later, in August 1994, the APCs were still in Entebbe. There were no trucks large enough to transport them to Rwanda.[38]

The UK offer for Rwanda was fifty Bedford trucks, but the money for them had to be paid by the UN up front. It was weeks before they arrived, and Dallaire recalled how they were fit only as museum relics.[39]

The possibility of Dallaire having to fight his way out of Rwanda was a very real and very desperate option that was prepared for, and nearly executed, on at least two occasions.[40] The tiny garrison ran out of all supplies at one point, and they packed everything up. There was pressure from New York to pull out, but Dallaire kept repeating that it was not an option.

The ghost of Gordon of Khartoum was watching over him, he said, for no one and no supplies were coming at all. 'Dying in Rwanda without sign or sight of relief was a reality that we faced on a daily basis for several desperate weeks,' he said.[41]

Annan and Riza respected his position and were prepared to listen to him. No matter how hard anyone tried, one of his officers said, there was nothing anyone could do to budge him. Dallaire said that his most powerful weapon in Rwanda had been his obstinacy.[42]

Another cable was sent from Kigali to headquarters, written on 15 May, pointing out that the ninety-one camps where people were trapped were desperately short of water, food and medical supplies.[43]

§ While the Rwandan government forces located their mortar base close to refugee camps the RPF was dug in near the Amahoro stadium, the King Faisal hospital and UN headquarters. This RPF position drew fire and there were daily casualties from shelling. The front line divided the city.[44] There were meetings between UNAMIR, the Rwandan army, the gendarmerie and the RPF to try to guarantee the safety of the imprisoned people. Dallaire continued his efforts to broker temporary ceasefires or truces, even for the shortest duration, to allow the rescue of civilians. Sometimes the peacekeepers were too late; one mission in early May to rescue a UN employee in hiding with her five children and five orphans found them all murdered. Neighbours described men with machetes in civilian clothes as the perpetrators.

The people sheltering in Kigali became hostages to be traded. The RPF was holding thousands of Hutu prisoners. It took endless discussions with the Rwandan government forces and the RPF and each person had to be counted, documented and verified with militias informed and trucks arranged. It could take days. One militia with one rifle could turn a transfer into disaster.[45] In one successful operation, peacekeepers escorted 300 Tutsi, exchanging them for 200 Hutu. Gerry McCarthy of UNICEF, who had come to Kigali as part of a four-man joint UN–agency cell, recalled that during one of these exchanges in which 200 Tutsi teenage boys were rescued, a group of Tutsi children had been left behind in a car park.[46] They were quickly surrounded by Interahamwe. McCarthy and colleagues negotiated their rescue. It took them more than an hour.[47]

On Tuesday, 17 May, the Security Council at last passed a resolution providing a first official recognition that the peacekeepers might have to take action to defend the people in their care. In Resolution 918, voted late at night, 5,500 reinforcements were authorized for UNAMIR. It was widely welcomed as a landmark, but in reality it was a sham. No equipped troops were available for Rwanda, and, even if there had been, there was no airlift. Nor was there an agreed plan for what they would do when they got there. The New Zealand ambassador wrote that night to his capital: 'As you will see, the US has essentially gutted the resolution ... in reality the expansion is a fiction.'[48]

Others were elated. The US historian and a board member of Human Rights Watch, an expert on Rwanda, Alison des Forges, heard about the resolution and immediately called the ambassador for the Czech Republic, Karel Kovanda. It was he who broke the news to her that there was little likelihood of anything happening for another three months. 'I threw up my hands in horror,' recalled des Forges. 'It was unacceptable: human lives were being lost. Why not tomorrow?'[49]

Dallaire believes that if the troops mandated in Resolution 918 had been speedily and effectively deployed, tens upon tens of thousands of people could have been saved. But the resolution was conditional; on US insistence, and as a first step, some 150 military observers were to be sent to Rwanda. The USA and the UK were now arguing that before troops were sent to Rwanda, the views of both armies in the civil war were needed and a ceasefire had to be brokered. The US ambassador, Karl Inderfurth, said that the Council had struggled to formulate a response that was both appropriate and effective. 'The key to the problems in Rwanda is in the hands of the Rwandese people. In Rwanda, this means that the killing – by all parties – must stop,' Inderfurth said. Dallaire quickly realized that with Resolution 918, Rwanda had been abandoned. The world had simply shut the door.

Afterwards there were claims that no troops had been available for Rwanda. This is not true. The government of Ghana had agreed to increase its battalion strength in Kigali to its original 800 soldiers. But without protective vehicles, or APCs, the troops would be unprotected, immobile and ineffective.[50] Ethiopia offered an 800-strong battalion and Malawi promised an infantry company. Offers of troops also came from Senegal, Nigeria, Zimbabwe, Zambia, Congo, Mali, Malawi and Tunisia. But all these countries wanted equipment for their troops and wanted the costs to be underwritten by the UN. Given the state of the UN finances, help for Rwanda quite obviously depended on Western states. No offers were forthcoming.[51]

Throughout May the USA blocked effective action for Rwanda by arguing against Dallaire's plan, devised weeks before, and which entailed airlifting a brigade to Kigali. The USA argued instead for a series of safe havens on Rwanda's borders with Tanzania and Zaire. A team of military experts from the Pentagon arrived at UN headquarters to persuade Kofi Annan of the merits of this idea, arguing that safe havens were cheaper to create, and would require fewer soldiers. If the safe-haven idea were to be accepted, then the USA would contribute to the costs. There could be buffer zones along the frontiers to keep people safe. Dallaire said this simply would not work: the people would be killed before they reached the borders – and those on the borders were not necessarily those most at risk. Keating described the situation as surreal: 'While thousands of human beings were hacked to death every day, ambassadors argued fitfully for weeks about military tactics.' The USA argued continually against wasting any money on failed missions.[52]

The French ambassador, Jean-Bernard Mérimée, told an informal meeting that the only way to resolve the crisis was to obtain a ceasefire within the framework of the Arusha agreement. And just prior to the vote on Resolution 918, on 16 May, Rwanda's own minister of foreign affairs, Jérôme Bicamumpaka, was allowed to address the Security Council. Bicamumpaka, already accorded full diplomatic honours in Paris at the end of April, told the Council that it would be naive to blame either the Rwandan army or the government for the massacres. The hatred, he said, was forged over four centuries of cruel and ruthless domination of the Hutu majority, the mental enslavement of an entire people. The assassination of President Habyarimana was no coincidence. It was part of a prepared plan by the RPF to take power, a plan coordinated with Ugandan authorities. There were large-scale massacres of Hutu civilians. It was an 'inter-ethnic war' of unbelievable cruelty.[53]

No adequate explanation has ever been offered as to why Bicamumpaka was allowed to address the Council, nor as to why, for the duration of the genocide, a representative of the interim government, Jean-Damascène Bizimana, was allowed to sit as Rwanda's ambassador in the Council.[54] The UK ambassador, David Hannay, said that unfortunately there was no procedure for getting rid of him.[55]

Ambassador Colin Keating described Bicamumpaka as the mouthpiece of a faction, not the representative of a state, and said he should not have been allowed to speak. He had given a shameful distortion of the truth. The UK ambassador, David Hannay, regretted 'the tone and the content' of Bicamumpaka's speech. 'We would have wished to see a condemnation of the atrocities that have taken place, many of them in parts of the country controlled by that government, in a less perfunctory manner than was done,' he said.

Karel Kovanda, the Czech ambassador, had by now been thoroughly briefed by Alison des Forges, and he had directly challenged the Rwandan foreign minister and reeled off a list of known massacre sites, giving an estimated casualty figure for each one: 4,000 in Kibeho; 5,500 in Cyahinda; 2,500 in Kibungo. The list went on. In the sports stadium in Cyangugu, he said, thousands of people were held captive and each day victims were pulled from the crowd: 'All reports indicate that these atrocities have been committed by Hutu cut-throats – and seldom has this word been so literally the right one – against their Tutsi neighbours,' he said. Kovanda added that there must have been Tutsi atrocities against Hutu, and human rights groups had assiduously sought direct evidence of massacres in territories controlled by the RPF. So far, they had found very little such evidence. Kovanda continued: 'This situation is being described as a humanitarian crisis as though it were … a natural disaster.' But the massacres were being committed on the orders of people close to Habyarimana and at the instigation of a radio station known for its incendiary broadcasts. The massacres were the work of Rwandan government forces, the militia and the gendarmerie. 'In the view of my delegation, the proper description is genocide,' Kovanda told the Council. The priority was not a ceasefire, but saving the lives of thousands of civilians.

§   The RPF steadily advanced. Colonel Théoneste Bagosora was seen less in Kigali. He made a trip to the Seychelles in May to buy weapons, but no one doubted who was in charge. Lieutenant General Dallaire said that whenever he attempted to establish communications with the Interahamwe leadership for ceasefires and humanitarian operations, the most sure and effective conduit to them was Bagosora. The Interahamwe was responsive to directions received from him.[56]

At one point, quite by chance, Philippe Gaillard had met Bagosora and Gaillard told him that he had to stop the killing. Civilians were being slaughtered, and all the time he was losing the war. 'Monsieur the delegate,' answered Bagosora, 'if I wanted to, I could conscript fifty thousand new men.' Gaillard's car was sometimes caught up in the fighting, and on one occasion, after leaving the Ministry of Defence, he had been obliged to run for cover behind a pillar on the front porch of a house. Mortars sliced through the trees. He was stopped later by the Interahamwe at a roadblock, and was asked to take one of their injured, a man with a bullet in his back, to hospital. Gaillard put the man in the front seat of his car, which became soaked with blood. The man was operated on at the ICRC hospital and some days later Gaillard saw him in the outpatients' room. 'We picked up the debris of genocide,' said Gaillard. 'First the Tutsi, and then little by little there were Hutu wounded.' There were the wounded from the war to treat, people with injuries from shelling and landmines, their limbs blown away. All the survivors in the hospital slept side by side, both Hutu and Tutsi. They talked to each other, worked together in the laundry and the kitchen, and dug holes in the garden to bury the dead. Eight more houses were requisitioned for the hospital. Only the children in the compound were spared any work.

Gaillard had to plead with both the RPF and the Rwandan army to spare the hospital. The Rwandan government army stationed heavy weapons behind it. The RPF asked Gaillard to move to another location but he refused. The hospital was shelled several times. On 25 May, two Rwandans were killed when a shell landed in their compound. Gaillard remembers a baby, aged just one month and a half, with shrapnel wounds to the face. Another child received serious injuries. The hospital was shelled again in June when two bombs fell in the emergency room, killing seven and injuring a dozen more. 'I kept insisting that the Rwandan staff who work in this hospital were both Hutu and Tutsi,' said Gaillard.

Only once did Gaillard call the UN for help. On 19 May, a Swiss medical coordinator, Pierre Gratzl, travelling on the road from Kigali to the south, received shrapnel wounds to his stomach from an RPF shell fired at the convoy. Gratzl was in the lead vehicle going to Kabgayi. He fell exactly on a front line between the two armies. It was impossible to rescue him because of shelling. Dallaire went himself, followed by a Tunisian APC. The road was a major exchange route for Rwandan government forces out of Kigali, with the RPF and the Rwandan army holding the high ground on either side.

Gratzl successfully underwent a major operation later that day. The ICRC stopped using the road, even though it was the principal resupply route. On 21 May, 7.2 tons of medical aid reached Kigali, but after that there were no more convoys, not until Kigali fell to the RPF on 4 July.[57]

An Interahamwe had once told Gaillard that the *Kalinga*, a sacred drum that was said to be a symbol of the Tutsi kings' supremacy, had passed into different hands. From the *Kalinga* were said to have hung the genitals of those killed in the conquered northern areas under the control of Hutu kinglets. Now the drum belonged to the Hutu. Gaillard was sickened. Some of the atrocities witnessed in Rwanda would never be seen by the rest of the world, he said, and he agreed with the self-censorship of the media. There was only one piece of TV footage broadcast to show an actual murder, a piece of film bravely snatched from a roof by British freelance cameraman, Nick Hughes. It was shot in April in central Kigali on the roof of the French school. 'I filmed across a valley to record a street that was being cleared of Tutsi. These images are among the only known pictures of the genocide ... if only there had been more ...' Hughes wrote a description some years later about exactly how this group of people was killed.

What is notable is that they weren't killed instantly; they were slowly beaten to death, tortured. Both women were kneeling. One was begging, arms outstretched ... Nonchalantly, the killer would come over and beat the men who were dying ... then stroll away. Finally, a man came across the street and hit one woman on the head with such a force that he broke the stick he was using. The second blow hit her on the side of her head and neck. I could see her head jerk away.

Hughes said the killing was not so sporadic. He had seen gangs, roaming in the street, looking for somebody to kill. People were brought out on to the street and killed. It was nonchalant and systematic. There was no other explanation.[58]

§ By mid-May the RPF was in control of almost half the country, from the north-west to the south-eastern corner, with the interim government and its army retreating east but managing to hold on to western Kigali, with the hilltops around the city under RPF control. When the RPF seized Kabuga, 16 kilometres east of Kigali, it opened the way for an offensive against both the main government army barracks at Kanombe and the airport. On 20 May, while the fighting continued for control of the capital, thirty people were killed when a mortar bomb hit the King Faisal hospital, where thousands of people were sheltering. At least twelve mortar bombs hit UN headquarters.

In those areas where the interim government and the Rwandan army were in control, the militia had created a dense network of roadblocks. Escape for Tutsi was virtually impossible. On 22 May, a nun and eleven novices, who had escaped from Kigali and were on their way to Kabgayi, arrived in Kamonyi, where they were caught, thrown into a pit and shot. There was an increasing number of people trapped in sites around the country: 38,000 people being held in Kabgayi; 3,000 at a stadium in Gitarama; 5,500 in a stadium in Cyangugu; 1,700 at Mibirizi; 400 at Sahngui, near Cyangugu; and 60,000 at Runda, near Kigali.[59]

From the Kamarampaka stadium near the cathedral in Cyangugu men and boys were regularly taken away by soldiers and militia. On 11 May, they took hundreds of people from the stadium to the countryside by bus and then murdered them. When delegates from the Red Cross had first arrived in Cyangugu on 20 April they had found 884 malnourished children needing special treatment. There was no food. There was one water tap. There were 7,889 people at this site; 500 of those needed urgent medical help. Two ICRC delegates and a nurse went there every day and distributed food and opened a pharmacy. A safe water supply was later ensured by an ICRC water engineer who came from Geneva.

The people in the stadium were later moved to a camp at Nyarushishi which had been used for refugees from Burundi who had fled to Rwanda in October 1993. As everywhere else, soldiers ostensibly guarding the refugees worked closely with the Interahamwe, who roamed the camp, abducting people. At Nyarushishi it is thought that most of the 10,000 refugees were saved from slaughter only because the gendarmes were under the command of a colonel called Innocent Bavugamenshi.

On 13 May, Dallaire received a telephone call from Washington, from Senator Paul Simon (Democrat, Illinois), a member of the Senate Committee on Foreign Relations, and chairman of the Subcommittee on African Affairs. Simon had received information – he does not recall whether it came from the State Department or the CIA – to the effect that in Rwanda hundreds of thousands of people were being killed. With the ranking Republican on the committee, Senator James Jeffords (Vermont), Simon placed a call to Dallaire. 'We asked what could be done to stop what was still in the initial stages,' Simon explained. 'Dallaire told us that if he could get eight thousand troops quickly he could put an end to it. Dallaire was very concerned about stopping the killing.' Dallaire indicated to the senators that 5,000 troops was his minimum requirement, but that these troops would be spread too thinly because the killing had extended to other parts of the country. Such reinforcements would need a mandate to stop the massacres, protect civilians and facilitate the delivery of humanitarian assistance. Simon remembered Dallaire as a compassionate, sensitive and sensible military commander.

Immediately after this conversation, Senators Jeffords and Simon wrote a letter to the White House, hand-delivered, with a copy to the State Department, asking for the USA immediately to request the Security Council to approve sending troops to Kigali to stop the senseless slaughter. 'Obviously there are risks involved but we cannot continue to sit idly by while this tragedy continues to unfold,' the letter stated. The failure of the international community to take decisive action had served to embolden the extremists; delay or simply doing nothing were not acceptable substitutes for a foreign policy of leadership. Human life was at stake, and swift and sound decision-making was needed.

There was no reply. Ten days later, Simon telephoned the White House but failed to speak to Anthony Lake at the National Security Council. Simon was put through to another official and told that there was no public support for US participation in such an operation. 'This might have been accurate,' said Simon, five years later, 'but this was a question of leadership, a case in which you have to build a public base.'

It took President Bill Clinton twenty-seven days to respond. On 9 June, he wrote to say that he was in full agreement that there should be action and he proceeded to list all those things he claimed his administration had done to alleviate the crisis: it had taken action in 'ensuring an effective UN peacekeeping force'; it had supported a UN resolution to authorize up to 5,500 troops for Rwanda and to reintroduce a full mechanized battalion and UN military observers as soon as possible.

'We have been contacting foreign governments to urge their rapid participation in the peacekeeping mission ... a number of countries have responded positively to these contacts,' the letter said. The USA had offered financial, logistical and material support, including fifty APCs; it was 'working with the UN to ensure that this force is effective, protects the maximum number of Rwandans at risk and meets the conditions set forth in my recent directive on peacekeeping'; it had sponsored a UN resolution to impose an arms embargo; it had committed more than US$50 million in humanitarian assistance for Rwanda, by far the largest amount of any donor, to ameliorate the crisis among the refugees on the borders with Tanzania and Burundi; it had strongly supported a negotiated settlement; Clinton's senior officials had been in almost daily contact with the leaders in the region to support diplomatic efforts for a ceasefire.

President Clinton wrote: 'I have spoken out against the killings ... we have called for a full investigation of these atrocities.' These initiatives, he claimed, had helped to relieve some of the suffering of the Rwandan people and supported a 'rapid introduction of an effective UN mission to protect people at risk'.

§   The RPF advance continued and the army took control of the airport at dawn on Sunday, 22 May, when 200 government soldiers fled their positions and the Kanombe barracks fell. The next day the RPF took over the presidential villa. The wreckage of the Falcon jet was still in the garden. There were hundreds of government soldiers leaving the city, and a column of people stretched for 32 kilometres on the road to Gitarama. The latest exodus would soon account for some 300,000 people, clogging the roads, fleeing an RPF advance.

Boutros-Ghali told reporters on 25 May that the real responsibility for what was happening lay with the Security Council: 'My role is to respect the decisions and the resolutions of the Security Council. I can suggest different solutions, but the decisions are taken by the Security Council.' When asked how he felt as a human being when seeing piles of corpses he said: 'I will try not to be emotional ... Let us recognize that this is a failure ... not only of the UN but also of the international community. All of us are responsible for this failure. I have tried. I was in contact with different heads of state and I begged them to send troops ... I failed. It is a scandal. I am the first one to say it and I am ready to repeat it.' Genocide had been committed, he said.[60]

Boutros-Ghali had by now sent two senior officials to Rwanda, ostensibly to try to get negotiations going between the Rwandan government forces and the RPF. They were Iqbal Riza, assistant secretary-general in DPKO, and Major General Maurice Baril, the secretary-general's military adviser. They visited Rwanda between 22 and 27 May, and when they returned to headquarters they wrote a report in which they described 'a frenzy of massacres', with 250,000 to 500,000 people killed in a systematic slaughter. There was little doubt that this was genocide. The UN peacekeepers were fulfilling two primary tasks: providing security to as many locations as possible where people were sheltering and facilitating the provision of humanitarian relief to these sites, even without a ceasefire.[61] On 30 May, in a report to the Council, the secretary-general told ambassadors: 'We must all realise that we have failed in our response to the agony of Rwanda and thus acquiesced in the continued loss of life.'[62]

In late May there was a determined counter-offensive in Kigali, with the Presidential Guard and four battalions of gendarmes combining together with Interahamwe.[63] On the last day of May, a military observer, Captain Mbaye Diagne, from Senegal, was killed, the twelfth peacekeeper to die since the crisis began.[64] Diagne had been driving a clearly marked UN vehicle, and was killed by an RPF mortar shell at an army checkpoint on the front line. He was negotiating, with his usual banter, his way back to UN headquarters, carrying a message from the government-held part of the city to the force commander in an attempt to allow refugees to cross the front line. Some six government soldiers had been the target and Diagne's car had effectively shielded them from the blast. Afterwards, Brigadier General Henry Anyidoho spent time with the peacekeepers. 'We tried to talk to both sides,' he told them quietly, 'but they just don't seem to be listening.' They suspended further rescue attempts. They wept as Diagne's body, wrapped in the blue sheeting used for refugee huts, there being no flags, was carried to a plane. He was, one of them said, the bravest of them all.[65] Diagne had protected the children of Prime Minister Uwilingiyimana in the Hôtel des Mille Collines; he was known for his fearless rescue missions and had single-handedly saved people from various hostage sites around the city.

When James Orbinski, a Canadian doctor with MSF, arrived overland in May, he was appalled at the state of the UN peacekeepers, astonished that they were obliged to limit their rescue attempts for lack of petrol. Their headquarters was constantly shelled. Lieutenant General Dallaire believes that he pushed his troops beyond decent limits in terms of the conditions they were forced to endure. He described: '... the acrid odours of death and starvation, to eat expired tinned rations and to cope with the resultant diarrhoea without toilet paper or running water'.

Orbinski was to join a team of five MSF staff who had recently established an operations centre in UNAMIR headquarters, next to the Amahoro stadium.[66] There were three MSF personnel working in the ICRC hospital on the other side of town. Orbinski was welcomed by a Canadian military observer, Major Don MacNeil, who was the deputy of UNAMIR's Humanitarian Action Cell. He told Orbinski that Kigali was hell with no fuel. MacNeil kept a map on his wall which showed the places where people were trapped – in churches, diplomatic compounds and orphanages. There were soldiers and militia surrounding them, and roadblocks and killing squads preventing their rescue. The killing of people from these sites took place between dusk and dawn. MacNeil held negotiations with the Rwandan army officers to try to organize rescue missions, and was sometimes told that the army did not always have control of the militia. There were notes taken at these encounters and the minutes were kept. Some of the meetings were filmed on videotape.[67]

The King Faisal hospital was at the margin of a shifting front line. On the other side of the valley, in the government zone, was the ICRC hospital. The King Faisal, a purpose-built hospital with 300 beds, was filthy and crammed with people. There was no sanitation, but a logistics expert from the ICRC had managed to create a clean area in the hospital containing 100 beds, a couple of wards and one operating theatre. The doctors and nurses from MSF were obliged to wear ICRC insignia, at risk of reprisals from Rwandan government soldiers. This was because of the MSF press campaign under way in Paris that continued to put pressure on the French government, calling for an end to genocide. By June, the King Faisal was functioning as a hospital with a ward for children, and carrying out up to thirty operations a day. There was rationing of morphine and the shelling and mortar fire around the hospital were a major problem.

The overcrowding in the ICRC hospital reached crisis point in June. Gaillard wanted to transfer patients across the front line to the King Faisal. Dallaire negotiated a two-hour ceasefire. Those patients considered fit enough to travel, both Hutu and Tutsi, were put in the back of a lorry and Gaillard led the convoy. One of UNAMIR's two APCs was parked at a crucial roundabout en route, with the other near the King Faisal.

Some days later, on 21 June, the ICRC hospital was again inundated with wounded. Orbinski remembers wounded people in their hundreds, so many needing medical help that they were laid out on the street outside. Orbinski took part in a roadside triage, treating as many as possible of those likely to die without immediate medical care. The ditches ran with blood. There were government soldiers, Interahamwe, and gunshot wounds, machete blows, shrapnel and blast injuries.

Orbinski tells of a woman, a victim of genocide, whose entire body had been systematically mutilated with a machete. Her ears had been cut off. Her face was carefully disfigured, and a pattern was obvious in the slashes. 'She was one among many, living an inhuman and indescribable suffering,' he recalled. There was little he could do for her other than try to stop the bleeding. She was slightly older than middle-aged and she had been raped. She was aware that all around her there were people in a similar condition. There were only six doctors in the ICRC–MSF team. Orbinski had faltered. 'She knew and I knew', Orbinski said, 'that we were completely overwhelmed.' And then the woman had released him from his own inescapable hell. She had looked up at him and said to him in the clearest voice he had heard: '*Allez, allez … ummera, ummera-sha*' (Go, go, my friend, find and let live your courage).[68]

They continued trying to alleviate the overcrowding in the ICRC hospital and a week later, on 27 June, forty-five more wounded people arrived at the King Faisal hospital. Other convoys tried but it was not always possible. The journey entailed crossing a bridge that spanned a valley; the bridge was exposed and was the most terrifying and dangerous place.

At the end of June a convoy with wounded was stopped on the bridge by Presidential Guards. Gaillard argued in vain as one of them climbed into the back of the lorry to 'inspect the wounded'. A crowd gathered and started shouting '*Inyenzi*'. Some brandished machetes. Gaillard jumped in his car, drove to the Ministry of Defence, waited for a piece of paper with a stamp, and then drove back to the bridge and showed the guard the paper. He watched while the guard radioed headquarters and was told to let the lorry through. When the convoy reached the other side there was another roadblock, this time with RPF soldiers. An RPF soldier insisted on inspecting the wounded and among them in the back of the lorry, he found his brother.

Gaillard travelled with Dallaire and a group of peacekeepers north to Buymba, and at one of the roadblocks Gaillard chatted with an Interahamwe. The man was dejected and exhausted. He was filthy, meagre and unshaven. Gaillard told him he was on his way to see Paul Kagame. 'Tell him to stop the war. We want to discuss everything,' the man said.

The RPF advance continued. On Thursday, 2 June, the RPF took Kabgayi. Before the government troops and Interahamwe fled, they had gone on a killing spree. The sight that greeted the rebel soldiers in this small and previously beautiful site was unforgettable. The Roman Catholic seminary, the home of the bishop, had been turned into a hell.[69] There were 30,000 people trapped in the town and 200,000 displaced people in the area.[70] On 9 June, RPF soldiers murdered the Catholic Archbishop of Kigali, Vincent Nsengiyumva, who had been Agathe Habyarimana's confessor and a member of the MRND central committee.[71] He was killed with the Bishop of Kabgayi, Thaddée Nsengiyumva, the Bishop of Byumba, Joseph Rusindana, and ten priests. The RPF claimed that the killings were carried out by young soldiers recently recruited, who disobeyed their orders to hold the clerics in protective custody.[72] Some two years later, a letter was sent to Pope John Paul II by a group of priests to explain that the clerics who were killed in Kabgayi were not in a state of grace for either their faith or their charity. The letter accused them of collusion with the regime.[73]

Although the RPF saved tens of thousands of people from extermination, rumours of summary executions by them began to spread and RPF soldiers were accused of committing war crimes.[74] The RPF were putting restrictions on where UN military observers could go. The RPF soldiers were discovering the fate of their families and friends. Their ranks were swollen by new recruits who were less disciplined. Sometimes the Interahamwe used the civilian population as a shield to protect them against the RPF. Special Rapporteur of the Commission on Human Rights, René Degni-Ségui, reported that the killing of civilians by the RPF was scattered, irregular and limited.[75] Later on, Ian Martin, who was the head of a UN Human Rights Field Operation created after the genocide, reported that thousands of civilians became victims of reprisal killings, in some cases amounting to massacres, which occurred during, and after, the RPF advance was complete.[76] Two months after the interim government had abandoned Kigali, it fled Gitarama, and on 12 June the ministers were on the road again to the Lake Kivu town of Kibuye, and eventually farther north to Gisenyi, their northern heartland.

Three days after the fall of Gitarama to the RPF, the French cabinet decided to send troops. The French military would mount a humanitarian operation to protect populations threatened with extermination. President François Mitterrand said there was not a moment to lose.

§ The French offer to the Security Council of a humanitarian operation for Rwanda was enthusiastically welcomed by the secretary-general, Boutros Boutros-Ghali, who took a keen interest in the resolution to authorize the French force. He argued that the French were acting out of 'bitter frustration with the US obstruction'.[1] Although the French government was seeking UN approval for the mission, it was made clear that its soldiers would not be 'shackled by the kind of restrictions that had turned UN soldiers into helpless bystanders'. France wanted a Chapter VII mandate to allow for the use of force, needed to protect French soldiers.[2] For some diplomats, Boutros-Ghali's decision to lobby for the return of the French military to a conflict that France had done so much to fuel was unspeakable. But Boutros-Ghali argued that he had no choice. France was the only country that had offered anything for Rwanda and at no cost to the UN. The USA was refusing to pay its UN debt and reluctant to incur peacekeeping bills. The French would be providing troops and picking up the bill.

A spokesperson for the French government, Nicolas Sarkozy, a later president of France, explained: 'We are not a middle power … we are a great power … if France does not react, Sarajevo falls; and finally Rwanda.'[3] French diplomats tried hard to obtain endorsement from their European allies and from African states. But there was a poor response. Only Senegal and Chad offered a few hundred soldiers, Congo and Niger about forty soldiers, and Mauritania four doctors. Although France said it would not act without UN endorsement, even before the Council had a chance to meet on the issue, an advance team of French troops had arrived at the Zairean border airfield of Goma to make preparatory plans for an intervention force. France had begun to position its forces in central Africa on 16 June.[4]

It would later emerge that the idea for French intervention may have been around longer than at first realized. On 9 May, General Jean-Pierre Huchon had received, in the Ministry of Cooperation in Paris, Lieutenant Colonel Ephrem Rwabalinda, adviser to the Rwandan chief of staff. Rwabalinda claimed later that among 'the priorities' of this meeting was 'the support of Rwanda by France at the level of international policy; the physical presence of the French soldiers in Rwanda ... for assistance in the framework of cooperation; the indirect use of regular or non-regular troops'.[5] Rwabalinda indicated that General Huchon had undertaken to supply ammunition, but also transmission equipment to facilitate secure communication with General Bizimungu, commander in chief of the Rwandan army. A secure telephone, to enable General Bizimungu and General Huchon to talk without being heard by a third party, was brought to Kigali. Seventeen small sets with seven frequencies were also sent to facilitate links between military units. The Kigali airport runway would be convenient as a secure and suitable landing site, as long as runway holes were filled and those spies moving around the airport were warded off. The purpose of the communications equipment was to provide Paris 'with protected information for the security of French soldiers of Opération Turquoise which was being prepared'.

The Security Council endorsed the French plan on 22 June, in Resolution 929. The troops would not be wearing blue berets but the mission was to be coordinated by the secretary-general, and was to last no longer than sixty days. It was hoped that by then a reinforced UNAMIR II, the mission that the Council had enthusiastically voted for on 17 May, would be operational.[6]

Not everyone believed that Opération Turquoise, as it was officially called, was a purely humanitarian exercise. In the Council five states abstained on the vote: Brazil, China, New Zealand, Nigeria and Pakistan. The New Zealand ambassador, Colin Keating, had urged that member states provide resources for a reinforced UNAMIR II.[7] But the USA argued in favour of French action, with Ambassador Madeleine Albright advising that the Council ought to be flexible enough to accept imperfect solutions – which this was. Albright said it was a way of bridging the gap until the arrival of the 5,500 troops authorized for a reinforced UNAMIR II, which Boutros-Ghali had warned could take three months. President Mitterrand did not understand the lack of enthusiasm and blamed the reluctance on RPF propaganda in Brussels, and he found the naivety of diplomats and journalists to be disconcerting. Mitterrand believed that the 'threatened Tutsi could eventually be sent to the RPF zone'.[8]

The French were mandated to secure humanitarian areas, and protect displaced people and relief workers. The idea, according to French military officials, was to set up security zones to protect fleeing refugees and to prevent warfare between the Rwandan military and the RPF from spreading into Burundi and Tanzania. With a Chapter VII mandate the French forces could disarm militia and arrest those responsible for massacres.

The French press was critical. In *Le Monde* there were warnings of a fiasco and accusations that once more France was riding to the rescue of the Rwandan government. In *Libération*, a letter from Jean Carbonare, the president of the French human rights group Survie, wrote that France had known for years what was happening in Rwanda. 'French intelligence services were running the whole country together with the Rwandese army,' he wrote.[9] *Libération* published an interview with someone who claimed to be from a Hutu Power death squad, who claimed that he had been trained by French instructors.[10] In New York, the RPF representative, Claude Dusaidi, shocked and angry at Opération Turquoise, told journalists outside the Council chamber that the sole purpose of the French mission was to save the perpetrators of the genocide.

§ In UNAMIR headquarters on the afternoon of 17 June, Lieutenant General Dallaire received a visit from Bernard Kouchner, a French internationalist, and one of the founder members of MSF. Kouchner had come at the behest of the French government.[11] He told Dallaire that the French were about to intervene and that while UNAMIR II could remain operational in the RPF zones, the French were going to sort out Rwandan government territory and create a safe area there. He showed Dallaire a map of Rwanda which was marked with a line designating the zone to be under French control, and it covered parts of Kigali. Kouchner said that orphans and missionaries were stuck behind the 'Interahamwe lines' in the capital, and that they could be saved. Any support Dallaire cared to give would help to persuade sceptics that French troops should return to Kigali. Dallaire immediately refused to give any support whatsoever. He was suspicious. Kouchner had come to Rwanda a few weeks earlier, from 12 to 16 May, when he had tried unsuccessfully to 'relocate' injured Rwandan orphans to France. Kouchner had negotiated with Colonel Théoneste Bagosora, and he had promised him media coverage and explained how the release of the orphans would be a public relations coup for the interim government. The French public, in a state of shock at the genocide, was demanding action. Kouchner told Dallaire that the release of the orphans was in his own interests; a gesture would help, as Dallaire was seen in a very bad light in Paris.[12]

Dallaire was appalled at the possibility of French intervention; he could not believe the effrontery of the French. If they really wanted to end genocide and support the aims of the UN, they should have reinforced UNAMIR II. His mission was further endangered now and he immediately stopped rescue missions.

In an angry cable to New York Dallaire wrote: 'UNAMIR had been waiting for expansion to help stop massacres ... the ineffective reaction to meeting the critical needs of the mission has been nothing less than scandalous ... this has directly led to the loss of many more Rwandese lives.'[13] The French deployment would reduce the chances of any other country donating either troops or equipment to UNAMIR II. With the French military making Goma, Zaire, on the western front, their headquarters, his UN force would now be in the middle. The UN peacekeepers were mostly confined to Kigali, in the centre of Rwanda, with the front line of the RPF and Rwandan government forces in between them. This farcical decision had placed a Chapter VI UN force between a Chapter VII force and one of the belligerents. The real reason the French were intervening, Dallaire believed, was in order to stop the RPF taking the whole country. The real intention was to split Rwanda in two, like Cyprus. There had been a suggestion that the French should land troops at Kigali airport and Dallaire had told New York that if his peacekeepers were ever intended to become subordinate to French command, he would resign. He learned that the French government had even held meetings with RPF representatives to discuss their plans.[14]

'I would never have guessed at the time', he wrote later, 'the extent to which the Interim Government, the RGF, Boutros-Ghali, France and even the RPF were already working together behind my back to secure a French intervention ... under the guise of humanitarian relief.'[15] When Kouchner returned to Paris he told Bruno Delaye, the head of the president's Africa Unit, that Dallaire was unsupportive and he advised that any initiative be portrayed as a brand-new phase in French policy towards Rwanda.[16] Kouchner thought it might be advisable to issue an avowal of regret for the past, and a public assurance that this mission was strictly humanitarian.

The RPF reaction came from Major General Paul Kagame, who called the French initiative a treacherous act of war. In *Le Figaro* on 25 June, Kagame was quoted: 'You have armed and trained the Presidential Guards; you have accepted that the Presidential Guards armed and trained, in front of you, the Hutu extremists.' Kigali would be able to absorb far more body bags than Paris, he warned. There were claims that the US government pressured the RPF to cooperate and there were secret assurances given to the RPF that the French would not go near Kigali, which the RPF was poised to capture.[17]

In Kigali now, with RTLM announcers repeating the news that the French were coming, new French flags appeared at every roadblock. The killers seemed invigorated. There was cheering and singing: 'Our French brothers are coming to save us.'[18]

The news of the French intervention put at risk the lives of UN military observers from Franco-African countries – from the Congo, Senegal and Togo – for their governments had initially considered providing troops for the French operation.[19] There were ninety of them, and as French speakers they had been an invaluable resource as liaison between UNAMIR and the government army. They had been vital for intelligence-gathering. They had come to Rwanda with an OAU mission, had solid contacts and knew the country well. They had played a key role in the protection of civilians in the Hôtel des Mille Collines. Now, many of them were being beaten and abused by RPF soldiers, and they had to be withdrawn. Brigadier Henry Anyidoho was given the task of escorting them safely out of the country, through RPF-held territory to Uganda, where they were to be picked up by Bell 212 helicopters in the Mirama hills and flown to Entebbe. But no sooner had they left Kigali on 21 June than they were stopped at a checkpoint, where an RPF second lieutenant insisted that they divert to the airport, and only after a thorough search of their luggage, during which anything of value was looted, were they sent on their way.[20] Some weeks later Dallaire travelled to Nairobi to present medals to them before their final repatriation. Among them were officers who had been exposed to extreme danger; some had seen comrades killed and others wounded. Many had fallen ill. Dallaire said they had shown commitment, determination and courage.

A further ceremony was held at UNAMIR headquarters in Kigali on 26 June. Dallaire, together with Brigadier General Henry Anyidoho, and the chief military observer, Colonel Isoa Tikoca from Fiji, pinned mission medals on sixty headquarters staff, the remaining military observers and the Tunisian contingent. Tikoca was a UN veteran who had served in Somalia, and he had been with the UN in Rwanda longer than any of them. Tikoca represented the UN as a military observer during the negotiations for the Arusha Accords. His team of unarmed military observers had been taken hostage, caught in crossfire, shot at and menaced by drunken Interahamwe. Tikoca had never once left any of his military observers in a precarious situation.[21] All of them testified to his bravery.[22]

The UNAMIR headquarters was beginning to change. Outsiders were arriving, a part of the slow build-up of UNAMIR II. A Canadian signals regiment had arrived along with a reconnaissance team to prepare for an Ethiopian battalion, and a Ghanaian company would soon be arriving. Military field hospitals were expected from Australia and Britain. All this had been made possible by Brigadier General Henry Anyidoho, who had successfully managed the Herculean task of organizing the logistics of an overland route from Nairobi to Kampala by air and then by road to Kigali. Anyidoho was never once ruffled by any situation, no matter how dangerous; he would say only that a military man had to get used to hazards.[23] All neighbouring governments and the RPF had agreed this overland ten-hour route by road. Anyidoho had personally led the first convoy of fifty Ghanaian troops, the first ever UNAMIR reinforcements, made possible only because the World Food Programme had provided heavy-lift trucks. 'We were no longer alone,' Dallaire wrote later on.[24] 'We had lived to see the cavalry.'[25]

Dallaire was asked to cooperate with the French mission. He travelled to Goma to meet the commander, Brigadier General Jean-Claude Lafourcade, who had set up an inter-service headquarters there. Dallaire was to be the link between this operation and the RPF. Lafourcade told Dallaire that in those parts of the country where the French were operational all non-combat troops would be disarmed. The French-led force would stop the killing taking place in the areas under their control. This never happened. Afterwards, Lafourcade wrote a letter to tell Dallaire that Opération Turquoise would not be disarming militias and military in their zone, not unless they posed a threat to the people they were protecting.[26]

Dallaire's visit to Lafourcade gave him an opportunity to see the well-equipped French headquarters in Goma.[27] Lafourcade had 2,500 elite troops, under the Commandement des Forces Spéciales (CFS), 100 armoured vehicles, a battering of heavy mortars, eight Super-Puma helicopters and four Jaguar fighter bombers, four Mirage ground-attack planes and four Mirage jets for reconnaissance.[28] There were communications vehicles, antennae, satellite dishes and landlines. Lafourcade had everything Dallaire needed, including a Chapter VII mandate. France spent 1 per cent of its annual defence budget on Opération Turquoise for its sixty-day duration. Dallaire thought it a lot of military power for what was strictly a humanitarian operation. And in his conversations with French officers, he noted their refusal to accept the reality of genocide, or that the perpetrators of genocide were former colleagues. They showed 'overt signs of wishing to fight the RPF', and thought that UNAMIR should have prevented the defeat of the Rwandan forces. Not many of them had a clear idea of the scale of the massacres.[29]

Some senior officers who served in Opération Turquoise had been in Rwanda previously, as advisers and trainers in Rwandan military units before the genocide began. One of them, known as Colonel Didier Thibaut, was now in charge of the south-western sector of the French operational zone.

Opération Turquoise officially began on Thursday, 23 June, when the French, accompanied by a truckload of Senegalese troops, crossed into Rwanda from Zaire at Bukavu. French soldiers conducted patrols in the prefectures of Gisenyi, Kibuye, Cyangugu and Gikongoro, all of which were controlled by the interim government. There were huge French flags to welcome them, and in Cyangugu their vehicles were garlanded with flowers. RTLM, broadcasting from Gisenyi, announced the French had arrived to help fight the RPF and would be giving them weapons. The Hutu girls should wear their best frocks to welcome the French soldiers.[30]

France maintained that its soldiers had come to rescue civilians, but as Gérard Prunier, an adviser at that time to the French government, wrote later, the first draft plan drawn up in Paris was for the French to enter through Gisenyi, in north-western Rwanda. Prunier had told government officials that in Gisenyi there were no Tutsi left alive to be paraded in front of the TV cameras as justification for intervention. An initial plan, which was presented at the UN by French diplomats, showed that the French desire was for a zone of control from the north and south-east to Kigali, and south-west to Butare. This was where the Rwandan government forces had troops and supplies. Dallaire had responded to this by telling New York that he did not want the French in Kigali; if the French wanted to help they should provide support for UNAMIR.[31]

Prunier argued that French troops should go to south-western Rwanda to Cyangugu and rescue the people trapped in the camp at Nyarushishi.[32] And so, accompanied by journalists, French troops went farther south, to two steep hillsides on a tea plantation at Nyarushishi, in the prefecture of Cyangugu, to the camp where 8,000 people were sheltering. When the terrified people first saw the French soldiers, they assumed they had come to kill them. Of an estimated 55,000 Tutsi in this prefecture, only 10,000 were left alive, and 8,000 of these were in the camp. 'Where were you in April?' someone asked a French soldier. By deciding to go to Nyarushishi, the French had tried to appear neutral. Thibaut, interviewed by a British journalist, said that the Tutsi in Nyarushishi were afraid of the RPF advance. In reality, what these people feared was a killing spree before the RPF had a chance to rescue them.[33]

In a less publicized move, French officers paid a courtesy call on the interim government at the Hôtel Méridien in Gisenyi and brought in supplies and equipment. There were schoolchildren lining up by the side of the road to cheer them. The commander of the Rwandan government troops, Major General Augustin Bizimungu, declared that his forces would soon launch an offensive against the RPF.

About a week after their arrival in Cyangugu, a group of French soldiers made the sickening discovery of hundreds of ill and frail Tutsis slowly emerging from a forest in a range of hills known as Bisesero, in the prefecture of Kibuye – the only survivors from an estimated fifty thousand in the region. Some of these people had been in hiding since April and had been under constant attack from militia and soldiers.[34] Some of them had suffered appalling wounds. There were few women and children among them because they had not been able to run fast enough. The area was littered with hundreds of bodies.[35] In the years to come Bisesero achieved a unique and important place in the history of the genocide. Bisesero was where there had been an organized resistance, albeit with stones, sticks, spears and a few guns, and where convoys of Interahamwe were sent as reinforcements into the hills, to try to finish off those people trying to survive.[36] The Tutsi of Bisesero were known as the Abasesero, and during previous violence they had defended themselves. This was the reason why, at the beginning, Tutsi from other regions had come here because they believed they would be safe.

On 26 June, when survivors realized French soldiers had arrived, they emerged, some of them after months in hiding, creeping out from under sheds, inside cupboards and attics, and there were stories of how some brave Hutu had sheltered them at risk to their lives. One of the French officers, Sergeant Major Thierry Prungnaud, said: 'This is not what we were led to believe. We were told that the Tutsi were killing Hutu.' Another soldier said: 'We have not a single wounded Hutu here, just massacred Tutsi.'[37] Two years earlier, Prungnaud had been helping to train the Presidential Guard. The French soldiers seemed to have believed that Hutu were the victims of civil war and that they had to be protected from the RPF, and the killing of Tutsi was a part of this war, and there were pockets of 'Tutsi resistance'.

The events in Bisesero have been widely investigated but they continue to present a lasting controversy with the most serious allegations levelled at French soldiers. These include a failure on the part of French officers to protect an estimated one thousand Bisesero survivors, people who had come out of hiding and who were told to wait by French soldiers for suitable transport. When the French soldiers returned three days later, the militia had killed most of them.[38] This claim first emerged in the French press in July 1994, and has subsequently been the subject of detailed work by French human rights groups.

In 2005 in Paris, a legal case was begun by a group of six Rwandans who accused certain French military officers who served with Opération Turquoise of complicity with genocide, and rape and murder.

§ On Friday, 1 July, with the RPF poised to take Kigali, and ten days after Opération Turquoise was launched, the French government informed Boutros-Ghali of an intention to establish a protection zone in south-western Rwanda where the population could be protected from the 'fighting'. This was a departure from the mandate. There were immediate concerns that this would serve only to protect those responsible for the genocide. But the French argued their own interpretation of Resolution 929, and the plan received the support of the secretary-general. Their zone would not allow an RPF presence. Boutros-Ghali argued that with a tide of refugees fleeing the RPF advance, France's only options were either to withdraw its troops or to establish a safe, humanitarian zone.[39]

With his endorsement, the French went ahead, and by 4 July had established a major base 10 kilometres from the RPF army's advanced line, manning it with paratroopers with heavy artillery. In drawing a line around south-western Rwanda, and declaring it a safe human-itarian zone, the French hoped to link what they were doing with the protection afforded by a no-fly zone. But the decision by the French to create a safe zone, an area comprising some 20 per cent of the country, was considered to be illegal under international law, particularly when French commanders announced that the RPF would be excluded from the safe zone by force. The French prime minister, Edouard Balladur, later told a meeting of the Security Council that everyone could see that without swift action the survival of an entire country was at stake and the stability of a region seriously compromised.[40] There are reports that the French and the RPF clashed in early July near Butare. Eighteen French soldiers were said to have been taken captive by the RPF, and after negotiations between the RPF and Paris they were released the following day. There was no publicity.[41]

The immediate effect of the French humanitarian zone was to provide a secure retreat for the Rwandan government army and the perpetra-tors of genocide – military, militia and civilian. French commanders maintained that because of limits to their mandate they could not arrest or detain anyone in their zone, whether or not they were war criminals.

Neither did they attempt to disarm the thousands of civilians who flooded the zone. The militia were still armed to the teeth. Nothing was done to stop the continuing pro-genocide transmissions of RTLM from within the zone.

There is a difference of opinion about French achievements during the sixty days of Opération Turquoise. Prunier writes that the importance and efficiency of the French mission were exaggerated for propaganda purposes. There are varying claims concerning the number of Tutsi saved by French soldiers. The French military claim that Opération Turquoise saved some 17,000 people, but Prunier maintains that when all the people at the Nyarushishi camp are taken into account, as well as people picked up elsewhere, then the figure is more like 10–13,000.[42] The French failed even to prevent massacres continuing in the zone.[43] The only French casualties of Opération Turquoise were soldiers who suffered from shock and trauma at what they had seen.[44]

Kigali fell to the RPF on Monday, 4 July, when at dawn the last Rwandan army contingents abandoned their positions. After three months the city was quiet. The Presidential Guard had held the RPF at the Kacyiru roundabout but now was in retreat, scurrying north to Ruhengeri. That same day a new UN Special Representative arrived, Shaharyar Khan, a former foreign minister of Pakistan.[45] He was greeted at UNAMIR headquarters by a Ghanaian guard of honour. Khan was given a tour of Kigali and taken to the ICRC hospital, its flags still flying over the hill. Khan described seeing hundreds of bodies. 'There was blood all over the floors and the terrible stench of rotting flesh.' Every inch of the site was taken up by patients, for as the Rwandan soldiers abandoned Kigali, they had fired mortars indiscriminately. One of them hit the ICRC casualty ward, killing seven patients.[46] A Rwandan officer had telephoned the ICRC, however, to thank Philippe Gaillard and the other ICRC delegates for helping with their wounded.

Gaillard left Rwanda the following day and, as in the past, he did not say goodbye to the other delegates. He did, however, have one last meal of emergency rations with Dallaire.[47] Three months before, Dallaire had promised that if and when the time came he would get the ICRC out of Rwanda. 'When you go is up to you,' Dallaire had told Gaillard. 'If I am here, I will move you.' He only had to ask. That night, Gaillard gave back to Dallaire the UN Motorola, and in a last gesture handed him an ICRC badge, and joked that although Dallaire had no right to wear it, it was appropriate that it belong to him. Dallaire had removed the UNAMIR ribbon that he wore on his shirt and handed it to Gaillard. He thought Gaillard deserved a medal.

Later on, Gaillard paid tribute to Dallaire's courage. He thought Dallaire's experiences were worse than his own. He had lost fourteen men, and ten of them in the most atrocious circumstances.[48] Hutu Power had put a price on his head. And he was abandoned by his own organization. The Security Council had not even bothered to assure supplies for its own force, let alone for the displaced people under UNAMIR protection. It was the ICRC which had supplied food to the people at the Amahoro stadium. It looked to one journalist, Aidan Hartley, as though the Security Council had deliberately starved UNAMIR.[49] The MSF doctor James Orbinski said that Dallaire had been left high and dry. 'His tenacity and sheer drive to maximize the impact of UNAMIR was extraordinary,' he said. Jean-Hervé Bradol, also of MSF, described how in Kigali, despite the danger to their own lives, some people in the UN mission had tried to bring help to threatened civilians. For UNICEF, Gerry McCarthy, who was the fund's representative in Rwanda, thought that in the entire UN, Dallaire was the one shining beacon.

In one of his last cables to UN headquarters, Dallaire wrote:

> What we have been living here is a disgrace. The international community and the UN member states have on the one hand been appalled at what has happened in Rwanda while, on the other hand, these same authorities, apart from a few exceptions, have done nothing substantive to help the situation ... the force has been prevented from having a modicum of self-respect and effectiveness on the ground ... FC [force commander] acknowledges that this mission is a logistical nightmare for your HQ, but that is nothing compared to the living hell that has surrounded us, coupled with the obligation of standing in front of both parties and being the bearer of so little help and credibility ... UNHQ, and sovereign countries, with few exceptions, have solidly failed in providing any reasonable/ tangible/timely support to the expanded UNAMIR so far. The APCs are still in Entebbe, we don't have water ... although Rwanda and UNAMIR have been at the centre of a terrible human tragedy, not to say Holocaust, and although many fine words have been pronounced by all, including members of the Security Council, the tangible effort on the ground to meet the minimum viable operational needs ... has been totally, completely ineffective.

§   A few days before the RPF took Kigali, thousands of people, incited by RTLM, took to the roads to flee the rebel advance. The radio, which remained the voice of authority, broadcast to the 'Hutu Nation' that the

RPF were devil-like fighters and were going to kill them all. A massive movement of people was predicted, by the ICRC, MSF-France and Oxfam. All of them warned of looming disaster. The roads were full of people. There were soldiers in lorries, people in cars, on bicycles, on foot with cows and chickens, and all surrounded by drunken Interahamwe who were 'organizing' the departure. Some 700,000 people were converging on the north-eastern border with Zaire, between Lake Kivu and the volcano of Nyiragongo.

The exodus to Goma, a town on the Zaire–Rwanda border, and the capital of Kivu Province, began on 14 July. It was witnessed by an information officer with MSF-France, Samantha Bolton. 'It was a silent line, a long, long black line of people, all of them walking silently, like machines,' Bolton described. All day people poured into Zaire, as though the whole country were emptying. 'We had known for two weeks that these people were coming,' Bolton said. She had called the BBC and CNN and told them that the 'floodgates of Rwanda have opened'. In two days, about a million people crossed into Zaire, dwarfing the previous refugee record set in April when Rwandans fled to Tanzania. It was the fastest and largest flight of people ever recorded. 'If they stay here,' Bolton wrote in her diary, 'thousands among them will die.' No one could cope. Oxfam and MSF began to distribute water but people were dying of dehydration and exhaustion. Bolton accurately predicted a cholera outbreak.[50] Some people claimed that the buses and the cars and the cattle carried what remained of President Juvénal Habyarimana.

The military moved with artillery, mortars and at least four anti-aircraft guns and anti-tank weapons. The chief of staff, Augustin Bizimungu, denied that his men were abandoning the battlefield. The prime minister, Jean Kambanda, said: 'We have lost the military battle but the war is by no means over because we have the people behind us.' He was right. Two million people had left the country. In Tanzania there were an estimated 500,000 at a camp called Benaco and 200,000 refugees had fled to Burundi. An estimated one million people had passed into Zaire at Goma and 200,000 more into Bukavu.[51] In Rwanda there were 600,000 refugees in Gikongoro, a further 800,000 in Cyangugu and 300,000 in Kibuye, and in these prefectures aid agencies were commencing relief distribution, hoping to avoid a similar exodus to the north-west. Sixty per cent of Rwanda's population was now either dead or displaced.[52]

Now, in a remote rural corner of Zaire, the horizon was black with people, with huge camps established in Goma and Bukavu. Hundreds of thousands of people settled on a barren plain surrounded by volcanoes, without food, water or shelter. Thousands died in appalling suffering in filthy overcrowded camps, walking in a mud of choleric vomit and diarrhoea, for the volcanic rock was as hard as concrete. People died from exhaustion, others from starvation, cholera or dysentery.[53] There were an estimated four thousand orphaned children. In one camp, boys were paid by French troops to collect the dead, ready to be tipped into vast graves. In other places the corpses stayed among the living.

The exodus would now push Rwanda to the top of the international agenda. By the end of July there were some five hundred journalists and technicians in the Goma area, and scores of satellite transmission dishes at the airport. In stark contrast to the reporting of the genocide, within three days of the exodus into Goma there was a media frenzy of graphic reports.

'The slaughter in Rwanda may have been an expression of the bestiality of man,' wrote one journalist. 'But what is happening in Zaire today is surely the wrath of God. Epidemics of biblical proportions sweep the land. Water is poison ... The dead are everywhere ... It is as if Mother Earth herself did not want to accept the remains of the Hutu refugees from Rwanda,' ran one story, which was accompanied by graphic photographs.[54] The catastrophe made for extraordinary television pictures, and from now on there was a blurring in the perception of events. The plight of the refugees became confused with the war and the genocide. The impression now was that this was yet more suffering in what appeared to be a long and complicated story. For Anne Mackintosh, who was the Oxfam regional representative for Rwanda, Burundi and Kivu (Zaire) from 1991 to 1994, the genocide was overshadowed by the refugee crisis. The refugees were not, as some journalists and aid agencies claimed, fleeing the genocide; instead, among those fleeing were thousands of those who had perpetrated it. A year earlier, Oxfam had even had to pay journalists to visit Rwanda and Kivu, and to help them place their stories, simply to ensure some serious coverage in the British media of the region and its latent conflicts. Mackintosh wrote that suddenly everyone was there writing stories.[55] In his book, the French expert Gérard Prunier noted how convenient for French policy-makers was the confusion that existed between the genocide and the refugees. By now Opération Turquoise soldiers were on every television screen, shown as trying to alleviate the terrible suffering in Goma.[56]

With an uproar of public outrage at the agony in these camps, the administration of President Bill Clinton decided now on a massive response. A US operation would be mounted. It would cost $US300–400 million, and some four thousand troops would be provided to help the by now hundreds of US civilian, and mostly independent, relief workers. A massive airlift began. It took just three days, once the orders had been issued by the White House to the Pentagon, for the first American troops to be on the ground and distributing fresh water to the refugees. The US military was under strict orders not to become involved in operations that could evolve into or be seen as peacekeeping, to limit its action to narrow technical humanitarian tasks and to leave as soon as possible. The US soldiers moved about in convoys of vehicles with heavy machine guns and wore helmets and flak jackets at all times. All US military personnel had to be back at the secure military compound by nightfall.

On 22 July, President Clinton said with some emotion how this was the worst humanitarian crisis in a generation. He described how one refugee was dying every minute, and the administration laid on special briefings for the press with J. Brian Atwood, appointed Clinton's special representative to Rwanda. It was announced that 1,200 tons of food a day was needed, on top of 3.8 million litres of clean water. This was more than twice the food that was needed in Somalia at the height of the famine.

'People had known what was going on earlier, but had done nothing,' said Tony Marley, a political military adviser in the State Department. The help provided to the refugees was a result of the 'CNN factor', whereby a certain level of media coverage prompts action by governments. Marley also perceived a sense of guilt on the part of those who had obstructed any US action, or any US response, during the genocide. In five months, from mid-July to the end of December, the UNHCR estimated that US$1 million a day was spent on relief efforts for Rwandan refugees.[57] Dallaire said that in the refugee camps in Goma, precious resources were wasted in fuelling a charade of political conscience-cleansing by the developed states in deference to the media and their constituencies.[58]

He relinquished his command of UNAMIR on 18 August. A parade was held at the entrance to the headquarters, and there was a Ghanaian brass band.[59] Dallaire left the following day, after strongly recommending that Anyidoho be appointed force commander, for there was no one in the world more qualified. Despite the deprivation Anyidoho had not been worn down. This last request was rejected out of hand by the office of the secretary-general.[60]

The mission that the ICRC operated during three months of genocide must rank as one of the world's most extraordinary humanitarian operations. It was thanks to Philippe Gaillard, chief delegate, that the ICRC remained operational. For three months, there was emergency medical help in Kigali and within weeks of the start of genocide the ICRC was present elsewhere in the country. When the RPF took Kigali on 4 July, there were 2,500 people living in the ICRC compound.

Gaillard estimated that between 10 April and 4 July the ICRC had looked after 9,000 injured in Kigali and that a further 100,000 people had been saved because of the work of ICRC delegates elsewhere in the country. During this period there had been 1,200 surgical operations and hundreds of people had been treated from the back of ambulances. Some 25,000 tons of food had been distributed. Water engineers repaired the Kigali hydraulic stations and those in Ruhengeri, Gisenyi and Butare.[61] Gaillard said it was no more than a drop of humanity in an ocean of blood.

'There were no deaths among the expats and that was a miracle ... neither were there casualties among our Rwandan collaborators,' he summed up. 'No armed militia ever entered our compound to threaten anyone although the Interahamwe often came to my office to talk to me.' He later gave a lecture in Geneva in which he paid tribute to the people in Rwanda who were moderate, who had been open to persuasion, and who had been 'desperate about the assassins among them'. Gaillard described how people had been prepared to save lives, particularly the lives of children, at great personal risk. There had been officials in the prefecture at Cyangugu, said Gaillard, who with patience and persuasion, and in spite of all the pressure they were under, tried to save the 8,000 people at the camp at Nyarushishi. The courage and exceptional vision of these people had put 'a flower of humanity in what they had all known was a veritable national charnel-house'.[62] Gaillard said that Rwanda now stood among the twentieth century's worst memories, including two world wars and Pol Pot, who killed between 2 and 3 million in Cambodia. In a country of 7 million people, 1 million people had died. There was a degrading of the values in our society, he said. 'It is terrible to see that in Europe we give power to the dishonest, and to cynics, people who put their own personal interests before the common good.'[63]

18 | STARTING FROM ZERO: 18 JULY 1994

§ The last Hutu Power stronghold in Rwanda fell on 18 July, and Kagame declared the civil war to be over. The next day in Kigali a broad-based government of national unity was sworn in comprising the representatives of all major political parties – apart from the MRND. Twelve of the eighteen ministers were Hutu. The president was Pasteur Bizimungu, who had fled to Uganda in August 1990, telling the RPF leadership that the rotten regime in Kigali was ready to collapse. The prime minister was Faustin Twagiramungu, who had escaped the elimination of the political opposition on 7 April, his appointment in accordance with provisions in the Arusha Accords. A new position of vice-president was created for Major General Paul Kagame.

There was no triumphant victory. The country had been ransacked. There was not a penny in the public coffers. There were no offices intact, no chairs, no desks, no paper, no telephones, nothing at all. The streets of Kigali were almost empty. From a previous population of 300,000, there were 50,000 people left, and half of these were displaced.[1] Their condition was disastrous, and they lacked adequate food and clean water. Outside the capital, whole families and communities had been destroyed. Livestock had been killed and crops laid to waste.[2] A once manicured landscape was overgrown and neglected. Everywhere there were ditches filled with rotting bodies. The people had been terrorized and traumatized. The hospitals and schools were destroyed or ransacked. Rwanda's health centres, one in each commune, were ruined. The stocks of basic drugs and health supplies had been looted. Water supply lines were non-operational. Qualified staff had been killed or had fled the country, including most of the teachers. An estimated 250,000 women had been widowed. In the whole country there were six judges and ten lawyers. There were no gendarmes.[3]

At least 100,000 children had been separated from their families, orphaned, lost, abducted or abandoned.[4] Most of Rwanda's children had witnessed extreme forms of brutality and 90 per cent of them had at some point thought they would die.[5] Most children felt they had no future. They did not believe that they would live to become adults.[6] More than three hundred children, some less than ten years old, were accused of genocide or murder. An estimated 300,000 children were thought to have been killed.[7]

Rwanda was divided, this time into victims, survivors, returnees and perpetrators. It was as though in 1945 the Jews and the Germans were to live together in Germany after the Holocaust, under a Jewish-dominated army, and with roughly a third of all Germans outside the country.

We will never know the exact number of victims in the genocide. A death toll of 1 million people is agreed by Gaillard, based on information gathered while the genocide unfolded. This was also the figure provided by Charles Petrie, the vice coordinator of the UN Rwandan Emergency Office (UNREO), who said on 24 August 1994 that he did not think that 1 million dead was an exaggeration.[8] In a report for the Commission on Human Rights, Special Rapporteur René Dégni-Ségui estimated that between 200,000 and 500,000 people had died. He reached this conclusion at the end of two months, saying he thought this far lower than the actual figure, adding that some observers thought the figure nearer one million.[9] A commission of experts, established by the Security Council to investigate the genocide, reported on 9 December 1994 that 500,000 unarmed civilians had been murdered.[10]

In December 2001 the Rwandan Ministry of Local Government produced a census carried out six years after the genocide during which the names of 951,018 victims were established. The ministry had determined that the genocide began in October 1990, in the prefectures of Gisenyi, Byumba and Ruhengeri, with the outbreak of civil war. The majority of victims were under twenty-four years old. For reasons that remain obscure, the figure generally used by news organizations is 800,000.

Hutu Power remained a threat, its adherents determined to continue their genocidal policies. From Zaire, and with the active support of the Zairean government, it did not take long for a plan to be devised to invade Rwanda, with a long-term strategy to destabilize the new government in Kigali.[11] There was a plan to continue to kill Tutsi – those people they termed 'rescapés', those who had survived, so that they could provoke the government in Kigali to retaliate against Hutu in Rwanda, thereby driving a wedge between the new government and the people and shifting attention away from the genocide. There are documents to show that an initial 'guerrilla phase' was going to cost an estimated US$6.3 million in arms and ammunition. The second phase, that of open classic warfare, would be decided when the guerrilla phase came to an end.[12] The total cost of an invasion was estimated at $50 million.[13]

The militias were integrated into the regular army forces and young recruits poured in from the refugee camps. Soon, the total number of soldiers under Hutu Power command had reached an estimated 50,000.[14] Among the flood of refugees were 30,000 soldiers and militia. The state structure had been left virtually intact, with local officials as well as national leaders. Military camps were established beside Lake Kivu at Manunga. Anything that could be carried had been removed from Rwanda: corrugated-iron sheets, window frames, door handles. Whole factories were dismantled and taken into exile along with every working vehicle.[15]

In the refugee camps, aid workers saw at first hand how local officials and the militia established their authority and control. There were gangs with guns, grenades and machetes. Some four thousand murders took place in Goma in the first month of the exodus. Killings, threats, extortions, rape and brutality were common. The Hutu Power ideology was as entrenched as ever, with people openly expressing the view that it was correct to kill Tutsi. The refugees spread over a network of 100 kilometres of roads, probably the largest group of fugitive murderers ever assembled, all fed and sheltered by the aid agencies. Hutu Power made a profit from refugee commerce, monopolizing the distribution of international aid, and creating a growing trade in purloined humanitarian provisions. There was even tax collection, the money quickly diverted into arms purchases. Richard McCall, chief of staff of the US Agency for International Development, described the camps as 'an unfettered corridor for arms shipment'. Goma settled down into a state within a state, a new 'Hutu land' carved out in Zaire.

In September 1994, a joint mission from the UNHCR and the government of Zaire considered separating the militia from the rest of the refugees. The UNHCR worked out that some 100,000 people would have to be moved – members of the militia and their families. The problems of identifying and relocating these people were immense. In November some of the aid agencies threatened to withdraw from the camps, for the people in them were no more than hostages, denied the right to return to their homes, denied equal access to aid and a guarantee of basic human rights. Some aid agency staff did walk out. MSF-France stated that the diversion of humanitarian aid by the same people who orchestrated the genocide, the lack of effective international action regarding impunity, and the fact that the refugees were held hostage presented a situation that was contradictory to the principles of humanitarian assistance. A plea was made by the agencies to the UN secretary-general to deploy a UN security force in the camps. But the Security Council dismissed a Secretariat plan that provided for 10,000–12,000 soldiers to separate the former political leaders, military and militia.[16] In any event, only one troop contributor, Bangladesh, came forward.[17]

While aid poured into the refugee camps in Zaire, and while Hutu Power rearmed and retrained, in Kigali there was nothing but debt. France was lobbying against the new regime in all international institutions, and would continue to do so for a long time to come. France tried to block aid from the European Union. France wanted money paid only when the refugees outside Rwanda had returned to their country. The main financial donors, however, insisted on negotiation as a prerequisite to aid. The World Bank had earmarked $140 million for Rwanda but wanted $4.5 million to be paid for the arrears; under the rules, new loans are not allowed unless other debts are paid, and the new government owed the World Bank US$6 million.[18] The new regime would have to repay money borrowed from international financial institutions, money that had been spent on the genocide. Having provided substantial assistance for the refugees, donors now held back, waiting until the new regime had 'established its credibility'.[19]

The new government in Kigali could not find $US4.5 million it owed, the debt that had accrued since the genocide began. What the donors were worrying about was RPF breaches of the Arusha Accords, and they wanted elections to be held. The new government argued that most moderate Hutu were dead. It was a mockery to insist that they negotiate with killers so as to form a broader-based government. There was nothing to negotiate; no one to negotiate with, apart from mass murderers.

19 | THE GENOCIDE CONVENTION

§ The Convention on the Punishment and Prevention of the Crime of Genocide of 9 December 1948 was the world's first human rights treaty, and it stood for a fundamental and important principle: whenever genocide threatened any group or nation or people, it was a matter of concern not just for that group, but for the whole of humanity. The Convention, which preceded the Universal Declaration of Human Rights by twenty-four hours, was the first truly universal, comprehensive and codified protection of human rights. While the Universal Declaration was an affirmation, the Genocide Convention was a treaty, which meant that compliance was not a choice but an obligation. The Security Council of the UN is entrusted with the application of the Genocide Convention: Article VIII states that any contracting party may call upon the competent organs of the UN to take such actions under the UN Charter as they consider appropriate for the prevention and suppression of the crime.

Following the Second World War it was intended that an international order should be created aimed at avoiding the recurrence of state-sanctioned racist policies directed against specific groups. On 11 December 1946, at its first session, the UN General Assembly adopted a resolution formally recognizing genocide as a crime under international law. Resolution 96(I) affirmed that:

> Genocide is a crime under international law which the civilized world condemns, and for the commission of which principals and accomplices – whether private individuals, public officials or statesmen, and whether the crime is committed on religious, racial, political or any other grounds – are punishable.[1]

In the 1948 Genocide Convention was enshrined the never-again promise, the world's response to the Nazi Holocaust in Europe and the revulsion at the systematic policy to exterminate the Jews.[2] The Genocide Convention was approved by the Assembly, in a unanimous vote, and it entered into force on 12 January 1951.[3]

Raphael Lemkin, a Polish lawyer, who coined the word genocide, and who is known as the father of the Genocide Convention, believed that the crime implied the existence of a coordinated plan of action, a conspiracy to be put into effect against people chosen as victims, purely, simply and exclusively because they were members of the target group. In his landmark book *Axis Rule in Occupied Europe*, published in 1944, Lemkin described the documentary evidence of genocide that he had accumulated; the copies of the laws and decrees that were part of the German technique to subjugate the peoples of Europe. Lemkin's book explained that genocide was not a sudden and an abominable aberration. It was a deliberate attempt to reconstruct the world. 'Genocide is a part of history,' Lemkin wrote. 'It follows humanity like a dark shadow from early antiquity to the present time.' Genocide could be predicted and, with an international early-warning system, it could be prevented. The key elements in genocide were effective propaganda to spread a racist ideology that defined the victim outside human existence, as vermin and subhuman, a dependence on military security and a certainty that outside interference would be at a minimum.

There were no sealed trains or secluded camps in Rwanda. A planned and political campaign, it began on 6 April 1994 and it lasted until 17 July, during which time up to one million people were murdered.[4] The methods of killing had been tried in the past and were documented in human rights reports.[5] Within a few days information was available that the killing was planned and coordinated. At the end of the first week the International Committee of the Red Cross (ICRC), which maintained a presence in the country throughout, estimated a death toll of 10,000 civilians murdered every day. After three weeks the ICRC, in an unprecedented statement, pleaded for the UN Security Council to act to protect civilians.

Throughout May reports continued to arrive at UN headquarters from the peacekeepers in Kigali that massacres continued and that there were preparations for more. At the end of May there was a two-day special session of the Human Rights Commission in Geneva with detailed testimony to the effect that the Rwandan government and military authorities were involved in the slaughter. The names of the perpetrators were known. It was possible to determine their identity from the highest to the lowest level.[6] Rony Zachariah, a doctor from Médecins Sans Frontières (MSF), described how Tutsi had been taken from the wards in his hospital in Butare and hacked and shot to death. Genocide was happening, he said. Alison des Forges from Human Rights Watch agreed that this was genocide and that the massacres had been prepared 'months in advance', with the aim of eliminating Tutsi.

A first official acknowledgement of genocide came at the end of May in a report to the Security Council from UN officials Iqbal Riza, Assistant Secretary-General for Peacekeeping, and Major General J. Maurice Baril, military adviser to the secretary-general. After a visit to Rwanda they blamed the huge civilian death toll on the government army, and in particular the Presidential Guard and youth militia.[7] More evidence arrived from the Commission on Human Rights, which reported that the massacres were planned and systematic. 'The victims are pursued to their very last refuge and killed there.'[8]

In possession of overwhelming proof of genocide, the UN Security Council thought of one action: on 1 July 1994, in Resolution 935, it established an Independent Commission of Experts, 'to evaluate the evidence'.[9] The Council mandated all organizations and agencies to provide to the Commission of Experts any evidence in their possession of breaches of the 1948 Genocide Convention. The Commission was to work with human rights monitors who were already establishing a Special Investigation Unit in Rwanda. They belonged to a newly created Human Rights Field Operation in Rwanda (HRFOR), launched in May by the Commission on Human Rights in Geneva. The Security Council wanted close coordination with them and with the Special Rapporteur on Rwanda, the Ivorian law professor Dégni-Ségui. The Commission of Experts was mandated by the Council to conduct its own investigations and reach its own conclusions. Almost at once the Commission was given an archive of evidence, from Rwanda's national archives and from other offices. This was provided by among others the staff of Amnesty International and Oxfam. Another team of investigators, including agents from the FBI, set up in the reopened US embassy and began to collect documentary evidence, which was shipped back to the US State Department. Once back in Washington some 27,000 pages of evidence were put on microfiche.[10]

The Commission of Experts would conclude that the documentary evidence collected 'proved the existence of a plan for genocide against Tutsi and the murder of moderate Hutu ... some documents reveal actual preparations for such actions, while others refer to lists of figures to be killed'.[11] The Special Rapporteur, Dégni-Ségui, gave the Commission of Experts a list of fifty-five people, those he considered chiefly responsible for the massacres, people against whom he said there was 'sufficient evidence' to prosecute for genocide.

Within three months there was a preliminary report showing that while both sides of the armed conflict had perpetrated serious breaches of international humanitarian law and crimes against humanity, there had been genocide of the Tutsi minority. There was 'overwhelming evidence' indicating that the extermination of the Tutsi had been premeditated, planned months in advance and it had been 'concerted, systematic and methodical'. It was motivated out of ethnic hatred and racist propaganda had been disseminated on a widespread basis; posters, leaflets and radio broadcasts had dehumanized the Tutsi as snakes, cockroaches and animals. A training camp existed where men had been indoctrinated in hatred against the Tutsi minority and given information about the methods of mass murder. The Commission of Expert's on-site investigation comprised specialized forensic and police teams, with prosecutors provided by member states. They located the sites of mass graves and photographs were taken. There was video recording of witnesses. In their final report they listed the dates of killings, the estimated number of victims and the sites where many people were buried or simply discarded. They found ample evidence to prove that the 1948 Genocide Convention had been massively violated between 6 April and 15 July.[12]

A part of the documentary evidence was transferred by the Commission of Experts to the office of a South African judge, Richard Goldstone. Goldstone had been appointed the first Chief Prosecutor of a newly created international tribunal, established by the Security Council on 8 November 1994, only the second such tribunal to be created.[13] Its mandate was to put on trial those responsible for genocide and other serious crimes against international humanitarian law in Rwanda in 1994. Its scope was limited. It was at French insistence in the Security Council that the court's temporal jurisdiction should run between 1 January and 31 December 1994. France also exerted pressure for the tribunal to investigate the violations of humanitarian law committed by the RPF during the genocide and afterwards.

The investigation into the genocide was continued under Judge Goldstone's direction. At the beginning, he said, he was visited by 'serious historians and professors from universities, particularly from Belgium and France', who wanted to tell him that stories of genocide were untrue. He was hampered by a lack of funding and had to argue with UN officials in New York for an adequate budget. He gradually assembled evidence and today he believes that the tribunal's work has established the 'historical truth'.[14] His strategy was to target those in command positions at national and local level including those who had fled Rwanda. Teams of investigators were established for each region, and with one team to concentrate solely on government and military leaders.[15] The Office of the Prosecutor would eventually evolve an agreed and unified case theory regarding the planning and implementation of the genocide with particular reference to the role of the military, the civilian interim government and the Interahamwe.[16]

The first trial at the ICTR began in January 1997. It resulted in a conviction in the case of a *bourgmestre* who was also a teacher and schools inspector, Jean-Paul Akayesu, from Taba commune, Gitarama. His life sentence, confirmed on appeal in September 1998, was for nine counts of genocide, direct and public incitement to commit genocide and crimes against humanity – extermination, murder, torture, rape and other inhumane acts. In a landmark ruling the judges had concluded that the crime of rape was 'a physical invasion of a sexual nature, committed on a person under circumstances which are coercive', and underscored that sexual assault constituted genocide in the same way as any other act as long as it was committed with the specific 'intent to destroy, in whole or in part, a particular group, targeted as such'.

A milestone on 1 May 1997 saw Jean Kambanda, the prime minister in the interim government, become the first person to plead guilty to the crime of genocide in an international court.[17] In an initial interview with Kambanda by ICTR investigators he acknowledged that the progress of genocide had been discussed in cabinet meetings.[18] There were guilty verdicts in December 2003 in the cases of Ferdinand Nahimana, Jean-Bosco Barayagwiza and Hassan Ngeze, who were held accountable for the racist campaign waged in *Kangura* and on RTLM.[19] By January 2009, as the fifteenth anniversary of the court approached, the ICTR had achieved thirty-six judgments, three defendants awaiting a verdict, and nineteen defendants with cases ongoing.[20]

There were formidable challenges for the Office of the Prosecution, which was to investigate all crimes, prepare indictments and prosecute offenders. The greatest problem, according to Justice Hassan B. Jallow, who was appointed the Prosecutor in 2003, was the lack of international cooperation, which he believed to be indispensable for the administration of international criminal justice.[21] Jallow thought there would be no successful outcome for the tribunal while several high-level fugitives remained at liberty. A continuing reluctance by governments to apprehend and put on trial in national courts those *génocidaires* who fled, he wrote, had not helped the course of international justice.[22]

Jallow said the French judiciary had been slow to proceed with Rwandan cases. A Catholic priest, Wenceslas Munyeshyaka, who had been at the St Famille church in Kigali, and Laurent Bucyibaruta, the prefect of Gikongoro, who is alleged to be responsible for the deaths of thousands of people, both live and work in France, and are the subject of ICTR arrest warrants, with their indictments under seal since 2005. The ICTR requested the French authorities to put them on trial in France but the French legal process showed little progress. The genocide financier, the Rwandan businessman Félicien Kabuga, remains a fugitive and is believed to be in Kenya.[23] Kabuga is named on the US State Department Rewards for Justice website, where there is a $US5 million reward offered for his capture.[24] There are thirteen fugitives named by the ICTR, a number of them who held command positions in 1994 and who are located in the neighbouring Democratic Republic of the Congo (DRC) by the ICTR Tracking Team, but there was thought to have been little cooperation from the authorities there in effecting their arrest.[25] The forces of the former Rwandan army and the Interahamwe, which fled in July 1994, had undergone several mutations. A new army called Force Démocratique pour la Libération du Rwanda (FDLR) included fugitives from justice, some of whom were involved in attempts to create a revitalized political opposition, coordinated from Europe and the USA. There remain thousands of suspects at large, including in the UK, where four Rwanda defendants won an appeal in the British courts to avoid extradition to stand trial for genocide in Rwanda on the grounds they would not get a fair trial in the current judicial system in Rwanda. They were released.[26]

While international support has fallen short of what was required, the ICTR is now under pressure to finish its work as the Security Council has imposed a completion strategy and the court is due to finish all trials at the end of 2009 and all appeals are to be concluded by 2010.[27] The tribunal has begun to reduce activities and staff, starting with the abolition of a number of posts at the Investigations Division in Kigali. The Office of the Prosecutor has been obliged to select targets, a difficult task given the number of people implicated and the fact that no country, other than Rwanda, had indicated a desire to receive any of the outstanding cases. The pressure to close the ICTR with a number of fugitives at large and the reluctance or perceived inability of many states, including Rwanda, to receive cases from the ICTR for prosecution has created an impunity gap through which many suspects will evade international justice.[28] Amnesty International has urged all countries 'which until now have declared that they do not have jurisdictions to take care of these kinds of cases, to re-examine their legislation and, if necessary, to modify it so that their national courts can try crimes falling within the jurisdiction of the ICTR'.

The ICTR came under the most severe criticism for bureaucratic inefficiency and for nepotistic and corrupt practices, and the government in Kigali was accused of controlling the use of witnesses who had to travel from Rwanda to the court.[29] But Arusha does represent the first time in Africa that an international court has called high-ranking officials to account for mass violation of human rights. The court has also achieved the largest electronic database of evidence of genocide and other international crimes. An invaluable resource, as Jallow explained in his report to the Security Council in June 2008, it would be used for years to come by national investigating and prosecuting authorities of UN member states, even after the closure of the ICTR, and for as long as the Rwandan fugitives remained at large. Long after the trials at the ICTR reached their conclusion there would be more investigators and researchers wanting to examine the existing evidence.

§ The Rwandan prisoners in the UN detention facility, built inside a top-security prison just outside Arusha, Tanzania, strenuously deny the accusations against them.[30] They maintain that the idea of genocide was a propaganda thesis. Their lawyers argue there never was a conspiracy and not one scintilla of evidence has ever been published anywhere in the world indicating that there was.[31] International opinion had been tricked into thinking that genocide took place by an effective and educated 'pro-Tutsi lobby'.

Colonel Théoneste Bagosora testified in his own defence and spent fifteen days in the box, beginning on 24 October 2005. 'Me, I don't believe that genocide took place. Most reasonable people think there were "excessive massacres",' he said. He blamed the people of Rwanda for the killing; it had been the result of their spontaneous reaction to the death of the president. Lieutenant General Dallaire was responsible for the deaths of the UN peacekeepers by failing to rescue them, and the murder of the prime minister was because the Belgian troops had abandoned her. The deaths of the opposition politicians were the fault of the UN peacekeepers through their lack of adequate protection. Bagosora was facing 'victor's justice', he said, and he was in the 'hands of the United States'.[32]

A fugitive for nearly two years, Bagosora had been arrested in Yaoundé, Cameroon, on 10 March 1996. He was transferred to the ICTR in January 1997. The trial took more than six and a half years, beginning on 2 April 2002 and lasting until 1 June 2007.[33] His defence counsel, Raphael Constant of French Martinique, maintained that his client, as the Director of Cabinet in the Ministry of Defence, had exercised no operational command.[34] Bagosora was joined in the dock by Colonel Anatole Nsengiyumva, who had been head of G2 intelligence and who was, on 7 April 1994, army commander in Gisenyi, Major Aloys Ntabakuze, the commander of the Para-commando unit, and Brigadier General Gratien Kabiligi. Their trial was known as Military One. More than thirteen different teams of investigators worked on the case over the years, based in the Investigations Division in Kigali.

Three judges took eighteen months to evaluate the prosecution evidence and on 18 December 2008 a verdict was given to a packed courtroom. Norwegian judge Erik Møse, presiding, reading from a prepared summary judgment, found three defendants, Bagosora, Nsengiyumva and Ntabakuze, guilty of genocide, crimes against humanity and war crimes.[35] They were sentenced to life imprisonment. Kabiligi was cleared of all the charges.

Judge Møse slowly read the details of the crimes for which Bagosora had been found guilty: the murders of the prime minister, Agathe Uwilingiyimana, the head of Rwanda's Constitutional Court, Joseph Kavaruganda, the opposition politicians Frédéric Nzamurambaho, Landoald Ndasingwa and Faustin Rucogoza, and a bank director, Augustin Maharangari. Bagosora was guilty of the murders of ten UN peacekeepers. He was guilty of extensive military involvement in the killing of civilians in Kigali, of the organized murders at roadblocks, of the massacres at the Centre Christus, at Gikondo, Nyundo and Kabeza and other places of sanctuary where people had gathered. Ntabakuze was found guilty of the crimes committed by the Para-commando battalion, including the massacre at the ETO.[36] Nsengiyumva was found guilty of targeted killings in Gisenyi on 7 April, at Mudende University, and for sending militia to Bisesero, in Kibuye.

A central and crucial accusation against the military officers, that they had conspired to commit genocide, was not proven. The judges determined that the evidence submitted for the charge of conspiracy to commit genocide was circumstantial and not sufficiently reliable.[37] Møse told the court that the defendants had 'not been found guilty of a considerable number of allegations with which they were charged'. There was, however, no doubt about the key findings, which formed the basis of their judgment – these men were guilty of genocide.[38] Bagosora had remained impassive throughout the hearing.[39]

That same day Protais Zigiranyirazo, the brother of Agathe Kanziga, the president's widow, was found guilty of genocide and extermination as a crime against humanity and sentenced to twenty years' imprisonment.[40] Other trials are ongoing; one of them, in which six defendants are charged with crimes in Butare, a case that began in 2001, is likely to be the longest in the history of international justice.

A network of ICTR lawyers, academics and journalists, in France, Belgium and Canada, continues to support the defence case in whole or in part.[41] There are expert witnesses called by the defence and their information spreads far beyond the courtrooms and is widely circulated on Internet sites. There are claims that the entire history of the genocide needs to be rewritten. There had been no planning; it had been a question of 'collective madness'; there was no *coup d'état* on 6 April; rather the Rwandan military had been obliged to take charge to avoid a state of anarchy. The massacres that followed were but one episode in a long and bloody civil war; the only conspiracy concerned Anglo-Saxons plotting against the Hutu by using the RFP to undermine French interests in Africa. There were claims of a 'double genocide' with Hutu as victims.[42]

The failure of the ICTR to put on trial RPF commanders for the crimes committed during the genocide, as described in the UN Commission of Experts report, continues to be used by the defence to challenge the legitimacy of the tribunal. The advocacy group Human Rights Watch believes that the tribunal has failed in its duty and continually reminds the court that the Commission of Experts had stipulated that there must be justice for all the victims. 'Although the crimes are not of the same nature or scale as the genocide they are serious crimes that fall under the ICTR jurisdiction,' the director, Kenneth Roth, wrote to the court in December 2008.[43] In Spain in 2007, Judge Fernando Andreu Merelles issued forty arrest warrants for Rwandan officials for murders committed by the RPF in Kabgaye on 2 June 1994, including '64 Hutu Priests'. This judge claimed evidence that, among other crimes, 'in the diocese of Byumba [...] a sector completely controlled by the RPA/RPF [...] several thousand people were killed'.[44] Merelles had relied on exiles from Rwanda and had not visited the country. He was using a law which holds that some crimes are so heinous that people accused of committing them can be tried anywhere, even in countries where the crimes did not take place. Spain has the broadest universal jurisdiction law in the world. 'This is the kind of thing that can and should happen when you have massive crimes that have essentially gone unpunished,' said Reed Brody, special counsel for Human Rights Watch when the Spanish report was released.[45]

In July 1994, the overwhelming need for justice in Rwanda had seemed an impossible task. No justice system or police force existed that could apply Rwandan law. The Kigali prosecutor, François-Xavier Nsanzuwera, was back in his office, and even the door frames had been looted. Thousands of people were being thrown into prison; more than 120,000 suspected perpetrators of genocide were detained in a system built for 15,000. Their conditions were appalling, and the ICRC made strenuous efforts to check the death rate, but this far exceeded the meagre volume of cases dealt with. In March 2001 the Rwandan government established the Gacaca courts, a system of justice based at community level using traditional methods and where suspects who confessed would have an automatic reduction in sentence. The regular Rwandan courts were used for those suspects deemed to have wielded power and influence; there were an estimated three thousand cases.

§   Few events have been the subject of as many rumours as the assassination, on 6 April 1994 of Rwanda's president, Juvénal Habyarimana. No international enquiry has even been held in spite of repeated calls at the time – including from the UN Security Council. The identity of those responsible for firing at the plane remains a mystery and we may never know who plotted to kill the president. A cornerstone of the defence case in Arusha is a denial that ICTR defendants had any role at all. Their lawyers have argued that the RPF was responsible in a cynical grab at power by Major General Paul Kagame, who had ordered the attack knowing full well that he would be sacrificing the Tutsi living in the country. In this case, Kagame was morally responsible for genocide.

For the ICTR prosecution a prime suspect was Lieutenant Colonel Théoneste Bagosora, who was accused of orchestrating a coup on 6 April 1994 and taking military command. Bagosora was a former commander of the anti-aircraft battalion in Camp Kanombe, and was well aware, as the prosecution lawyer Drew White reminded the court, that the flight path for the one runway went directly over the Kanombe military camp. A prosecutor in his trial, US attorney Barbara Mulvaney, said after the verdict that Habyarimana was flying back to Kigali to implement the peace deal. If the plane had landed Bagosora would have lost his house, his job and his position. He would have had to demobilize the Rwandan army and integrate with the RPF. 'Bagosora needed a big event to mobilise people, to spark the bloodlust,' she said.[46]

Bagosora told the court that it was 'common knowledge' that Kagame, the current president of Rwanda, had ordered the president's assassination. The continuing failure of the ICTR to investigate the assassination, said Bagosora, was a way to stifle the truth; the USA was preventing an inquiry as a way to protect its new ally, the RPF leadership in Kigali. Bagosora had relied in court on a French judicial report which had first surfaced in March 2004 in *Le Monde* just weeks before the tenth commemoration of the genocide.[47] A celebrated French judge, Jean-Louis Bruguière, had, for six years, been investigating the missile attack on behalf of the families of three French crew members who had died on board the jet.[48] Bruguière had obtained testimony from a series of witnesses who claimed to have been RPF soldiers, and one of them, Lieutenant Abdul Joshua Ruzibiza, had provided the names of two men who fired the missiles. Ruzibiza claimed to be a member of a secret RPF death squad called Network Zero, a group of killers that was responsible for the murder of the MDR politician Félicien Gatabazi.[49] In Bruguière's final report, published two years later in November 2006, there was a claim that Gatabazi was killed because he had refused to take part in an RPF *coup d'état* that was being prepared. No mention was made of the UN CIVPOL investigation into the assassination of Gatabazi, which had implicated the Presidential Guard, nor the arrest made in that case.

Belgian intelligence experts were quick to point to the lack of information about how RPF operatives managed to gain access to Masaka, from where, they claim, the missiles were fired. One of the most fortified areas in Kigali, it was where the families of Presidential Guards had their homes, and the farm, said to have been the location for the assassins, and where there is a cattle dip, belonged to Agathe Habyarimana, the president's wife. There was criticism of Bruguière's failure to visit the crash site, where the wreckage was visible in the garden of Habyarimana's abandoned villa.[50] Nor had Bruguière provided any ballistic evidence. There were no interviews with any of the Belgian army officers who had seen the missiles in the night sky, although Bruguière had been to Arusha to interview several defendants, including Bagosora. And although Bruguière claimed that the cockpit voice recorder and the relevant recording from Kigali International Airport control tower were available, his report was silent about what these tapes might contain.[51] No one seemed sure what to believe. The advocacy group Human Rights Watch, which had initially welcomed both the French and the Spanish judicial reports, a year later was not so certain. It determined only that parts of the French and Spanish inquiries were based on serious investigations and had merit; but that other parts were 'not fully substantiated'.[52]

Other stories emerged, one of them from an ICTR prosecution witness known as XXQ, who said that the plot involved a French mercenary.[53] According to XXQ, who had been a gendarmerie officer and is currently serving a life sentence for genocide in a Rwandan military prison, the assassins had tried to implicate UNAMIR. This involved painting army trucks white with UN markings. Protais Mpiranya, the commander of the Presidential Guard, and a senior French officer embedded in the Rwandan army living in Camp Kanombe, were also involved.[54] This same French officer, so other sources claimed, had supervised the installation of a 14.5mm anti-aircraft gun less than one hundred metres from the airport on 5 April 1994.

More than twelve years after the event, on 27 November 2006, the first international arrest warrants were issued for the terrorist attack on the plane, at the request of Judge Bruguière. They named nine senior officials who were currently serving in the Rwandan government as responsible. Only the immunity accorded by French law to serving heads of state prevented the authorities from issuing a warrant for Kagame. These officials would now face restrictions on travel, especially within the European Union. They included Major General James Kabarebe, chief of staff of the Rwandan army.[55] The Rwandan government immediately severed diplomatic relations; the French ambassador was expelled and the Rwandan ambassador in Paris was recalled. There was no basis to these allegations, an official statement noted. Rwanda was being subjected to a 'super-power, diplomatic and political war'. The first arrest came on 9 November 2008 when Rwanda's head of state protocol, Rose Kabuye, was detained at Frankfurt airport under a European arrest warrant issued by France for her alleged part in the assassination. She was extradited to France and her case is pending. Any discreet warnings there may have been beforehand were ignored, and speculation grew that the Rwandan government wanted to test the Bruguière thesis in open court.[56]

Only a matter of days later the Bruguière case was seriously weakened when Abdul Ruzibiza, the investigation's key witness, retracted his testimony. In an interview broadcast on 15 November 2008 on a Rwandan radio station, Ruzibiza said he had fabricated the whole story. The RPF Network Commando death squad was a fiction and he had never mentioned the name Rose Kabuye to anyone.[57] He was the third witness to retract.[58] An investigation is now under way in Rwanda which seeks to establish, using ballistic research and witness testimony, exactly how many missiles were fired at the plane, and the precise location of the assassins.[59]

§ A true reckoning of French involvement in Rwanda may never be possible. The French policy was largely determined within the confines of a special office in the president's Elysée Palace. It was known as the Africa Unit.[60] It operated through a network of military officers, politicians, diplomats, businessmen and senior intelligence operatives, and at its centre was President François Mitterrand.[61] Mitterrand had operated through senior army officers: General Christian Quesnot, Admiral Jacques Lanxade and General Jean-Pierre Huchon. There was some input from the French ministries of defence, finance, cooperation and foreign affairs, and from the intelligence service, DGSE.

There have been a number of investigations to try to unravel the extent of French influence. French journalist Patrick de Saint-Exupéry, in June 1994 in *Le Figaro*, blamed President Mitterrand and his Africa Unit for a total policy failure; he had reported from the hills of Bisesero, from the Opération Turquoise zone, where he had described how Rwandan survivors were abandoned by the French army. In a series for *Le Figaro* four years later, in January 1998, and in a book published in 2004, the journalist showed that France had provided weapons before, during and after the genocide. He concluded: 'We poured petrol on an immense fire.'[62] Saint-Exupéry showed how a secret army had been created for Rwanda by French officers who worked directly with what he called a '*légion présidentielle*'.[63] These elite operatives, answerable only to Mitterrand, had created a secret command for the Rwandan army, and built within it a psychological warfare capability with operatives trained in the manipulation of public opinion based on fear and terror. Rwanda was like a military laboratory.[64] This unit of elite troops, the Commandement des Opérations Spéciales (COS), which was created in 1992, was not subject to usual military controls.

It was in response to mounting evidence of French influence in Rwanda that, in March 1998, the senate established a 'Mission of Information' (Mission d'Information Parlementaire), a parliamentary investigation into the military operations of France and other countries in Rwanda from 1990 to 1994. This inquiry was unprecedented but, as its title suggested, it was intended to gather information only, and there were no judicial procedures, nor did it have the legal authority of a commission of inquiry. A series of public and private hearings took place and the senate report, published in December 1998, concluded that French policy had been intended to encourage political reform, and ensure a respect for human rights – as well as to avoid a military victory by the RPF – and it was based on the assumption that the Arusha Accords could work. France 'in no way incited, encouraged, helped or supported those who orchestrated the genocide'. There had been some actions that were 'regrettable' and the threat of genocide had been 'underestimated' at a time when 'openly racist extremist branches multiplied in most of the political parties'.[65] The policy had been guided by Mitterrand and the senate recommended that there would have to be better control by parliament over military operations. The senate did confirm that the Rwandan army had been a 'military protégé' of the French army and this had involved certain officers who were determined to prevent an RPF victory at no matter what cost. The policy had been unaccountable to either parliament or the press.

No part of French political life was untouched. When the genocide happened the French government was a left–right cohabitation between a socialist head of state, François Mitterrand, and a Gaullist prime minister, Edouard Balladur. Four former ministers testified to the senate inquiry: Edouard Balladur, Gaullist prime minister between 1993 and 1995, and three of his ministers, François Léotard, who was minister of defence, Alain Juppé, who was minster for foreign affairs (later prime minister), and Michel Roussin, minister of cooperation. Balladur, who assumed office in March 1993, was indignant at suggestions that France was as deeply involved as suggested. Only limited quantities of arms had been shipped to the Hutu regime. There was an attempt to discredit the only country that had tried to stop the genocide. Hubert Védrine, who was secretary-general at the presidency and Mitterrand's diplomatic adviser, said the French had put pressure on President Habyarimana to accept the Arusha Accords, the only possible solution.[66]

The Rwandan government's own investigation into the role of France was established during the tenth commemoration on 14 April 2004 when the cabinet adopted a draft law establishing an Independent National Commission. This was required to collect and examine documents, hear testimonies and any other evidence showing the involvement of the French state in the 1994 genocide, as well as its role in the period after the genocide in all areas – in politics, diplomacy, media, judiciary and the military.[67] The commission was chaired by a former minister of justice, Jean de Dieu Mucyo, a lawyer and genocide survivor. A detailed and lengthy report, published in August 2008, contained a damning indictment of French policy and cited thirteen senior French politicians and twenty members of the armed forces with cases to answer for their role in events. The report included witness testimony of the training of Interahamwe by French officers and alleged human rights abuses by French troops from 1990, and during Opération Turquoise, including murder and rape. This report confirmed evidence from a 2004 Citizens' Commission of Inquiry that took place in France, a collaborative effort of French human rights groups.[68] A body of evidence about French involvement continues to grow with ongoing investigations by researchers and journalists.[69]

One of the more contentious issues is likely to remain the extent of influence of senior French officers who, on 6 April 1994, were embedded in the elite units of the Rwandan army.[70] Four of them have testified at the ICTR but this was anonymously and in camera. Their evidence – given for the defence – is publicly unavailable.[71]

The first significant release of material from French government archives came in 2007, and the documents from the presidency confirmed what officials had been privately claiming: that François Mitterrand had been obsessed with Rwanda to the point of interrupting cabinet meetings to talk about it.[72] Mitterrand had truly believed that the rebel RPF was part of an 'Anglophone plot', involving the president of Uganda, Yoweri Museveni, whose ultimate aim was the creation of a regional and English-speaking 'Tutsi-land'. Mitterrand feared that this would be helped by the 'complicity of false French intellectuals' and a 'pro-Tutsi lobby'. Rwanda was a key ally, a regional and strategic base. The RPF were not freedom fighters but battle-scarred soldiers from the Ugandan army. In October 1990 Rwanda had been invaded by a foreign power, a clear case of external aggression by an 'Anglophone' neighbour attempting to seize power by stealth and military prowess. No one had ever threatened the sizeable Western aid allocation to Uganda from its US and UK allies when it failed to use its leverage to compel the RPF to withdraw its troops.

In July 1994, when a conquering RPF army had taken the whole country, the worst fears must have been realized. Mitterrand did not live to see how fifteen years later Rwanda's closest allies had become the USA and the UK, providing the bulk of foreign aid; in 2003 Rwanda had applied to join the British Commonwealth and English is now the language of commerce, education and the media.

§ A formal apology to Rwanda came from Belgium in April 2000 at a ceremony in Kigali, when the prime minister, Guy Verhofstadt, on behalf of his government, asked forgiveness from the Rwandan people.[73] 'I accept ... the responsibility of my country ... Belgium was at the heart of the UN mission ... we should have done more,' he said. Verhofstadt had served on an earlier senate inquiry into Belgium's role in Rwanda, and he said that what he had learned had changed him for ever.[74] The Senate Commission report, published in December 1997, had shown how soon this government was really well informed – given the intelligence available – about the possibility of genocide.[75] There was a cable written in 1992, sent by Johan Swinnen, the Belgian ambassador, stating that a 'secret command exists which is planning the total extermination of the Tutsis in order to resolve, once and for all, the ethnic problem and to destroy the Hutu opposition'.[76]

The Senate Commission was given access to cables, letters and reports, both confidential and secret, from the archives of the foreign and defence ministries. There were nineteen documents in which a Machiavellian plot was described, intended to terminate the peace process and destabilize the country. Two documents made specific references to the possibility of genocide. From 15 January 1994 there were twenty-nine intelligence reports from Kigali containing warnings of arms caches, the distribution of weapons to civilians, and huge quantities of weapons in houses owned by the president and in Kanombe army camp. There were warnings about the risks to Belgian troops. A note by Belgian intelligence dated 28 December 1993 claimed that French advisers who had remained in Rwanda that month after the withdrawal of the French troops had 'organised a campaign of denigrating the Belgian blue helmets [...]' and that two French experts had 'put taps on the Kigali telephone exchange, more particularly telephones in embassies'.[77] Another inquiry took place within the Belgian military, but this was held in secret and the eventual report was classified. It is understood to have concluded that UN peacekeeping had been completely inappropriate for Rwanda. The senior officers of UNAMIR, Lieutenant General Dallaire and Colonel Luc Marchal, were blamed for being too optimistic and putting too much faith in the Rwandans.[78] In later journalistic descriptions of the part played by UNAMIR officers they would be described as cowards.[79]

A UN inquiry was established in March 1999, nearly five years after the genocide began, by Kofi Annan, the former head of the Department of Peacekeeping Operations (DPKO), who had become UN secretary-general in January 1997.

Annan chose a former prime minister of Sweden, Ingvar Carlsson, to head a three-person team. The inquiry was limited in scope from October 1993, when UNAMIR was created, to the military conquest of the RPF in July 1994.[80] The eventual report was critical of the Security Council, describing a preoccupation, led by the USA, with minimizing costs and commitments. A deliberately weakened UNAMIR, a feeble UN effort, had proved to the Hutu Power faction that it had nothing to fear from the outside world. A force capable of dealing with the growing violence and eventual genocide had been required. When the genocide began, the rapid dismantling of UNAMIR ruled out any chance of re-equipping it with a mandate and the capacity to protect sites where people had sought refuge. A grave error was to have insisted on negotiations to restore a ceasefire, when what had been needed was a plan to protect civilians.[81]

The secretary-general, Boutros Boutros-Ghali, the UN report concluded, 'should have done more' to argue for reinforcements. The sole power given to the secretary-general under the UN Charter is to bring to the attention of the Council any matter that threatens international peace and security. He could have had a decisive influence. Yet Boutros-Ghali was absent from New York during the first weeks and had missed what may have been the optimum time to intervene. The report concluded: 'the Secretary-General cannot be present at every meeting ... and although Boutros-Ghali was kept informed of key developments ... the role of the Secretary-General is limited if performed by proxy'.[82]

Boutros-Ghali would angrily blame the USA and describe how he had argued for action in individual private meetings with the ambassador, Madeleine Albright, and the UK's David Hannay.[83] Boutros-Ghali mimicked their reaction: 'Come on, Boutros, relax ... Don't put us in a difficult position ... the mood is not for intervention, you will obtain nothing ... we will not move.' Boutros-Ghali denies that the Security Council was inadequately informed. 'Everybody knew that the people coming from Uganda were Tutsi and the people in power were Hutu and that it was a war between Hutu and Tutsi. We did not need to tell them that, it was evident. What was not evident was that there was a plan of genocide.' He said the entire Council meekly followed the US lead.[84] Had the Council created the UN stand-by force which he had asked for two years earlier, then the genocide might never have taken place. His own failure was to convince governments to act. 'But believe me,' he said, 'I tried.'[85]

Colin Keating, the permanent representative for New Zealand, and the president of the Council in April 1994, did not think the Council was ready to cope at ambassadorial level with professional military issues. The situation had cried out for military and technical advisers to sit together to discuss the options. No one was listening to Lieutenant General Dallaire.[86] Kofi Annan said that he believed the time had come for the member states to take stock, and to determine that sufficient resources were made available for all UN operations. Large-scale field operations needed advanced planning, clear mandates, trained peacekeepers and assured financing, an effective and integrated UN command and logistical support. At the time UNAMIR was in the field there had been 71,543 peacekeepers in seventeen different trouble spots around the globe, with 300 officials coping with logistics for them; there was no genuine peacekeeping headquarters, there were too few planning staff, no timely intelligence, no adequate command-and-control operations room. The UN had been in crisis management for as long

as anyone could remember with years of cutbacks and job losses.[87]
Scores of officials spent entire months juggling funds simply to keep
the doors open. There were institutional weaknesses, no infrastructure
for emergency operations, and no contingency planning.

The Organization of African Unity (OAU), which had played a central
role in the negotiations in Arusha, launched its own report in Addis
Ababa in July 2000.[88] Its title, *Rwanda, the Preventable Genocide*, reflected
the main conclusion – that the genocide could have been entirely prevented and, once allowed to start, could have been significantly reduced.
The Security Council, led unremittingly by the USA, simply 'did not
care enough about Rwanda'. All that had been required was a reasonably
sized international military force with a strong mandate to enforce the
peace agreement; nothing of the kind had ever been authorized by the
Security Council either before or during the genocide. Many aspects
of the story defied understanding, notably how the victims had been
'betrayed repeatedly by the international community'.[89]

The OAU itself did not escape criticism for its silence, and a large
majority of African heads of state were also found to be guilty of a
'shocking moral failure'. A large part of the responsibility rested with
France for giving 'unconditional public support' to President Juvénal
Habyarimana, this accusation also being levelled at the Anglican and
Catholic Churches. The OAU report described how in an overwhelmingly Christian population, the religious leaders had failed to use their
unique moral positions to denounce ethnic hatred and human rights
abuses. With some heroic exceptions, Church leaders played a 'conspicu-
ously scandalous role', at best remaining silent or neutral. This had been
interpreted as an implicit endorsement of the killing. There were priests
and nuns who delivered people to the killers.[90] For the OAU panel, the
'great mystery' of the genocide was the way in which Hutu Power had
managed to make so many people accomplices to their crime; this was
how people had been killed so swiftly.[91]

The OAU inquiry, with a broader remit than others, addressed the
catastrophic economic influences on events. In the late eighties Rwanda's
individual and productive farmers had been pushed to breaking point
because of drought.[92] There had been the collapse of the coffee price,
and a structural adjustment regime which had thrown people into
poverty. There were an increasing number of landless and unemployed
youths.[93] The soaring population, the soil erosion, the land scarcity – all
were relevant factors.

A key part of the role of the West had been the provision of aid.
Rwanda was one of the poorest but best-aided countries in the world.[94]

When the genocide began there had been thousands of Western technical assistants and expert expatriates training staff and advising in government ministries, or taking part in developmental cooperation.[95] While the political violence worsened and as society became militarized, the practice of aid development had continued business as usual.[96] All but one of the foreign donors increased its bilateral aid.[97] The racist policies against Tutsi seem to have been viewed by some with a quiet acceptance. A Swiss official wrote to his capital: 'while the Tutsi are excluded from political life, they more than make up for it with their role in commerce'. Switzerland, an important donor to Rwanda for thirty years, held its own inquiry into the circumstances of the genocide.[98] It laid the blame on those governments that had tried to impose a democratic system of government on a country with no organized middle class and where there was the bare minimum of economic and political control. The result was a multitude of polarized political parties, none of them with any real democratic support, and all of them either regionally or ethnically based.

Some donors, such as the US Agency for International Development (USAID), the European Union and the German government, did withhold all development aid in early 1994, just a few months before the genocide began. Each cited constraints such as a lack of Rwandan administrative capacity as a reason for suspension.[99]

§ Rwanda had been an issue requiring leadership as Senator Paul Simon (Democrat, Illinois) and Senator Jim Jeffords (Republican, Vermont) had reminded President Bill Clinton in their letter to him on 13 May 1994.[100] The senators had pleaded for help for UNAMIR, to get troops to Lieutenant General Dallaire to stop the slaughter.[101] Three days afterwards a delegation from the State Department and the Pentagon arrived at the UN in New York. While the USA was willing to help, this was on the condition that UNAMIR was bypassed and safe havens were created on Rwanda's borders, an idea that had been enthusiastically suggested by Ambassador Madeleine Albright at an informal meeting of the Security Council on 11 May.[102] The UN's Assistant Secretary-General for Peacekeeping, Iqbal Riza, told the US delegation that the problem was not on the borders.[103] He said the UN was morally obligated to stop the killing of civilians where it was taking place and urgently needed troops, transport and equipment for Lieutenant General Dallaire.

Richard Clarke, as the head of international and global issues at the National Security Council (NSC), whose remit covered UN peacekeeping, would later defend the US record. Clarke had largely been responsible for the post-Somalia policy directive towards multilateral operations, a policy that was widely interpreted as a manifesto for inaction.[104] He believes that if the UN had adopted the US idea to create safe havens lives may have been saved.[105] In the NSC, in the heart of the US government, neither Don Steinberg, senior Director for Africa, nor the National Security Adviser, Anthony Lake, formulated any policy other than to do nothing. Not one top-level meeting was held to discuss Rwanda. The Secretary of Defense, William Perry, theorized later that had Rwanda happened before Somalia there was 'a probability that a symbolic force' would have been sent, but post-Somalia most senior officials did not even want to discuss intervention.[106] The Secretary of State, Warren Christopher, apparently never once sent for contingency plans or even analysis concerning a response to Rwanda.[107] He continued to distort the reality of Rwanda as late as 24 July 1994, when he told a television programme that there had been a 'tremendous civil war' in Rwanda and that the USA had done all it could to try to support the UN, but that this had not been a time for the USA to try to intervene.[108]

Only a fraction of the government documents concerning Rwanda have been declassified under the US Freedom of Information Act, but these clearly show how from the beginning, and at all levels of government, there was significant intelligence about a huge number of civilian deaths nowhere near the civil war.[109] One of them, dated 28 April 1994, a top-secret National Intelligence Daily, routinely sent to President Clinton and other top officials, gave an estimate of 'probably 500,000 people killed' and projected that thousands more were going to die.

A US-trained marine, Allen Campbell, with over thirty years of flying experience in Africa, in the first week of June was reporting back directly to the US embassy in Kampala, Uganda, that genocide was taking place. During the third week of June he was in Kibuye, negotiating to save the lives of nuns and orphans under his protection, attempting to evaluate battle conditions, do a body count and rescue different families. At the request of the US embassy in Kampala, he evaluated reports that numerous bodies were in Lake Victoria and circulating around the lake towards the inlet source of fresh water for the capital city. Campbell was able to borrow a Ugandan police helicopter at Entebbe Airport and, with two USAID staff members on board, started to count the bodies along the shoreline of the lake, where they were stacked six deep with heads and legs missing. Some women still had their children strapped to their backs with their heads gone. The skids of the helicopter were sometimes used to separate the bodies to get an accurate count. The aircraft was used to chase away the dogs and pigs that were eating the bodies. They were entering the lake from the Kagara river in Rwanda. The body count was over ten thousand.[110]

There were detailed briefings given by the ICRC directly to US government officials in New York and in Geneva. The ICRC Director of Operations, Jean de Courten, in regular contact with Philippe Gaillard in Kigali, made it clear to Under Secretary-General for Global Affairs in the Department of State Tim Wirth that the killing would not stop without military action.

But there was reluctance even to jam the hate-radio station, RTLM. The question was raised several times in Washington during daily video conferences held in May 1994. The Defense Department's official response was that jamming the broadcasts was technically and legally impossible, but there were objections that the cost, at US$8,500 per flight, was too high. In any event, this was the decision of the State Department or the NSC. According to James Woods, deputy Assistant Secretary of Defense, the fact of genocide was known as early as the second week.[111] Recalling the misery of that time, Woods said: 'I think it was sort of a formal spectacle of the US in disarray and retreat, leading the international community away from doing the right thing and I think that everybody was perfectly happy to follow our lead – in retreat.' Everyone knew about the genocide. No official in the US administration could claim not to have known. Yet in 1998 that is precisely what President Bill Clinton did during a first visit to Kigali. In an apology to Rwanda, used to skilfully minimize his own shameful role, and attempting to rewrite history, Clinton declared:

> ... all over the world there were people like me sitting in offices, day after day after day, who did not fully appreciate the depth and speed with which you were being engulfed by this unimaginable terror. The international community, together with nations in Africa, must bear its share of responsibility for this tragedy, as well. We did not act quickly enough after the killing began ... we did not immediately call these crimes by their rightful name, genocide. Never again must we be shy in the face of the evidence.

As permanent members of the Security Council, the UK and the USA could have taken action in accordance with the 1948 Genocide Convention. But both states, from the beginning to the end, had recognized as legitimate the interim government of Rwanda, a government perpetrating genocide, hastily sworn into office to replace Rwanda's pro-democracy movement, whose members had been murdered. No attempt was made to remove this government's ambassador from the Security Council. In the Council they argued that without a ceasefire in the civil war it was militarily impossible to do anything. Both governments seemed to have wanted to undermine all attempts at strengthening UNAMIR, opposing any expansion of the mandate to allow the peacekeepers to protect Rwandans. They even failed to resupply their own volunteer garrison of UN peacekeepers and little discussion took place about what UNAMIR was achieving.[112] 'There is no magic keeping troops there,' said the UK ambassador, David Hannay, 'if there is nothing useful that they can do.'

Even after the US government had determined that genocide was happening, the Clinton administration sought to play down what was occurring.[113] The relevant memorandum from the US Office of the Legal Advisor shows that by 20 May 1994 it had been determined that 'acts of genocide' had taken place.[114] Some acts had been committed with the intent to destroy, in whole or in part, the Tutsi group. The State Department's Bureau of Intelligence had concluded that Rwandan government and military authorities were implicated in widespread, systematic killing of ethnic Tutsi, those who had Tutsi physical characteristics and those who supported Tutsi. National and local officials had exhorted civilians to take part in massacres and the campaign appeared well planned and systematic.

We may never know whether the obligations of the British government, as a signatory to the 1948 Genocide Convention, were raised in government in 1994. When the UK government determined that genocide was taking place is unclear. The principal function of the Legal Adviser at the Foreign and Commonwealth Office is to provide legal advice to ministers and officials, including on international human rights law. This department was represented at the UK mission to the UN in Geneva. What advice the Legal Adviser, Sir Franklin Berman, may have offered ministers about their responsibilities is apparently, according to him, protected by 'client privilege', irrespective of any official secrets considerations.[115] This reveals a secret process whereby officials work without any kind of scrutiny or accountability.

After weeks of genocide, on 9 May 1994 the House of Commons was informed only that 200,000 people 'may have perished in the recent fighting' in Rwanda and that a horrific and tragic civil war was happening.[116] There was little interest in the Commons; a debate did not take place until 24 May 1994, when Tony Worthington, MP (Labour, Clydebank and Milngavie), who had spoken to Oxfam, expressed shock at how little attention had been given to Rwanda. 'It is inconceivable that an atrocity in which half a million white people had died would not have been extensively debated in the House,' Worthington told an almost empty chamber, and he added that the press had a terrible tendency to dismiss the events as tribalism. But this was genocide and Britain was a signatory to the Genocide Convention; had there ever been a clearer example, he asked.

In the case of the prime minister, John Major, the Rwandan genocide has completely vanished from the public version of his period in office and there is, for instance, no reference to the Rwandan genocide in the index, chronology or the chapter on 'The wider world' in his autobiography.[117] 'Of course we didn't [do anything],' said a senior diplomat, now retired, when asked about Rwanda. 'Neither the press nor the public was interested.' Rwanda was not in the British sphere in Africa. The UK was extremely 'unsighted'; there was no British embassy in Kigali, and there were no British interests. The telegrams about Rwanda, received from British embassies in Brussels, Paris and Washington, were not treated as of high importance. 'We tended to believe what the French were telling us,' said another. The time and resources were being channelled into the problems of Bosnia, and the UK was trying to disarm Iraq. The UK mission in New York was overwhelmed with other issues.

Ambassador David Hannay complained later that the UN Secretariat had failed to provide an independent, objective flow of information. 'Events proved we were looking in the wrong direction and that the Secretariat was telling us to look in that direction,' he said. The Council was not involved in the day-to-day running of peacekeeping missions and so he never saw the UN force commander's cables.[118] The entire focus had been on how to implement the Arusha Accords. 'We really were groping around in the dark,' he said. A lack of information, however, did not prevent the UK playing a leading role in the Security Council in the shaping of UN policy towards the crisis. It was the UK which had first suggested 'a small interim presence' in Rwanda and a 'British compromise resolution' which mandated the removal of most of UNAMIR. British diplomats had argued that anything other than massive military intervention was impossible.[119]

A similar lack of information was apparently the case in Whitehall, where, according to the British journalist and executive director of the Royal African Society, Richard Dowden, as the crisis developed the Foreign Secretary, Douglas Hurd, was being briefed by officials whose only source of information was CNN.[120] 'It is hard to judge whether leaders such as John Major, François Mitterrand and Bill Clinton would have taken a different stand had they known what was going on,' Dowden wrote. But there was reliable and relevant information available and, as in the USA, this was collated at many different levels of government. At the UK mission to the UN in New York there were briefings at senior level from Belgian diplomats trying to convince the UK, a permanent member of the Council, why UNAMIR urgently needed more troops and a robust mandate. The RPF representative in New York, Claude Dusaidi, briefed UK officials about militia training, political murders, hate propaganda and death lists. The situation was discussed during meetings of the Security Council, even before the establishment of UNAMIR. In the offices of the Department of Peacekeeping Operations (DPKO) there were eight British military officers on secondment. There was UK representation in Washington, DC, at the World Bank, which had sent successive missions to Rwanda as the situation deteriorated.

There were briefings from Oxfam, including with Foreign Secretary Douglas Hurd. There were reports sent to London from the UK high commissioner in Kampala, Edward Clay. He was given information by regional Oxfam experts, one of whom accurately predicted in April 1994 that neighbouring states would be inundated with refugees. Clay visited Rwanda only weeks before genocide began; he sent cables to Whitehall before and during the genocide. Clay obtained information from UNAMIR situation reports and he met with RPF representatives. Between 21 and 23 April 1994 the UK government, involved in a ceasefire initiative for Rwanda headed by President Yoweri Museveni, was preparing briefing documents.[121] Information came from the president of the ICRC, Cornelio Sommaruga, directly to the UK government's Overseas Development Administration. This office also received intelligence from the European Community Humanitarian Office (ECHO). The UK embassy in Brussels was actively collecting information about Rwanda, from both open and more secret sources.

By late April, along with Human Rights Watch and Amnesty International, Oxfam repeatedly and publicly called on the British government for immediate action to protect civilians.[122] On 3 May the director of Oxfam, David Bryer, delivered a petition to 10 Downing Street with the British actor Helen Mirren. An accompanying letter told the prime minister that the genocide was potentially on a scale not seen since Cambodia. The UN could not stand idly by. A relatively small UN force could offer protection.[123] Bryer later recalled being 'fobbed off with all sorts of platitudes'. Ed Cairns, who was an Oxfam policy adviser, said that anyone other than a fool knew that military intervention was what was needed.[124] There were regrets later at the lack of time to devise a strategy, and they believed they should have tried to shame the politicians and officials responsible for the decision-making.

The Foreign Secretary, Douglas Hurd, admitted that in 1994 Bosnia had been the priority; it was 'in our continent'. In the House of Commons Hurd said: 'they are close to us. It is right that we should be devoting such effort to them.'[125] Some years later he wrote: 'It never occurred to us, the Americans or anyone to send combatant troops to Rwanda to stop the killing. I record this as a bleak fact.'[126] In 2004 Hurd explained that the UK government 'had been slow to realize the enormity of what had happened'.[127] The UN inquiry, however, found that states should have been ready to identify genocide and assume the responsibility to act.[128] The UK had depicted events as an ethnic civil war between morally equivalent factions, reflecting Britain's preferred solution, to seek a ceasefire.

Were there departments in the Foreign Office with information, not passing that information to ministers? Perhaps the information in Whitehall was not sent to New York. But even if all the information had reached him, Hannay remains convinced that there was nothing the UN could have done to prevent the genocide in Rwanda, not with the Hutu-led government intent upon it. He was not a lawyer and was therefore not in a position to decide whether or not what was happening was genocide. 'We knew a lot of Tutsi were being killed by a lot of Hutu,' he said. The Council could not conjure up troops, and although he believes that Dallaire did a fantastic job, Hannay remains deeply sceptical of Dallaire's belief that 5,500 troops could have prevented much of the slaughter. In any case, to have mounted an enforcement mission with so few troops was totally against US military doctrine.[129] This is not an isolated view.[130] There were analysts at the Pentagon who believed that military intervention would not have been able to stop it. Only early reinforcements of UNAMIR would have stood any chance of averting the killing.[131] In the USA, a report published in 2008, *Preventing Genocide, a Blueprint for US Policymakers*, claimed that 'leaders within the US and elsewhere still debate whether robust military action could have thwarted the massacres'. This genocide prevention initiative was co-chaired by Madeleine Albright, who in 1994 was the US ambassador to the UN.[132] The 2008 report maintains that it had been difficult to get critical information about the grave risks of genocide or mass atrocities to key decision-makers before they were full blown, and that they were 'distracted by other crises'. There was a 'lack of understanding' of the range of military options that could help prevent or stop genocide. Hannay later spoke specifically about the Genocide

Convention in relation to Rwanda. In December 1998, in a BBC Radio 4 interview, he said: 'Nobody ever started to say and who will actually do the intervening and how will it be done.'[133]

The Labour Party waited until May 1994 before pressuring the government, and then only after Oxfam telephoned the office of David Clark, the shadow defence minister. Clark responded by calling for the UN and the OAU to organize an immediate deployment of forces to try to end the mass killing of civilians, and appealed to the minister of defence, Malcolm Rifkind, for advice and expertise to be made available to the UN. Rifkind wrote back to say troops for Rwanda would 'probably come from regional forces in Africa'. The UK had not been asked to provide any personnel for the operation.[134] It was an extraordinary claim. A few days earlier, on 17 May, the UK had voted in the Security Council to authorize troops for UNAMIR, knowing that UN officials were pleading for soldiers from member states. Annan sent a list of urgently needed troops and equipment to every member government known to have spare military capacity. At that time the UK had 3,800 troops serving in peace operations. The British army had two main units that could have been rapidly mobilized for deployment overseas, each occupying a very different niche in low-to-mid-intensity combat capabilities.[135]

Some years afterwards the then Labour prime minister, Tony Blair, said that in retrospect, if nearly a million people were being murdered in Rwanda, as they had been in 1994, then the British government would have a political and moral duty to prevent or suppress the killing.[136] And yet there seemed no apparent understanding of his predecessor's failure, or how it might help to formulate government policy for the future, or any active promotion of international practices and procedures that could build up a prevention capability in the UN.

In July 1994 Britain's overseas development minister, Baroness Lynda Chalker, had visited Kigali. She asked Dallaire what he needed. Dallaire had shown Chalker his list of basic requirements, which by then had been faxed around the world. 'I gave her my shopping list,' he remembered. 'I was up to my knees in bodies by then.' The fifty trucks the UK had promised had not materialized.[137] Speaking later on a BBC TV *Newsnight* programme, Chalker would blame Dallaire's lack of resources on 'the UN', which, she said, must 'get its procurement right'.[138] Only after the genocide was over did Britain become more generous, and on 28 July offered military assistance to Rwanda in the form of 600 personnel from the Royal Electrical and Mechanical Engineers (REME) to repair the large number of unroadworthy vehicles that belonged to the mission, as well as a field ambulance and a field squadron of Royal Engineers to repair roads and drill wells.[139]

As a matter of record, the offers to UNAMIR during the genocide were fifty trucks from the UK; a promise from Italy of one C-130 aircraft plus crew, and six water trucks; a signals squadron plus aircraft from Canada; from the USA fifty armoured personnel carriers, leasehold; and from Japan, US$3 million towards the cost of equipment.[140]

'Those who were critical did not offer,' said Kofi Annan in July 1994. 'The sceptical did not offer, and the silent did not offer. What choice did we have?'

Annan had clearly believed that, whatever had happened, UNAMIR would never have overcome the fundamental problem – that the extremists did not want reconciliation with the RPF.[141] Once the genocide started, had Kigali been reinforced, then the militia would have been intimidated. In this event the Belgian UN peacekeepers would never have withdrawn from the ETO and would have stayed to protect the families in their care. But there had never been hope of reinforcements. 'If we had gone to the Council at the beginning to ask for reinforcements for UNAMIR,' one official said, 'we would have been laughed out of the chamber.'[142] Annan concluded in July 1994: 'Nobody should feel he has a clear conscience in this business ... If the pictures of tens of thousands of human bodies rotting and gnawed on by dogs ... do not wake us up out of our apathy, I don't know what will.' He found it difficult to accept that member states with more intelligence-gathering capabilities than the UN did not know what was happening. Was it really a lack of understanding of something so totally unbelievable? No. In this case no one could credibly claim ignorance. Everyone involved would be harshly judged by history. Of the part played by the USA and the UK, two powerful states with abundant means to have made a difference, Lieutenant General Dallaire would conclude that they had done everything possible to sabotage the fulfilment of the UNAMIR mission.[143] Their selfish and racist policies had aided and abetted genocide.[144]

Since 1994 there has been an almost continuous series of debates, studies and resolutions on the role of the West in Rwanda's genocide. These have shown how little true humanitarianism there is at the heart of even states that both possess abundant resources and profess a commitment to human rights.[145] Neither the US nor the UK government has answered the accusations levelled at them, including a failure to abide by their obligations under the 1948 Genocide Convention. There has been no official inquiry into this failure by either state, and today the blame has simply slid away from the officials and politicians responsible for the decision-making.

The 1994 genocide in Rwanda is one of the most horrible crimes of our age.[146] It contributed to the destabilization of an entire region and it was followed by years of war, human deprivation, rape and misery, with untold and unimaginable brutality, and an incalculable number of victims. The story has not ended.

CHRONOLOGY

1500   It is believed that from 1506 there was increasing unification of the kingdom of Rwanda. A society was created which would be compared with those in European feudal states.

1885   The Berlin Conference agrees that Ruanda-Urundi should become a German protectorate.

1894   The first European, a German, Count Gustav Adolf von Götzen, arrives in Rwanda.

1900   The Missionaries of Africa (White Fathers) found their first mission in Rwanda.

1907   The Germans establish a post in Kigali and a prominent explorer, Richard Kandt, is appointed the first Resident.

1910   The frontiers of the Belgian Congo, British Uganda and German East Africa – including Ruanda-Urundi – are fixed at a conference in Brussels.

1911   A popular uprising in northern Rwanda is crushed by the German Schutztruppe and Tutsi chiefs, leaving bitterness among northern Hutu.

1913   Coffee introduced as a cash crop.

1914   German control strengthens with the introduction of a head tax.

1916   Belgian troops chase out the Germans and occupy both Ruanda and Urundi.

1923   Ruanda-Urundi becomes a mandated territory of the League of Nations under the supervision of Belgium.

1931   *November* King Musinga is deposed by the Belgian administration and replaced with one of his sons.

1933   The Belgian administrators organize a census and everyone is issued with an identity card classifying them as Hutu, Tutsi or Twa.

1945   Transfer of the Belgian mandate to a UN Trust Territory.

1946   Dedication of Rwanda to Christ the King.

1948   The Convention on the Punishment and Prevention of the

Crime of Genocide, 1948, voted by the General Assembly on 9 December.

First UN Trusteeship Council visiting mission goes to Ruanda-Urundi and Tanganyika.

1957   Publication of the Hutu Manifesto.

1959   *July* King Mutara Rudahigwa dies in suspicious circumstances.

August–September Political parties are created.

November The Hutu rebel, supported by Belgium, and thousands of Tutsi flee for their lives to Burundi.

Belgium places Rwanda under military rule.

Hutu now favoured by Belgian administrators.

1960   Rwanda's first municipal elections give Hutu a large majority.

1961   *January* The monarchy is formally abolished by a referendum and a republic is proclaimed.

A new wave of violence against Tutsi. More people flee the country.

1962   Armed attacks by Tutsi exiles from Burundi. There are internal reprisals and 2,000 Tutsi are killed.

Proclamation of the independence of Rwanda.

Grégoire Kayibanda is declared president.

1963   Further armed attacks from Tutsi.

Violence against Tutsi escalates and there are further massacres. A new wave of refugees.

1964   British philosopher Lord Bertrand Russell calls the killing of Tutsi in Rwanda the most horrible extermination of a people since the killing of the Jews.

UN report by Max Dorsinville estimates a few hundred killed and repeats government claims that the culprits will be punished.

1967   Renewed massacres of Tutsi.

1972   Massacres of Hutu in Burundi.

Tutsi are purged from the administration in Rwanda.

1973   A purge of Tutsi from schools and the National University of Rwanda, Butare. More killings of Tutsi.

Coup d'état by Major Juvénal Habyarimana.

1975   Creation of the one-party MRND. France and Rwanda sign a military assistance agreement.

1978	Habyarimana promulgates a new constitution and becomes president of Rwanda after an election in which he is the sole candidate. Northern Hutu are favoured in government.
1979	The Rwandan Alliance for National Unity (RANU) is created in Kenya.
1980	An attempted coup by Colonel Théoneste Lizinde, ex-security chief, and thirty conspirators.
1982	The Rwandan refugee communities in Uganda are attacked. Those who flee to the border are trapped.
1983	Re-election of President Juvénal Habyarimana with 99.98 per cent of the vote.
1986	The government in Kigali announces that Rwandan refugees will not be allowed home because the country is not big enough.
1987	*1 July* Celebrations of twenty-five years of independence.
1988	International conference held by Rwandan refugees in Washington, DC. The RPF is created in Uganda.
	Re-election of Habyarimana with more than 99 per cent of the vote.
1989	First meeting of a Rwanda–Uganda ministerial committee to discuss the refugee problem.
	The price of coffee collapses.
1990	*July* Habyarimana concedes the principle of multiparty democracy.

September Thirty-three intellectuals publish a letter to denounce the one-party system.

Pope John Paul II visits Rwanda.

October The RPF invades Rwanda, starting a civil war. France, Belgium and Zaire send troops.

Rwanda's ambassador to Egypt requests Boutros Boutros-Ghali, a minister of state, to help Rwanda obtain arms.

First Egyptian weapons sold to Rwanda.

South Africa starts to sell arms to Rwanda.

Thousands of people, most of them Tutsi, are arrested in Rwanda.

More than three hundred Tutsi are killed in Gisenyi.

Structural Adjustment Programme (SAP) for Rwanda is agreed.

| 1991 | *January* RPF attack Ruhengeri prison. |

Massacres of Tutsi take place in the prefectures of Gisenyi, Ruhengeri, Kibuye and Byumba.

A further arms deal is concluded with Egypt.

February Guerrilla attack by RPF in response to massacres.

Summit in Dar es Salaam to discuss Rwanda crisis.

March A ceasefire agreement is signed in N'sele, Zaire, under OAU supervision, between the Rwandan government and the RPF, but it soon breaks down.

April A further arms deal is concluded between Egypt and the Rwandan government.

June A new constitution adopted bringing in multipartyism.

A French intelligence report warns that an extremist group surrounding Agathe Habyarimana is encouraging ethnic hatred and is determined to resist democracy.

August Creation of political parties, the MDR, PSD, PL.

September The OAU creates a Neutral Military Observer Group (NMOG) to monitor the border between Rwanda and Uganda.

November A demonstration organized by government opposition brings thousands on to the streets of Kigali. Habyarimana sets up commission to look into possible democratic system.

December Pro-democracy demonstrations take place.

1992 *January* Boutros Boutros-Ghali takes office as the sixth secretary-general of the UN.

The UN Security Council meets at summit level for the first time and Western leaders promise to equip the UN to deal with crisis prevention.

On-and-off talks continue between the Rwandan government and the RPF at various locations for over a year and another ceasefire is signed; this one is largely observed.

Assistant Secretary of State for Africa Herman Cohen convenes an inter-agency forum in Washington to discuss Rwanda.

February Massacres of Tutsi take place in the Bugesera. Radio Rwanda is blamed for incitement by human rights groups.

CDR and MRND militias are built up by Hutu Power supporters.

March Rwandan human rights group links deaths in the Bugesera to local officials.

A further arms deal is concluded between Egypt and the Rwandan government.

April   A new government with increased representation of the opposition. MDR given Foreign Affairs Ministry.

The president of the World Bank, Lewis Preston, writes to Habyarimana to ask him to stop military spending.

May   Violent demonstrations by militia.

Agathe Uwilingiyimana, minister of education, attacked in her home.

Pitched battles between supporters of the MRND and the PL.

The RPF meets with the OAU in Kampala.

June   A further arms deal is concluded between Egypt and the Rwandan government. RPF and political opposition agree formula for power sharing.

August   A defector, Christophe Mfizi, reveals that Rwanda is run by a ruthless and greedy oligarchy from the north.

Formal opening of the peace conference in Arusha, Tanzania.

October   Professor Filip Reyntjens gives a press conference in Brussels to warn of death squads in Rwanda.

November   The planning for a new radio station begins.

Political violence. Hutu extremist militia activity escalates. Government opponents continue to demonstrate.

A prominent Hutu, Dr Leon Mugesera, appeals to Hutu to send Tutsi back to Ethiopia via the rivers.

A further arms deal is concluded between Egypt and the Rwandan government.

December   Fringe elements unite. US troops storm Somali beaches – a groundbreaking humanitarian intervention.

1993   *January* The composition of a Broad-based Transitional Government is agreed at the negotiations at Arusha.

More than three hundred Tutsi killed in the north-west.

International human rights experts visit Rwanda.

Weapons are distributed to communal police in certain communes.

20–22 January MRND organizes pro-government demonstrations.

February RPF launches a fresh offensive and their soldiers reach the outskirts of Kigali. French forces again called in to help.

More than one million people displaced because of the fighting.

March   A new ceasefire is agreed.

At the UN Security Council in New York, France suggests the creation of a UN peacekeeping mission for Rwanda.

A human rights report is published revealing that 2,000 Tutsi have been killed since 1990.

A further arms deal is concluded between Egypt and the Rwandan government.

The Security Council passes Resolution 814 to restore law and order in Somalia.

April   The ICRC warns that because of the displaced people in Rwanda there is the risk of a major humanitarian catastrophe. Famine is imminent.

Bacre Waly Ndiaye, UN Human Rights Commission special rapporteur on extrajudicial, summary or arbitrary executions, visits Rwanda.

May   The Habyarimana regime enters into an arms deal for US$12 million with a French arms dealer.

The secretary-general, in a report to the Security Council, recommends the creation of a UN observer mission for the Rwanda–Uganda border.

June   The Security Council adopts Resolution 846 creating the United Nations Observer Mission Uganda–Rwanda (UNOMUR).

Brigadier General Roméo A. Dallaire appointed commander of UNOMUR.

In Mogadishu, Somalia, twenty-three Pakistani UN peacekeepers are killed.

July   A new government is formed with Agathe Uwilingiyimana as prime minister. This results in divisions within the MDR.

August   The Arusha Accords are signed between the Rwandan government and the RPF. Multiparty elections, which are to include the RPF, are scheduled to be held within twenty-two months.

Dallaire arrives in Kigali with a reconnaissance mission to evaluate the possible role of international peacekeepers.

Bacre Waly Ndiaye publishes a report for the UN Human Rights Commission which reveals that in Rwanda the Convention on the Prevention and Punishment of the Crime of Genocide, 1948, is applicable.

September The secretary-general recommends to the Security Council that a peacekeeping force be provided for Rwanda without delay.

October   Eighteen elite US troops are killed in Somalia.

The UN Security Council passes Resolution 872 creating the UN Assistance Mission for Rwanda (UNAMIR), which is to help implement the Arusha Accords. UNOMUR is integrated into UNAMIR.

Dallaire is appointed force commander of UNAMIR.

President Melchior Ndadaye of Burundi is assassinated. Thousands of people flee from Burundi to Rwanda.

Political violence in Rwanda escalates.

November   The Organization of African Unity (OAU) Neutral Military Observer Group (NMOG) is integrated into UNAMIR.

The Belgian battalion arrives in Kigali.

The secretary-general's Special Representative, Jacques-Roger Booh-Booh, arrives.

A series of killings takes place in northern communes.

December   UNAMIR peacekeepers are in place in Rwanda. As part of the Arusha Accords a contingent of RPF troops is deployed in Kigali.

French troops withdraw. A few remained with the Détachement d'assistance militaire d'instruction.

Dallaire and diplomats in Kigali receive an anonymous letter from within the Rwandan army warning of a plan to kill Tutsi in order to prevent the implementation of the Arusha Accords.

1994   *January*   Rwanda takes its seat as a non-permanent member of the Security Council.

The Security Council adopts Resolution 893 approving deployment of a second infantry battalion to the demilitarized zone.

Investiture of Habyarimana as president.

The Broad-based Transitional Government fails to take off, with each side blaming the other for blocking its formation.

Human Rights Watch Arms Project publishes a report on the continuing arming of Rwanda.

The Belgian ambassador in Kigali, Johan Swinnen, warns Brussels that the new hate-radio station is destabilizing Rwanda.

Violent demonstration takes place in Kigali by the Interahamwe.

Dallaire informs UN headquarters there is an informer from the heart of Hutu Power who warns that a genocide against Tutsi is planned.

Dallaire tries to persuade UN headquarters that he be allowed to conduct arms seizures.

21 February Félicien Gatabazi of the PSD is assassinated.

22 February Martin Bucyana, the president of the CDR, is lynched.

3 February, 24 February–5 April Dallaire warns New York of the deteriorating situation, the weapons distribution, death squad target lists, and pleads for reinforcements.

USA issues a travel advisory for Rwanda.

The ICRC and MSF stockpile medicines and prepare for large numbers of casualties.

Belgian Foreign Minister Willy Claes visits Rwanda. He warns Boutros-Ghali that Dallaire needs a stronger mandate. Claes warns the USA that Habyarimana could be playing a double game.

March A joint communiqué is issued by the Kigali diplomatic community asking for acceptance of the CDR. The manager of the Las Vegas bar, a local leader of the Interahamwe, is taken into custody for the killing of Gatabazi.

15 March US troops withdraw from Somalia.

Boutros-Ghali's report to the Security Council states that the security situation is deteriorating and requests an extension of the mandate of UNAMIR for six months.

31 March Alphonse Ingabire, CDR, assassinated in Kigali.

1–5 April Boutros-Ghali visit to Moscow.

2 April Booh-Booh threatens that the UN will pull out unless the peace agreement is implemented.

5–7 April Boutros-Ghali visit to Minsk.

5 April The Security Council, with Resolution 909, renews the mandate for UNAMIR with a threat to pull out in six weeks unless the Arusha Accords are applied.

6 April President Habyarimana and President Ntaryamira of Burundi and a number of government officials returning from negotiations in Tanzania are killed when the plane in which they are travelling is shot out of the sky on its approach to Kigali airport.

7–12 April Boutros-Ghali visit to Geneva.

7 April   Systematic killing of opposition politicians, pro-democracy Hutu and Tutsi, begins.

Ten peacekeepers guarding the prime minister are killed in a Rwandan army barracks in Kigali.

RPF troops in Kigali engage Presidential Guard.

Armed militias begin an organized round-up and slaughter of Tutsi and political moderates in Kigali. The violence escalates and spreads.

RTLM broadcasts that the RPF and the Belgian peacekeepers are responsible for the death of the president.

8 April   Telephone lines are progressively cut.

Increasing numbers of people are killed.

Former parliament speaker Théodore Sindikubwabo announces the formation of an interim government and declares himself president.

9 April   Interahamwe and Presidential Guard conduct massacre at Gikondo. Evacuation of foreign nationals starts.

The RPF leaves its northern bases and attacks Byumba and Ruhengeri.

Sindikubwabo meets Dallaire and asks him to negotiate a ceasefire with the RPF.

10–11 April   NATO launches air strike against Serb positions after Bosnian Serb assault against UN safe area of Gorazde.

10 April   Prisoners are put to work with dustcarts picking up bodies.

Ambassador David Rawson closes the US embassy in Kigali.

11 April   Dallaire obtains a ceasefire to facilitate the evacuation of expatriates.

The Belgian peacekeepers pull out of Kicukiro, abandoning 2,000 people.

12–13 April   Boutros-Ghali visit to Bonn.

12 April   French embassy closes its doors.

The interim government flees to Gitarama as the RPF moves on the capital.

Claes meets Boutros-Ghali in Bonn to tell him that Belgium is withdrawing soldiers from UNAMIR.

13–15 April   Boutros-Ghali visit to Madrid.

13 April   ICRC–MSF convoy arrives in Kigali from Bujumbura with doctors and medicines.

14 April   Belgium announces it is withdrawing its troops from

UNAMIR. In Kigali wounded people are dragged from a Red Cross ambulance and killed. An ICRC estimate is that 10,000 people are being killed every day.

15–16 April Boutros-Ghali visit to Barcelona.

18 April An attempt by the RPF to silence RTLM fails.

The interim government dismisses the prefect of Butare.

19 April The last Belgian peacekeepers leave Kigali.

21 April The UN Security Council votes Resolution 912 to withdraw the bulk of UNAMIR peacekeepers from Rwanda, authorizing 270 to remain.

The RPF takes Byumba.

22 April A second ICRC road convoy reaches Kigali from Burundi.

23–26 April Boutros-Ghali visit to Barbados.

24 April MSF pulls its medical team from Butare.

Oxfam emergencies officer Maurice Herson telephones Oxfam headquarters to say that genocide is taking place in Rwanda.

27 April Worldwide news coverage as South Africa holds first fully multiracial elections, marking the end of apartheid.

28 April Oxfam issues a press release stating that the killing in Rwanda amounts to genocide.

28–29 April An estimated 250,000 people crossed the Rwandan border into Tanzania. This is reportedly the largest mass exodus of people ever witnessed by the UNHCR.

29 April A debate in the Security Council to discuss the use of the word genocide in a Presidential Statement takes eight hours. The UK and the USA resist the use of the word.

The secretary-general asks the Security Council to re-examine its decision to reduce UNAMIR.

30 April The RPF takes the town of Rusumo close to the Tanzanian border.

1 May Rwanda is on top of news schedules owing to massive exodus of Rwandans into Tanzania.

1–3 May Boutros-Ghali visit to Oslo.

3 May Oxfam deliver letter to Prime Minister John Major at 10 Downing Street, urging military intervention in Rwanda.

4 May Boutros-Ghali appears on ABC *Nightline* and says that it is a question of genocide in Rwanda.

5 May The PDD-25 presidential directive on peacekeeping is launched.

In Kampala, Museveni accuses the interim government of Rwanda of genocide.

6 May   UN Commissioner for Human Rights José Ayala Lasso says he is going to Rwanda.

7–9 May   Boutros-Ghali visit to Pretoria.

9 May   Inauguration of Nelson Mandela as president of South Africa.

11–13 May   Boutros-Ghali visit to Paris.

13 May   Boutros-Ghali suggests to the Security Council Dallaire's original plan to airlift 5,500 troops to Kigali.

Dallaire speaks to Senators Paul Simon and James Jeffords, who write to the White House.

16 May   The RPF cuts the road between Kigali and Gitarama.

17 May   The Security Council votes Resolution 918 approving the deployment of 5,500 troops to Rwanda. No troops are available.

19 May   Lasso produces a report that calls Rwanda a human rights tragedy.

21 May   An ICRC convoy with medical aid reaches Kigali.

22 May   The RPF takes control of the airport and the Kanombe military camp and extends control over the north and eastern part of the country. The government forces continue to flee south in front of an RPF advance.

22–27 May   Assistant Secretary-General Iqbal Riza and the secretary-general's military adviser, Major General J. Maurice Baril, visit Rwanda.

23 May   The RPF overruns the presidential villa.

24 May   The UN Commission on Human Rights holds its third special session to discuss human rights violations in Rwanda.

25 May   The UN Commission on Human Rights appoints René Dégni-Ségui as special human rights envoy to Rwanda.

Ghana, Ethiopia and Senegal make a firm commitment to provide 800 troops each to the UN effort. Zimbabwe and Nigeria make similar commitments soon after.

26–28 May   Boutros-Ghali visit to Washington.

29 May   The RPF takes Nyanza.

31 May   The secretary-general reports to the Council on the special mission by Riza and Baril, recommending that the Council authorize an expanded mandate for UNAMIR.

2 June   The RPF takes Kabgayi.

5 June   The Canadian relief flight is forced to stop flying relief supplies into Kigali owing to heavy fighting around the airport.

6–10 June   Boutros-Ghali visit to Geneva.

6 June   Normandy, France. International ceremony with the heads of state of the UK, France, the USA, Canada, Netherlands, Norway, Poland and Luxembourg to commemorate the fiftieth anniversary of the D-Day landings and the defeat of fascism. Opening of the thirtieth OAU summit in Carthage, Tunisia.

8 June   The Security Council adopts Resolution 925, which extends the UNAMIR mandate until December 1994.

10–13 June   Boutros-Ghali visit to Tunis.

10 June   Some members of the interim government leave Gitarama for Gisenyi.

11 June   Special Rapporteur Dégni-Ségui begins a week-long field mission to Rwanda to investigate violations of human rights.

13 June   The RPF takes Gitarama.

14–15 June   Boutros-Ghali visit to Geneva.

17 June   France announces its plan to deploy troops to Rwanda as an interim peacekeeping force to the UN Security Council. The secretary-general and the USA support the idea.

21 June   First French troops arrive on the Zaire–Rwanda border.

22 June   The UN Security Council, in Resolution 929, approves the French proposal to dispatch troops to Rwanda under a UN humanitarian mission.

24 June   French military forces are deployed into western Rwanda through Goma and Bukavu in eastern Zaire.

28 June   The report of the UN Commission on Human Rights Special Rapporteur is published in Geneva stating that the massacres that occurred throughout Rwanda were pre-planned and a systematic campaign of genocide.

1 July   Security Council sets up a commission of experts to investigate acts of genocide in Rwanda.

Booh-Booh is replace by Mohamed Shaharyar Khan of Pakistan as Special Representative.

2 July   Boutros-Ghali supports the French proposal for a designated 'safe zone' in south-western Rwanda to protect vulnerable populations in the region.

3 July   The RPF takes Butare.

4 July   The RPF wins control of Kigali. The RPF leadership states that it intends to establish a new government based on the framework of the Arusha Accords.

5 July   The French establish a humanitarian zone in the south-west corner of the country.

6 July   Canadian relief flights into Kigali are resumed.

7 July   Kigali airport reopens.

13 July   Ruhengeri is captured by the RPF.

13–14 July An estimated one million people begin to flee towards Zaire.

14 July   An estimated six thousand people per hour file into the French safe zone, including members of the militia and interim government officials.

15 July   The Clinton administration publicly declares that it no longer recognizes the interim government of Rwanda.

16 July   Thirteen ministers of the interim government take refuge in the French safe zone.

17 July   The RPF takes Gisenyi, the last Rwandan stronghold of Hutu Power.

18 July   The war comes to an end with the RPF defeat of the remnants of Rwandan government troops still in Rwanda.

19 July   A new government of national unity is created and announces the end of compulsory identity cards.

22 July   Clinton announces that US troops will be deployed to help the refugees who have fled the country.

16 August Dallaire leaves Rwanda. Canadian General Guy Tousignant takes command of UNAMIR, which has 1,624 soldiers.

October   An interim report is produced by the Commission of Experts which concludes that a genocide had been perpetrated against Tutsi.

8 November UN Security Council adopts Resolution 955 on the establishment of an international criminal court for the criminals of Rwanda.

1996   *10 March* Bagosora arrested in Yaoundé, Cameroon.

1997   *January* Bagosora transferred to the ICTR.

2001   Zigiranyirazo arrested in Belgium.

2002   *2 April* Bagosora trial begins at ICTR, lasting until 1 June 2007. Bagosora is joined in the dock by Colonel Anatole Nsengiyumva, head of G2 intelligence, who in April 1994 was army commander in Gisenyi, Major Aloys Ntabakuze, commander of the Para-commando unit, and Brigadier General Gratien Kabiligi.

2008   *18 December* Bagosora, Nsengiyumva and Ntabakuze are found guilty of genocide, crimes against humanity and war crimes. They are sentenced to life imprisonment. Kabiligi is cleared of all charges. Protais Zigiranyirizo is found guilty of genocide and extermination as a crime against humanity and sentenced to twenty years.

Convention on the Prevention and Punishment of the Crime of Genocide, 1948

The Contracting Parties,

Having considered the declaration made by the General Assembly of the United Nations in its resolution of 96 (I) dated 11 December 1946 that genocide is a crime under international law, contrary to the spirit and aims of the United Nations and condemned by the civilized world:

Recognizing that at all periods of history genocide has inflicted great losses on humanity; and

Being convinced that, in order to liberate mankind from such an odious scourge, international co-operation is required, Hereby agree as hereinafter provided:

ARTICLE I

The Contracting Parties confirm that genocide, whether committed in time of peace or in time of war, is a crime under international law which they undertake to prevent and to punish.

ARTICLE II

In the present Convention, genocide means any of the following acts committed with intent to destroy in whole or in part, a national, ethnical, racial or religious group, as such:

a) Killing members of the group;
b) Causing serious bodily or mental harm to members of the group;
c) Deliberately inflicting on the group conditions of life calculated to bring about its physical destruction in whole or in part;
d) Imposing measures intended to prevent births within the group;
e) Forcibly transferring children of the group to another group.

ARTICLE III

The following acts shall be punishable:

a) Genocide;
b) Conspiracy to commit genocide;
c) Direct and public incitement to commit genocide;

d) Attempt to commit genocide;

e) Complicity in genocide.

ARTICLE IV

Persons committing genocide or any of the other acts enumerated in Article III shall be punished, whether they are constitutional responsible rulers, public officials or private individuals.

ARTICLE V

The Contracting Parties undertake to enact, in accordance with their respective Constitutions, the necessary legislation to give effect to the provisions of the present Convention and, in particular, to provide effective penalties for persons guilty of genocide or of any of the other acts enumerated in Article III.

ARTICLE VI

Persons charged with genocide or any of the other acts enumerated in Article III shall be tried by a competent tribunal of the State in the territory of which the act was committed, or by such international penal tribunal as may have jurisdiction with respect to those Contracting Parties which shall have accepted its jurisdictions.

ARTICLE VII

Genocide and the other acts enumerated in Article III shall not be considered as political crimes for the purpose of extradition.

The Contracting Parties pledge themselves in such cases to grant extradition in accordance with their laws and treaties in force.

ARTICLE VIII

Any Contracting Party may call upon the competent organs of the United Nations to take such action under the Charter of the United Nations as they consider appropriate for the prevention and suppression of acts of genocide or any of the other acts enumerated in Article III.

ARTICLE IX

Disputes between the Contracting Parties relating to the interpretation, application or fulfilment of the present Convention, including those relating to the responsibility of a State for genocide or for any of the other acts enumerated in Article III, shall be submitted to the International Court of Justice at the request of any of the parties to the dispute.

ARTICLE X

The present Convention, of which the Chinese, English, French, Russian and Spanish texts are equally authentic, shall bear the date of 9 December 1948.

ARTICLE XI

The Present Convention shall be open until 31 December 1949 for signature on behalf of any Member of the United Nations and of any non-member State to which an invitation to sign has been addressed by the General Assembly.

The present Convention shall be ratified, and the instruments of ratification shall be deposited with the Secretary-General of the United Nations.

After 1 January 1950 the present Convention may be acceded to on behalf of any Member of the United Nations and of any non-member State which has received an invitation as aforesaid.

Instruments of accession shall be deposited with the Secretary-General of the United Nations.

ARTICLE XII

Any Contracting Party may at any time, by notification addressed to the Secretary-General of the United Nations, extend the application of the present Convention to all or any of the territories for the conduct of whose foreign relations that Contracting Party is responsible.

ARTICLE XIII

On the day when the first twenty instruments of ratification or accession have been deposited, the Secretary-General shall draw up a *procès-verbal* and transmit a copy thereof to each Member of the United Nations and to each of the non-member States contemplated in Article XI.

The present Convention shall come into force on the twentieth day following the date of deposit of the twentieth instrument of ratification or accession.

Any ratification or accession effected subsequent to the latter date shall become effective on the ninetieth day following the deposit of the instrument of ratification or access.

ARTICLE XIV

The present Convention shall remain in effect for a period of ten years as from the date of its coming into force.

It shall thereafter remain in force for successive periods of five years for such Contracting Parties as have not denounced it at least six months before the expiration of the current period.

Denunciation shall be effected by a written notification addressed to the Secretary-General of the United Nations.

ARTICLE XV

If, as a result of denunciations, the number of Parties to the present Convention should become less than sixteen, the Convention shall cease to be in force as from the date on which the last of these denunciations shall become effective.

ARTICLE XVI

A request for the revision of the present Convention may be made at any time by a Contracting Party by means of a notification in writing addressed to the Secretary-General.

The General Assembly shall decide upon the steps, if any, to be taken in respect of such request.

ARTICLE XVII

The Secretary-General of the United Nations shall notify all Members of the United Nations and the non-member States contemplated in Article XI of the following:

a) Signatures, ratification and accessions received in accordance with Article XI;

b) Notifications received in accordance with Article XII;

c) The date upon which the present Convention comes into force in accordance with Article XIII;

d) Denunciations received in accordance with Article XIV;

e) The abrogation of the Convention in accordance with Article XV;

f) Notification received in accordance with Article XVI.

ARTICLE XVIII

The original of the present Convention shall be deposited in the archives of the United Nations.

A certified copy of the Convention shall be transmitted to each Member of the United Nations and to each of the non-member States contemplated in Article XI.

ARTICLE XIX

The present Convention shall be registered by the Secretary-General of the United Nations on the date of its coming into force.

NOTES

I GENOCIDE, APRIL 1994

1 Hutu Power is the name given to an ideology whose adherents were rabidly anti-Tutsi. Racist and nationalistic, they were opposed to the Arusha Accords, the international peace agreement that provided for the creation in Rwanda of a power-sharing democracy. Hutu Power sought the elimination of all Tutsi and all pro-democracy Hutu.

2 Testimony of Captain Luc Lemaire, in Belgian Senate, Commission d'Enquête, p. 267.

3 Interview, Lieutenant Luc Lemaire, November 1996. Lemaire said he had just enough ammunition – nine machine guns, a grenade per soldier – to get his men to the airport.

4 Lt-Col. J. Dewez, *Chronique*, 6–19 April 1994 (author's archive).

5 Ibid., p. 2.

6 Ibid., p. 25.

7 Ibid.

8 Ibid., p. 32.

9 In Rwanda there were eleven prefectures, each governed by a *préfet* (prefect). The prefectures were further subdivided into *communes* that were placed under the authority of *bourgmestres*. The *bourgmestre* of each commune was appointed by the president, upon the recommendation of the minister of the interior. In Rwanda, the *bourgmestre* was the most powerful person in the commune. His de facto authority in the area was significantly greater than that conferred upon him *de jure*. A *bourgmestre* was responsible for public order within his commune, with exclusive control over the communal police as well as any gendarmes put at the disposal of the commune. He was responsible for the execution of laws and regulations and the administration of justice, subject only to the prefect's authority.

10 Rusatira was arrested in Belgium on 15 May 2000 and later released when an ICTR indictment was withdrawn through lack of evidence against him.

11 Dewez, *Chronique*, p. 32.

12 African Rights, *Rwanda. Death, Despair and Defiance*, African Rights, London, 1995, pp. 567–71. All the quotes of survivors of the genocide are taken from this book unless otherwise stated.

13 African Rights, *Left to Die at ETO and Nyanza*, 11 April 2001.

14 Rutaganda was the second vice-president of the National Committee of the militia known as the Interahamwe. ICTR case number ICTR-96-3-1. Witness statements attached to the indictment of Georges Rutaganda, dated 12 January 1996. (Rutaganda was arrested in 1995 in Zambia.) The indictment presented by the Prosecutor of the International Criminal Tribunal for Rwanda (ICTR) on 13 February 1996 contained eight counts, including genocide, crimes against humanity and violations of the Geneva Conventions. On 6 December 1999, the Trial Chamber of the ICTR found Georges Rutaganda guilty of offences including genocide and war crimes. He was sentenced to life imprisonment. Rutaganda appealed this judgment and on 26 May 2003

the Appeal Chamber confirmed his conviction. Rutaganda was the first defendant at the ICTR to receive a war crimes conviction.

15 ICTR Judgment and Sentence. Georges Rutaganda. 6 December 1999.

16 ICTR Military One trial. Case number ICTR-98-41-T. Théoneste Bagosora, Gratien Kabiligi, Aloys Ntabakuze, Anatole Nsengiyumva. Closing submissions by Prosecutor. 28 May 2007. Summary Judgment 18 December 2008. Ntabakuke, as the commander of the Para-commando unit, was found guilty of genocide, crimes against humanity and war crimes, including the crimes committed in Nyanza on 11 April. Bagosora and Nsengiyumva were found guilty of genocide, crimes against humanity and war crimes. Each was sentenced to a single life term (subject to appeal). Kabiligi was acquitted.

17 Ibid., Closing submission.

18 Interview with a survivor of the ETO massacre, Kigali, April 2004.

19 The massacre at ETO was the subject of a BBC-financed film, *Shooting Dogs* (2007). Director: Michael Caton-Jones. It was said to have been based on the story of ETO but it grossly misrepresents what happened. There was no British priest, no British journalist and no BBC film crew at the ETO.

2 THE PAST IS PROLOGUE

1 The UN Trusteeship Council chose as commissioners: Henri Laurentie (France), E. W. P. Chinnery (Australia), Lin Mousheng (China) and R. E. Woodbridge (Costa Rica). They were accompanied by the distinguished American anthropologist Jack Harris, Political Affairs Officer, territorial research and analysis section of the UN Division of Trusteeship.

2 Linda Melvern, *The Ultimate Crime. Who Betrayed the UN and Why*, Allison and Busby, London, 1995, pp. 52–61.

3 UN Trusteeship Council, Report of the Visiting Mission to the Trust Territory of Ruanda-Urundi under Belgian Administration (T/217), 31 October 1948 (author's archive).

4 Jan Vansina, *Antecedents to Modern Rwanda. The Nyiginya Kingdom*, James Currey, Oxford, 2004.

5 John Middleton (editor-in-chief), *Encylopaedia of Africa South of the Sahara*, vol. 4, Simon and Schuster, New York, 1997.

6 C. Wrigley, *Kingship and State: The Buganda Dynasty*, Cambridge University Press, Cambridge, 1996.

7 Each district had two chiefs appointed by the Mwami, the king. There was a land chief in charge of agricultural levies and a cattle chief who collected cattle taxes. The hills were administered by hill chiefs who were responsible for landholdings, taxation and grazing rights.

8 Vansina, *Antecedents to Modern Rwanda*, p. 80.

9 Ibid., p. 11.

10 Ibid., p. 4.

11 David Newbury, *Kings and Clans. Iwji Island and the Lake Kivu Rift, 1780–1840*, University of Wisconsin Press, 1991.

12 Vansina, *Antecedents to Modern Rwanda*, p. 75.

13 Ibid., p. 133.

14 David Newbury, 'Les campagnes de Rwabugiri', *Cahiers d'étude africaines*, 14 (1974), pp. 181–91.

15 Vansina, *Antecedents to Modern Rwanda*, pp. 185–6.

16 Ibid., p. 181.

17 I. Reisdorf, 'Enquête Foncières au Ruanda, Kigali, Rwanda, 1952', Mimeograph, pp. 43–4. Quoted in Vansina, *Antecedents to Modern Rwanda*, p. 75.

18 Vansina, *Antecedents to Modern Rwanda*, p. 135.

19 Antoine Lema, *Africa Divided: The Creation of Ethnic Groups*, Lund University Press, Sweden, 1993, p. 43.

20 Catharine Newbury, *The Cohesion of Oppression. Clientship and Ethnicity in Rwanda, 1860–1960*, Columbia University Press, 1988, p. 10.

21 For an exploration of these historical processes, see D. Newbury, *The Invention of Rwanda: The Alchemy of Ethnicity* (paper presented at the ASA annual meeting, Orlando, 1995).

22 C. Newbury, *The Cohesion of Oppression*, p. 51.

23 D. Newbury, *The Invention of Rwanda*.

24 Gérard Prunier, *The Rwanda Crisis 1959–1994. History of a Genocide*, Hurst and Company, London, 1995, p. 12.

25 Jacques J. Maquet, *Le Système des relations sociales dans le Ruanda ancien*, Tervuren, 1954.

26 Lema, *Africa Divided*, p. 43.

27 J.-B. Piollet, *Les Missions catholiques françaises au XiXe siècle*, Les Missions d'Afrique, 1902.

28 Vansina, *Antecedents to Modern Rwanda*, pp. 37–8.

29 C. Newbury, *The Cohesion of Oppression*, p. 11.

30 Vansina, *Antecedents to Modern Rwanda*, p. 81.

31 Ibid., p. 197.

32 Lema, *Africa Divided*, p. 59. He sources this to a confidential memorandum of the Ministère des Colonies, dated 15 June 1920, from Archives Africaines, AE/II no. 1849 (3288).

33 Belgian Senate, Commission d'enquête parlementaire concernant les événements du Rwanda. *Rapport.* Brussels: Sénat de Belgique, 6 December 1997, p. 107.

34 René Lemarchand, *Rwanda and Burundi*, Pall Mall, London, 1970, p. 73.

35 C. Newbury, *The Cohesion of Oppression*, p. 153.

36 Ibid., p. 207.

37 In the genocide in 1994, physical traits rather than an identity card could spell the difference between death and survival.

38 Lemarchand, *Rwanda and Burundi*, pp. 74–5 and 137–9.

39 C. Newbury, *The Cohesion of Oppression*, p. 116.

40 Ibid., p. 148.

41 Ibid., p. 150.

42 Lemarchand, *Rwanda and Burundi*, p. 106.

43 Petition from B. K. Kavutse from Kigeri High School, Kigezi, Uganda (T/PET.3/107).

44 C. Newbury, *The Cohesion of Oppression*, p. 196.

45 Ibid.

46 Ibid., p. 197.

47 Kigeli V lives today in Washington, DC.

48 Kayibanda was born in 1924 and educated in a seminary at Nyakibanda. He had been the chief editor of a Catholic magazine and ran TRAFIPRO, a coffee cooperative.

49 UN General Assembly, Question of the Future of Ruanda-Urundi. Report of the UN Commission for Ruanda-Urundi established under General Assembly resolution 1743 (XVI) (A/5126), 30 May 1962.

50 Ibid.

51 Aaron Segal, *Massacre in Rwanda*, Fabian Society, April 1964. The origin of the name is also in Lema, *Africa Divided*, p. 71.

52 Gabriel Périès and David Servenay, *Une Guerre Noire. Enquête sur les origines du génocide rwandais (1959–1994)*, Editions La Découverte, Paris, 2007, p. 130.

53 Lema, *Africa Divided*, p. 72. See also Lemarchand, *Rwanda and Burundi*, p. 224.

54 *Le Monde*, 6 February 1964.

55 'De sanglants incidents auraient lieu au Ruanda', *Le Monde*, 17 January 1964.

56 'L'Extermination des Tutsi', *Le Monde*, 4 February 1964.

57 Max Dorsinville, Report of the Officer-in-Charge of the UN Operation in the Congo to the Secretary-General, 29 September 1964 (declassified at the request of the author: UN Archives, 11 November 1999).

58 Périès et Servenay, *Une Guerre Noire*, p. 138.

59 The Atlantic Report, *Rwanda*, June 1964.

60 Guy Theunis, 'Le rôle de l'église catholique dans les événements récents', in André Guichaoua (ed.), *Les Crises Politiques au Burundi et au Rwanda (1993–1994)*, Université des Sciences et Technologies de Lille, Karthala, 1995, p. 289.

61 Ibid.

62 Middleton, *Africa South of the Sahara*, 'Regional Surveys of the World', has the percentage of people with Hutu identity cards in Rwanda as 85 per cent.

63 Leo Kuper, *The Prevention of Genocide*, Yale University Press, New Haven, CT, and London, 1985, p. 154.

64 Michael Bowen, Gary Freeman and Kay Miller, *Passing By. The United States and Genocide in Burundi*, Special Report, Humanitarian Policy Studies, Carnegie Endowment for International Peace, 1972.

65 Kuper, *The Prevention of Genocide*, p. 161.

66 Ibid., p. 162.

67 Prunier, *The Rwanda Crisis*, p. 60.

68 Copies of some of these lists are in the author's archive.

69 The first military training of Rwandans in the use of guns came from the German administration at the outbreak of the First World War in 1914. It was called the Indugaruga.

See C. Newbury, *The Cohesion of Oppression*, p. 128.

70 There had been three military forces in the UN territory Ruanda-Urundi before independence in 1962. These were comprised uniquely of soldiers from the neighbouring Congo (DCR): the Force Publique Congolaise; the Garde Territoriale (GT); and the Forces Metropolitaines, based in the Congo. See Patrick and Jean-Noel Lefèvre, *Les Militaires Belges et le Rwanda 1916-2006*, Editions Racine, Brussels, 2006.

71 Périès and Servenay, *Une Guerre Noire*.

72 The Bushiru, a region in the north-west of Rwanda, was claimed by Ferdinand Nahimana, Rwandan historian and Hutu Power ideologue, to have been for many centuries a purely Hutu kingdom.

73 Vanderstraeten's archive is located in Belgium. It is a valuable contribution to studies of this period. Louis-François Vanderstraeten, Archives privées, Brussels. See: 'La force publique et le maintien de Pax Belgica 1944–janvier 1959'. Recueil d'études, 'Congo 1955–1960', Arsom, Brussels, 1992.

74 Logiest stayed on in Kigali as High Representative of Belgium and left the country on 5 June 1963 to become military adviser to President Sese Seko Mobutu of Zaire (DRC).

3 THE RWANDAN PATRIOTIC FRONT

1 François-Xavier Verschave and Claudine Vidal, 'France-Rwanda: l'engrenage d'un genocide', 19 September 1994 (author's archive).

2 Gabriel Périès and David Servenay, *Une Guerre Noire. Enquête sur les origines du génocide rwandais (1959–1994)*, Editions La Découverte, Paris, 2007, p. 146.

3 Interviews, Kigali, June 2006.

4 Linda Melvern, *The Rwandan Government Archives* (limited circulation, unpublished), 2007.

5 Gérard Prunier, *The Rwanda Crisis 1959–1994. History of a Genocide*, Hurst and Company, London, 1995, p. 76n.

6 Catherine Watson, *Exile from Rwanda. Background to an Invasion*, US Committee for Refugees, Issue Paper, Washington, DC, February 1991.

7 Jean-Paul Gouteux, *Un Génocide secret d'état*, Editions Sociales, Paris, 1998, p. 104. While the percentage of Tutsi in Rwanda was officially 9 per cent, research by the UNDP showed this figure to be nearer 20 per cent. In some places the number of Tutsi was as high as 30 per cent, principally in the west, in Kibuye. There were just 5 per cent in other parts of Rwanda, most notably in the north-west, in Gisenyi and Ruhengeri.

8 Olivier Thimonier, 'Aux sources de la cooperation franco-rwandaise', *Golias* magazine, 101, March/April 2005.

9 Patrick de Saint-Exupéry, 'Les relations franco-africaines sont essentiellement fondées sur des liens de famille', *Le Figaro*, 3 June 1994.

10 Gérard Prunier, 'The Rwandan Patriotic Front', in Christopher Clapham (ed.), *African Guerrillas*, James Currey, Oxford, 1998, p. 121.

11 Dismas Nsengiyaremye, 'La Transition démocratique au Rwanda (1989–1993)', in André Guichaoua (ed.), *Les Crises Politiques au Burundi et au Rwanda (1993–1994)*, Université des Sciences et Technologies de Lille, Karthala, 1995 (2nd edn), p. 246.

12 Stephen Kinzer, *A Thousand Hills. Rwanda's Rebirth and the Man Who Dreamed It*, John Wiley and Sons Inc., Hoboken, NJ, 2008, p. 52.

13 Ibid., p. 1.

14 The National Resistance Army of Uganda was the military wing of the National Resistance Movement.

15 Pascal Ngoga, 'Uganda. The National Resistance Army', in Clapham, *African Guerrillas*, p. 95.

16 Prunier, 'The Rwandan Patriotic Front', p. 125.

17 Watson, *Exile from Rwanda*, p. 11.

18 Ogenga Otunnu, 'An historical analysis of the invasion by the Rwanda Patriotic Army', in Howard Adelman and Astri Suhrke (eds), *The Path of a Genocide. The Rwanda Crisis from Uganda to Zaire*, Transaction, New Brunswick, NJ, 1999, p. 33. Watson, *Exile from Rwanda*, p. 13.

19 Watson, *Exile from Rwanda*, p. 14.

20 Interviews, Kigali, June 2007.

21 Rwandan Republic, Independent National Commission to Collect Proof of the Implication of the Government of France in the 1994 Genocide in Rwanda, 15 November 2007. Report published August 2008, p. 23.

22 Christophe Mfizi, *Le Réseau Zero. Fossoyeur de la démocratie et de la République au Rwanda (1975–1994)*, Consultation Report requested by the prosecutor's office. ICTR, Arusha, March 2006.

23 *The International Response to Conflict and Genocide: Lessons from the Rwanda Experience, Joint Evaluation of Emergency Assistance to Rwanda*, Copenhagen, March 1996, ch. 2, p. 19.

24 Fred Rwigyema was elected president of the RPF.

25 Interview, Patrick Mazimhaka, London, September 1999.

26 Every president, from de Gaulle to Chirac, had retained a presidential prerogative in African policy-making. The president had the power to dispatch troops overseas without reference to parliament or ministers,

advised only by the unelected head of the Africa Unit attached to the Elysée Palace.

27 Prunier, *The Rwanda Crisis*, p. 100. Jean-Christophe acquired his knowledge of Africa while a correspondent for Agence France-Presse, including in Togo. He is the eldest of Mitterrand's children. He was appointed to his father's Africa Unit in October 1986, having been deputy in the office since August 1982. He left this office in July 1992, handing over to Bruno Delaye, a career diplomat whose previous posting had been in Togo.

28 Gabriel Périès and David Servenay, *Une Guerre Noire*, p. 183.

29 Patrick de Saint-Exupéry, *L'inavouable. La France au Rwanda*, Editions des Arènes, Paris, 2004, pp. 279–80.

30 *Kangura*, 6, December 1990 (author's archive).

31 The Rwandan army's most significant weaponry had included eight 81mm mortars, six 57mm anti-tank guns, French 8mm Blindicide rocket launchers, twelve French armoured cars and sixteen French M-3 armoured personnel carriers.

32 There were seven bilateral donors, as well as the African Development Bank and the European Union, in a co-financing arrangement.

33 Pierre Galand and Michel Chossudovsky, *L'Usage de la dette extérieure du Rwanda (1990/1994). La responsabilité des bailleurs de fonds*, Brussels and Ottawa, 1996 (author's archive).

34 Minister of Defence Abu Ghazala, a presidential adviser, had built up a network of army enterprises in weapons and had recently been made responsible for selling off some of these to the private sector. Egypt ranked fifteenth in the league of world arms exporters (1989) and exported arms essentially to make domestic defence industries less of a financial drain.

35 On 3 October, President Habyarimana had appealed to Belgium for help and 500 Para-commandos had been sent to Kigali. Troops witnessed brutality and massacres committed by the Rwandan army and this led to a parliamentary debate on 9 October. On 11 October military aid was suspended by Belgium.

36 The letters, contracts and minutes of meetings concerning Rwanda's arms deals with Egypt were abandoned in the Rwandan embassy in Cairo when the genocide was over. Copies of these documents are in the author's archive.

37 Casimir Bizimungu, a medical doctor from Ruhengeri in north-west Rwanda, was arrested in Nairobi on 11 February 1999, and is currently on trial at the International Criminal Tribunal for Rwanda on charges of genocide and crimes against humanity in Rwanda in 1994. He was minister of health in the interim government that took power when the genocide began.

38 Interview, Boutros Boutros-Ghali, Paris, December 1999.

39 Diplomatic relations between Rwanda and Egypt were opened in May 1975.

40 Boutros Boutros-Ghali, *Unvanquished. A US–UN Saga*, I.B.Tauris, London, 1999.

41 ADL, *Rapport sur les droits de l'homme au Rwanda, Kigali*, Association Rwandaise pour la défense des droits de la personne et des libertés publiques (ADL), December 1992. See also Amnesty International, *Rwanda: Amnesty International's Concerns since the Beginning of an Insurgency in October 1990*, AI Index, AFR 47/05/91, March 1991.

42 Amnesty International, *Rwanda: Persecution of Tutsi Minority and Repres-*

NOTES TO 3 AND 4 | **303**

sion of Government Critics, 1990–1992,
May 1992.

43 Visit by author in June 2007 to
the former presidential office in Kigali
and interviews with former prisoners
arrested in October 1990.

44 Amnesty International, *Rwanda:
Amnesty International's Concerns since
the Beginning of an Insurgency in
October 1990.*

45 Gabriel Périès and David
Servenay, *Une Guerre Noire*, p. 183.

46 Ibid., p. 184.

4 AKAZU

1 François Misser, *Vers un nouveau
Rwanda? Entretiens avec Paul Kagame,*
Editions Luc Pire, Brussels, 2000,
p. 62.

2 Stephen Kinzer, *A Thousand
Hills. Rwanda's Rebirth and the Man
Who Dreamed It,* John Wiley and Sons
Inc., Hoboken, NJ, 2008, p. 84.

3 Ibid., p. 92.

4 Interview with Colonel Charles
Uwihoreye, minister for prisons,
Ministry of Internal Affairs, Kigali,
December 2001.

5 On 21 November 2001, seven
people from the Kinigi commune
were convicted by a Rwandan court
of genocide of the Bagogwe. See www.
hirondelle.org, Rwanda/Justice files
1999/2001.

6 André Gakwaya, Rwandan
journalist. Unpublished manuscript
(author's archive).

7 Michel Chossudovsky, 'Les
Fruits empoisonnés de l'adjustement
structurel', *Le Monde Diplomatique,*
November 1994.

8 Belgian senate, Commission
d'enquête parlementaire concernant
les événements du Rwanda, Report,
6 December 1997, p. 82.

9 According to the World Bank, the
growth of GDP per capita declined
from 0.4 per cent in 1981–86 to −5.5

per cent in the period immediately
following the slump of the coffee
market (1987–91).

10 Commission of a Citizens'
Inquiry into the role of France during
the genocide of the Tutsi in 1994.
Public session 22–26 March 2004.
Report, 'L'horreur qui nous prend
au visage'. Testimony Pierre Galand,
p. 186.

11 Private visit to the former
presidential villa in Kanombe, June
2007. Courtesy Ministry of Youth,
Culture and Sport.

12 Interviews with former staff,
presidential villa, Kanombe, June
2007.

13 There are no surnames in
Rwanda. Women do not take the name
of their husbands and children do not
bear the name of their parents.

14 Gérard Prunier, *The Rwanda
Crisis 1959–1994. History of a Genocide,*
Hurst and Company, London, 1995,
pp. 23–5.

15 Her father was Gervaise
Magera.

16 René Lemarchand, 'Rwanda:
the rationality of genocide', *Issue: A
Journal of Opinion,* XXIII(2), 1995.

17 Filip Reyntjens, *L'Afrique des
Grands Lacs en crise. Rwanda, Burundi:
1988–1994,* Karthala, Paris, 1994.

18 This information was confirmed
during testimony at the International Criminal Tribunal for Rwanda
(ICTR), Case Military One. Cross-
examination of Théoneste Bagosora.

19 Zigiranyirazo was arrested in
Belgium in 2001. He was sentenced
to twenty years in jail for genocide
and extermination at the ICTR on
18 December 2008.

20 Rwabukumba reportedly lives
in Belgium.

21 Rwagafilita's whereabouts are
unknown.

22 CRR, 15 February 2007,
564776, Mme Habyarimana.

23 Evaluation of Emergency Assistance to Rwanda. Study 2: *Early Warning and Conflict Management*, Copenhagen, 1996, p. 28.

24 RFP Press Release, 'Death commando unit and massacres of civilians in Rwanda', Paris, 4 November 1991. Signed: Dr Jacques Bihozagara (author's archive).

25 Jean-Pierre Chrétien, *Le Défi de l'ethnisme. Rwanda et Burundi, 1990–1996*, Karthala, Paris, 1997, p. 136.

26 Sagatwa died on 6 April 1994, in the missile attack on the private Falcon jet of President Juvénal Habyarimana.

27 François Karera was arrested in Kenya in 2001. His trial began at the ICTR in January 2006.

28 Simbikangwa, who is on the Interpol wanted list for genocide, was arrested on 28 October 2008 in the French overseas territory of Mayotte. A month later a French court ruled against his extradition to Rwanda.

29 Nsengiyumva was arrested in Cameroon in 1996. He was found guilty of genocide and war crimes charges on 18 December 2008 and sentenced to a life trem.

30 Renzaho was arrested in Kinshasa in September 2002 and his trial on genocide charges began at the ICTR in November that year.

31 Belgian senate, Commission d'enquête, p. 493.

32 Jean-François Dupaquier, 'Rwanda. La France au chevet d'un fascisme africain', *L'Evénement du Jeudi*, July 1992.

33 Email correspondence with Dupaquier, September 2008.

34 Christophe Mfizi, 'Le Réseau Zéro', Lettre ouverte à Monsieur le Président du Mouvement Républicain National pour la Démocratie et le Développement (MRNDD), Editions Uruhimbi, Kigali, 1992.

35 Professor Filip Reyntjens. Bulletin Cridef: 'Donneés sur les escradons de la mort', October 1992 (copy provided to author by Professor Reyntjens).

36 Ibid.

37 Nzirorera was arrested in Benin in June 1998. His trial opened in November 2003 at the ICTR and he pleads not guilty to genocide and related charges.

38 ICTR testimony of Professor Filip Reyntjens, Military One, 16 September 2004.

39 Afrika further alleged that Monsieur Z, Protais Zigiranyirazo, was implicated in the murder of Dian Fossey, the American ecologist whose passion for the silverback gorillas in northern Rwanda was internationally known.

40 Janvier Afrika, 'Ibikorwa bya escradon de la mort byashyizwe ahagaragara', published in Kinyarwanda in *Umurava* magazine, 14, 25 December 1992.

41 Laurent Bijart, quoted in Citizens' Inquiry, Report, p. 329.

42 ADL, *Rapport sur les Droits de l'Homme au Rwanda. September 1991–September 1992*, Association Rwandaise pour la défense des droits de la personne et des libertés publiques (ADL), Kigali, December 1992. There had been killing of Tutsi by now in Kibilira, Mutara, Nasho, Bigogwe and Murambi.

43 Stephen Smith, 'Massacre au Rwanda: le réseau zero du général président', *Le Monde*, 9 February 1993.

44 Marc Sommers, 'Fearing Africa's young men. The case of Rwanda', Social Development Papers, 32, World Bank, January 2006.

45 Interviews, Kigali, October 1997.

46 Afrika, 'Ibikorwa bya escradon de la mort byashyizwe ahagaragara'.

47 Two men ran these camps: a

Belgian-trained former Presidential Guard chief, Colonel Leonard Nkundiye, and the American-trained Lieutenant Colonel Innocent Nzabanita, who was nicknamed Gisinda (wild animal).

48 Filip Reyntjens. 'Akazu, "escadrons de la mort" et autres. "Réseau Zéro": un historique des résistances au changement politique depuis 1990', in André Guichaoua (ed.), *Les Crises politiques au Burundi et au Rwanda (1993–1994)*, Université des Sciences et Technologies de Lille, Karthala, Paris, 1995 (2nd edn), p. 265.

49 Belgian senate, Commission d'enquête, p. 495.

50 In the Bugesera, Hassen Ngeze, the editor-in-chief of the extremist journal *Kangura*, was seen distributing copies of anti-Tutsi leaflets. Colette Braeckman, *Rwanda, histoire d'un génocide*, Fayard, Paris, 1994.

51 The homes of Tutsi were looted in the communes of Kanzenze, Gashora and Ngenda.

52 The Parti Libéral had the largest Tutsi membership. The Parti Social Démocrate, recruited from among Hutus from the south, was more intellectual. The oldest opposition party was the Mouvement Démocratique Républicain.

53 Lucie Edwards, the Canadian ambassador, operated from the Canadian embassy in Kenya.

54 Georges Martres served from September 1989 until March 1993 and was replaced by Jean-Michel Marlaud.

55 The MRND changed its name in April 1992 to the Mouvement Républicain National pour la Démocratie et le Développement (MRNDD).

56 Uwilingiyimana was prime minister in a transitional government, and while holding this office she was assassinated when the genocide began.

Belgian peacekeepers, part of her security detail, were killed trying to protect her.

57 The International Development Agency contributed $19 million as part of a coordinated relief programme with the UNDP. The UNDP pledged $3.1 million and the World Food Programme $16 million.

58 Interview, Michel Chossudovsky, Professor of Economics, University of Ottawa, December 1999. La Coopération Suisse au Rwanda, Rapport du Groupe d'Etude institué par le Départment Fédérale des affaires Etrangères (FAE), January 1996. (See Chapter 19.)

59 Leon Mugesera lives in Quebec, Canada, where he is fighting a deportation order.

60 The complete text of the Mugesera speech can be found in Guichaoua, *Les Crises politiques au Burundi et au Rwanda.*

61 Chrétien, *Le Défi de l'ethnisme*, p. 143.

62 Citizens' Inquiry, p. 109.

63 Assemblée Nationale. Mission d'Information Commune. *Enquête sur la Tragédie Rwandaise (1990–1994)*, p. 187.

64 Citizens' Inquiry, p. 111.

65 Mel McNulty, 'France's Rwanda débâcle', *War Studies*, 2(2), Spring 1997, p. 10.

66 Patrick de Saint-Exupéry, *L'inavouable. La France au Rwanda*, Editions des Arènes, Paris, 2004, pp. 267–71, 276–7.

67 Nsabimana was killed on 6 April 1994 in a missile attack on the president's private Falcon jet.

68 McNulty, 'France's Rwanda Débâcle', p. 12. Paul Barril, former head of the GIGN (Groupe d'intervention de la gendarmerie nationale), is currently director of the private security firm SECRETS (Société d'études de conception et de

réalisation d'équipements techniques et de sécurité), one of five constituent companies of Groupe Barril Sécurité.

69 François-Xavier Verschave and Claudine Vidal, 'France–Rwanda: l'engrenage d'un genocide', Rapport préparé pour l'observatoir permanent de la cooperation française, 19 September 1994 (author's archive).

70 Senate Report, p. 351. Roux was later responsible for the security at the Elysée Palace. See Citizens' Inquiry, p. 134.

71 Assemblée Nationale, vol. 2, p. 183.

72 Human Rights Watch Arms Project, *The Arms Trade and Human Rights Abuses in Arming Rwanda*, 6(1), January 1994.

73 Prunier, *The Rwanda Crisis*, p. 164.

74 Interviews, Kigali European airport technicians, June 2007.

5 PEACE IN RWANDA?

1 In June 1992, Salim Ahmed Salim had presented a proposal to create an OAU Mechanism for Conflict Prevention, Management and Resolution, and a year later this was established by the Assembly of Heads of States and Government. A peace fund was launched in 1993 to pay for it but African funding was not available. The OAU was not provided with enough money by its member states to finance military operations.

2 NMOG had a mandated strength of fifty-five soldiers from Mali, Nigeria, Senegal and Zimbabwe.

3 Twagiramungu lacked the support of the majority of his party, which was badly divided. A pro-reform Hutu, he was accused of having sided with the RPF and was therefore seen by the extremists as corrupted.

4 Testimony of Eric Gillet. Belgian senate, Commission d'enquête parlementaire concernant les evénéments du Rwanda. Report, 6 December 1997, p. 193.

5 Interview, Patrick Mazimhaka, London, September 1999.

6 Interview, Major General Paul Kagame, Kigali, October 1997.

7 The CDR's militia was the Impuzamugambi.

8 Bruce D. Jones, 'The Arusha peace process', in Howard Adelman and Astri Suhrke (eds), *The Path of a Genocide. The Rwanda Crisis from Uganda to Zaire*, Transaction, New Brunswick, NJ, 1999, p. 141.

9 Barayagwiza was arrested in Cameroon in 1996 and taken to the ICTR. He was found guilty of genocide and related charges in December 2003 in the Media Trial and sentenced to life in prison. This was reduced on appeal in 2007 to thirty years.

10 Contrat pour la fourniture de matériels techniques militaires. Contrat No. 01/93 Dos 0384/06.1.9. Pour l'acheteur: le Ministre de la Défense, Dr James Gasana. Le Ministre des Finances, Marc Rugenera. Pour le vendeur: Dominique Lemonnier (author's archive).

11 Jones, 'The Arusha peace process', p. 135.

12 International Federation of Human Rights (FIDH), Africa Watch, InterAfrican Union of Human Rights, and International Centre of Rights of the Person and of Democratic Development. Report of the International Commission of Investigation of Human Rights Violations in Rwanda since October 1, 1990 (7–21 January 1993).

13 Professor Schabas is currently the director of the Irish Centre for Human Rights at the National University of Ireland, Galway.

14 For the text of the 1948 Genocide Convention, see pp. 293–6.

15 Nahimana was arrested in

Cameroon in 1996. His trial at the ICTR lasted from 2000 to 2003, when he was convicted on genocide charges. See Chapter 7.

16 A sub-commission on Prevention of Discrimination and Protection of Minorities was created in 1946 to undertake studies to make recommendations to protect racial, national, religious and linguistic minorities. This sub-commission meets at least once a year. Members are nominated by governments and elected by the Commission on Human Rights but serve in a personal capacity.

17 The USA, the UK, France and Canada were members of the commission. Belgium was not.

18 In the first set of confidential discussions with the commission in 1992, the Rwandan judge who appeared for the government was notable for his incompetence. In 1993, the Rwandan government sent a member of the democratic opposition, Agathe Uwilingiyimana, minister of education, who was one of the first politicians to be assassinated on the morning when the genocide began. She gave evidence on 8 March 1993 in Geneva.

19 UN Commission on Human Rights, *Report by Mr. B. W. Ndiaye, Special Rapporteur, on his mission to Rwanda from 8 to 17 April 1993* (E/CN. 4/1994/7/Add. 1), 11 August 1993.

20 Interview, Paul Kagame, Kigali. October 1997.

21 The peace agreement was concluded on 12 July 1992 during the negotiations that led to the Arusha Accords.

22 Jean-Hervé Bradol, 'Rwanda, Avril–Mai 1994. Limites et ambiguités de l'action humanitaire. Crises politiques, massacres et exodes massifs', *Les Temps Modernes*, 583, 1995, p. 126.

23 Jones, 'The Arusha peace process', p. 141.

24 Note dated 15 February 1993 to the President of the Republic. Institut François Mitterrand. As quoted in Rwandan Republic, Independent National Commission to Collect Proof of the Implication of the Genocide in Rwanda, Kigali, 2008.

25 Report by Mr B. W. Ndiaye.

26 Serubuga is reportedly living in Strasbourg, France.

27 Letters dated 12 October 1991 and 29 November 1991 (author's archive).

28 Immediately after the genocide, the RPF gave the Special Rapporteur for the UN Commission on Human Rights, René Dégni-Ségui, a list of names of fifty-five people considered to be the core group of *génocidaires*. The International Criminal Tribunal for Rwanda later prepared an unofficial list of some five hundred people involved. See para. 144, Report of the Special Representative of the Commission on Human Rights, 17 September 1999. A provisional list of 220 people who allegedly organized the genocide, published by the RPF in July, is reproduced in André Guichaoua (ed.), *Les Crises politiques au Burundi et au Rwanda (1993–1994)*, Université des Sciences et Technologies de Lille, Karthala, Paris, 1995 (2nd edn), pp. 723–7.

6 PREPARING THE GENOCIDE

1 ICTR Indictment. The Prosecutor against Augustin Bizimungu, Augustin Ndindiliyimana, Protais Mpiranya, François-Xavier Nzuwonemeye and Innocent Sagahutu. Amended 25 September 2002, ICTR 200-56-1.

2 Document from Case no. ICTR 96.7.D. The Prosecutor of the International Criminal Tribunal for Rwanda against Théoneste Bagosora.

3 Bagosora was arrested in Cameroon in 1996 and transferred to the

ICTR in January 1997. He was given a life sentence on 18 December 2008 for genocide, crimes against humanity and war crimes. Summary judgment: The summary found that several elements underpinning the prosecution case about conspiracy were not supported by sufficiently reliable evidence.

4 Colonel B. E. M. Théoneste Bagosora, 'L'Assassinat du President Habyarimana ou l'Ultime Opération du Tutsi pour sa reconquête du pouvoir par la force au Rwanda', Unpublished (author's archive).

5 ICTR Prosecution Witness, statement, GS (author's archive).

6 Bagaragaza surrendered to the ICTR in August 2005. Negotiations for a guilty plea agreement broke down in October 2008.

7 Musabe was arrested in Cameroon in 1996 but later released. He was assassinated in February 1999.

8 Interview with witnesses by ICTR investigator, Kigali, 1997.

9 ICTR Judgment and Sentence, Media Trial, December 2007, Summary, p. 29.

10 Navanethem Pillay, of South Africa, was chosen as the UN High Commissioner for Human Rights in September 2008.

11 Dina Temple-Raston, *Justice on the Grass. Three Rwandan journalists, their trial for war crimes, and a Nation's quest for redemption*, Simon and Schuster, New York, 2005.

12 ICTR Testimony of Professor Filip Reyntjens. Cross-examination of Reyntjens by Defence attorney Raphael Constant, 16 September 2004.

13 Genocide Prevention Task Force. Preventing Genocide: A Blueprint for U.S. Policymakers Madeleine K. Albright • William S. Cohen. Co-Chairs John Danforth • Thomas Daschle Stuart Eizenstat • Michael Gerson Dan Glickman • Jack Kemp Gabrielle Kirk McDonald • Thomas R. Pickering Julia Taft • Vin Weber • Anthony Zinni Brandon Grove, Executive Director. United States Institute of Peace, 2008 by the United States Holocaust Memorial Museum, the American Academy of Diplomacy, and the Endowment of the United States Institute of Peace.

14 ICTR Court Transcript. Testimony of ZF. Prosecution witness. Military One. Bagosora et al.

15 Ntabakuze was arrested in Kenya in 1997. After a trial lasting six and a half years, on 18 December 2008 he was sentenced to life imprisonment for genocide, crimes against humanity and war crimes. An appeal is likely.

16 ICTR Prosecution witness statement, DAT (author's archive).

17 Amnesty International, *Rwanda: Amnesty International's Concerns since the Beginning of an Insurgency in October 1990*, AI Index AFR 47/05/91, March 1991.

18 Afrika reportedly fled Rwanda in 1996 and went to live in Cameroon. See ICTR Testimony. Professor Filip Reyntjens. Cross-examination by Defence attorney Raphael Constant. 16 September 2004.

19 Quoted in François-Xavier Verschave and Claudine Vidal, 'France–Rwanda: l'engrenage d'un genocide', Rapport préparé pour l'observatoir permanent de la cooperation française, 19 September 1994 (author's archive).

20 Ngirumpatse was arrested in Mali in 1998. He is currently on trial for genocide and related charges at the ICTR.

21 Interviews, Kigali, June 2004. As far as can be ascertained, no complete copy was found.

22 Christophe Mfizi, 'Le Réseau Zéro. Fossoyeur de la démocratie et de la République au Rwanda (1975–1994)', Consultation Report requested by the Prosecutor's office. ICTR, Arusha, March 2006.

23 Interviews, Kigali, June 2007, with survivors of the October 1990 arrests.

24 Assemblée Nationale, Mission d'Information Commune, *Enquête sur la tragédie Rwandaise (1990–1994)*, Paris, p. 276.

25 The letters: Ministère de la Défense Nationale. Armée Rwandaise. Etat-Major. G2 Secret. Note au Chef. EM AR Objet: Sûreté Intérieure de l'Etat. Letter dated 2 July 1992; Objet: Etat d'esprit des militaires et de la population civile. 27 July 1992. Signed: A. Nsengiyumva Lt Col. Copie: SEM le Président de la République (author's archive).

26 Nsengiyumva was arrested in Cameroon in March 1996. He was convicted of genocide and related charges 18 December 2008.

27 Human Rights Watch/Fédération Internationale des Ligues des Droits de l'Homme, *Leave none to tell the story. Genocide in Rwanda*, 1999, p. 107.

28 Bagosora, 'L'Assassinat du Président Habyarimana' (author's archive).

29 ICTR. Interrogation transcript of Jean Kambanda. Prime Minister. Interim Government. (April 1994–October 1995) (author's archive). Kambanda was the first head of government to plead guilty to the crime of genocide. He is serving a life term in a prison in Mali.

30 Jean Kambanda, 'Les circonstances entourant mon arrestation le 15 July 1997 à Nairobi, au Kenya, mon detention en Tanzanie, mon transfert au pays-bas et mon procès en appel', 19 October 1999. Quoted in 'The Rwandan genocide. How it was prepared', Human Rights Watch Briefing Paper, April 2006.

31 Jacques Castonguay, *Les Casques Bleus au Rwanda*, Editions l'Harmattan, Paris, 1998, p. 68.

32 Oxfam-Belgium pulled out of Rwanda in 1994, before the genocide, because of the racist policies of the government.

33 Commission of a Citizens' Inquiry into the role of France during the genocide of the Tutsi in 1994. Public session 22–26 March 2004. Report, 'L'horreur qui nous prend au visage'. Testimony Pierre Galand, p. 186.

34 Pierre Galand and Michel Chossudovsky, 'L'Usage de la dette extérieure du Rwanda (1990/1994). La responsabilité des bailleurs de fonds. Analyse et recommandations', Preliminary report, Brussels and Ottawa, November 1996, unpublished (author's archive). A list of machete and agricultural-tools importers is listed in this report together with invoice amounts.

35 Kabuga is currently at large, and one of the principal targets of the ICTR. He was indicted in 1998 on eleven counts including genocide. In August 1994 he was deported from Switzerland and allowed to fly to Zaire. He is thought to be resident in Kenya under the protection of certain political leaders. The USA has offered a reward of $US5 million for information leading to his arrest.

36 IMF Rwanda. Briefing Paper – 1992 Article IV Consultation and Discussions on a Second Annual Arrangement. May 14, 1992. Confidential (author's archive).

37 In December 1991, Colonel A. Ndindiliyimana went to Cairo. In February 1992, President Habyarimana visited Cairo on a two-day official visit. Documents, Cairo Embassy (author's archive).

38 United States Congress, Committee on International Relations, House of Representatives, Rwanda: Genocide and the Continuing Cycle of Violence. Hearing before

the Subcommittee on International Operations and Human Rights, 5 May 1998. Addendum, The Nature of the Beast – Arms Trafficking to the Great Lakes Region of Africa, Kathi Austen.

39 See Gérard Prunier, *The Rwanda Crisis 1959–1994. History of a Genocide*, Hurst and Co., London, 1995, p. 148. In France, after the legislative election of March 1993, the new conservative majority in the French parliament started to investigate the operation of Crédit Lyonnais and found it to have undertaken a number of operations that were politically motivated and without justifiable business reasons. Accounts were in the red for over $9 billion. Its general manager, Jean-Yves Haberer, was dismissed. (See *Le Nouvel Observateur*, 29 September–5 October 1994.)

40 During the genocide Cairo airport was used as a staging post for arms deliveries to Rwanda; a Boeing 707, registered in Nairobi and chartered by the British company Mil-Tec, called in at Cairo.

41 'Regional survey of the world', *Africa South of the Sahara*, 1994.

42 Funds were blocked for some months between 1992 and 1993 and resumed after the signing of the Arusha Accords.

43 Interviews, Washington, DC, January 1998.

7 THE HATE RADIO

1 Human Rights Watch, 'Leave none to tell the story. Ten years later', *Propaganda and Practice*, 1 April, 2004, hrw.org.

2 Article 19, *Broadcasting genocide: censorship, propaganda and state-sponsored violence in Rwanda 1990–1994*, International Centre against Censorship, London, October 1996, pp. 85–6.

3 Ferdinand Nahimana, *Le Rwanda. Emergence d'un état*,

L'Harmattan, Paris, 1993. Nahimana was evacuated with French embassy staff from Kigali to Burundi on 8 April 1994. He was arrested in Cameroon in March 1996. After a three-year trial at the ICTR he was sentenced to life imprisonment for incitement to genocide and related charges in December 2003. The sentence was reduced to a thirty-year term by the court of appeal in 2007.

4 Serugendo was arrested in Gabon in 2005 and transferred to the ICTR. He was charged with conspiracy to commit genocide and cooperated with the court. He received a six-year sentence. He died in 2006.

5 In June 2000, the ICTR sentenced Ruggiu to twelve years in prison on two counts of directly and publicly inciting people to commit genocide.

6 Radio-Télévision Libre des Mille Collines Société Anonyme (RTLMC SA), Statutes (author's archive).

7 There were 20,000 shares at 5,000 Rwanda francs each. No one could own more than 1,000 shares. Company Statutes (author's archive).

8 Liste des Actionnaires de la Radio-Télévision des Mille Collines (RTLMC), unpublished (author's archive).

9 ICTR Judgment and Sentence. Media Trial. December 2003.

10 Reporters sans Frontières, 'Rwanda: médias de la haine ou presse démocratique?', Rapport de mission, 16–24 September 1994.

11 ICTR Judgment and Sentencing. Media Trial. December 2003. Summary, p. 14.

12 Ngeze was arrested in Kenya in 1997. He was convicted of incitement to genocide and related crimes at the ICTR in December 2003. His sentence was reduced from life to thirty-five years on appeal in 2007.

13 *Kangura*, 53, December 1993.

See André Guichaoua (ed.), *Les Crises politiques au Burundi et au Rwanda (1993–1994)*, Université des Sciences et Technologies de Lille, Karthala, Paris, 1995.

14 *Kangura*, 6, December 1990 (author's archive).

15 Georgina Holmes, 'The postcolonial politics of militarizing women's lives. An analysis of the extremist magazine *Kangura* and the gendering of a genocidal nation-state', *Minerva Journal of Women and War*, 2(2), 2008, pp. 26–63.

16 ICTR Media Trial Summary, p. 24.

17 Human Rights Watch, *Propaganda and Practice*.

18 Roger Mucchielli, *Psychologie de la publicité et de la propaganda*, Editeur ESF, Paris, 1970, p. 74.

19 MRND. Secrétariat National. Militant(e) Membre du Comité National du MRND. Object: Transmission d'un document. Kigali. 24 August 1991. Signed Edouard Karemera. Copied to the President (author's archive).

20 ICTR Media Trial. Summary, p. 18.

21 Belgian senate, Commission d'enquête parlementaire concernant les événements du Rwanda, Report, 6 December 1997, p. 607.

22 Ibid., p. 599.

23 'Evaluation of emergency assistance to Rwanda: lessons from the Rwanda experience', *Joint Evaluation of Emergency Assistance to Rwanda*, Copenhagen, 1996, ch. 2, p. 19.

24 Jared Cohen, *One Hundred Days of Silence. America and the Rwanda Genocide*, Rowman and Littlefield, 2007, p. 19.

8 NEW WORLD ORDER

1 Council of Ministers. 3 March 1993. Note taken by Françoise Carle. Institut François Mitterrand. See: Rwandan Republic, Independent National Commission to Collect Proof of the Implication of the Government of France in the 1994 Genocide in Rwanda. November 15, 2007. Report published August 2008, p. 218.

2 Howard Adelman, 'Canadian policy in Rwanda', in Howard Adelman and Astri Suhrkei (eds), *The Path of a Genocide. The Rwanda Crisis from Uganda to Zaire*, Transaction, New Brunswick, NJ, 1999.

3 There was an OAU neutral military observer group in 1991–92 of forty observers called NMOG. NMOG II, officially 240 observers, operated 1992–93.

4 Agnes Callamard, 'French policy in Rwanda', in Adelman and Suhrke, *The Path of a Genocide*, p. 170.

5 Ibid., p. 171.

6 The missions were: UNPROFOR (former Yugoslavia); UNOSOM II (Somalia); UNOMOZ (Mozambique); UNIFIL (Lebanon); UNICYP (Cyprus); UNIKOM (Iraq Kuwait); UNDOF (Golan Heights); MINURSO (Western Sahara); ONUSAL (El Salvador); UNTSO (Israel Palestine); UNAVEM (Angola); UNMOGIP (India Pakistan).

7 UN General Assembly. Effective planning, budgeting and administration of peacekeeping operations. Report of the Secretary-General, A/48/1994, 25 May 1994. Nearly all post-cold-war operations concerned the transition from civil war to civil society: Namibia (UNTAG); Cambodia (UNTAC); El Salvador (ONUSAL); and Haiti (UNMIH). El Salvador, Mozambique and Namibia were successful although a peaceful solution for Angola remained impossible. See also: Alex Bellamy, Paul Williams and Stuart Griffin, *Understanding Peacekeeping*, Polity Press, London, 2004.

8 American diplomats in Rwanda funded conferences on constitutional reform and paid for printing the government's constitutional literature. The USA encouraged human rights groups. The US Information Service had organized and facilitated a study tour of the USA for representatives of Rwanda's political parties in order to explain the role parties played in a democracy. See Jared Cohen, *One Hundred Days of Silence. America and the Rwanda Genocide*, Rowman and Littlefield, 2007, p. 19.

9 Report of the Secretary-General on Rwanda, requesting establishment of a UN Assistance Mission for Rwanda (UNAMIR) and the Integration of UNOMUR into UNAMIR (S/26488), 24 September 1993. *The United Nations and Rwanda, 1993–1996*, UN Blue Book series, vol. 10, UN Department of Public Information, New York, 1996, p. 221.

10 'New chief of UN pyramid', Profile of Boutros Boutros-Ghali, *Observer*, 24 November 1991.

11 A former assistant secretary-general, Giadomenico Picco, wrote a strong criticism of Boutros-Ghali in *Japan Times*, 10 November 1996.

12 Linda Melvern, Obituary, Sadruddin Aga Khan, *Independent*, 14 May 2003.

13 Boutros Boutros-Ghali, *Unvanquished. A US–UN Saga*, I.B.Tauris, London, 1999, p. 9.

14 Ibid., p. 23.

15 Ibid., p. 7.

16 *Secretariat News*, September 1991.

17 Linda Melvern, *The Ultimate Crime. Who Betrayed the UN and Why*, Allison and Busby, London, 1995, p. 84–5.

18 US Department of State Dispatch, Address to the Nation. Washington, DC, 4 December 1992.

19 Troops came from the USA,

Italy, Morocco, France, Pakistan, Nigeria, Egypt, Malaysia and Turkey.

20 Michael Barnett, *Eyewitness to a Genocide. The United Nations and Rwanda*, Cornell University Press, 2002.

21 UN troops did serve in the UN Preventive Deployment Force in the former Yugoslav Republic of Macedonia (UNPREDEP), 1993–99.

22 In October 1993, the non-permanent members of the Security Council were: Cape Verde, Djibouti, Japan, Morocco, Pakistan, Hungary, Brazil, Venezuela, New Zealand and Spain.

23 UN Security Council. Report of the Commission of Inquiry Established Pursuant to Security Council Resolution 885 (1993), 4 February 1994.

24 Interview, Secretariat official, DPKO, July 1994.

25 Steven A. Dimoff, 'Congress's budget-cutting fervor threatens US standing at UN', *Interdependent*, 19, United Nations Association of the US, Autumn 1993.

26 Interviews, DPKO, March 1996.

27 Statement, 'The Security Council role in the Rwanda crisis', by Ambassador Colin Keating, Permanent Representative of New Zealand to the UN, at Comprehensive Seminar on Lessons Learned from UNAMIR, 12 June 1996. Unpublished (author's archive).

28 David Hannay, *New World Disorder. The UN After the Cold War – An Insider's View*, I.B.Tauris, London, 2008.

9 PEACEKEEPERS

1 Assemblée Nationale, Mission d'Information Commune, Enquête sur la Tragédie Rwandaise (1990–1994), Book III: Auditions, p. 396.

2 The observers were to patrol, observe and make sure the buffer zone was not breached. See *The United Nations and Rwanda, 1993–1996*, Blue Book series, vol. 10, 1996. The observers came from Bangladesh, Botswana, Brazil, Hungary, the Netherlands, Poland, Senegal, Slovakia and Zimbabwe.

3 Dallaire was appointed force commander on 18 October 1993. He was promoted to major general on 1 January 1994.

4 Report of the Secretary-General on Rwanda, requesting establishment of a UN Assistance Mission for Rwanda (UNAMIR) and the integration of UNOMUR into UNAMIR (S/26488), 24 September 1993, in *The Blue Helmets. A Review of UN Peacekeeping* (3rd edn), UN Publications, New York, p. 221.

5 Paul LaRose-Edwards, *The Rwandan Crisis of April 1994: The Lessons Learned*, International Human Rights, Democracy and Conflict Resolution, Ottawa, 1994.

6 'Remember Rwanda, Dallaire pleads', *Globe and Mail*, Toronto, 2 February 1998.

7 Interviews, Washington, DC, January 1998.

8 Karamira was arrested in Bombay, India, in 1996. He was extradited to Rwanda and found guilty of genocide and related charges on 15 February 1997. He was executed by firing squad in the Nyamirambo stadium on 24 April 1998.

9 Jean-Paul Kimonyo, *Rwanda. Un Génocide populaire*, Karthala, Paris, 2008.

10 Human Rights Watch/Fédération Internationale des Ligues des Droits de l'Homme, *Leave none to tell the story. Genocide in Rwanda*, 1999, p. 138.

11 Kimonyo, *Rwanda*, p. 126.

12 Belgian senate, Commission d'enquête parlementaire concernant les événements du Rwanda. Report. 6 December 1997, p. 194.

13 Article 19, *Broadcasting genocide: censorship, propaganda and state-sponsored violence in Rwanda 1990–1994*, International Centre against Censorship, London, October 1996.

14 Bruce D. Jones, 'The Arusha peace process', in Howard Adelman and Astri Suhrke (eds), *The Path of a Genocide. The Rwanda Crisis from Uganda to Zaire*, Transaction, New Brunswick, NJ, 1999, p. 153n.

15 Michael N. Barnett, 'The politics of indifference at the UN and genocide in Rwanda and Bosnia', in Thomas Cushman and Stjepan Mesrovic (eds), *This Time We Knew: Western Responses to Genocide in Bosnia*, New York University Press, New York, 1996.

16 Susan D. Moeller, *Compassion Fatigue*, Routledge, New York and London, 1999, p. 286. Moeller quotes Steven Weisman, the *New York Times* deputy foreign editor, who said Somalia had used up a lot of the news resources.

17 Guy Theunis, 'Le rôle de l'église catholique dans les événements récents', in André Guichaoua (ed.), *Les Crises politiques au Burundi et au Rwanda (1993–1994)*, Université des Sciences et Technologies de Lille, Karthala, Paris, 1995, p. 289.

18 Jean-Hervé Bradol, 'Rwanda, Avril–Mai 1994. Limites et ambiguïtés de l'action humanitaire. Crises politiques, massacres et exodes massifs', *Le Temps Moderne*, 583, 1995.

19 Interview, Lieutenant General Roméo A. Dallaire, London, November 1994.

20 Roméo A. Dallaire, 'End of innocence: Rwanda, 1994', in Jonathan Moore (ed.), *Hard Choices: Moral Dilemmas in Humanitarian Intervention*, Rowman and Littlefield, Oxford, 1998.

21 In Kigali during the UN reconnaissance mission, a French attaché had argued for 500 UN observers.

22 Dallaire, 'End of innocence'.

23 Jacques Castonguay, *Les Casques Bleus au Rwanda*, Editions L'Harmattan, Paris, 1998.

24 Venuste Nshimiyimana, *Prélude de Génocide Rwandais. Enquête sur les circonstances politique et militaires du meurtre du Président Habyarimana*, Quorum, Brussels, 1995, p. 66.

25 UNAMIR, coded cable, 6 January 1994 (author's archive).

26 Brent Beardsley. Statement to ICTR. Military One (author's archive).

27 UN Archives. UNAMIR Force Commander's papers. Box G60132. To Maurice Baril. From Dallaire. Subject: Military Situation Overview. 30 November 1993. MIR 144.

28 UN Doc. To Annan from Booh-Booh. Assessment of Political Situation. 28 November 1993.

29 The best the Bangladeshi troops managed was to construct a volleyball pitch and a soccer field for themselves in Byumba. They were there because their government was paid $1,000 a month for each soldier by the UN (the Bangladeshi government paid their troops $10 a month).

30 James Orbinski, *An Imperfect Offering. Dispatches from the Medical Frontline*, Random House, 2008, p. 129.

31 Lieutenant General Roméo Dallaire, *Shake Hands with the Devil. The Failure of Humanity in Rwanda*, Random House, Canada, 2003, p. 185.

32 Rwandan Army Command. Letter to Minister of Defence. August 28, 1993. Signed Nsabimana (author's archive).

33 UNAMIR observers were with the RPF battalion and UN military observers were alongside the RPF and Rwandan government army in some outlying areas.

34 Mel McNulty, 'France's Rwanda débâcle', *War Studies*, 2(2), Spring 1997, p. 12.

35 Stephen Kinzer, *A Thousand Hills. Rwanda's Rebirth and the Man Who Dreamed It*, John Wiley and Sons Inc., Hoboken, NJ, 2008, p. 101.

36 Genocide in Rwanda. Documentation of Two Massacres during April 1994. Issue Brief, US Committee for Refugees, November 1994, p. 11 (author's archive).

37 David Waller, *Rwanda: Which Way Now?*, Oxfam, Oxford, 1993.

38 Theunis, 'Le rôle de l'église catholique'.

39 Dallaire, Police Forces' Reconnaissance Mission Report 1993 (author's archive).

40 Bizimana is the subject of an ICTR indictment containing eleven counts including genocide. He is a fugitive.

41 Kajuga was killed during the genocide.

42 Human Rights Watch/Fédération Internationale des Ligues des Droits de l'Homme, *Leave none to tell the story*, p. 149.

43 Major General Roméo Dallaire, 'Military aspects', in Dick A. Leurdijk (ed.), *A UN Rapid Deployment Brigade*, Netherlands Institute of International Relations, The Hague, 1995.

44 Twagiramungu was the first post-genocide prime minister, serving from July 1994 to August 1995. He resigned and lived in Brussels until 2003, when he unsuccessfully stood against President Paul Kagame in a presidential election.

45 Gatabazi was killed on 22 February 1994.

46 Guichaoua, *Les Crises politiques au Burundi et au Rwanda*, pp. 653–4.

47 The force commander did not know of this slush fund. He knew only that one request for cash had been denied.

48 Dallaire, *Shake Hands*, p. 122.

49 ICTR Prosecution witness UB would later claim that Jean-Pierre had been Ngirumpatse's intermediary with the Interahamwe. Trial Chamber Government II. Testimony, 24 February 2007.

50 Interview, Colonel Luc Marchal, December 1999.

51 Dallaire, *Shake Hands*, p. 144.

52 Philip Gourevitch, *We wish to inform you that tomorrow we will be killed with our families. Stories from Rwanda*, Picador, London, 1999, pp. 104–5.

53 Riza had been Special Representative with the UN Observer Mission in El Salvador (ONUSAL), to monitor the end of a decade-long civil war, the reform of the armed forces, the judiciary and the electoral system. ONUSAL ran from July 1991 to April 1995. See *The Blue Helmets*, p. 737.

54 UN Security Council, Report of the Independent Inquiry into the Actions of the UN during the 1994 Genocide in Rwanda, 15 December 1999, p. 26.

55 Frontline Transcript, www.pbs. org/wgbh/pages.

56 In his reconnaissance report, Dallaire had recommended a military Special Representative leading a French-language mission. Instead it was decided to have a civilian Special Representative leading an English-language mission in a French-speaking country.

57 UN Security Council, Report of the Independent Inquiry, 15 December 1999, p. 10.

58 Ibid., p. 11.

59 The cable: Annan, UNATIONS, New York to Booh-Booh/Dallaire, UNAMIR, Kigali, no. 100, 11 January 1994 (see Castonguay, *Les Casques Bleus*).

60 Human Rights Watch/Fédération Internationale des Ligues des Droits de l'Homme, *Leave none to tell the story*, p. 156.

61 Filip Reyntjens, *Rwanda. Trois jours qui on fait basculer l'histoire*, Editions l'Harmattan, Paris, 1995, p. 19.

62 Ibid., p. 154.

63 UN Security Council, Report of the Independent Inquiry, p. 11.

64 Human Rights Watch Arms Project, *Arming Rwanda. The Arms Trade and Human Rights Abuses in the Rwandan War*, 6(1), January 1994.

10 PEACEKEEPERS IN TROUBLE

1 Interview, Major General Roméo Dallaire, London, November 1994.

2 UN Doc. DPKO. UNAMIR outgoing Code Cable. To Annan from Booh-Booh. 21 January, 1994 Attachment: Inter-office memo: To SRSG. From FC. 21 January, 1994 (author's archive).

3 UN Doc. Force Commander's Documents. 'Notes on Meeting with Kagame'. Mulindi. 22 January, 1994 (author's archive).

4 UN Doc. From Booh-Booh to Annan. Political/Military Option Estimate. 21 January, 1994. CRN 22 (author's archive).

5 Lt Gen. Roméo Dallaire, *Shake Hands with the Devil. The Failure of Humanity in Rwanda*, Random House, Canada, 2003, p. 161.

6 UN Doc. From Annan to Booh-Booh. 24 March. UNAMIR 858. UNAMIR Security Responsibility (author's archive).

7 Dallaire, *Shake Hands*, p. 147.

8 Interview, Major General Roméo A. Dallaire, 23 September 1994.

9 Jacques Castonguay, *Les Casques Bleus au Rwanda*, Editions L'Harmattan, Paris, 1998, p. 140.

10 UN Archives. UNAMIR Force Commanders Papers. Box 1. G60132. Interoffice Memorandum. From FC to Distribution List. 4 February, 1994 (author's archive).

11 UNAMIR CIVPOL. Police

Observers Staff List shows the following contingents: Austria (20), Bangladesh (2), Belgium (5), Guyana (2), Mali (5), Togo (15) (author's archive).

12 Nzansuwera is today a Legal Officer, Appeals Section, ICTR.

13 Dallaire, *Shake Hands*, p. 187.

14 André Guichaoua, *Rwanda 1994: Les Politiques du génocide à Butare*, Karthala Editions, 2005, p. 99.

15 Interviews, Gikondo, December 2001.

16 Interview, Major General Paul Kagame, Kigali, October 1997.

17 Guichaoua, *Rwanda 1994*, p. 114.

18 Dallaire, *Shake Hands*, p. 200.

19 The State Department report for 1994 noted that in January and February government militiamen killed several dozen citizens, blocked streets, searched cars, beat perceived opposition supporters and damaged property. US Department of State, Country Reports on Human Rights Practices for 1994 (US Government Printing Office, Washington, DC, 1995).

20 UN Security Council, Report of the Independent Inquiry into the Actions of the UN during the 1994 Genocide in Rwanda, 15 December 1999, p. 12.

21 UN Doc. Force Commander's documents. To Annan. From Dallaire. 'Withdrawal patrols on night of February 22'. 3 March, 1994 (author's archive).

22 UN Doc. To Annan from Booh-Booh. UNAMIR Civilian Police. 8 March, 1994 (author's archive).

23 UN Doc. To Annan from Dallaire. Attention Major-General Baril. MIR 437 CRN 65. 27 February, 1994 (author's archive).

24 UN Doc. To Annan from Booh-Booh. The Current Situation in Rwanda. MIR 409. 24 February, 1994 (author's archive).

25 UN Doc. To Annan from Booh-

Booh. Current Situation. MIR 418. 25 February, 1994 (author's archive).

26 Interviews, Brussels, October 2007.

27 Civilian Police (Investigative Section) Special Report. To SRSG. Through Police Commissioner. Subject: 'Shooting of the Minister of Public Works and Energy, Mr. Gatabazi, Félicien.' No date (author's archive).

28 CIVPOL Special Report. Last page: List of names of people said to have organized and carried out the assassination of Gatabazi. There are also the names of those people who allegedly interfered with the investigation (author's archive).

29 UN Doc. Weekly Sit Rep. To Annan and Goulding from Booh-Booh. MIR 715. 5 April, 1994 (author's archive).

30 Avocats sans Frontières. Chronique Judiciaire. Assises Rwanda 2007, no. 2.

31 Dallaire, *Shake Hands*, p. 180.

32 Belgian senate, Commission d'enquête parlementaire concernant les événements du Rwanda. Report, 6 December 1997, p. 242. In the UN Independent Inquiry the date is given as 14 February.

33 Ibid., pp. 392–3. The telex was sent by the *chef de cabinet*, M. Willems.

34 Holly J. Burkhalter, 'The question of genocide. The Clinton administration and Rwanda', *World Policy Journal*, 11(4), Winter, 1994/95, p. 45.

35 Belgian senate, Commission d'enquête, p. 394.

36 Under J.-R. Booh-Booh there were four subordinate commands: Mission HQ, Military Division, Police Division and Administration and Management Division. In his reconnaissance report, Dallaire had recommended that they be under military command in accordance with the principle of unity of command.

37 Dallaire, *Shake Hands*, p. 114.

38 Vénuste Nshimiyimana, *Prélude du genocide rwandais. Enquête sur les circonstances politiques et militaires du meurtre du President Habyarimana*, Quorum, Brussels, 1995, p. 35.

39 Dallaire, *Shake Hands*, p. 118.

40 Ingrid A. Lehmann, *Peacekeeping and Public Information. Caught in the Crossfire*, Frank Cass, London, 1999, p. 101.

41 Dallaire, *Shake Hands*, p. 208.

42 Ibid., p. 209.

43 Human Rights Watch Arms Project, *Arming Rwanda. The Arms Trade and Human Rights Abuses in the Rwandan War*, 6(1), January 1994.

44 Lindsey Hilsum, 'Fears of new wave of tribal killings', *Guardian*, 23 February 1994.

45 Richard Dowden, 'Comment: the Rwandan genocide: how the press missed the story. A memoir', *African Affairs*, 103: 283–90. Dowden is the executive director of the Royal African Society.

46 Eric Bertin, Unpublished report, Kigali, 28 February 1994.

47 UN Doc. To Annan from Dallaire. Reinforcement of the KWSA. MIR 437. 27 February, 1994 (author's archive).

48 The Rwandan government forces numbered 40,000 soldiers, with some 6,000 gendarmes, while the RPF was estimated at some 20,000 strong.

49 Interview, Major General Paul Kagame, Kigali, October 1997.

50 Bruce D. Jones, 'The Arusha peace process', in Howard Adelman and Astri Suhrke (eds), *The Path of a Genocide. The Rwanda Crisis from Uganda to Zaire*, Transaction, New Brunswick, NJ, 1999, pp. 142–3.

51 Dallaire, *Shake Hands*, p. 205.

52 UN Doc. To Annan/Goulding. Weekly sit-rep. NB 23. 15 March–21 March, 1994 (author's archive).

53 Dallaire, *Shake Hands*, p. 201.

54 UN Commission on Human Rights, *Report on the situation of human rights in Rwanda submitted by Mr. René Dégni-Ségui, Special Rapporteur, under paragraph 20 of resolution S-3/1 of 25 May, 1994* (E/CN.4/1995/7), 28 June 1995, p. 9.

55 Colette Braeckman, 'Jean Birara', *Le Soir*, 8 May 1994.

56 ICTR Prosecution anonymous witness. XXQ.

57 Interview, Major Stefan Stec (UNAMIR). The Hague, October 1997.

58 Belgian senate, Commission d'enquête, p. 334.

59 Summary of World Broadcasts. AL/1962 A/3. 4 April 1994.

60 The communiqué was signed by Dr Jacques-Roger Booh-Booh; Monsignor Giuseppe Bertello, dean of the Diplomatic Corps; the US ambassador, David Rawson; the French ambassador, Jean-Michel Marlaud; the Belgian ambassador, Johan Swinnen; the German ambassador, Dieter Holscher; the Zairean ambassador, M. Kokule; the Ugandan ambassador, Ignatius B. Katetegirwe; the chargé d'affaires from Burundi, Severin Mfatiye; and the representative of Tanzania and the facilitator to Arusha, Saleh Tambwe (author's archive).

61 UN Doc. DPKO Files. RPF. Letter to the Secretary-General of the UN. Subject: Complaint Against Dr. Booh-Booh, Mulindi. 5 April, 1994 (author's archive).

62 ICTR witness statement, Jacques-Roger Booh-Booh (author's archive).

63 André Guichaoua (ed.), *Les Crises politiques au Burundi et au Rwanda (1993–1994)*, Université des Sciences et Technologies de Lille, Karthala, Paris, 1995, p. 694.

64 François Ryckmans, *Chapeau* magazine, Rwanda, 15 March 1994. Broadcast, Radio Télévision de la

Communauté Française de Belgique (RTBF).

65 Dallaire, *Shake Hands*, p. 190.

66 International Centre Against Censorship, *Broadcasting Genocide: Censorship, Propaganda and State-sponsored Violence in Rwanda 1990–1994*, Article 19, London, October 1996.

67 Nshimiyimana, *Prélude du génocide rwandais*.

68 ICTR Indictment. Georges Rutaganda, 12 January 1996.

69 African Rights, *Rwanda. Death, Despair and Defiance*, London, 1995, p. 574.

70 Alain Destexhe, *Qui a tué nos paras?*, Editions Luc Pire, Brussels, 1996, p. 33.

71 ICTR witness statement, Luc Marchal. 11 February 1997 (author's archive).

72 See Filip Reyntjens, *Rwanda. Trois jours qui on fait basculer l'histoire*, Editions L'Harmatttan, Paris, 1995, p. 34. Author's interviews, Brussels, June 2007.

73 The commander at Camp Kacyiru was Colonel Aloys Ntiwiragabo, an officer from Gisenyi who had received military training in France.

74 Belgian senate, Commission d'Enquête, p. 345.

11 THE UN SECURITY COUNCIL

1 Rwanda's candidacy for a non-permanent seat was put forward to the General Assembly in October 1993. Its candidacy was endorsed at the summit meeting of the Organization of African Unity held in Cairo at the end of June 1993.

2 'The United Nations and Rwanda, 1993–1996', United Nations Blue Book series, vol. 10, UN Department of Public Information, New York, 1996.

3 Marrack Goulding, Under Secretary-General for Political Affairs, claims that his documents for this period were shredded.

4 Boutros Boutros-Ghali, *Unvanquished. A US–UN Saga*, I.B. Tauris, London, 1999, p. 130.

5 Chinmaya Gharekhan, *The Horseshoe Table: An Inside View of the UN Security Council*, Dorling Kindersley (India), New Delhi, 2006.

6 Statement. *The Security Council Role in the Rwanda Crisis*. Ambassador Colin Keating, Permanent Representative of New Zealand to the UN, at a Comprehensive Seminar on Lessons Learned from UNAMIR, 12 June 1996 (author's archive).

7 Interview, Colin Keating, New York, December 1996.

8 UN Commission on Human Rights, *Report by Mr. B. W. Ndiaye, Special Rapporteur, on his mission to Rwanda from 8–17 April, 1993* (E/CN. 4/1994/7/Add. 1), 11 August 1993, p. 22.

9 Interview, Colin Keating, New York, 13 September 1994.

10 Gharekhan had served for six years as India's permanent representative to the UN.

11 Gharekhan, *The Horseshoe Table*, p. 125.

12 Marrack Goulding, 'The UN Secretary-General', in David Malone (ed.), *The UN Security Council from the Cold War to the 21st Century*, Lynne Rienner, Boulder, CO, 2004.

13 Address to the UN General Assembly by the Rt Hon. Don McKinnon, Deputy Prime Minister and Minister of Foreign Affairs and Trade of New Zealand, 27 September 1994.

14 Report of the Commission of Inquiry Established Pursuant to Security Council Resolution 885 (1993) to investigate armed attacks on UNOSOM II. 24 February, 1994. Unpublished (author's archive).

15 Colin Keating, 'Rwanda: an insider's account', in Malone, *The UN Security Council*.

16 Goulding, 'The UN Secretary-General'.

17 Linda Melvern, *The Ultimate Crime. Who Betrayed the UN and Why*, Allison and Busby, London, 1995, p. 326.

18 Madeleine Albright, *Madame Secretary: A Memoir*, Talk Miramax, New York, 2003, p. 145.

19 Security Council Resolution 824, May 1993.

20 Interview, David Hannay, December 1999, London.

21 Transcript of interview with senior FCO official, February 2003 (author's archive).

22 Carne Ross, 'Decline and fall', *New Statesman*, 4 September 2008.

23 David Hannay, *New World Disorder*, I.B.Tauris, London, 2008, p. 166.

24 Declassified FCO documents (complete): FCO O14/1 (12) 'Travels in Rwanda', from Edward Clay to FCO, 1 March 1994. FCO Documents (portions deleted): FCO 55 'Rwanda – Sir Edward Clay visit to present credentials from Kampala to FCO (routine)', 1 March 1994. FCO 014.1/15 'Rwanda: Impressions from E Clay visit' from Kampala to FCO.

25 As of this date, UNAMIR had a strength of 2,539 military personnel from twenty-four nations: Austria (15), Bangladesh (942), Belgium (440), Botswana (9), Brazil (13), Canada (2), Congo (26), Egypt (10), Fiji (1), Ghana (843), Hungary (4), Malawi (5), Mali (10), Netherlands (9), Nigeria (15), Poland (5), Romania (5), Russian Federation (15), Senegal (35), Slovakia (5), Togo (15), Tunisia (61), Uruguay (25) and Zimbabwe (29).

26 In early April, President Juvénal Habyarimana made a series of visits to neighbouring states. On the day before the crucial Security Council meeting, Monday, 4 April, he was in Zaire, at Gbadolite, visiting President Mobutu.

27 Summary of World Broadcasts. AL/1966 A/3. 8 April 1994.

12 FOUR DAYS IN KIGALI

1 Lowell Blankfort, 'Almost a million dead, Rwanda seeks justice', *World Outlook*, UNA-US, 2 December 1995.

2 Simbizi was the secretary-general of the CDR and a shareholder in RTLM. He fled Rwanda after the genocide and is thought to have died in the DRC in 1998.

3 Colette Braeckman, 'J'ai vu partir trois missiles', *Le Soir*, 6 May 2006. The air traffic controller and the president's son, Jean-Luc Habyarimana, claim that three and not two missiles were fired.

4 Patrice Munyaneza, *Déroulement des faits marquant le TIR sur l'avion transportant l'ex-Président Rwandais Juvénal Habyarimana*. Signed statement, 28 November 2006 (author's archive).

5 UN Doc. UNAMIR code cable. Attack on Presidential aircraft. MIR-772. To Annan from Booh-Booh (author's archive).

6 Lt-Col. J. Dewez, *Chronique 6 Avril-19 Avril, 1994* (author's archive).

7 Jean Birara, Statement. La Commission Rogatoire Internationale execute au Rwanda du 5 Juin au 24 Juin 1995 (author's archive).

8 Unless otherwise stated, survivor statements are taken from African Rights, *Rwanda. Death, Despair and Defiance*, London, 1995.

9 Henry Kwami Anyidoho, *Guns over Kigali*, Woeli Publishing Services, Accra, 1997, p. 23.

10 André Guichaoua (ed.), *Les Crises politiques au Burundi et au Rwanda (1993–1994)*, Université des

Sciences et Technologies de Lille, Karthala, Paris, 1995, p. 705.

11 Interview, Major General Roméo Dallaire, London, November 1994.

12 Filip Reyntjens, *Rwanda. Trois jours qui on fait basculer l'histoire*, Editions L'Harmattan, Paris, 1995.

13 Interviews, Kigali, December 2001.

14 Colonel Théoneste Bagosora, *L'Assassinat du Président Habyarimana ou l'ultime opération du Tutsi pour sa reconquête du pouvoir par la force au Rwanda*, Unpublished MS (author's achive).

15 Lt Gen. Roméo Dallaire, *Shake Hands with the Devil. The Failure of Humanity in Rwanda*, Random House, Canada, 2003, p. 225.

16 Interview, Valérie Bemeriki, Kigali, March 2007.

17 Interview, Colonel Luc Marchal, December 1999.

18 Summary of World Broadcasts, AL/1996, 8 April 1994.

19 Dewez, *Chronique*.

20 Summary of World Broadcasts, AL/1966 A/2, 8 April 1994.

21 ICTR Prosecution witness statement, LS (author's archive).

22 In 2001 the USA offered rewards of $US5 million for information on the whereabouts of thirteen Rwandan fugitives. This list included Cedeslas Kabera.

23 Statement, Death of Joseph Kavaruganda (author's archive).

24 ICTR Prosecution witness statement, GS (author's archive).

25 Interviews, Gikondo, December 2001.

26 African Rights, *Rwanda*, p. 557.

27 Dewez, *Chronique*.

28 Théophile Umuhire, aged three, Michel Hirwa, aged five, Christine Gasare, aged thirteen, Marie-Christine Umuraza, aged fifteen, Aimé Barahira, aged nineteen. They eventually escaped thanks to help from Professor André Guichaoua and were granted asylum in Switzerland.

29 Samantha Power, *A Problem from Hell: America and the Age of Genocide*, Basic Books, New York, 2002, p. 332.

30 Astri Suhrke, 'Dilemmas of protection: the log of the Kigali Battalion', *Security Dialogue*, 29(1), March 1998.

31 Belgian senate, Commission d'enquête parlementaire concernant les événements du Rwanda. Report, 6 December 1997, p. 437.

32 Testimony of Major Timsonet during the court martial of Luc Marchal, Unpublished (author's archive).

33 Interview, Colonel Luc Marchal, December 1999.

34 Anyidoho, *Guns over Kigali*, p. 27.

35 The Ghanaian peacekeepers were overpowered and were reported missing. They arrived back at headquarters later that morning.

36 Excerpt from the interviews on Frontline's website for *The Triumph of Evil*, www.pbs.org/WGBH/Pages/Frontline/shows/evil. Copyright WGBH/Frontline, 1999.

37 UN Security Council, Report of the Independent Inquiry into the Actions of the United Nations during the 1994 Genocide in Rwanda, 15 December 1999, p. 20.

38 Memorandum. From Yvon Le Moal, Acting Designated Official, Rwanda. To Mr. Benon Sevan, UN Security Co-ordinator and Mr. G. Speth, the Administrator, the UN Development Programme. 20 April 1994, unpublished (author's archive).

39 Nubaha died in Brussels in May 2007 just prior to testifying for the defence in the case against Bernard Ntuyahaga for the murder of the ten Belgian peacekeepers.

40 Reyntjens, *Rwanda*, p. 76.

41 Written answer to questions put to General Roméo Dallaire by the *juge-avocat général* of the Belgian military court. Belgian senate, Commission d'enquête, p. 423 (author's archive).

42 Interview, Major General Roméo Dallaire, London, November 1994.

43 The ten UN peacekeepers: Lt Thierry Lotin, Sgt Yannick Leroy, Cpls Bruno Bassine, Alain Debatty, Christophe Dupont, Stéphane Lhoir, Bruno Meaux, Louis Plescia, Christophe Renwa, Marc Uyttebroeck.

44 Avocats sans Frontières, *Chronique Judicaire, Assises Rwanda 2007*, 3, www.asf.be./.

45 Ibid., 5.

46 Ibid., 2.

47 Temmerman has managed the affairs of the family of President Habyarimana and has represented Colonel Théoneste Bagosora.

48 Interview, Luc de Temmerman, Rwanda News Agency, 20 June 2007.

49 Avocats sans Frontières, *Chronique Judicaire, Assises Rwanda, 2007*, 4, www.asf.be./.

50 Bagosora was found guilty at the ICTR on 18 December 2008 of the murders of the ten Belgian peacekeepers.

51 Dallaire, *Shake Hands*, p. 215.

52 Interview, Colonel Luc Marchal, November 1999.

53 Avocats sans Frontières, *Chronique Judicaire, Assises Rwanda 2007*, 5, www.asf.be./.

54 Colette Braeckman, 'Rwanda: l'attaché de presse de la MINUAR se sourvient du tout', *Le Soir*, 4 June 2007.

55 The Parti Libéral lost nearly all its members, as did the Parti Social Démocrate. MDR members who had advocated links with the RPF were killed, as were most of the militants in the party opposed to the dictatorship of the northern Hutu. See African Rights, *Rwanda*.

56 Interview, Marcel Gatsinzi, Kigali, October 1997.

57 *Genocide in Rwanda. Documentation of Two Massacres during April 1994*. Issue Brief, US Committee for Refugees, November 1994, p. 12.

58 Mahmood Mamdani, *From Conquest to Consent as the Basis of State Formation: Reflections on Rwanda*, Paper presented to the conference Crisis in the Great Lakes Region, organized by the Council for the Development of Social Research in Africa, Arusha, Tanzania, 4–7 September 1995.

59 Human Rights Watch/Fédération Internationale des Ligues des Droits de l'Homme, *Leave none to tell the story. Genocide in Rwanda*, 1999, p. 209.

60 Jacques Castonguay, *Les Casques Bleus au Rwanda*, Editions l'Harmattan, Paris, 1998, p. 145.

61 Interview, Major General Paul Kagame, Kigali, October 1997.

62 Dallaire, *Shake Hands*, pp. 318–19, 320n.

63 Interview, Marcel Gatsinzi, Kigali, October 1997.

64 Reyntjens, *Rwanda*, p. 89.

65 Assemblée Nationale, Mission d'Information Commune, Enquête sur la Tragédie Rwandaise (1990–1994). Book III: *Auditions*, vol. 1, p. 296.

66 Article 19, *Broadcasting Genocide: Censorship, Propaganda and State-sponsored Violence in Rwanda 1990–1994*, 1996, pp. 110–11.

67 The International Criminal Tribunal for Rwanda. Case ICTR 97-23-S. Judgment and Sentence. 23 September 1998. Jean Kambanda received a life sentence for six counts including genocide, conspiracy to commit genocide, direct and public incitement to commit genocide, complicity in genocide, and two counts of crimes against humanity.

68 Radio Rwanda, Summary of World Broadcasts. AL/1968 A/2, 11 April 1994.

69 ICTR interrogation of Jean Kambanda (author's archive).

70 Commission of a Citizens Enquiry into the role of France during the genocide of the Tutsi in 1994. Report, *L'horreur qui nous prend au visage*, Survie, p. 213.

71 Rwandan Republic. Independent National Commission to Collect Proof of the Implication of the Government of France in the 1994 Genocide in Rwanda. November 15, 2007. Report published August 2008, p. 146.

72 UN Doc. DPKO Outgoing Code Cable. To the SG, Geneva from Annan. Subject: Rwanda. Continuation of our earlier cable of today. 8 April 1994 (author's archive).

73 The text of the 8 April cable is published in Belgian senate, Commission d'Enquête, pp. 508–15.

74 Human Rights Watch/Fédération Internationale des Ligues des Droits de l'Homme, *Leave none to tell the story*, p. 600.

75 Interview, Major General Paul Kagame, Kigali, October 1997.

76 In March, a Major Podevijn had reported to UN HQ that weapons had been distributed to the members of the Interahamwe militia there.

77 Genocide in Rwanda, Documentation of Two Massacres during April 1994. Issue Brief. US Committee for Refugees, November 1994, pp. 4–9.

78 Some of them were evacuated when the genocide started but others stayed on and formed a team of liaison officers who were attached to the headquarters of the RGF and RPF. Others were formed into rapid-reaction teams for information-gathering.

79 Jerzy Maczka. Statement, Military Trials – Gikondo Parish, Cracow, 13 March 2000 (author's archive).

80 Interviews, Stefan Stec, The Hague, 10 April 1996 and 2004; Major Brent Beardsley, Montreal, 20 March 1996; Marec Pazik, The Hague, 6 April 1996.

81 Ibid.

82 Jonathan Moore (ed.), *Hard Choices, Moral Dilemmas in Humanitarian Intervention*, Rowman and Littlefield, Oxford, 1998.

83 The bodies were taken to a mass grave at Nyamirambo.

84 Interview with Colonel Quist, transcript, tape 28. Twenty-Twenty Television, July 1994 (author's archive).

13 THE GENOCIDE EXPOSED

1 Belgian Senate, Commission d'enquête parlementaire concernant les événements du Rwanda. Report, 6 December 1997, p. 523. Also interviews with UN officials in DPKO, New York, July 1994 and October 1996.

2 Ibid., p. 526.

3 Ibid., p. 536.

4 There are two versions of this letter. One, a copy given to the author by the president of the Security Council, Colin Keating, and the second, a version printed in *The United Nations and Rwanda, 1993–1994*, UN Blue Book Series, vol. 10, p. 255. The difference between the two versions is that the letter in the Blue Book series does not mention the evacuation from Rwanda of UNAMIR. In the letter sent to the president of the Council a sentence reads: 'It is quite possible that the evacuation of UNAMIR and other United Nations personnel might become unavoidable, in which event UNAMIR would be hindered in providing assistance under its present mandate and rules of engagement.' The letter in the Blue Book series reads: 'It is quite possible that the

evacuation of civilian staff from the United Nations system, as well as other foreign nationals, might become unavoidable, in which event UNAMIR would be hindered in providing assistance under its present mandate and rules of engagement.'

5 A list of the capitals visited by Boutros Boutros-Ghali, from April to June 1994, can be found in 'Travels of the Secretary-General', Press information, 1 July 1994 (DPI/1557).

6 Interview, Boutros Boutros-Ghali, Paris, December 1999.

7 Belgian Senate, Commission d'enquête, p. 532.

8 Ibid., Chronology, p. 519.

9 Major Brent Beardsley, Dallaire's staff officer, had prepared a plan for total UN evacuation. A US special forces officer had requested certain details from him for the US plan.

10 Hotel register, Hôtel des Mille Collines, 5–12 April. Plan Hotel. Reservations (author's archive). Interviews, Brussels and Ottawa, September 1997.

11 Email correspondence, Ambassador David Rawson, November 2008.

12 Belgian Senate, Commission d'enquête, p. 535.

13 Ibid., p. 565.

14 Ibid., p. 535.

15 Ibid., p. 537.

16 Olivier Lanotte, *La France au Rwanda (1990–1994). Entre abstention impossible et engagement ambivalent*, PIE Peter Lang, SA, Brussels, 2007.

17 UN Security Council, Report of the Independent Inquiry into the Actions of the United Nations during the 1994 Genocide in Rwanda, 15 December 1999, p. 16.

18 Ibid., p. 27.

19 A list of the Rwandans flown out of Rwanda is to be found in André Guichaoua (ed.), *Les Crises politiques au Burundi et au Rwanda, (1993–1994)*, Université des Sciences et Techno-

logies de Lille, Karthala, Paris, 1995, pp. 697–701.

20 James Orbinski, *An Imperfect Offering. Dispatches from the Medical Front Line*, Random House, Canada, 2008.

21 There were fourteen MSF staff who stayed behind in Rwanda.

22 A small UNICEF emergency operations team returned to Kigali on 22 April to distribute airlifted supplies. See UNICEF, Rwanda Emergency Programme: Progress Report No. 1, Kigali.

23 Interview, Eric Bertin, December 1999. Also interview with Bertrand des Moulins, New York, December 1999.

24 The president of Burundi, Cyprien Ntaryamira, was killed with Habyarimana in the plane crash. In the days immediately following his death, local newspapers reported calm, allaying fears of further violence. The government took steps to strengthen national security. There was violence later in April but the situation was calm as the month ended.

25 Interview, Gerry McCarthy (consultant, UNICEF), December 1999.

26 The French evacuated 1,238 people by air, and of these 454 were French, 784 were other nationalities and 394 were Rwandans. A further 115 French nationals were taken by road to Bujumbura in Burundi. Belgium evacuated 1,226 people, of whom 1,026 were Belgian. Italy and Canada took out about one hundred people.

27 Interview, Tito Rutaremara, Kigali, October 1997.

28 Philippe Gaillard, *Rwanda 1994: La vraie vie est absente* (Arthur Rimbaud). Cycle des Conferences les Mardi de Musée. M. Philippe Gaillard, délégué du CIRC, chef de délégation au Rwanda de juillet 1993 à juillet 1994. www.ICRC.org.

29 Gérard Delaloye and Elisabeth Levy, 'Philippe Gaillard, après Kigali, pouvez-vous encore croire en l'humanité', *Le Nouveau Quotidien*, 30 December 1994.

30 Gaillard, *Rwanda 1994*.

31 Delaloye and Levy, 'Philippe Gaillard, après Kigali'.

32 Orbinski, *An Imperfect Offering*, p. 192.

33 Ibid., p. 175.

34 Interview, Jean-Hervé Bradol, November 1999.

35 Assemblée Nationale, Mission de'Information Commune, Enquête sur la Tragédie Rwandaise (1990–1994), Paris.

36 Friday, 15 April 1994.

37 Jean-Hervé Bradol, 'Rwanda, avril–mai 1994. Limites et ambiguïtés de l'action humanitaire. Crises politiques, massacres et exodes massifs', *Le Temps Moderne*, 583, 1995.

38 Jean-Philippe Ceppi, 'Kigali livré à la fureur des tueurs Hutus', *Libération*, 11 April 1994.

39 Jean Hélène, 'Le Rwanda à feu et à sang', *Le Monde*, 12 April 1994.

40 Elaine Sciolino, 'For West, Rwanda is not worth the political candle', *New York Times*, 15 April 1994.

41 The international reporting of Rwanda has been the subject of a number of studies which have shown that the coverage of these crises was ambiguous, unclear and often misconstrued. Ingrid A. Lehmann, *Peacekeeping and Public Information. Caught in the Crossfire*, Frank Cass, London, 1999.

42 Roger Winter, 'Power, not tribalism, stokes Rwanda's slaughter', *Globe and Mail*, Toronto, 14 April 1994.

43 Interview with Professor Catharine Newbury and Professor David Newbury. Radcliffe Institute for Advanced Study, Harvard University, October 2008.

44 The International Response to Conflict and Genocide: Lessons from the Rwandan Experience. Joint Evaluation of Emergency Assistance to Rwanda. Copenhagen, March 1996, ch. 2, p. 36.

45 Interview, Major Brent Beardsley, December 1999, and Major General Dallaire, November 1994.

46 Interview, Boutros Boutros-Ghali, Paris, December 1999.

47 The text of this cable is given in full in Belgian Senate, Commission d'enquête, pp. 508–15.

48 Colonel Scott R. Feil, *Preventing Genocide. How the Use of Force Might Have Succeeded in Rwanda*. Pre-publication draft, December 1997, Carnegie Commission on Preventing Deadly Conflict, New York. This report contains a detailed description of Dallaire's plan, devised in three phases (author's archive).

14 SECRET MEETINGS

1 A copy of this document is in the author's archive.

2 Interview, Ambassador Karel Kovanda, 2 June 1994.

3 Belgian Senate, Commission d'enquête parlementaire concernant les événements du Rwanda. Report, 6 December 1997, p. 543.

4 Boutros Boutros-Ghali, *Unvanquished. A US–UN Saga*, I.B.Tauris, London, 1999, p. 132.

5 Doubts have been raised about this claim. Belgian opinion polls showed no overwhelming demand for withdrawal. See Human Rights Watch/ Fédération Internationale des Ligues des Droits de l'Homme, *Leave none to tell the story. Genocide in Rwanda*, 1999, pp. 617–18.

6 *The United Nations and Rwanda, 1993–1996*, UN Blue Book series, vol. 10, UN Department of Public Information, New York, p. 259.

7 Letter from the Permanent Representative of Cameroon to the UN addressed to the President of the Security Council, 11 April 1994. S/1994/420, 12 April 1994.

8 Radio Muhabura, Summary of World Broadcasts. AL/1968 A/4, 11 April 1994.

9 Interview, Major General Paul Kagame, October 1997.

10 Article 19, *Broadcasting Genocide: Censorship, Propaganda and State-Sponsored Violence in Rwanda 1990–1994*, October 1996, pp. 146–7.

11 Ibid., p. 101.

12 J.-P. Chrétien et al., *Rwanda: Les Médias du Génocide*, Karthala, Paris, 1995, p. 331.

13 Article 19, *Broadcasting Genocide*, p. 120.

14 André Guichaoua (ed.), *Les Crises politiques au Burundi et au Rwanda (1993–1994)*, Université des Sciences et Technologies de Lille, Karthala, Paris, 1995, p. 526.

15 Gérard Delaloye and Elisabeth Levy, 'Philippe Gaillard, après Kigali, pouvez-vous encore croire en l'humanité?', *Le Nouveau Quotidien*, 30 December 1994.

16 Frederic Fischer, 'The Season in Hell', *Guardian Europe*, 7 July 1994.

17 Interview, Philippe Gaillard, July 1998. In *Cycle des Conférences* Gaillard quotes Federico García Lorca's 'Enfance et Mort'. García Lorca, *Poeta en Nueva York* (Poet in New York), English and Spanish edn, trans. G. Simon and S. F. White, ed. C. Maurer, Monday Press, New York, 1998.

18 Aidan Hartley, *The Zanzibar Chest. A Memoir of Love and War*, HarperCollins, London, 2003, p. 382.

19 ICTR interrogation of Jean Kambanda (author's archive).

20 Mark Doyle, BBC Radio, 13 April 1994. Transcripts (author's archive).

21 Interview, Major General Marcel Gatsinzi, Kigali, October 1997.

22 For the duration of the genocide and some weeks after it, Hutu Power kept its worldwide government banking network operational and a total of US$17.8 million was spirited away with US$6.4 million taken out in traveller's cheques. 'Le financement de l'ancien régime après avril 1994', in Pierre Galand and Michel Chossudovsky, *L'Usage de la Dette Extérieure du Rwanda (1990/1994). La Responsabilité des Bailleurs de Fonds*, Brussels and Ottawa, 1996.

23 Bizimungu fled Rwanda in July 1994. He was arrested in Angola, in July 2002, and transferred to the ICTR. His trial for genocide and related charges began in 2004.

24 Human Rights Watch/Fédération Internationale des Ligues des Droits de l'Homme, *Leave none to tell the story*, pp. 270–78.

25 UN Commission on Human Rights, *Report of the Special Rapporteur on violence against women, its causes and consequences, Ms. Radhika Coomaraswamy* (E/CN.4/1998/54/Add. 1), 4 February 1998, p. 10.

26 Interviews, Ambassador Karel Kovanda (permanent representative to the UN, Czech Republic), New York, July 1995, and Colin Keating (permanent representative to the UN, New Zealand), July 1995. Michael N. Barnett, Department of Political Science, University of Wisconsin, July 1994. See also M. N. Barnett, 'The UN Security Council: indifference and genocide in Rwanda', *Cultural Anthropology*, 12(4), 1997.

27 *The United Nations and Rwanda, 1993–1996*, p. 259.

28 Boutros-Ghali, *Unvanquished*, p. 132.

29 Rwanda had officially put forward its candidacy as a non-permanent member at the General

Assembly of October 1993. Its candidacy had been endorsed at the summit meeting of the OAU in June 1993.

30 The letter is dated 15 April 1994 (reference S.1168). Trans. from French (author's archive).

31 Chinmaya Gharekhan, *The Horseshoe Table: An Inside View of the UN Security Council*, Dorling Kindersley (India), New Delhi, 2006, p. 243.

32 UNAMIR created a humanitarian assistance cell (HAC) with six military staff. Major Don MacNeil, a Canadian, was operations officer.

33 Mark Doyle, BBC Radio, 15 April 1994.

34 Madeleine Albright, *Madame Secretary: A Memoir*, Talk Miramax, New York, 2003, p. 150.

35 The National Security Council (NSC) has responsibility for policy coordination on issues related to national security, including conflict, genocide and mass atrocities. See Jared Cohen, *One Hundred Days of Silence. America and the Rwanda Genocide*, Rowman and Littlefield, MD, 2007, p. 6.

36 All prefects but three attended: those from Ruhengeri, Cyangugu and Butare were absent. The meeting was held on 11 April.

37 The Prosecutor versus Jean Kambanda. Case No. ICTR 97-23-S, Judgment and Sentence.

38 Speech by Philippe Gaillard at the Genocide Prevention Conference, Nottingham. January 2002. Aegis Trust/FCO. See: ICRC.Org./web/Eng/.

39 Interview, Didier Grond (ICRC delegate), Geneva, 12 December 1998. The checkpoint was at Myambo.

40 Associated Press, Nairobi, 'Tribes battle for Rwandan capital: new massacres reported', *New York Times*, 16 April 1994.

41 Donatella Lorch, 'UN in Rwanda says it is powerless to halt the violence', *New York Times*, 15 April 1994.

42 Jacques Castonguay, *Les*

Casques Bleus au Rwanda, Editions L'Harmattan, Paris, 1998, p. 134. Interview, Major Brent Beardsley, December 1999.

43 Outgoing coded cable. To: Baril, UNATIONS. From: Dallaire, UNAMUIR, Kigali, 17 April 1994.

44 Castonguay, *Les Casques Bleus*, p. 133.

45 Report of the Independent Inquiry into the Actions of the United Nations during the Genocide in Rwanda, 15 December 1999, December 1999, p. 17.

15 GENOCIDE SPREADS

1 Interview, Colonel Luc Marchal, November 1999.

2 Canada had forty-five pilots and two C-130s in Nairobi. These planes, throughout the genocide, transported 6,315 passengers from Kigali and brought in supplies, often to be greeted at Kigali airport by missiles and bombs. They also evacuated the majority of the peacekeepers after the 21 April decision of the Security Council.

3 On 5 June, a C-130 made an emergency departure, forced to take off after a mortar bomb exploded 400 yards away. The plane was hardly in the air when a second bomb exploded on the tarmac. Then the airport finally closed. Attempts were made to resupply the peacekeepers through Entebbe and then overland to Kigali, through RPF territory, about a ten-hour journey. This was the only resupply and casualty evacuation.

4 The technicians who stayed behind were: Per Einarson from Norway, Richard Gregoive from Trinidad and Tobago, Paul Martin from Australia and Shuji Ashiama from Japan.

5 Donatella Lorch, 'The massacres in Rwanda: hope is also a victim', *New York Times*, 21 April 1994.

6 Excerpt taken from interviews published on Frontline's website for *The Triumph of Evil*. www.pbs.org/ WGBH/Pages/Frontline/shows/evil. Copyright WGBH/Frontline, 1999.

7 Jared Cohen, *One Hundred Days of Silence. America and the Rwanda Genocide*, Rowman and Littlefield, MD, 2007, p. 135.

8 Another prefect was killed: Godefroid Ruzindana of Kibungo.

9 Human Rights Watch/Fédération Internationale des Ligues des Droits de l'Homme, *Leave none to tell the story. Genocide in Rwanda*, 1999, p. 456.

10 ICTR 98-42-T Butare trial. Defendents on genocide and related charges regarding crimes committed in the prefecture of Butare: Pauline Nyiramasuhuko, Arsène Shalom Ntahobali, Sylvan Nsabimana, Alphonse Nteziryayo, Joseph Kanyabashi, Elie Ndayambaje. This trial began in April 2001, and it is ongoing.

11 Human Rights Watch/Fédération Internationale des Ligues des Droits de l'Homme, *Leave none to tell the story*, p. 488.

12 African Rights, *Rwanda. Death, Despair and Defiance*, London, 1995, pp. 345–51.

13 After the Belgian contingent withdrew, the troop numbers decreased from 2,165 to 1,515 and the number of military observers from 321 to 190.

14 *The United Nations and Rwanda, 1993–1996*. The UN Blue Book series, vol. 10, UN Department of Public Information, New York, pp. 62–5.

15 David Hannay, *New World Disorder. The UN After the Cold War – An Insider's View*, I.B.Tauris, London, 2008, p. 168.

16 Chinmaya Gharekhan, *The Horseshoe Table: An Inside View of the UN Security Council*, Dorling Kindersley (India), New Delhi, 2006.

17 Although most of the Bangladeshi contingent left, the chief of operations and two other officers of the staff remained with a senior non-commissioned officer.

18 Email correspondence with General Henry Anyidoho, Deputy Joint Special Representative of the AU–UN Hybrid Operations in Darfur, November 2008.

19 Jonathan Moore (ed.), *Hard Choices, Moral Dilemmas in Humanitarian Intervention*, Rowman and Littlefield, Oxford, 1998, p. 81. See also Human Rights Watch/Fédération Internationale des Ligues des Droits de l'Homme, *Leave none to tell the story*, p. 320.

20 Ibid., p. 216.

21 'Cold choices in Rwanda', Editorial, *New York Times*, 23 April 1994.

22 Eye Witness Accounts of Massacres/Human Rights Violations (Chronological Recollection of Events) Butare, Rwanda. April, 1994. Dr Rony Zachariah, medical coordinator. Wauter Van Emplem, Emergency desk, MSF-Holland. Unpublished.

23 Testimony of Dr Rony Zachariah, ICTR94-4-T. In the trial of Jean-Paul Akayesu.

24 James Orbinski, *An Imperfect Offering. Dispatches from the Medical Front Line*, Random House, Canada, 2008, p. 177.

25 Excerpt taken from interviews published on Frontline's website for *The Triumph of Evil*. www.pbs.org/ WGBH/Pages/Frontline/shows/evil. Copyright WGBH/Frontline, 1999.

26 Rwandan Republic. Ministry of Defence. Military Intelligence Report. Secret (author's archive).

27 Steven Livingstone and Todd Eachus, 'Rwanda: US policy and television coverage', in Howard Adelman and Astri Suhrke (eds), *The Path of a Genocide. The Rwanda Crisis from Uganda to Zaire*, Transaction, New Brunswick, NJ, 1999, p. 209.

28 Human Rights Watch/Fédération Internationale des Ligues des Droits de l'Homme, *Leave none to tell the story*, p. 282. Also, testimony of Alison des Forges in Assemblée Nationale, Mission d'Information Commune, Enquête sur la Tragédie Rwandaise (1990–1994). Book III: Auditions.

29 Interview, Major Brent Beardsley, staff officer, UNAMIR, December 1999.

30 Jacques Castonguay, *Les Casques Bleus au Rwanda*, Editions L'Harmattan, Paris, 1998, p. 89.

31 D. Orr, *From Landmines to Genocide: Analysing the influence of non-state actors upon state decision-making in the security issue area*, Unpublished MSc human rights and international politics dissertation, University of Glasgow, 2006.

32 Human Rights Watch/Fédération Internationale des Ligues des Droits de l'Homme, *Leave none to tell the story*, p. 211.

33 *The United Nations and Rwanda, 1993–1996*, UN Blue Book series, vol. 10, p. 271.

34 Gharekhan, *The Horseshoe Table*.

35 Ibid., p. 245.

36 Human Rights Watch/Fédération Internationale des Ligues des Droits de l'Homme, *Leave none to tell the story*, p. 766.

37 Letters from the Rwanda embassy, Cairo, to the Department of Protocol at the Egyptian Ministry of Foreign Affairs, 13 and 24 June 1994 (author's archive).

38 Human Rights Watch/Fédération Internationale des Ligues des Droits de l'Homme, *Leave none to tell the story*, p. 662.

39 Ibid., p. 278.

40 Statement by the Political Bureau of the Rwandese Patriotic Front on the Proposed Deployment of a UN Intervention Force in Rwanda. RPF. New York, 30 April 1994. Signed by Claude Dusaidi and Gerald Gahima.

41 The South African arms industry, which until 1994 operated covertly, was being brought under increasing government control. But some individuals involved in the arms trade or the armed forces during the apartheid regime were still active in an individual capacity or in private industry. Their activities included dealing arms and providing mercenaries.

42 Shipping documents show that Mil-Tec used an aircraft registered in Nigeria but leased from a company in the Bahamas to make the deliveries.

43 Mil-Tec was set up as a shell company in February 1993 by BDO Binder in Douglas, Isle of Man.

44 A Whitehall committee set up after the Mil-Tec deals came to light concluded that there were no structured arrangements in Britain for ensuring the timely and accurate imposition of embargoes. It found a lack of consistency in implementing embargoes in the UK and its dependent territories – such as Bermuda, Gibraltar and Hong Kong. The Home Office, which is responsible for Crown dependencies, was not informed of the embargoes until August 1994, and they had still not been applied by January 1997. The committee found gaps in government controls on arms exports and recommended that all future UN and other arms embargoes should be applied promptly in Britain, the Crown dependencies and the dependent territories.

45 Documents reveal the exact amounts paid to Mil-Tec during the genocide. On 14 April, Mil-Tec received US$1,621,901, via the Bank Belgolaise in Brussels, and later, on 17 May, a further US$300,000. From the Cairo embassy, on 19 April, US$667,120 was paid to Mil-Tec through the National Westminster

Bank; on 26 April, US$596,120 was transferred to Mil-Tec, and on 8 May the sum of US$130,120.

46 Security Council Resolution 1013, 7 September 1995. International Commission of Inquiry (Rwanda).

47 The other members of the commission were: Inspector Jean-Michel Hanssens (Canada); Colonel Jürgen G. H. Almeling (Germany); Lieutenant-Colonel Jan Meijvogel (Netherlands); Brigadier Mujahid Alam (Pakistan); and Colonel Lameck Mutanda (Zimbabwe).

48 Human Rights Watch Arms Project, *Rwanda/Zaire: Rearming with Impunity*, 7(4), May 1995.

16 THE WORLD SHUTS THE DOOR

1 René Caravielhe, 'Dans le témoignage, l'horreur', 13 April–19 May. MSF Info. no. 30, May–June 1994 (author's translation).

2 ICRC, *Cri d'alarme du CICR au no des victims de la tragédie Rwandaise*. Geneva, 28 April 1994 (author's archive).

3 Jacques Castonguay, *Les Casques Bleus au Rwanda*, Editions L'Harmattan, Paris, 1998, p. 166.

4 Human Rights Watch/Fédération Internationale des Ligues des Droits de l'Homme, *Leave none to tell the story. Genocide in Rwanda*, 1999, p. 494.

5 Peter Smerdon (Reuters), 'Rwanda refugees trapped and orphans massacred', *Independent*, 4 May 1994.

6 André Guichaoua (ed.), *Les Crises politiques au Burundi et au Rwanda (1993–1994)*, Université des Sciences et Technologies de Lille, Karthala, Paris, 1995, p. 696.

7 African Rights, *Rwanda. Death, Despair and Defiance*, London, 1995, p. 719. This incident occurred on 18 April 1994.

8 Serious doubts have been raised about the role played by Rusesabagina. See Alfred Ndahiro and Priva Rutazibwa, *Impostor Made Hero in Hollywood. The True Story of Paul Rusesabagina and the Film Hotel Rwanda*, Editions L'Harmattan, Paris, 2008.

9 Obituary, Major Stefan Stec, *Independent*, 29 September 2005. And author's interviews 1997–2005.

10 A group of forty Tunisian peacekeepers was responsible for the security at the Hôtel des Mille Collines under their company commander, Major M'fareng Belgacem, an air defence artillery expert. When the genocide was over Dallaire paid tribute to the bravery of these men. Nsazuwera, Rwanda's deputy attorney-general, described the UN protection of the hotel as 'wholly inadequate'.

11 Lt Gen. Roméo Dallaire, *Shake Hands with the Devil. The Failure of Humanity in Rwanda*, Random House, Canada, 2003, p. 398.

12 African Rights, *Rwanda*, p. 723.

13 Ibid., p. 689.

14 Dallaire, *Shake Hands*, p. 421.

15 Edgar Roskis, 'A genocide without images: white film noirs', in Allan Thompson (ed.), *The Media and the Rwandan Genocide*, International Development Research Centre, Ottawa, 2007.

16 Paul Lewis, 'U.S. examines way to assist Rwanda without troops. Direct action rejected', *New York Times*, 1 May 1994.

17 Tom Giles, 'Media failure over Rwanda's genocide', in Allan Thompson (ed.), *The Media and the Rwandan Genocide*, International Development Research Centre, Ottawa, 2007.

18 Richard Dowden, 'Sweet sour stench of death fills Rwanda', *Independent*, 7 May 1994.

19 Interview, Paul Kagame, Kigali, October 1997.

20 *Nightline* (ABC), 4 May 1994. Transcript 3378 (author's archive).

21 White House, Press briefing. Policy on Multilateral Peacekeeping Operations, Washington, DC, 5 May 1994. Transcript by Federal News Service, Washington, DC, document number WL-05-01, 5 May 1994.

22 Ivo H. Daalder, 'US policy for peacekeeping', in William J. Durch (ed.), *UN Peacekeeping: American Politics and the Uncivil Wars of the 1990s*, Henry L. Stimson Center, St Martin's Press, New York, 1996, p. 42.

23 The unclassified text of the Presidential Decision Directive was released as 'The Clinton Administration's policy on reforming multilateral peace operations' (White House, Washington, DC, May 1994).

24 'Press Briefing by the High Commissioner for Human Rights, Mr. José Ayala Lasso, Regarding his mission to Rwanda. 6 May 1994.' UN Information Service; for use of the UN Secretariat only (author's archive).

25 Lasso assumed the post on 5 April 1994. He resigned in 1997 to broker talks between Ecuador and Peru, which led to a treaty in 1998.

26 UN Commission on Human Rights, *Report of the UN High Commissioner for Human Rights, Mr. José Ayala Lasso, on his mission to Rwanda 11–12 May, 1994* (E/CN.4/S-3/3), 19 May 1994.

27 After the genocide, Lasso appealed for 147 human rights observers to be sent to Rwanda. Two months later, in September, there was only one, an Irish national, Karen Kenny. She had no phone, no car, no way to make a recording of an interview, and after two months she resigned.

28 Cornelio Sommaruga, 'For urgent action to stop the massacres in Rwanda', *International Herald Tribune*, 5 May 1994.

29 UN Doc. UNAMIR Outgoing Code Cable. To Annan from Dallaire.

Security Council Consultations. 15 May 1994 (author's archive).

30 James Schofield, *Silent over Africa. Stories of War and Genocide*, HarperCollins, Sydney, 1996, pp. 158–9.

31 Sam Kiley, 'Tutsi refugees face choice of starvation or being murdered', *The Times*, 14 May 1994.

32 *20 heures* (TFI), 16 May 1994. Patrick Poivre d'Arvor.

33 UNAMIR Code Cable. To Annan. Informal Consultations of the Non-paper. MIR 952. 12 May 1994 (author's archive).

34 The plan was: Proposed Future Mandate and Force Structure of UNAMIR. See Dallaire, *Shake Hands*, p. 354.

35 *The United Nations and Rwanda, 1993–1996*. UN Blue Book series, vol. 10, UN Department of Public Information, New York, 1996, pp. 277–82.

36 Boutros Boutros-Ghali, *Unvanquished. A US–UN Saga*, I.B. Tauris, London, 1999, p. 136.

37 Ibid., p. 141.

38 Linda Melvern, *The Ultimate Crime: Who Betrayed the UN and Why*, Allison and Busby, London, 1995, pp. 19–20.

39 Dallaire, *Shake Hands*, p. 376.

40 Ibid., p. 80.

41 Jonathan Moore (ed.), *Hard Choices: Moral Dilemmas in Humanitarian Intervention*, Rowman and Littlefield, Oxford, 1998, p. 82.

42 Interview, Major General Roméo Dallaire, London, November 1994.

43 UN Outgoing Code Cable. To Hein, Nairobi, Kenya. From Hansen. DHA New York. Attachment. Humanitarian Situation in Rwanda (15 May 1994). From FC. 19 May 1994 (author's archive).

44 Ibid., p. 1.

45 James Orbinski, *An Imperfect*

Offering. Dispatches from the Medical Front Line, Random House, Canada, 2008, p. 205.

46 The four were: Gerry McCarthy and Roger Carter, consultants for UNICEF; Pierre Honorat, World Food Programme; and Gregory Alex 'Gromo' of the UN Development Programme.

47 Interview, Gerry McCarthy, December 1999.

48 New Zealand Mission to the UN, New York, Fax. 17 May 1994. Subject: Security Council: Rwanda.

49 Interview, Alison des Forges, New York, July 1994. Transcript. 20/20 Television.

50 These Ghanaian troops arrived in Kigali on 15 August after the genocide was over, but only in late October 1994 did some small-arms ammunition arrive for them. Tents, night-vision aids, radios and defence stores did not come until much later.

51 Nigeria was an obvious candidate as one of Africa's foremost military powers, but it was preoccupied with events in Liberia, where it was leading a West African intervention force sponsored by the Economic Community of West-African States. Troops from Nigeria, Mali and Zambia arrived in Rwanda in October as part of UNAMIR II.

52 The estimated budget for UNAMIR II was US$115 million for six months, or slightly under US$20 million a month. UNAMIR I cost US$10 million a month. Boutros-Ghali, in order to get around this problem, had suggested a voluntary fund of some US$80 million, but no UN member came forward and the USA was not keen on the idea.

53 Security Council. S/PV.3377. Monday, 16 May 1994.

54 Not until 15 July did the USA close its Rwandan embassy in Washington and order diplomats to leave the country in five days. At the same time it began steps to remove Rwandan representatives from the Security Council. 'The US cannot allow representatives of a regime that supports genocidal massacres to remain on our soil,' President Bill Clinton said.

55 Interview, Sir David Hannay, London, 9 November 1999.

56 Human Rights Watch/Fédération Internationale des Ligues des Droits de l'Homme, *Leave none to tell the story*, p. 228.

57 Between 6 April and 23 May, the food supplies which the ICRC provided for Rwanda were as follows: 254.84 tons by air and 1,744.2 tons by road. Medical supplies: 677.76 tons by air and 1.25 tons by road. Water and sanitation equipment: 26.5 tons by air, none by road. Other equipment amounted to 1.6 tons by air. All supplies were initially sent from Nairobi to three locations in neighbouring countries – Bujumbura in Burundi, Ngara in Tanzania and Kabale in Uganda. From there road convoys or planes took them to Kigali with some supplies provided for a Red Cross team in Cyangugu.

58 Nick Hughes, 'Exhibit 467: genocide through a camera lens', in Allan Thompson (ed.), *The Media and the Rwandan Genocide*, International Development Research Centre, Ottawa, 2007. Hughes testified for the prosecution at the ICTR in the trial of Georges Rutaganda and his footage was used in evidence. He later produced the film *100 Days*, the first cinematic treatment of the Rwanda genocide.

59 UN Commission on Human Rights, *Report of the UN High Commissioner for Human Rights, Mr. José Ayala Lasso, on his mission to Rwanda 11–12 May, 1994.*

60 Transcript of Press Conference

by Secretary General Boutros Boutros-Ghali held at headquarters on May 25, 1994 (SG/SM/5297/REV.1). Press release (author's archive).

61 Report of the Independent Inquiry into the Actions of the United Nations during the 1994 Genocide in Rwanda, 15 December 1999, p. 25.

62 *The Blue Helmets: A Review of United Nations Peacekeeping* (3rd edn), United Nations, New York, 1996, p. 285.

63 Orbinski, *An Imperfect Offering*, p. 187.

64 A Ghanaian soldier was killed in the Amahoro stadium when a mortar round was fired at refugees.

65 In June UN military observer Major Manuel Sosa from Uruguay was killed by an RPF shell in Kigali.

66 Orbinski, *An Imperfect Offering*, p. 184.

67 Note de Service Interne. To Force Commander. 21 May, 1994. Signed D. J. MacNeil CHO.

68 The Nobel Lecture given by the Nobel Peace Prize laureate, Dr James Orbinski, Médecins Sans Frontières, Oslo, 10 December 1999.

69 According to the Vatican, three bishops and nearly 250 priests, nuns and missionaries were killed in the genocide.

70 The ICRC hospital at Kabgayi was moved, under orders from the RPF, to Nyanza, and then at the beginning of July the patients were moved once more, many of them dying en route to Rilima in the Bugesera. This extraordinary convoy arrived there on 5 July 1994.

71 Guy Theunis speculates that the archbishop may have had a change of heart, for he remained behind in Kabgayi, knowing that the RPF was approaching. He could have left and gone with the interim government to Gisenyi. See Guichaoua, *Les Crises politiques au Burundi at au Rwanda*.

72 In October 2008, a military court in Kigali acquitted two army officers, but convicted two junior officers for these crimes. The RPF officers, John Butera and Dieudonne Rukeba, pleaded guilty and were sentenced to eight years in prison.

73 Colette Braeckman, *Terreur Africaine. Burundi, Rwanda, Zaire: les racines de la violence*, Fayard, Paris, 1996, p. 82.

74 Human Rights Watch/Fédération International des Ligues des Droits de l'Homme, *Leave none to tell the story*. A UNHCR report apparently found evidence of an unmistakable pattern of killing and persecution by the RPF. Few have seen the document. Named after its principal author, Robert Gersony, it was rumoured to contain a section which stated that the RPF had murdered 30,000 Hutus in revenge killings between July and September 1994. These claims ran counter to reports from UN military observers, and UN agency field representatives. Brigadier General Henry Anyidoho and Colonel Iosa Ticoka rejected the contention that 30,000 Hutu people had been massacred in a systematic and preordained campaign.

75 Report on the situation of human rights in Rwanda, submitted by Mr. R. Degni-Ségui, under paragraph 20 of commission resolution E/CN.4/5.3/1 of 25 May 1994. Gérard Prunier, *The Rwanda Crisis, 1959–1994. History of a Genocide*, Hurst and Co., London, 1995.

76 Ian Martin, *After Genocide. The UN Field Operation in Rwanda*, Human Rights Centre, University of Essex. Ian Martin was secretary-general of Amnesty International, 1986–92. He is currently the UN secretary-general's Special Representative in Nepal.

17 FOR VALOUR

1 Boutros Boutros-Ghali, *Unvanquished. A US–UN Saga*, I.B.Tauris, London, 1999, p. 140.

2 William Drozdiak, 'No rescue for Rwanda', *Washington Post*, 18 June 1994.

3 Monique Mas, *Paris–Kigali 1990–1994*, Editions L'Harmattan, Paris, 1999. Sarkozy was minister for the budget 1993–95, and spokesperson in the cabinet of Prime Minister Edouard Balladur.

4 J. Matthew Vaccaro, 'The politics of genocide: peacekeeping and Rwanda', in William J. Durch (ed.), *UN Peacekeeping, American Politics and the Uncivil Wars of the 1990s*, Henry L. Stimson Center, St Martin's Press, New York, 1996.

5 The report can be accessed on the site of the Voltaire agency: www.voltaire.org/article5869.html. See also: Assemblée Nationale, Mission d'Information Commune, *Enquéte sur la Tragédie Rwandaise (1990–1994)*, vol. 2, Paris, p. 572.

6 UNAMIR II did not reach full strength until December 1994.

7 Security Council (S/PV.3392), 22 June 1994.

8 French document: Confidentiel Défense. 22 June, 1994. Quoted in Gabriel Périès and David Servenay, *Une Guerre Noire. Enquête sur les origines du genocide rwandais (1959–1994)*, Editions La Découverte, Paris, 2007, p. 383.

9 Letter, *Libération*, 14 June 1994.

10 Stephen Smith, 'Rwanda. Un ancien des escadrons de la mort accusé', *Libération*, 21 June 1994.

11 Kouchner was French minister of state for humanitarian affairs (1988–91), and minister of health (1992–93). In July 1994 he became a member of the European Parliament. He was appointed minister for foreign affairs by President Nicolas Sarkozy in May 2007.

12 ICTR Prosecution testimony. Lt-General Dallaire. Military One. January 2004.

13 Boutros-Ghali, *Unvanquished*, p. 139.

14 Lt Gen. Roméo Dallaire, *Shake Hands with the Devil. The Failure of Humanity in Rwanda*, Random House, Canada, 2003, p. 425.

15 Ibid., p. 418.

16 Institut François Mitterrand: Présidence de la République. Le Conseiller à la Présidence. Object: Rwanda – B. Kouchner. Note à l'attention de Monsieur le Président de la République. Paris, 21 June 1994.

17 Telephone interview, former US government official, Washington, DC, October 2007.

18 James Orbinski, *An Imperfect Offering. Dispatches from the Medical Front Line*, Random House, Canada, 2008, p. 221.

19 Jonathan Moore (ed.), *Hard Choices: Moral Dilemmas in Humanitarian Intervention*, Rowman and Littlefield, Oxford, 1998, p. 81.

20 Henry Kwami Anyidoho, *Guns over Kigali*, Woeli Publishing Services, Accra, 1997, pp. 77–8.

21 Dallaire, *Shake Hands*, p. 408.

22 Tikoca is today Fiji's high commissioner to Papua New Guinea.

23 Aidan Hartley, *The Zanzibar Chest. A Memoir of Love and War*, HarperCollins, London, 2003, p. 375.

24 Dallaire, *Shake Hands*, p. 443.

25 Ibid., p. 458.

26 Ibid., p. 457.

27 Ibid., p. 481.

28 Ibid., p. 449. See also Vaccaro, 'The politics of genocide'.

29 Dallaire, *Shake Hands*, p. 451.

30 Human Rights Watch/Fédération Internationale des Ligues des Droits de l'Homme, *Leave none to tell the story. Genocide in Rwanda*, 1999, p. 678.

31 Ibid., pp. 671–2.

32 Gérard Prunier, *The Rwanda Crisis 1959–1994. History of a Genocide*, Hurst and Co., London, 1995, pp. 281–7.

33 Chris McGreal, 'French compromised by collaboration in Rwanda', *Guardian*, 1 July 1994.

34 See ICTR Prosecution cases against Edouard Karemera, Yussuf Munyakazi, Clément Kayishema, Obed Ruzindana, Eliezer Niyitegeka and Alfred Musema.

35 Philip Verwimp, 'Death and survival during the 1994 genocide in Rwanda', *Population Studies*, 58(2), 2004, pp. 233–45.

36 African Rights, *Resisting Genocide. Bisesero April–June 1994*, April 1998.

37 Robert Block, 'Pattern of slaughter confounds French', *Independent on Sunday*, 3 July 1994.

38 Commission of a Citizens' Enquiry into the role of France during the genocide of the Tutsi in 1994. Report, *L'horreur qui nous prend au visage*. Survie. (The soldiers were from the Commandos Parachutiste de l'Air de Nîmes.) See also African Rights, *Rwanda. Death, Despair and Defiance*, London, 1995.

39 *The United Nations and Rwanda, 1993–1996*, UN Blue Book series, vol. 10, UN Department of Public Information, New York, 1996, p. 55.

40 Security Council (S/PV.3402), 11 July 1994.

41 Mel McNulty, 'France's Rwanda débâcle', *War Studies*, 2(2), Spring 1997, p. 16.

42 Gérard Prunier, 'Operation Turquoise: a humanitarian escape', in Howard Adelman and Astri Suhrke (eds), *The Path of a Genocide. The Rwanda Crisis from Uganda to Zaire*, Transaction, New Brunswick, NJ, 1999, p. 303.

43 Human Rights Watch/Fédération Internationale des Ligues des Droits de l'Homme, *Leave none to tell the story*, pp. 679–81.

44 McNulty, 'France's Rwanda débâcle', p. 18.

45 Jacques Roger Booh-Booh was replaced on 1 July 1994. He had left Rwanda on 24 April, and made Nairobi his base.

46 Shaharyar Khan, *The Shallow Graves of Rwanda*, I.B.Tauris, London, 2000, p. 16.

47 Philippe Gaillard, *Rwanda 1994: la vraie vie est absente (Arthur Rimbaud). Cycle des Conférences les Mardi de Musée. M. Philippe Gaillard, délégué du CIRC, chef de délégation au Rwanda de juillet 1993 à juillet 1994*. See also: ICRC.Org./web/Eng/, Speech made by Philippe Gaillard at the Genocide Prevention Conference, Nottingham, January 2002. Aegis Trust/FCO.

48 The fourteen UN personnel were ten Belgian peacekeepers on 7 April; Captain Mbabye Diagne, of Senegal, who died in a mortar bomb attack on 31 May; Private Mensah-Baidoo, of Ghana, who died in a mortar shell attack on 9 May; Lance Corporal Ahedor, of Ghana, killed in action, 17 April 1994; and Captain Ankah, of Ghana, killed in action, 8 July.

49 Hartley, *The Zanzibar Chest*, p. 375.

50 Samantha Bolton, 'J'ai vu arriver le choléra', *Le Nouvel Observateur*, 28 July–3 August 1994.

51 Larry Minear and Philippe Guillot, *Soldiers to the Rescue. Humanitarian Lessons from Rwanda*, Development Centre of the Organization for Economic Cooperation and Development, Paris, 1996, p. 63.

52 *The International Response to Conflict and Genocide: Lessons from the Rwanda Experience*. Joint Evaluation of Emergency Assistance to Rwanda. Copenhagen, March 1996, study

3, p. 43. On 24 July, the UNHCR reported 2.1 million refugees and 1.4 million displaced within the French zone, and 1.2 million displaced in the rest of the country.

53 An estimated 20,000 people died of cholera, a disease easily treated with a simple remedy costing less than 50p a day. Oral rehydration salts replace the vital mineral and fluids lost in violent diarrhoea and vomiting.

54 Robert Block, 'A week in Goma', *Independent on Sunday*, 31 July 1994.

55 Anne Mackintosh, 'Rwanda: beyond "ethnic conflict"', *Development in Practice*, 7(4), November 1997, p. 466.

56 Prunier, 'Operation Turquoise', p. 303.

57 Excerpts taken from interview published on Frontline's website for *The Triumph of Evil*, www.pbs.org/ WGBH/Pages/Frontline/shows/evil. Copyright WGBH/Frontline, 1999.

58 Moore, *Hard Choices*, p. 72.

59 The last UNAMIR II soldier left Rwanda in March 1996.

60 Dallaire returned home to an appointment as deputy commander of the army and commander of the 1st Canadian Division. Canada gave him the Meritorious Service Cross. He was medically released from the Canadian armed forces in April 2000. In January 2004 Lt Gen. Dallaire testified at the ICTR in the trial Military One. He became a Canadian senator in March 2005.

61 By July 1994, there were the following ICRC operations in Rwanda: there was a seven-strong medical team in Bukavu working across the Zaire border in Cyangugu and helping those who had escaped the massacres in the Nyarushishi camp in the hills; there was a five-strong medical team in Gikongoro; there were two ICRC delegates in Rusumo. A delegation in Kabgayi was displaced because of the fighting. In Kigali there were ten delegates when the city fell.

62 Gaillard, *Rwanda 1994*.

63 Gérard Delaloye and Elisabeth Levy, 'Philippe Gaillard, après Kigali, pouvez-vous encore croire en l'humanité?', *Le Nouveau Quotidien*, 30 December 1994.

18 STARTING FROM ZERO

1 US Agency for International Development. Bureau for Humanitarian Response. Office of US Foreign Disaster Assistance. Situation Report no. 4, 25 July 1994.

2 Nigel Cantwell, *Starting from Zero: The Promotion and Protection of Children's Rights in Post-genocide Rwanda*, July 1994–December 1996, UNICEF and International Child Development Centre, Florence, 1997.

3 Françoise Bouchet-Saulnier, *Mission Rwanda. Juriste*, MSF, p. 4.

4 Rwanda Emergency Programme. Progress Report no. 1, UNICEF, Kigali, Reporting Period: May 1994–March 1995 (author's archive).

5 Cantwell, *Starting from Zero*, p. 46.

6 See Suzanne Kaplan, *Children in Genocide. Extreme traumatisation and affect regulation*, International Psychoanalytical Association, London, 2008, pp. 171–83, 201–25.

7 The UK Committee for UNICEF, *Annual Review 1994/1995*, p. 5.

8 'Rwanda toll could top 1 million', *Guardian*, 25 August 1994. The UN Rwandan Emergency Office (UNREO) was created by the UN Department of Humanitarian Affairs and UNDP to coordinate relief efforts. See also Jean-Paul Gouteux, *Un Génocide secret d'état. La France et le Rwanda 1990–1997*, Editions Sociales, 1998, p. 104. While the percentage of

Tutsi in Rwanda was officially 9 per cent, research by the UNDP showed this figure to be nearer 20 per cent.

9 UN Commission on Human Rights, *Report on the situation of human rights in Rwanda submitted by Mr. René Dégni-Ségui, Special Rapporteur, under paragraph 20 of resolution S-3/1 of 25 May, 1994* (E/CN.4/1995/7). 28 June 1994.

10 *The United Nations and Rwanda, 1993–1996*, UN Blue Book series, vol. 10, UN Department of Public Information, New York, 1996, p. 415.

11 Report signed Col. Gasake. For the attention of the FAR Commander. Goma, 12 May 1995 (author's archive).

12 Memorandum Presented by the Rwanda Armed Forces (in exile) for the Liberation of Their Country. Signed: Major-General Augustin Bizimungu. Chief of Staff. Goma, 1 June 1996 (author's archive).

13 Report signed Col. Gasake. For the attention of the FAR Commander. Goma, 12 May 1995 (author's archive).

14 William Cyrus Reed, 'Guerrillas in the midst', in Christopher Clapham (ed.), *African Guerillas*, James Currey, Oxford, 1998, p. 140.

15 Ibid., p. 139.

16 Eventually, the issue of camp security was made the responsibility of the UNHCR, which contracted with the Zairean government to provide an elite force to police the camps. It took until the end of January 1995 before the Zairean Camp Security Operation was agreed. The UNHCR signed a deal whereby Zaire would provide troops and the UNHCR would pay for salaries, food and healthcare, and the troops would liaise with an international group of civilians who had police and military backgrounds. By the end of April, the contingent from Zaire had reached 1,500. As a result, the killing and thuggery were reduced but the core problem was not addressed.

17 *The United Nations and Rwanda, 1993–1996*, pp. 80–83.

18 Mark Huband, 'France blocks Rwanda aid in cynical power game', *Observer*, 10 October 1994.

19 Larry Minear and Philippe Guillot, *Soldiers to the Rescue. Humanitarian Lessons from Rwanda*, Development Centre of the Organization for Economic Cooperation and Development, Paris, 1996, p. 66.

19 THE GENOCIDE CONVENTION

1 *Year Book of the United Nations, 1946–7*, p. 255; Patrick Thornberry, *International Law and the Rights of Minorities*, Oxford University Press, 1993, p. 64.

2 Raphael Lemkin, *Axis Rule in Occupied Europe. Laws of Occupation, Analysis of Government, Proposals for Redress*, Carnegie Endowment for International Peace, Washington, DC.

3 The resolution was passed by fifty-five votes to none with no abstentions. See Thornberry, *International Law*, p. 67.

4 The death toll estimate was provided to this author by Philippe Gaillard, chief delegate, International Committee of the Red Cross (ICRC), Rwanda, 1993–94. This was the estimate used by Charles Petrie, deputy coordinator of the UN Rwanda Emergency Office (UNREO).

5 UN Commission on Human Rights, *Report by Mr. B. W. Ndiaye, Special Rapporteur, on his mission to Rwanda from 8–17 April 1993* (E/CN. 4/1994/7/Add. 1), 11 August 1993. International Federation of Human Rights (FIDH), Report of the International Commission to Investigate Human Rights Violations in Rwanda since October 1, 1990, 7–21 January 1993.

6 United Nations Press Release. Special Session of Human Rights Commission continues discussion of Rwandan Conflict. DPI New York HR/CN/568. May 25, 1994 (author's archive).

7 Report of the Secretary-General on the situation in Rwanda, covering the political mission he sent to Rwanda to move the warring parties towards a ceasefire and recommending that the expanded mandate for UNAMIR be authorized for an initial period of six months, S/1994/640. 31 May, 1994. Blue Book Series, p. 290.

8 UN Commission on Human Rights, *Report on the situation of human rights in Rwanda submitted by Mr. R. Dégni-Ségui, Special Rapporteur of the Commission on Human Rights*, 28 June 1994.

9 Security Council Resolution 935 of 1 July 1994 mandated the creation of an impartial commission of experts to examine and analyse information concerning serious violations of international law, including genocide. The experts were Astu-Koffi Amega, a former president of the Supreme Court of Togo; Habi Dieng, a former attorney-general of Guinea; and Salifou Fomba, a law professor in Mali who was a member of the UN International Law Commission.

10 Interview, London, 10 February 2009. Also ICTR investigator, February 2003. A part of this archive was subsequently given to prosecution lawyers at the ICTR and was used as evidence in the Media Trial.

11 Final report of the Commission of Experts established in accordance with Security Council Resolution 935 (S/1994/1405), 9 December 1994.

12 Interim report of the Commission of Experts established in accordance with Security Council Resolution 935 (S/1994/1125), 4 October 1994.

13 The first such tribunal was the International Criminal Tribunal for Former Yugoslavia (ICTY), created on 25 May 1993.

14 Richard Goldstone, 'Justice now, and for posterity', *International Herald Tribune*, 15–16 October 2005.

15 Honoré Rakotomanana. Judge. Deputy Prosecutor. 'Résumé of Official Responses given by the Deputy Prosecutor to the OIS Draft Report on the ICTR'. Kigali, 31 January 1997 (author's archive).

16 Justice Hassan B. Jallow, *The OTP-ICTR: on-going challenges of completion*, The Hague. International Criminal Court. Office of the Prosecutor. Guest Lecture Series. 1 November 2004.

17 Kambanda was arrested on 18 July 1997 in Nairobi. Transcript of ICTR interrogation of Kambanda (author's archive).

18 Kambanda was sentenced on six counts, including genocide, and sentenced to life imprisonment.

19 Ferdinand Nahimana was sentenced to thirty years, Hassan Ngeze to thirty-five years and Barayagwiza to twenty-seven years in prison.

20 ICTR. See www.ictr. orgS/2008/322.

21 Justice Jallow is a former minister of justice of the Gambia.

22 Jallow, *The OTP-ICTR*.

23 After the genocide, Kabuga had been given a visa to enter Switzerland and, having withdrawn money from a bank, had flown from Zurich airport to the safety of the Democratic Republic of Congo (DRC). On 6 May 2008, the Kenyan government applied for a court order to seize property in Nairobi that purportedly belonged to him. Kabuga's son-in-law, Augustin Ngirabatware, a former minister of planning, was arrested in Germany in September 2007.

24 The US State Department Rewards for Justice programme has

seen the arrests of Tharcisse Renzaho, who had been the prefect in Kigali, Jean-Baptiste Gatete, the prefect of Murambi, and Yusuf Munyakezi, a trader.

25 Statement by Justice Hassan B. Jallow, Prosecutor of the ICTR, to the UN Security Council, 4 June 2008.

26 The Government of the Republic of Rwanda versus Vincent Bajinya, Charles Munyaneza, Emmanuel Nteziryayo, Celestin Ugirashebuja, City of Westminster Magistrates' Court, 6 June 2008.

27 Security Council Resolution 1503, 28 August 2003.

28 The judges at the ICTR have so far refused to approve applications from the prosecutor to transfer genocide cases to Rwanda, although Kigali was said to have made 'remarkable' progress in improving its judicial system. Rwanda's prosecutor general, Martin Ngoga, has announced a determination by the government to remove the final judicial obstacles to the prosecutor's referral strategy. See News@Hirondelle.org, 'Weekly summary', 21 November 2008. The four targeted by transfer requests to Rwanda are Lieutenant Ildephonse Hategekimana, Yussuf Munyakazi, Gaspard Kanyarukiga and Jean-Baptiste Gatete. The ICTR was hoping that the transfers to Rwanda would reduce its workload. News@Hirondelle.org, 'ICTR trials. Extremely challenging judicial year begins with trial delays', 6 January 2009.

29 Gérard Prunier, *From Genocide to Continental War. The 'Congolese' Conflict and the Crisis of Contemporary Africa*, Hurst Publishers Ltd, London, 2009, pp. 349–50.

30 One notable exception is Michel Bagaragaza, the former managing director of a Rwandan tea organization, who was a close acquaintance of former President Juvénal Habyarimana. Bagaragaza has testified against other ICTR defendants, including Protais Zigiranyirazo.

31 Christopher Black, defence lawyer, in the trial of General Augustin Ndindiliyimana, March 2005.

32 Allan Thomson, 'Rwanda kingpin plays it cool', *Toronto Star*, 10 July 2005.

33 There are sixteen judges at the ICTR chosen by the UN General Assembly. There are three permanent judges of each of the trial chambers and seven permanent judges of the appeals chamber. The story of the ICTR and the controversies that surround it is beyond the scope of this book.

34 Kabiligi's lead counsel was Paul Skolnik of Canada. Professor Erlinder of the USA led Ntabakuze's team and Nsengiyumva's defence was led by Kennedy Ogetto of Kenya.

35 Judge Jai Ram Reddy of Fiji and Judge Sergei Alekseevich Egorov of Russia were the other two judges in the trial.

36 See Chapter 1.

37 The case law of the International Criminal Tribunals has now made it clear that proving 'intent' is no barrier to prosecution. To prove genocide, it is enough to prove actions that any reasonable person would conclude were intended to kill or otherwise destroy, in whole or in part, an ethnic, national, racial or religious group. Dr Gregory H. Stanton, President, International Association of Genocide Scholars and President of Genocide Watch.

38 The Prosecutor v. Théoneste Bagosora et al. Case No. ICTR-98-41-T. Oral Summary.

39 Reuters live feed to the offices of al-Jazeera International, Knightsbridge, London, 18 December 2008.

40 Zigiranyirazo was arrested in Belgium in 2001 and his trial began

on 3 October 2005. The judges were
Judge Inés Mónica Weinberg de Roca,
presiding, Judge Khalida Rachid Khan
and Judge Lee Gacuiga Muthoga.

41 Among these, but not exclusively, are: French historian Bernard
Lugan, Associate Professor of African
History at the Jean Moulin University,
Lyon, with thirty years of study of the
countries of Africa; Peter Erlinder, 'No
conspiracy, no genocide planning ...
no genocide?', *Jurist Legal News and
Research*, 24 December 2008. (Erlinder
is lead defence counsel at the ICTR,
from the William Mitchell College of
Law.) See also www.taylor-report.com
and Edward S. Herman, 'Genocide
inflation is the real human rights
threat', www.coldtype.net. Also: No
Justice, 'A letter to the UN from some
of its political prisoners in Arusha',
2 January 2008, published on www.
cirqueMinime/Paris. Sites accessed
January 2009. Barrie Collins, 'Rwanda:
obscuring the truth of genocide',
13 August 2008, www.spiked-online.
org.

42 Pierre Péan, 'Noires fureurs,
blancs menteurs, Rwanda 1990–1994',
Mille et une nuits, November 2005.

43 Human Rights Watch. *Address
Crimes Committed by RPF*. Letter to
the ICTR Prosecutor. 11 December
2008.

44 On 6 February 2008, the Spanish judge issued forty arrest warrants
against officials serving in the Rwandan government in connection with
crimes of genocide, crimes against
humanity, war crimes and terrorism
committed between 1990 and 2002.
The crimes, he argues, fall under the
jurisdiction of the ICTR.

45 Tracy Wilkinson, 'Spain indicts
40 Rwandan officials', *Los Angeles
Times*, 7 February 2008.

46 Chris McGreal, 'If Tutsi died it
was because the people were angry with
them', *Guardian*, 19 December 2008.

47 Stephen Smith, *Révélations
sur l'attentat qui a déclenché le genocide
rwandais*, 10 March 2004.

48 Bruguière was best known
for tracking the Venezuelan terrorist
known as 'Carlos the Jackal', Ilich
Ramírez Sánchez, one of the most
wanted terrorists in the world for the
bombing of the OPEC headquarters in
Vienna in 1975. He was sentenced to
life imprisonment by a French court
in December 1994, found guilty of the
murders of two French policemen.

49 Ruzibiza wrote a book about his
experiences. Abdul Ruzibiza, *Rwanda
L'Histoire Secret*, Editions du Panama,
Paris, 2005.

50 See Colette Braeckman,
Archives.

51 Georges Kapler (cinéaste),
Jacques Morel (ingénieur CNRS à
la retraite). The complete analysis
of Judge Bruguière's order by these
authors can be read at La Nuit
Rwandaise no. 1, izuba.info/
Nuitrwandaise/spip.php?article6.

52 Human Rights Watch, *Equal
Access to Justice: Prosecuting Crimes by
RPF Soldiers*, 24 July 2008.

53 Linda Melvern, 'A perfect
crime', *Prospect*, February 2008. There
were attempts to prevent publication
of XXQ's story by British journalists,
one of them a specialist in African
affairs, who was sure that the RPF was
responsible for the attack on the plane.
(Email correspondence, September
2007–January 2008. Printed version in
author's archive.)

54 Mpiranya sought refuge with
Bagosora in Cameroon. He escaped
capture, leaving the capital two days
before Bagosora was arrested on
10 March 1996 to go to the west of the
country, where he hid in the home of
a French DGSE agent. Sources within
the Rwandan government claim that
Mpiranya died in Zimbabwe in 2006.

55 Tribunal de Grande Instance

de Paris. Cabinet de Jean-Louis Bruguière. Delivrance de mandats d'arrêt internationaux. Parquet: 97.295.2303/0.

56 Interview with anonymous source, London, 9 January 2008.

57 Contact FM Kigali. The interview was with journalist Albert Rudatsimburw, 15 November 2008 (translation Serge Farnel). See also: Christoph Ayad, 'Le témoin-clé du Juge Bruguière se rétracte', *Libération*, 19 November 2008.

58 The two other witnesses were Deus Kagiraneza and Emmanuel Ruzingana.

59 The commission was established in October 2007. High Court Judge Jean Mutsinzi heads a seven-person investigation team. Other commissioners are Dr Jean Damascene Bizimana (vice-president), Alice Rugira (secretary), Augustin Mukama, Jean Baptiste Mvano, Judith Mbabazi and Peter Mugenzi.

60 Roland Marchal, 'France and Africa: the emergence of essential reform?', *International Affairs*, 74(2), 1998, p. 357.

61 Mitterrand was in his second seven-year term of office as president (1988–95). He was in office longer than any other democratic president. He died 8 January 1996.

62 Patrick de Saint-Exupéry, *Les Détectives de l'histoire. Rwanda, la France coupable?*, 8 December 2008, www.dailymotion.com.

63 Patrick de Saint-Exupéry, *L'Inavouable: La France au Rwanda*, Les Arènes, Paris, 2004.

64 Ibid., pp. 277–8. See also: Gabriel Périès and David Servenay, *Une Guerre Noire. Enquête sur les origines du genocide rwandais (1959–1994)*, Editions La Découverte, Paris, 2007.

65 Assembléé Nationale, Mission d'Information Commune, *Enquête sur la tragédie rwandaise (1990–1994)*, Paris, pt 1, p. 363.

66 Védrine became foreign minister in the government of Lionel Jospin, 1997–2002.

67 Rwandan Republic. Independent National Commission to Collect Proof of the Implication of the Government of France in the 1994 Genocide in Rwanda. November 15, 2007. Report Published August 2008, p. 23. The commission was given a six-month mandate; this was renewed twice, in October 2006 and April 2007.

68 Commission of a Citizens' Inquiry into the role of France during the genocide of the Tutsi in 1994. Report, 'L'horreur qui nous prend au visage', p. 257, www.cec.rwanda.free.fr.

69 Serge Farnel, Rwanda News Agency. Georges Kapler, Jacques Morel, Survie. Commission d'Enquête Citoyenne, www.cec.rwanda.free.fr. La Nuit Rwandaise was created in 2007 and is dedicated to the study of the French involvement in the Rwandan genocide. It produces a yearly journal and the website is: www.lanuitrwandaise.net.

70 Stéphanie Maupas, 'Three Rwandan officers testified in favour of the colonel', *Le Monde*, 19 January 2007. In January 2007, three of them appeared for General Gratien Kabiligi. In December 2006, a French colonel testified for three defendants in Military One – Bagosora, Anatole Nsengiyunva and Aloys Ntabakuze. See also Rwandan Republic. Independent National Commission to Collect Proof of the Implication of the Government of France in the 1994 Genocide in Rwanda. November 15, 2007.

71 Jean Chatai, 'Omerta à la française', *L'Humanité*, 23 October 2006.

72 Saint-Exupéry, *Les Détectives de l'histoire*.

73 Verhofstadt was the prime

minister between July 1999 and March 2008.

74 Joseph Ndahimana, 'Les effets indésirables d'une demande de pardon', *Le Libre Belgique*, 8–9 April 2000. Full text p. 10.

75 Avocats sans Frontières. Chronique Judicaire. Assises Rwanda 2007 no. 5.

76 Telex de l'ambassadeur Swinnen du 27 Mars, 1992, in Belgian senate, Commission d'enquête parlementaire concernant les événements du Rwanda. Report, 6 December 1997, pp. 493–4.

77 Belgian Senate Parliamentary Commission of Inquiry, report of the Rwanda ad hoc group, p. 84.

78 Marchal, the commanding officer of the Kigali Weapons Secure Area and the Belgian contingent, was later subject to a court martial for failing to protect his men. He was acquitted.

79 An American journalist, Philip Gourevitch, has written how in the summer of 1994 UN troops had killed the dogs feeding off the corpses. Gourevitch noted: 'After months during which Rwandans had been left to wonder whether the UN troops knew how to shoot, because they never used their excellent weapons to stop the extermination of civilians, it turned out that the peacekeepers were very good shots.' Philip Gourevitch, *We wish to inform you that tomorrow we will be killed with our families*, Picador, London, 1998, p. 148. See also the feature film *Shooting Dogs* (2007).

80 The other members of the panel were Han Sung-Joo, former foreign minister of the Republic of Korea, and Lieutenant General Rufus Kupolati of Nigeria, the former head of the UN Truce Supervision Organization (UNTSO) in Jerusalem.

81 Report of the Independent Inquiry into the Actions of the United Nations during the 1994 Genocide in Rwanda, 15 December 1999.

82 The USA vetoed a second term for him. In January 1997 Boutros-Ghali moved to Paris to take up a post as secretary-general of Francophonie, a grouping of French-speaking countries, and he became the head of an international panel on democracy-building created by UNESCO (the UN Educational, Scientific and Cultural Organization).

83 Interview, Boutros Boutros-Ghali, Paris, December 1999.

84 Boutros Boutros-Ghali, *Unvanquished. A US–UN Saga*, I.B.Tauris, London, 1999, p. 140.

85 Interview, Boutros Boutros-Ghali.

86 Statement of New Zealand to Open-Ended Working Group on the Question of Equitable Representation on and Increase in the Membership of the Security Council. April 1994. Unpublished (author's archive). Interview, Colin Keating on UN reform, 16 January 1996.

87 See Linda Melvern, *The Ultimate Crime*, Allison and Busby, London, 1995.

88 Both the UN and the OAU reports owe much information to *The International Response to Conflict and Genocide: Lessons from the Rwanda Experience.* Joint Emergency Assistance to Rwanda. Copenhagen, March 1996. Study I: 'Historical Perspective: Some Explanatory Factors', Tor Sellström and Lennart Wohlgemuth. Study II: 'Early Warning and Conflict Management', Howard Adelman. Study III: 'Humanitarian Aid and Effects', John Bourton, Emery Brusset, Alistair Hallam'. Study IV: 'Rebuilding Post-War Rwanda', Krishna Kumar, David Tardif-Douglin, Kim Maynard, Peter Manikas, Annette Sheckler and Carolyn Knapp. Synthesis Report John Eriksson. (This study was initiated

in 1995 by the Nordic countries and was eventually sponsored by nineteen countries and eighteen international agencies. France withdrew its support for the report after examining the draft.)

89 The members of the International Panel of Eminent Personalities to Investigate the 1994 Genocide in Rwanda and the Surrounding Events were: Q. K. J. Masire, Botswana, Amadou Toumani Toure, Mali, Lisbet Palme, Sweden, Ellen Johnson-Sirleaf, Liberia, Hocine Djoudi, Algeria, Stephen Lewis, Canada, and P. N. Bhagwati, India. *Rwanda, the Preventable Genocide* was written by a Canadian, Gerry Caplan. Canada contributed financially to both the OAU and the UN inquiries.

90 Groupe Golias, *Rwanda, l'horreur perdu de l'église*, Editions Golias, 1999. See also Timothy Longman, 'Church politics and the genocide in Rwanda', *Journal of Religion in Africa*, 31(2), 2001.

91 Organization of African Unity, *Rwanda, the Preventable Genocide.*

92 Charles Jeanneret, 'Rwanda: land of a thousand hills', *UNESCO Courier*, November 1991.

93 Charles Jeanneret, 'Economie de développement et réalité. Interrogations et interpellations', *IFDA Dossier*, July–September 1990.

94 Interim report, p. 40.

95 Peter Uvin, *Aiding Violence: The Development Enterprise in Rwanda*, Kumarian Press, New York, 1998, pp. 1–4.

96 Howard Adelman and Astri Suhrke with Bruce D. Jones, *Early Warning and Conflict Management in Rwanda: Report of Study II of the Joint Evaluation of Emergency Assistance in Rwanda*, DANIDA, Copenhagen, 1996.

97 Organization for Economic Cooperation and Development (1988–1993), Informal Task Force on Conflict, Peace and Development Cooperation, OECD, 1999. Anton Baaré, David Shearer and Peter Uvin, *The Limits and Scope for the Use of Development Assistance Incentives for Influencing Conflict Situations: Case Study Rwanda*, OECD, Paris, 1999.

98 La Coopération Suisse au Rwanda. Rapport du Groupe d'Etude institué par le Département Fédérale des Affaires Etrangères (FAE), January 1996.

99 Matthew Ripley, 'Putting the politics back in: a study of bilateral development aid and donor policy in Rwanda, up to 1994', MA Thesis, King's College London, Department of War Studies, 2007.

100 Simon was a member of the Senate Committee on Foreign Relations, and chairman of the Subcommittee on African Affairs, US Senate. See Committee on Foreign Relations, Subcommittee on African Affairs, *Crisis in Central Africa*, Hearings, 26 July 1994.

101 Interview with Senator Paul Simon, 3 December 1999.

102 UN Doc. Outgoing Code Cable. From Annan to Dallaire. UNAMIR 1584, 11 May 1994 (author's archive).

103 The secretary-general was in Paris.

104 Presidential Decision Directive (PDD-25), 3 May 1994, www.fas.org/irp/offdocs/pdd25.htm.

105 Samantha Power, 'Bystanders to genocide', *Atlantic Monthly*, September 2001. See also Jared Cohen, *One Hundred Days of Silence: America and the Rwanda Genocide*, Rowman and Littlefield, MD, 2007.

106 Cohen, *One Hundred Days of Silence*, p. 114.

107 Ibid., p. 103.

108 *This Week* with David Brinkley, 24 July 1994. Transcript 665. Quoted

in Susan D. Moeller, *Compassion Fatigue*, Routledge, New York and London, 1999, p. 296.

109 William Ferroggiaro, *The US and the Genocide in Rwanda, 1994*, 24 March 2004. See www.gwu.edu. The National Security Archive is a research group at George Washington University that specializes in collecting government documents through Freedom of Information requests. See also: Samantha Power, *A Problem from Hell: America and the Age of Genocide*, Basic Books, New York, 2002.

110 Email correspondence with author, December 2008.

111 Excerpts from the interviews on Frontline's website for *The Triumph of Evil*, www.pbs.org/WGBH/Pages/Frontline/shows/evil. Copyright WGBH/Frontline, 1999.

112 The UNAMIR troops in Rwanda during the genocide were, on 25 May 1994, from the following countries: Ghana 334, Tunisia 40, Canada 11, Togo 18, Senegal 12, Bangladesh 11, Zimbabwe 8, Mali 9, Austria 7, Congo 7, Nigeria 7, Russia 4, Poland 3, Egypt 2, Malawi 2, Fiji 1.

113 A first description of what happened within the administration of President Bill Clinton can be found in Holly J. Burkhalter, 'The question of genocide. The Clinton Administration and Rwanda', *World Policy Journal*, 11(4), Winter 1994–95.

114 Memorandum from George E. Moose, John Shattuck, Douglas J. Bennett and Conrad K. Harper to the Secretary of State. The declassified US documents are available at www.gwu.edu.

115 Email correspondence with Sir Franklin Berman, 10 May 2003. The Legal Adviser, who holds the rank of director general within the FCO, is the head of the Legal Advisers. The Legal Advisers are members of the Diplomatic Service. The Legal Adviser

reports directly to the Permanent Under-Secretary. The Advisers are the main centre of expertise on public international law within the UK government.

116 Written answer: Mark Lennox-Boyd, the Parliamentary Under-Secretary of State for Foreign and Commonwealth Affairs, 9 May 1994.

117 John Major, *John Major: The Autobiography*, HarperCollins, London, 1999.

118 This directly contradicts a claim in a speech by Peter Hain, MP, that the UK government did have access to Dallaire's cables. 22 January 2002.

119 Lillian Wong, former British ambassador to Rwanda. Presentation. Rwanda Forum. Imperial War Museum. March 2004. One anonymous source, FCO, 21 November 2003.

120 Richard Dowden, *Africa: Altered States, Ordinary Miracles*, Portobello Books, London, 2008.

121 Paul Williams, 'The peacekeeping system, Britain and the 1994 Rwandan genocide', in Phil Clark and Zachary D. Kaufman (eds), *After Genocide: Transitional Justice, Post-Conflict Reconstruction and Reconciliation in Rwanda and Beyond*, Columbia University Press/C. Hurst and Co., New York, 2008, www.aftergenocide.com.

122 Stewart Wallis, Overseas Director, Oxfam, 'Looking the other way in Rwanda', Letter to the Editor, *Guardian*, 16 April 1994.

123 Letter from David Bryer, director, Oxfam, to Prime Minister the Rt Hon. John Major, MP, 3 May 1994 (author's archive).

124 D. Orr, 'From Landmines to genocide: analysing the influence of non-state actors upon state decision-making in the security issue area',

Unpublished MSc Human Rights and International Politics dissertation, University of Glasgow, 2006.

125 House of Commons, Hansard, Debates for 12 April 1994.

126 Douglas Hurd, *Memoirs*, Little, Brown, London, 2003, p. 489.

127 BBC Radio 4, *The World at One*. Interview, Douglas Hurd with James Cox, 4 August 2004.

128 Report of the Independent Inquiry into the Actions of the United Nations during the 1994 Genocide in Rwanda, 15 December 1999, pp. 53–5.

129 Interview with Sir David Hannay, London, December 1999.

130 Alan J. Kuperman, *The Limits of Humanitarian Intervention. Genocide in Rwanda*, Brookings Institution, Washington, DC, 2001.

131 Ibid., p. 99.

132 Madeleine K. Albright and William S. Cohen (co-chairs), *Preventing Genocide, a A Blueprint for US Policymakers*, Genocide Prevention Task Force, 2008, www.usip.org/genocide_taskforce.

133 Misha Glenny, *War Radio*, BBC Radio 4, 10 December 1998. In 2001 Hannay was created a life peer and in 2006 was appointed chair of the United Nations Association of Great Britain and Northern Ireland (UNA-UK).

134 This phrase was repeated in the House of Commons on 14 June when, in a written answer, Douglas Hogg claimed that the UK government had not been asked to contribute troops to the UN peacekeeping operation in Rwanda.

135 The 5th Airborne Brigade and the Special Air Service (SAS). The level of readiness of the 5th Airborne Brigade, the only airborne and air-trained brigade in the British army, was routinely set at five days and fewer in a crisis. The brigade consisted of two battalions of parachutists plus a command structure – a total of about five thousand – men. It was to be integrated into a NATO rapid deployment force.

136 Prime Minister Tony Blair. Speech to the Labour Party Annual Conference, Brighton, 2 October 2001.

137 Interview, Major General Roméo Dallaire, November 1994.

138 BBC *Newsnight* Special on Rwanda, 27 July 1994.

139 Melvern, *The Ultimate Crime*, p. 355.

140 Written answers, House of Commons, Hansard, 21 July 1994, p. 473.

141 Interviews, DPKO, New York, July 1994.

142 Ibid., 29 March 1996.

143 The last UNAMIR soldier left Rwanda on 8 March 1996 when UNAMIR II withdrew from the country at the request of the Rwandan government.

144 Lt Gen. Roméo Dallaire, *Shake Hands with the Devil. The Failure of Humanity in Rwanda*, Random House, Canada, 2003, p. 5.

145 Ken Booth, *Theory of World Security*, Cambridge Studies in International Relations, 105, Cambridge University Press, 2007.

146 Martin Gilbert, *Auschwitz and the Allies*, Michael Joseph, 1981, p. 341. Prime Minister Winston Churchill to Anthony Eden in July 1944 had described the Holocaust in the following terms: '... this is probably the greatest and most horrible single crime ever committed in the whole history of the world'.

SOURCES

The archives consulted in the research for this book include the records of the United Nations Department of Peacekeeping Operations, Rwanda, October 1993–July 1994. The Force Commanders Papers are in the UN Archives and Records Management Section. A large collection of UNAMIR coded cables from Kigali and the responses to them from UN headquarters was passed to the author by UN Military Observer Major Stefan Stec, who was part of a Humanitarian Action Cell during the genocide.

The author's archive includes comprehensive files on UN peacekeeping, the UN missions in the former Yugoslavia, UNPROFOR, and Somalia, UNOSOM II. In Kigali, Rwanda, the author was given access to the Rwanda National Archives, which included a part of the Rwandan government's Ministry of Defence files 1990–94, including general administration and military intelligence. The author's archive includes copies of documents from the administration of the interim government, April–July 1994, and from the offices of the Kigali Ville prefecture, and a collection from the office of President Juvénal Habyarimana.

UN BOOKS, AVAILABLE REPORTS AND DOCUMENTS

Security Council

An Agenda for Peace: Preventive Diplomacy, Peacemaking and Peacekeeping. Report of the Secretary-General pursuant to the statement adopted by the Summit Meeting of the Security Council on January 31, 1992 (A/47/277-S/24111), 17 June 1992.

Effective Planning, Budgeting and Administration of Peacekeeping Operations. Report of the Secretary-General (A/48/1994), 25 May 1994.

Rwanda

Interim report of the Commission of Experts established in accordance with Security Council Resolution 935 (S/1994/1125), 4 October 1994.

Final report of the Commission of Experts established pursuant to Security Council Resolution 935 (S/1994/1405), 9 December 1994.

Report of the Independent Inquiry into the Actions of the United Nations during the 1994 Genocide in Rwanda. 15 December 1999.

Somalia

Report of the Commission of Inquiry Established Pursuant to Security Council Resolution 885 (1993) to Investigate Armed Attacks on UNOSOM II Personnel Which

Led to Casualties Among Them.
24 February 1994.

Economic and Social Council. Commission on Human Rights
Report by Mr. B. W. Ndiaye, Special Rapporteur, on his mission to Rwanda from 8–17 April, 1993 (E/CN4/1994/7/Add 1), 11 August 1993.

Report of the United Nations High Commissioner for Human Rights, Mr. José Ayala Lasso, on his mission to Rwanda 11–12 May, 1994 (E/CN.4/S-3/3), 19 May 1994.

Revised and updated report on the question of the prevention and punishment of the crime of Genocide. B. Whitaker (E/CN.4/1985/6), 2 July 1985.

Report on the situation of human rights in Rwanda submitted by Mr. René Dégni-Ségui, Special Rapporteur, under paragraph 20 of Resolution 8-3/1 of 25 May, 1994 (E/CN.4/1995/7), 28 June 1994. Further reports: 12 August 1994 (E/CN.4/1995/12) and 11 November 1994 (E/CN.4/1995/70).

Books
The United Nations and Rwanda, 1993–1996. The United Nations Blue Book series, vol. 10. New York: UN Department of Public Information, 1996 (contains all the secretary-general's reports and letters to the Security Council in relation to UNAMIR together with all relevant resolutions).

The Blue Helmets: A Review of United Nations Peacekeeping (3rd edn). New York: UN Publications, 1996.

Comprehensive Report on Lessons Learned from United Nations Assistance Mission for Rwanda (UNAMIR), October 1993–April 1996. New York: United Nations, 1996.

REPORTS
ADL, *Rapport sur les Droits de l'homme au Rwanda. September 1991–September 1992.* Kigali: Association Rwandaise pour la défense des droits de la personne et des libertés publiques (ADL), December 1992.

Albright, Madeleine K., William S. Cohen, co-chairs: *Preventing Genocide. A Blueprint for US Policymakers,* Genocide Prevention Task Force. With Thomas Daschle, Stuart Eizenstat, Michael Gerson, Dan Glickman, Jack Kemp, Gabrielle Kirk McDonald, Thomas R. Pickering, Julia Taft, Vin Weber, Anthony Zinni, Brandon Grove, Executive Director. United States Institute of Peace, the United States Holocaust Memorial Museum, the American Academy of Diplomacy, and the Endowment of the United States Institute of Peace, 2008.

Amnesty International, *Rwanda: Amnesty International's Concerns Since the Beginning of an Insurgency in October,* March 1991 (/~ Index: AFR 47/05/91).

— *Rwanda: Persecution of Tutsi Minority and Repression of Government Critics, 1990–1992,* May 1992.

— *Rwanda: Mass Murder by Government Supporters and Troops in April and May, 1994,* 23 May 1994.

— *A Call for UN human rights action on Rwanda and Burundi,* May 1994.

Article 19, *Broadcasting Genocide: Censorship, Propaganda and State-Sponsored Violence in Rwanda 1990–1994,* October 1996.

Assemblée Nationale, Mission d'Information Commune, *Enquête sur la Tragédie Rwandaise (1990–1994),* Paris.

Belgian senate, Commission d'enquête parlementaire concernant les événements du Rwanda. *Rapport.* Brussels: Sénat de Belgique, 6 December 1997.

Chossudovsky, Michel and Pierre Galand, *L'Usage de la Dette Extérieure du Rwanda (1990/1994). La Responsabilité des Bailleurs de Fends. Analyse et Recommandations.* Brussels and Ottawa. Rapport Preliminaire, November 1996.

Commission of a Citizens' Inquiry into the role of France during the genocide of the Tutsi in 1994. Report, 'L'horreur qui nous prend au visage'. Survie.

La Coopération Suisse au Rwanda. Rapport du Groupe d'Etude institué par le Départment Fédérale des Affaires Etrangères (FAE), January 1996.

Fédération Internationale des Droits de l'Homme (FIDH), *Rapport sur la Commission d'enquête sur les violations des droits de l'homme au Rwanda depuis le 1er October 1990.* Paris and New York.

Feil, Colonel Scott R., *Preventing Genocide. How the Use of Force Might Have Succeeded in Rwanda.* Pre-publication draft, December 1997. New York: Carnegie Commission on Preventing Deadly Conflict.

Genocide in Rwanda. Documentation of Two Massacres during April 1994. Issue Brief, US Committee for Refugees, November 1994.

Human Rights Watch, *Genocide in Rwanda April–May 1994*, May 1994.

— *Rwanda: Talking Peace and Waging War*, 27 February 1992.

— *World Report, 1994*, December 1993.

Human Rights Watch Arms Project, *Arming Rwanda. The Arms Trade and Human Rights Abuses in the Rwandan War*, 6(1), January 1994.

International Federation of Human Rights (FIDH), Africa Watch, InterAfrican Union of Human Rights, and International Centre of Rights of the Person and of Democratic Development, *Report of the International Commission of Investigation of Human Rights Violations in Rwanda since October 1, 1990*, 7–21 January 1993.

International Monetary Fund, *Rwanda. Briefing Paper – 1992 Article IV Consultation and Discussions on a Second Annual Arrangement under the Structural Adjustment Facility*, 14 May 1992.

The International Response to Conflict and Genocide: Lessons from the Rwanda Experience. Joint Emergency Assistance to Rwanda. Copenhagen, March 1996. Study I: 'Historical Perspective: Some Explanatory Factors', Tor Sellström and Lennart Wohlgemuth. Study II: 'Early Warning and Conflict Management', Howard Adelman. Study III: 'Humanitarian Aid and Effects', John Bourton, Emery Brusset, Alistair Hallam. Study IV: 'Rebuilding Post-War Rwanda', Krishna Kumar, David Tardif-Douglin, Kim Maynard, Peter Manikas, Annette Sheckler and Carolyn Knapp. Synthesis Report: John Eriksson (ISBN 87 7265 335). (This study was initiated in 1995 by the Nordic countries and was eventually sponsored by nineteen countries and eighteen international agencies. France withdrew its support for the report after examining the draft.) See also: John Borton and John Eriksson, *Lessons from Rwanda*

– Lessons for Today. Assessment of the Impact and Influence of Joint Evaluation of Emergency Assistance to Rwanda, December 2004.

Minear, Larry and Philippe Guillot, *Soldiers to the Rescue. Humanitarian Lessons from Rwanda*. Paris: Development Centre of the Organization for Economic Cooperation and Development, 1996.

OECD. Informal Task Force on Conflict, Peace and Development Cooperation. Anton Baaré, David Shearer and Peter Uvin. *The Limits and Scope for the Use of Development Assistance Incentives for Influencing Conflict Situations: Case Study Rwanda*, Paris: OECD, 1999.

Organization of African Unity, *Rwanda. The Preventable Genocide*, Report of the International Panel of Eminent Personalities to Investigate the 1994 genocide in Rwanda and the surrounding events, July 2000.

Reporters sans Frontières, *Rwanda: Médias de la haine ou presse démocratique?* Report of mission, 16–24 September 1994.

Rwandan Republic, *Independent National Commission to Collect Proof of the Implication of the Government of France in the 1994 Genocide in Rwanda*. November 15, 2007. Report published August 2008.

Segal, Aaron, *Massacre in Rwanda*. Fabian Society, April 1964.

Sommers, Marc, *Fearing Africa's Young Men. The Case of Rwanda*. World Bank. Social Development Papers no. 32, January 2006.

UN, *Report on the Fifth Annual Peacekeeping Mission 3–11 November 1995*, United Nations Association of the USA, January 1996.

US Department of State, *Annual Report on Human Rights, 1993*.

Watson, Catherine, *Exile from Rwanda. Background to an Invasion*, US Committee for Refugees, Issue Paper, Washington, DC, February 1991.

PAPERS

Fein, Helen, *Patrons, Prevention and Punishment of Genocide: Observation on Bosnia and Rwanda*, Paper prepared for presentation at the annual meeting of the Amercian Sociological Association, Los Angeles, 5 August 1994.

Galliard, Philippe, *Rwanda 1994: La vraie vie est absent (Arthur Rimbaud). Cycle de Conference les Mardi de Musée. M. Philippe Gaillard, délégué du CIRC, chef de délégation au Rwanda de juillet 1993 à juillet 1994*, Unpublished.

Jallow, Justice Hassan B., *The OTP-ICTR: on-going challenges of completion*, The Hague. International Criminal Court. Office of the Prosecutor. Guest Lecture Series, 1 November 2004.

Kamali, Jean Baptiste, *Le Génocide au Rwanda. Un Silence complice ou inefficacité de la loi?* Licencié en Droit, Université Libre de Kigali, Kigali, March 2004.

Kroslak, Daniela, *The Media in Wartime. International History and International Politics*, University of Wales, Aberystwyth, 1997. Unpublished.

— *Evaluating the Moral Responsibility of France in the 1994 Rwandan Genocide*, Paper presented to the 23rd annual conference of the British International Studies Association (BISA), 14–16 December 1998. Unpublished.

— *The Responsibility of External Bystanders in Cases of Genocide: The French in Rwanda, 1990–1994*,

Unpublished PhD thesis, University of Wales, Aberystwyth, 2002.

Longman, Timothy, 'Church politics and the genocide in Rwanda', *Journal of Religion in Africa*, 31(2), 2001.

Mamdani, Mahmood, *From Conquest to Consent as the Basis of State Formation: Reflections on Rwanda*, Paper presented to the conference Crisis in the Great Lakes Region, organized by the Council for the Development of Social Research in Africa, Arusha, Tanzania, 4–7 September 1995.

Mfizi, Christophe, *'Le Réseau Zéro'*, *Lettre Ouverte de M. le Président du Mouvement Republicain National pour la Démocratie et le Développement (MRNDD)*, Editions Uruhimbi, BP 1067, Kigali, Rwanda, 1992.

Orr, D., *From Landmines to Genocide: Analysing the influence of non-state actors upon state decision-making in the security issue area*, Unpublished MSc Human Rights and International Politics dissertation, University of Glasgow, 2006.

Ripley, Matthew, *Putting the politics back in: a study of bilateral development aid and donor policy in Rwanda, up to 1994*, MA thesis, King's College London, Department of War Studies, 2007.

Tarling, Serena I. M., *Blinkered vision: how British journalists saw and reported the Rwandan genocide*, MA thesis, Print, Media and Communications Department, Napier University, Edinburgh.

JOURNALS

Africa Confidential, 'Rwanda: civilian slaughter', 35(9), 6 May 1994.

Barnett, Michael N., 'The UN Security Council, indifference, and the genocide in Rwanda', *Cultural Anthropology*, 12(4), 1997.

Blankfort, Lowell, 'Almost a million dead, Rwanda seeks justice', *World Outlook*, 2 December 1995 (UNA-US).

Bradol, Jean-Hervé, 'Rwanda, avril–mai 1994. Limites et ambiguités de l'action humanitaire. Crises politiques, massacres et exodes massifs', *Le Temps Modernes*, 583, 1995.

Burkhalter, Holly J., 'The question of genocide. The Clinton Administration and Rwanda', *World Policy Journal*, 11(4), Winter 1994/95.

Clapham, Christopher, 'Rwanda. The perils of peacemaking', *Journal of Peace Research*, 35(2), 1998.

Destexhe, Alain, 'The third genocide', *Foreign Policy*, 97, Winter 1994/95.

Hannay, David, 'The UN: mission impossible', *Prospect*, February 1996.

Heusch, Luc de, 'Rwanda. Responsibilities for a genocide', *Anthropology Today*, II(4), August 1994.

Hintjens, Helen M., 'Explaining the 1994 genocide in Rwanda', *Journal of African Studies*, 37(2), 1999, pp. 241–86.

Jones, Bruce, '"Intervention without borders". Humanitarian intervention in Rwanda, 1990–94', *Millennium*, 24(2), Summer 1995.

Leitenberg, Milton, 'Rwanda, 1994: international incompetence produces genocide', *Peacekeeping and International Relations*, November/December 1994.

Lemarchand, René, 'The apocalypse in Rwanda', *Cultural Survival Quarterly*, Summer/Fall 1994.

McNulty, Mel, 'France's Rwanda debacle', *War Studies*, 2(2), Spring 1997.

Mamdani, Mahmood, 'From conquest

to consent as the basis of state formation: reflections on Rwanda', *New Left Review*, 216, 1996.

Melvern, Linda, 'The UN and Rwanda', *London Review of Books*, 12 December 1996.

— 'Genocide behind the thin blue line', *Security Dialogue*, 28(3), September 1997.

— 'Is anyone interested in Rwanda?', *British Journalism Review*, July 2001.

— 'The Security Council: behind the scenes', *International Affairs*, 77, 2001.

Melvern, Linda with Paul Williams, 'Britannia waived the rules: the Major government and the 1994 genocide in Rwanda', *African Affairs*, 103(410), January 2004.

Schabas, William, 'Justice, democracy, and impunity in post-genocide Rwanda: searching for solutions to impossible problems', *Criminal Law Forum*, 7(3), 1996.

Smith, David Norman, 'The genesis of genocide in Rwanda: the fatal dialectic of class and ethnicity', *Humanity and Society*, 19(4), November 1995.

Suhrke, Astri, 'Dilemmas of protection: the log of the Kigali Battalion', *Security Dialogue*, 29(1), March 1998.

Thimonier, Olivier, 'Aux sources de la coopération franco-rwandaise', *Golias*, 101, March/April 2005

Van Hoyweghen, Saskia, 'The disintegration of the Catholic Church of Rwanda. A study of the fragmentation of political and religious authority', *African Affairs*, 95, 1996, pp. 379–401.

Verwimp, Philip, 'Machetes and firearms: the organisation of massacres in Rwanda', *Journal of Peace Research*, 43(1), 2006.

— 'Death and survival during the 1994 genocide in Rwanda', *Population Studies*, 58(2). 2004.

BOOKS

Abdulai, Napoleon (ed.), *Genocide in Rwanda*, Africa Research and Information Centre, 1994.

Adelman, Howard and Astri Suhrke (eds), *The Path of a Genocide. The Rwanda Crisis from Uganda to Zaire*, New Brunswick, NJ: Transaction, 1999.

African Rights, *Rwanda. Death, Despair and Defiance*, London: African Rights, 1995.

Albright, Madeleine, *Madame Secretary: A Memoir*, New York: Talk Miramax, 2003.

Anyidoho, Henry Kwami, *Guns over Kigali*, Accra: Woeli Publishing Services, 1997.

Barnett, Michael, 'The politics of indifference at the United Nations and genocide in Rwanda and Bosnia', in Thomas Cushman and Stjepan Mestrovic (eds), *This Time We Knew: Western Responses to Genocide in Bosnia*, New York: New York University Press, 1996.

— *Eyewitness to a Genocide. The UN and Rwanda*, Ithaca, NY: Cornell University Press, 2002.

Bellamy, Alex, Paul Williams and Stuart Griffin, *Understanding Peacekeeping*, Polity Press, 2004.

Berry, John A and Carol Pott Berry (eds), *Genocide in Rwanda. A Collective Memory*, Washington, DC: Howard University Press, 1999.

Blumenthal, Sydney, *The Clinton Wars. An Insider's Account of the White House Years*, London: Viking, 2003.

Booth, Ken, *Theory of World Security*, Cambridge Studies in International Relations, 105,

Cambridge: Cambridge University Press, 2007.

Boutros-Ghali, Boutros, *Unvanquished. A US–UN Saga*, London: I.B.Tauris, 1999.

Bowen, Michael, Gary Freeman and Kay Miller, *Passing By. The United States and Genocide in Burundi, 1972*, Special Report, Humanitarian Policy Studies, Carnegie Endowment for International Peace.

Braeckman, Colette, *Rwanda, histoire d'un génocide*, Paris: Fayard, 1994.

— *Terreur Africaine. Burundi, Rwanda, Zaire: les racines de la violence*, Paris: Fayard, 1996.

Castonguay, Jacques, *Les Casques Bleus au Rwanda*, Paris: Editions L'Harmattan, 1998.

Chrétien, Jean-Pierre, *Le Défi de l'ethnisme. Rwanda et Burundi, 1990–1996*, Paris: Karthala, 1997.

Chrétien, Jean-Pierre, Jean-François Dupaquier, Marcel Kabanda and Joseph Ngarambe (Reporters sans Frontières), *Rwanda: les médias du génocide*, Paris: Karthala, 1995.

Clapham, Christopher (ed.), *African Guerrillas*, Oxford: James Currey, 1998.

Clark, Phil and Zachary D. Kaufman (eds), *After Genocide: Transitional Justice, Post-Conflict Reconstruction and Reconciliation in Rwanda and Beyond*, New York: Columbia University Press/C. Hurst and Co., 2008.

Cohen, Herman J., *Intervening in Africa. Superpower Peacemaking in a Troubled Continent*, Basingstoke: Macmillan, 2000.

Cohen, Jared, *One Hundred Days of Silence. America and the Rwanda Genocide*, Maryland: Rowman and Littlefield, 2007

Dallaire, Lt Gen. Roméo, *Shake Hands with the Devil. The Failure of Humanity in Rwanda*, Canada: Random House, 2003.

Destexhe, Alain, *Rwanda: essai sur le génocide*, Editions Complexe, 1994.

— *Qui a tué nos Paras?*, Brussels: Editions Luc Pire, 1996.

Dowden, Richard, *Africa: Altered States, Ordinary Miracles*, London: Portobello Books, 2008.

Durch, William J. (ed.), *UN Peacekeeping: American Politics and the Uncivil Wars of the 1990s*, Henry L. Stimson Center, New York: St Martin's Press, 1996.

Espelund, Görrel (with Jesper Strudsholm and Eric Miller), *Reality Bites. An African Decade*, Cape Town: Double Storey, 2003.

Les Familles des Para, Rwanda. Lettre Ouverte aux parlementaires. Le texte du rapport du group 'Rwanda' du Senat, Brussels: Editions Luc Pire, 1997.

Fein, Helen, *Accounting for Genocide after 1945. Theories and Some Findings*, International Journal on Group Rights, vol. 1, Amsterdam: Martinus Nijhoff, 1993.

— *Human Rights and Wrongs: Slavery, Terror, Genocide*, New York: Paradigm Books, 2007.

Gharekhan, Chinmaya, *The Horseshoe Table: An Inside View of the UN Security Council*, New Delhi: Dorling Kindersley (India), 2006.

Gordon, Nick, *Murders in the Mist*, London: Hodder and Stoughton, 1993.

Gourevitch, Philip, *We wish to inform you that tomorrow we will be killed with our families. Stories from Rwanda*, London: Picador, 1999.

Gouteux, Jean-Paul, *Un Génocide secret d'état*, Editions Sociales, 1998.

Guichaoua, André (ed.), *Les Crises*

politiques au Burundi et an Rwanda (1993–1994), Université des Sciences et Technologies de Lille, Paris: Karthala, 1995.

— Rwanda 1994: Les Politiques du génocide à Butare, Paris: Karthala, 2005.

Hannay, David, New World Disorder. The UN after the Cold War – An Insider's View, London: I.B. Tauris, 2008.

Hartley, Aidan, The Zanzibar Chest. A Memoir of Love and War, London: HarperCollins, 2003.

Horowitz, Irving, Taking Lives: Genocide and State Power, New Brunswick, NJ: Transaction, 1981.

Human Rights Watch/Fédération Internationale des Ligues des Droits de l'Homme, Leave none to tell the story. Genocide in Rwanda, 1999.

Jefremovas, Villa, Brickyards to Graveyards. From Production to Genocide in Rwanda, Albany: State University of New York Press, 2002.

Jones, Bruce D., Peacemaking in Rwanda: The Dynamic of Failure, Boulder, CO: Lynne Rienner, 2001.

Keane, Fergal, Season of Blood, London: Penguin, 1995.

Khan, Shaharyar, The Shallow Graves of Rwanda, London: I.B. Tauris, 2000.

Kimonyo, Jean-Paul, Rwanda. Un Génocide populaire, Paris: Karthala, 2008.

Kinzer, Stephen, A Thousand Hills. Rwanda's Rebirth and the Man Who Dreamed It, Hoboken, NJ: John Wiley and Sons Inc., 2008.

Klinghoffer, Arthur Jay, The International Dimension of Genocide in Rwanda, London: Macmillan, 1998.

Kuper, Leo, The Prevention of Genocide, New Haven, CT, and London: Yale University Press, 1985.

Kuperman, Alan J., The Limits of Humanitarian Intervention. Genocide in Rwanda, Washington, DC: Brookings Institution, 2001.

Kroslak, Daniela, The Role of France in the Rwandan Genocide, London: Hurst and Co., 2007.

Lanotte, Olivier, La France au Rwanda (1990-1994). Entre abstention impossible et engagement ambivalent, Brussels: P. I. E. Peter Lang, SA, 2007.

Lefèvre, Patrick and Jean-Noel, Les Militaires belges et le Rwanda 1916–2006, Brussels: Editions Racine, 2006.

Lema, Antoine, Africa Divided, Sweden: Lund University Press, 1993.

Lemarchand, René, Rwanda and Burundi, London: Pall Mall, 1970.

McInnes, Colin and Nicholas J. Wheeler (eds), Dimensions of Western Military Intervention, London: Frank Cass, 2002.

Malone, David M. (ed.), The UN Security Council from the Cold War to the Twenty-first Century, Boulder, CO: Lynne Rienner, 2004.

Marchal, Colonel Luc, Rwanda: la descente aux enfers. Témoinage d'un paecekeeper decembre 1993–avril 1994, Brussels: Labor, 2001.

Marrus, Michael, The Holocaust in History, Harmondsworth: Penguin, 1996.

Mas, Monique, Paris–Kigali 1990–1994, Paris: Editions L'Harmattan, 1999.

Melvern, Linda, The Ultimate Crime. Who Betrayed the UN and Why, London: Allison and Busby, 1995.

— A People Betrayed. The Role of the West in Rwanda's Genocide, London: Zed Books, 2000.

— Conspiracy to Murder. The Rwandan Genocide, London: Verso, 2004 (paperback 2006).

Misser, François, Vers un nouveau Rwanda? Entretiens avec Paul Kagame, Brussels: Editions Luc Pire, 2000.

Moore, Jonathan (ed.), Hard Choices, Moral Dilemmas in Humanitarian Intervention, Oxford: Rowman and Littlefield, 1998.

Mushikiwabo, Louise and Jack Kramer, Rwanda Means the Universe. A Native's Memory of Blood and Bloodlines, New York: St Martin's Press, 2006.

Ndahiro, Alfred and Priva Rutazibwa, Impostor Made Hero in Hollywood. The True Story of Paul Rusesabagina and the film Hotel Rwanda, Paris: Editions L'Harmattan, 2008.

Newbury, Catharine, The Cohesion of Oppression: Clientship and Ethnicity in Rwanda, 1860–1960, Columbia University Press, 1988.

Newbury, David, Kings and Clans. Iwji Island and the Lake Kivu Rift 1780–1840, University of Wisconsin Press, 1991.

Nshimiyimana, Venuste, Prélude de génocide Rwandais. Enquête sur les circonstances politique et militaires du meurtre du President Habyarimana, Brussels: Quorum, 1995.

Orbinski, James, An Imperfect Offering. Dispatches from the Medical Front Line, Canada: Random House, 2008.

Ould-Abdallah, Ahmedou, Burundi on the Brink 1993–95, Washington, DC: US Institute of Peace, 2000.

Péan, Pierre, Noires fureurs, blancs menteurs Rwanda 1990–1994, Mille et une nuits, 2005.

Périès, Gabriel et David Servenay, Une Guerre Noire. Enquête sur les origines du génocide rwandais (1959–1994), Paris: Editions La Découverte, 2007.

Petersen, Scott, Me against My Brother, London: Routledge, 2001.

Piollet, J.-B., Les Missions catholiques françaises au XIXe siècle, Les Missions d'Afrique, 1902.

Porter, Jack Nusan, Genocide and Human Rights, a Global Anthology, University Press of America, 1982.

Power, Samantha, A Problem from Hell: America and the Age of Genocide, New York: Basic Books, 2002.

Prunier, Gérard, The Rwanda Crisis 1959–1994. History of a Genocide, London: Hurst and Co., 1995.

— From Genocide to Continental War. The 'Congolese' Conflict and the Crisis of Contemporary Africa, London: Hurst and Co., 2009.

Reyntjens, Filip, L'Afrique des Grands Lacs en crise. Rwanda, Burundi: 1988–1994, Paris: Karthala, 1994.

— Rwanda. Trois jours qui on fait basculé l'histoire, Paris: Editions L'Harmattan, 1995.

Saint-Exupéry, Patrick de, L'Inavouable: la France au Rwanda, Paris: Les Arènes, 2004.

Schabas, William A., Genocide in International Law, Cambridge: Cambridge University Press, 2000.

Schofield, James, Silent over Africa. Stories of War and Genocide, Sydney: HarperCollins, 1996.

Semujanga, Josia, Origins of Rwandan Genocide, New York: Humanity Books, 2003.

Speke, J. H., Journal of the Discovery of the Source of the Nile, London: J. M. Dent, 1969 (1st edn 1863).

Tadjo, Veronique, The Shadow of Imana. Travels in the Heart of Rwanda, trans. Veronique Wakerley, London: Heinemann, 2002.

Temple-Raston, Dina, Justice on the

Grass. Three Rwandan Journalists, Their Trial for War Crimes, and a Nation's Quest for Redemption, New York: Simon and Schuster, 2005.

Thompson, Allan (ed.), *The Media and the Rwandan Genocide*, Ottawa: International Development Research Centre, 2007.

Thornberry, Patrick, *International Law and the Rights of Minorities*, Oxford: Oxford University Press, 1993,

Uvin, Peter, *Aiding Violence: The Development Enterprise in Rwanda*, New York: Kumarian Press, 1998.

Vansina, Jan, *Le Rwanda ancien: le Royaume Ngiyinya*, Paris: Karthala, 2001.

— *Antecedents to Modern Rwanda. The Nyiginya Kingdom*, Oxford: James Currey, 2004 (trans. from French by the author).

Vassall-Adams, Guy, *Rwanda: An Agenda for International Action*, Oxford: Oxfam Publications, 1994.

Vincelet, Christophe, *La Mort des dix Casques Bleus belges à Kigali ou le belgocentrisme dans la crise rwandaise*, Paris: Editions L'Harmattan, 2004.

Waugh, Colin, *Power, Genocide and the Rwandan Patriotic Front*, Jefferson, NC: McFarland, 2004.

Wheeler, Nicholas J., *Saving Strangers: Humanitarian Intervention in International Society*, Oxford: Oxford University Press, 2000.

Wrigley, C., *Kingship and State: The Buganda Dynasty*, Cambridge: Cambridge University Press, 1996.

ACKNOWLEDGEMENTS

I began to investigate the circumstances of the genocide in Rwanda in April 1994 when I was at the United Nations Secretariat in New York, completing a book on the fifty-year history of the United Nations. I published a first account of the decision-making within the Security Council in the *Scotsman* in January 1995. This article described the first critical hours of the crisis, the murder of ten United Nations peacekeepers and the rapid elimination of almost all of Rwanda's political opposition.

Since *A People Betrayed* was first published in April 2000 new information has become available. This includes seven collections in the Rwandan National Archives to which I was given unprecedented access. At the UN Secretariat in New York I was allowed to study the files of the Department of Peacekeeping Operations, including the daily situation reports sent from the UN Assistance Mission for Rwanda as the genocide progressed. These reports must rank as one of the world's most extraordinary collections on genocide.

There is still much that remains hidden from public scrutiny. More research needs to be undertaken in order to advance our knowledge and understanding of the failure over Rwanda. I have been encouraged in the past few years by how many students, academics and investigators have sought my assistance in their determination to investigate the subject in all aspects. I hope that my own archive, described in the 'Sources' section of this edition, will one day be widely available in an academic centre of excellence as a digitized resource for use worldwide.

This revised and updated edition of *A People Betrayed* would not have been possible without the crucial assistance of Alan McClue, a Fellow of Cranfield University Forensic Institute. I am most grateful to him. It has been a privilege for me to have had sustained encouragement for my project from Professor Ken Booth, Department of International Politics, University of Wales, Peter Greaves and Magnus Linklater. I thank Doris Hollander and Martin Page for their dedication to the subject and their painstaking help with the manuscript.

I thank David MacRae and Genevieve-Anne Dehoux, who helped me in so many ways. I greatly value their friendship.

My nephew, Michael Melvern, is a skilled computer consultant whose help and advice at the most crucial moments saved the manuscript and many hours of work. I am no less indebted to Becky and Henry Tinsley for their help. I thank Georgina Holmes, Nick Webb, Charlotte Welsh, Sam Westcott and Paul Williams. I thank Raymond Lloyd, whose service to history is tireless. Polly Low, Sue Snell and S. J. Taylor have been the most supportive of friends.

My partner Phill Green and our son Laurence have shown extraordinary forbearance and good nature. Their support for my work has been unyielding.

Linda Melvern
London, 2009

INDEX